LOUIS KRONENBERGER was born in Cincinnati, Ohio. He has been an editor at Alfred A. Knopf and at *Fortune* magazine, and from 1938 to 1961 he was the drama critic for *Time* magazine. From 1940 until 1948 he was drama editor for the newspaper *PM*. He has been a lecturer in English at Columbia University, was a Lawrence Lowell visiting professor at Harvard in 1959, and gave the Christian Gauss Lectures at Princeton in 1960–61. Among his many books are *Kings and Desperate Men, Grand Right and Left, The Pleasure of Their Company, Company Manners,* and *A Month of Sundays.* He was the editor of *An Anthology of Light Verse, An Eighteenth Century Miscellany, The Viking Portable Reader's Companion,* and *G. B. Shaw: A Critical Survey.* He contributed to *Books That Changed Our Minds* and has edited the Best Play Series.

Novelists on

NOVELISTS

An anthology edited by

LOUIS KRONENBERGER

Anchor Books

DOUBLEDAY & COMPANY, INC.

GARDEN CITY, NEW YORK

1962

ACKNOWLEDGMENTS

"Seventh Essay on Jane Austen" by Elizabeth Bowen. Reprinted by permission of the author.

"Turgenev" from *Notes On Life and Letters* by Joseph Conrad; "Essay on Stephen Crane and the Red Badge of Courage" from *Last Essays* by Joseph Conrad. Reprinted by permission of J. M. Dent & Sons, Ltd.

"Note—On Arnold Bennett" from *The Traveller's Library* by W. Somerset Maugham, copyright 1933 by Doubleday and Company, Inc. Reprinted by permission of the publisher.

"Defoe" from *The Common Reader* by Virginia Woolf, copyright 1925 by Harcourt, Brace & World, Inc.; renewed 1953 by Leonard Woolf; "The Novels of George Meredith" from *The Second Common Reader* by Virginia Woolf, copyright 1932 by Harcourt, Brace & World, Inc.; renewed 1960 by Leonard Woolf; "Proust" from *Abinger Harvest* by E. M. Forster, copyright 1936 by E. M. Forster; "Virginia Woolf" from *Two Cheers for Democracy*, copyright 1951 by E. M. Forster; "Reflections on Willa Cather," copyright 1952 by Katherine Anne Porter. Reprinted from her volume, *The Days Before*. All selections reprinted by permission of Harcourt, Brace & World, Inc.

"D. H. Lawrence" from *The Olive Tree* by Aldous Huxley. Copyright 1937 by Aldous Huxley. Reprinted by permission of Harper & Brothers.

"Henry James and the Russian Novelists" from *Confessions to a Jacobite*, by Louis Auchincloss. Reprinted by permission of Houghton Mifflin Company.

"Anna Karenina" from *Thomas Mann: Essays of Three Decades*, copyright 1947 by Alfred A. Knopf, Inc. Reprinted by permission of the publisher.

Owing to one or two names in it, strict accuracy would have imposed on this book the unwieldy title of *Writers of Fiction on Writers of Fiction*. But the actual title is so nearly comprehensive as, I would think, to need no defense, and the book itself offers novelists on novelists in a variety of forms. The rule I *have* obeyed is that all authors represented be best known as novelists. Surely this applies by a very wide margin to a Henry James or a D. H. Lawrence and by a very safe one to a Virginia Woolf or an Aldous Huxley. Perhaps, here, Rebecca West is the exception that proves the rule, but she is at least as much known for her novels as for her other writings. Obeying this rule has meant, of course, omitting many excellent critics who have also written novels; but to violate the book's guiding principle would be to vitiate its special temper.

Moreover, by honoring that principle I have felt free to abandon most other restraints, and have included—along with a preponderant number of critical pieces—various reminiscences, character sketches, personal estimates, memorial tributes, and short reviews of work as it emerged. I have done this not just because most of the novelists considered here have been widely appraised elsewhere by critics, but also because critical talent is not what we would particularly look for—any more than consistently find—in novelists. Their insight into character, their powers of observation, their almost creative gifts of memory, their craft rather than critical understanding of their fellows—and sometimes their mere reactions to their fellows—have a special, often unique, interest and value. Still, I have drawn only moderately from a great storehouse of such material, since to have allotted reminiscence or personal reaction the primary place would have defeated my primary concern—an emphasis on the novelist and his work rather than on the human being as such.

While naturally delighting in the well-proportioned 5000 word essay, I have not greatly penalized longer or shorter writings, and have also—in the form of salted almonds at the feast—introduced some very brief novelists' observations on other novelists. Along with much writing that, had space allowed, it would have been pleasant to include, essays by Robert Penn Warren have been specifically omitted because for one reason or another it was impossible to obtain permission.

L. K.

CONTENTS

Novelists on

NOVELISTS

Virginia Woolf on

DANIEL DEFOE

The fear which attacks the recorder of centenaries lest he should find himself measuring a diminishing spectre and forced to foretell its approaching dissolution is not only absent in the case of *Robinson Crusoe* but the mere thought of it is ridiculous. It may be true that *Robinson Crusoe* is two hundred years of age upon the twenty-fifth of April 1919, but far from raising the familiar speculations as to whether people now read it and will continue to read it, the effect of the bi-centenary is to make us marvel that *Robinson Crusoe*, the perennial and immortal, should have been in existence so short a time as that. The book resembles one of the anonymous productions of the race itself rather than the effort of a single mind; and as for celebrating its centenary we should as soon think of celebrating the centenaries of Stonehenge itself. Something of this we may attribute to the fact that we have all had *Robinson Crusoe* read aloud to us as children, and were thus much in the same state of mind towards Defoe and his story that the Greeks were in towards Homer. It never occurred to us that there was such a person as Defoe, and to have been told that *Robinson Crusoe* was the work of a man with a pen in his hand would either have disturbed us unpleasantly or meant nothing at all. The impressions of childhood are those that last longest and cut deepest. It still seems that the name of Daniel Defoe has no right to appear upon the title-page of *Robinson Crusoe*, and if we celebrate the bi-centenary of the book we are making a slightly unnecessary allusion to the fact that, like Stonehenge, it is still in existence.

The great fame of the book has done its author some injustice; for while it has given him a kind of anonymous glory it has obscured the fact that he was a writer of other works which, it is safe to assert, were not read aloud to us as children. Thus when the Editor of the *Christian World* in the year 1870 appealed to "the boys and girls of England" to erect a monument upon the grave of Defoe, which a stroke of lightning had mutilated, the marble was inscribed to the memory of the author of *Robinson Crusoe*. No mention was made of *Moll Flanders*. Considering the topics which are dealt with in that book, and in *Roxana, Captain Singleton, Colonel Jack* and the rest, we need not be surprised, though we may be indignant, at the omission. We may agree with Mr. Wright, the biographer of Defoe, that these "are not works for the drawing-room table". But unless we consent to make that useful piece of furniture the final arbiter of taste, we must deplore the fact that their superficial coarseness, or the universal celebrity of *Robinson Crusoe*, has led them to be far less widely famed than they deserve. On any monument worthy of the name of monument the names of *Moll Flanders* and *Roxana*, at least, should be carved as deeply as the name of Defoe. They stand among the few English novels which we can call indisputably great. The occasion of the bicentenary of their more famous companion may well lead us to consider in what their greatness, which has so much in common with his, may be found to consist.

Defoe was an elderly man when he turned novelist, many years the predecessor of Richardson and Fielding, and one of the first indeed to shape the novel and launch it on its way. But it is unnecessary to labour the fact of his precedence, except that he came to his novel-writing with certain conceptions about the art which he derived partly from being himself one of the first to practise it. The novel had to justify its existence by telling a true story and preaching a sound moral. "This supplying a story by invention is certainly a most scandalous crime," he wrote. "It is a sort of lying that makes a great hole in the heart, in which by degrees a habit of lying enters in." Either in the preface or in the text of each of his works, therefore, he takes pains to insist that he has not used his invention at all but has depended upon facts, and that his purpose has been the highly moral desire to convert the vicious or to warn the innocent. Happily these were principles that tallied very well with his natural disposition and endowments. Facts had been drilled into him by sixty years of varying fortunes before he turned his experience to account in fiction. "I have some time ago summed up the Scenes of my life in this distich," he wrote:

> No man has tasted differing fortunes more,
> And thirteen times I have been rich and poor.

He had spent eighteen months in Newgate and talked with thieves, pirates, highwaymen, and coiners before he wrote the history of Moll Flanders. But to have facts thrust upon you by dint of living and accident is one thing; to swallow them voraciously and retain the imprint of them indelibly, is another. It is not merely that Defoe knew the stress of poverty and had talked with the victims of it, but that the unsheltered life, exposed to circumstances and forced to shift for itself, appealed to him imaginatively as the right matter for his art. In the first pages of each of his great novels he reduces his hero or heroine to such a state of unfriended misery that their existence must be a continued struggle, and their survival at all the result of luck and their own exertions. Moll Flanders was born in Newgate of a criminal mother; Captain Singleton was stolen as a child and sold to the gipsies; Colonel Jack, though "born a gentleman, was put 'prentice to a pickpocket"; Roxana starts under better auspices, but, having married at fifteen, she sees her husband go bankrupt and is left with five children in "a condition the most deplorable that words can express".

Thus each of these boys and girls has the world to begin and the battle to fight for himself. The situation thus created was entirely to Defoe's liking. From her very birth or with half a year's respite at most, Moll Flanders, the most notable of them, is goaded by "that worst of devils, poverty", forced to earn her living as soon as she can sew, driven from place to place, making no demands upon her creator for the subtle domestic atmosphere which he was unable to supply, but drawing upon him for all he knew of strange people and customs. From the outset the burden of proving her right to exist is laid upon her. She has to depend entirely upon her own wits and judgement, and to deal with each emergency as it arises by a rule-of-thumb morality which she has forged in

her own head. The briskness of the story is due partly to the
fact that having transgressed the accepted laws at a very early
age she has henceforth the freedom of the outcast. The one
impossible event is that she should settle down in comfort
and security. But from the first the peculiar genius of the
author asserts itself, and avoids the obvious danger of the
novel of adventure. He makes us understand that Moll Flanders was a woman on her own account and not only material
for a succession of adventures. In proof of this she begins, as
Roxana also begins, by falling passionately, if unfortunately,
in love. That she must rouse herself and marry some one else
and look very closely to her settlements and prospects is no
slight upon her passion, but to be laid to the charge of her
birth; and, like all Defoe's women, she is a person of robust
understanding. Since she makes no scruple of telling lies
when they serve her purpose, there is something undeniable
about her truth when she speaks it. She has no time to
waste upon the refinements of personal affection; one tear is
dropped, one moment of despair allowed, and then "on with
the story". She has a spirit that loves to breast the storm. She
delights in the exercise of her own powers. When she discovers that the man she has married in Virginia is her own
brother she is violently disgusted; she insists upon leaving
him; but as soon as she sets foot in Bristol, "I took the diversion of going to Bath, for as I was still far from being old
so my humour, which was always gay, continued so to an extreme". Heartless she is not, nor can any one charge her with
levity; but life delights her, and a heroine who lives has us
all in tow. Moreover, her ambition has that slight strain of
imagination in it which puts it in the category of the noble
passions. Shrewd and practical of necessity, she is yet haunted
by a desire for romance and for the quality which to her
perception makes a man a gentleman. "It was really a true
gallant spirit he was of, and it was the more grievous to me.
'Tis something of relief even to be undone by a man of honour rather than by a scoundrel," she writes when she had misled a highwayman as to the extent of her fortune. It is in
keeping with this temper that she should be proud of her
final partner because he refuses to work when they reach the
plantations but prefers hunting, and that she should take

pleasure in buying him wigs and silver-hilted swords "to make him appear, as he really was, a very fine gentleman". Her very love of hot weather is in keeping, and the passion with which she kissed the ground that her son had trod on, and her noble tolerance of every kind of fault so long as it is not "complete baseness of spirit, imperious, cruel, and relentless when uppermost, abject and low-spirited when down". For the rest of the world she has nothing but goodwill.

Since the list of the qualities and graces of this seasoned old sinner is by no means exhausted we can well understand how it was that Borrow's applewoman on London Bridge called her "blessed Mary" and valued her book above all the apples on her stall; and that Borrow, taking the book deep into the booth, read till his eyes ached. But we dwell upon such signs of character only by way of proof that the creator of Moll Flanders was not, as he has been accused of being, a mere journalist and literal recorder of facts with no conception of the nature of psychology. It is true that his characters take shape and substance of their own accord, as if in despite of the author and not altogether to his liking. He never lingers or stresses any point of subtlety or pathos, but presses on imperturbably as if they came there without his knowledge. A touch of imagination, such as that when the Prince sits by his son's cradle and Roxana observes how "he loved to look at it when it was asleep", seems to mean much more to us than to him. After the curiously modern dissertation upon the need of communicating matters of importance to a second person lest, like the thief in Newgate, we should talk of it in our sleep, he apologises for his digression. He seems to have taken his characters so deeply into his mind that he lived them without exactly knowing how; and, like all unconscious artists, he leaves more gold in his work than his own generation was able to bring to the surface.

The interpretation that we put on his characters might therefore well have puzzled him. We find for ourselves meanings which he was careful to disguise even from himself. Thus it comes about that we admire Moll Flanders far more than we blame her. Nor can we believe that Defoe had made up his mind as to the precise degree of her guilt, or was unaware that in considering the lives of the abandoned he raised many deep questions and hinted, if he did not state, answers quite at variance with his professions of belief. From the evidence supplied by his essay upon the "Education of Women" we know that he had thought deeply and much in advance of his age upon the capacities of women, which he rated very high, and the injustice done to them, which he rated very harsh.

I have often thought of it as one of the most barbarous customs in the world, considering us as a civilised and a Christian country, that we deny the advantages of learning to women. We reproach the sex every day with folly and impertinence; which I am confident, had they the advantages of education equal to us, they would be guilty of less than ourselves.

The advocates of women's rights would hardly care, perhaps, to claim Moll Flanders and Roxana among their patron saints; and yet it is clear that Defoe not only intended them to speak some very modern doctrines upon the subject, but placed them in circumstances where their peculiar hardships are displayed in such a way as to elicit our sympathy. Courage, said Moll Flanders, was what women needed, and the power to "stand their ground"; and at once gave practical demonstration of the benefits that would result. Roxana, a lady of the same profession, argues more subtly against the slavery of marriage. She "had started a new thing in the world" the merchant told her; "it was a way of arguing contrary to the general practise". But Defoe is the last writer to be guilty of bald preaching. Roxana keeps our attention because she is blessedly unconscious that she is in any good sense an example to her sex and is thus at liberty to own that part of her argument is "of an elevated strain which was really not in my thoughts at first, at all". The knowledge of her own frailties and the honest questioning of her own motives, which that knowledge begets, have the happy result of keeping her fresh and human when the martyrs and pioneers of so many problem novels have shrunken and shrivelled to the pegs and props of their respective creeds.

But the claim of Defoe upon our admiration does not rest

upon the fact that he can be shown to have anticipated some of the views of Meredith, or to have written scenes which (the odd suggestion occurs) might have been turned into plays by Ibsen. Whatever his ideas upon the position of women, they are an incidental result of his chief virtue, which is that he deals with the important and lasting side of things and not with the passing and trivial. He is often dull. He can imitate the matter-of-fact precision of a scientific travel-ler until we wonder that his pen could trace or his brain conceive what has not even the excuse of truth to soften its dryness. He leaves out the whole of vegetable nature, and a large part of human nature. All this we may admit, though we have to admit defects as grave in many writers whom we call great. But that does not impair the peculiar merit of what remains. Having at the outset limited his scope and confined his ambitions he achieves a truth of insight which is far rarer and more enduring than the truth of fact which he professed to make his aim. Moll Flanders and her friends recommended themselves to him not because they were, as we should say, "picturesque"; nor, as he affirmed, because they were examples of evil living by which the public might profit. It was their natural veracity, bred in them by a life of hardship, that excited his interest. For them there were no excuses; no kindly shelter obscured their motives. Poverty was their taskmaster. Defoe did not pronounce more than a judgement of the lips upon their failings. But their courage and resource and tenacity delighted him. He found their so-ciety full of good talk, and pleasant stories, and faith in each other, and morality of a home-made kind. Their fortunes had that infinite variety which he praised and relished and be-held with wonder in his own life. These men and women, above all, were free to talk openly of the passions and de-sires which have moved men and women since the beginning of time, and thus even now they keep their vitality undimin-ished. There is a dignity in everything that is looked at openly. Even the sordid subject of money, which plays so large a part in their histories, becomes not sordid but tragic when it stands not for ease and consequence but for honour, honesty and life itself. You may object that Defoe is hum-drum, but never that he is engrossed with petty things.

He belongs, indeed, to the school of the great plain writers, whose work is founded upon a knowledge of what is most persistent, though not most seductive, in human nature. The view of London from Hungerford Bridge, grey, serious, massive, and full of the subdued stir of traffic and business, prosaic if it were not for the masts of the ships and the towers and domes of the city, brings him to mind. The tattered girls with violets in their hands at the street corners, and the old weatherbeaten women patiently displaying their matches and bootlaces beneath the shelter of arches, seem like characters from his books. He is of the school of Crabbe, and of Gissing, and not merely a fellow pupil in the same stern place of learning, but its founder and master.

Trollope ON Samuel Richardson:	*Richardson laid himself out to support high-toned feminine virtue. The praise of strict matrons and of severe elders was the very breath of his nostrils. He placed himself on a pedestal of morality, and dictated to Propriety at large what should and what should not be considered becoming for young women. . . .* *Richardson's men are fiends—such as men I think never were.*
George Moore ON Fielding:	*Fielding seems to have been without sensibility of any kind, mental or physical. . . . He writes with gusto, a quality we seldom meet with in modern literature, perhaps we are becoming more thoughtful; and he keeps it up like an actor who knows he is playing in a bad play.*

Jane Austen, who died a hundred and eighteen years ago, brought the English novel to a point nearer perfection than it has reached since. As a form, the novel has several parts or aspects—social photography, charted emotion, dialogue, delineation of people. Each of these has been made, from time to time, by (in her sense) "respectable" novelists his or her main province. It is possible to give a fair, if flattish, picture of life by approaching one's subject ably on any one of these sides. But Jane Austen's ability was comprehensive: she did more than approach a subject, she surrounded it. Thus her novels are novels in the most classic sense.

Their Englishness is, moreover, their peculiar triumph. The English novel has, on the whole, suffered from having been written after writers' glory in being English had begun to decline. The most minor Elizabethan play has a quality —a kind of absoluteness or thoroughgoingness—that the most distinguished novel too often lacks. (*Wuthering Heights* is the best exception to this.) There is a great drop in pressure: greater, I think, than the change of medium—prose for verse—accounts for. In this field, the nineteenth-century Russians succeeded to what properly should have been the English heritage: heroicness, a kind of overbearing spirituality. Tolstoy is in the succession of Shakespeare, Dostoëvsky of Webster. English novelists, whether consciously or unconsciously, wear their nationality as a shackle rather than as a decoration of honour. Moral strife is, largely, their subject: it is the greatest of subjects, but in approaching it they suffer from moral cramp. With the close of the eighteenth century, French classical influence with its restraints gone, fancy, let loose again, showed a good deal of weakness. Enforced form had bolstered this weakness up. But now columns gave

place to arches and tracery: one no longer built to enclose
light but to cast gothic shadows. Life is always impinged upon
by a literary fashion, and Jane Austen saw round her a world
in which, genteel and orderly as it was, the new sensibility
began to luxuriate. On what promised to be a kind of garden
jungle, a sinister dusk of ferns, she imposed her two twin
orders, Elegance and Propriety. Qualities one would be prepared, in the last resort, to die for, that one would be prepared, at least, to sacrifice a life to, take on an ideality of
their own. Her sense of values was more than positive; it
would have been passionate once put to the proof. The un-
changingness of her characters' moral colour, the unswerving-
ness of their pursuit of an aim, would make them major,
apart from anything else. Her people are so relentlessly
thoroughgoing—Anne Eliot in her regret, Miss Bates in her
power to bore, Fanny in her humility, Mr Darcy in his pride,
Elinor in her stability, Harriet in her goosishness, Mrs Bennett in her desire to get her girls off, Emma in her determination to rule—that she creates, in the heart of the mannered
Regency, a muted Elizabethan world of her own. On the
polite plane, violence has its equivalent. Witty, detached,
engaging and travelling lightly, her pen has been dipped in
the purest English ink. *Persuasion* and *Emma* are as out-
standingly English as *War and Peace* is Russian or *L'Éduca-
tion sentimentale* French. Her keen eye is for the manner,
but sees the spirit behind.

She lived, it is true, in a small and very secure world, in
which values were not questioned: nothing got dragged up.
Her unperplexity—or the resentment it arouses—is perhaps at
the root of many objections to her. The charge of tameness
against her is in itself so wild, the charge of triviality so
trivial, that there must be something rather deeper behind
them. She has been more fairly, perhaps, disliked than pa-
tronized—her own ironic remark about the two inches of ivory
always pursuing her. No woman had ever less the provinciality
of her sex, no lady less the provinciality of her sphere. It is
all very well to talk grandiosely about the world in general:
one's nearest hope of knowing the world in general is to syn-
thesize one's knowledge of the particular. Accident—the accident of her birth—dictated the scene and scope of her novels

but did not restrict their power. She was a very rare example —perhaps Proust was another—of intelligence articulating with the social personality; she was one of those happy natures whose very stuff is intelligence, with which nothing goes to waste, that everything aliments. Provinciality is a malady bred of being too much engaged with one's surroundings: the provinciality of Bohemia is well known. To be unprovincial is to know what is important, to see the exact importance of everything that you see. To underrate a deliberately quiet life is, absurdly, to confuse experience with knowledge. Every writer is born with something to find out, and Jane Austen, by dancing circumspectly at county balls, chatting with people in drawing-rooms, staying with her relations and visiting Bath and London, found out what it was necessary for her to know.

She enjoyed being a woman, and being a gentlewoman. Emulativeness and the succeeding antagonisms did not distort her view of the other sex. Her men characters appear in company only, and are present only in relation to women —as hosts (Sir John Middleton, Mr Weston), fathers (Mr Bennett, Mr Woodhouse), uncles (Sir Thomas Bertram), suitors (Mr Elton, Mr Collins), flirts (Frank Churchill, Mr Wickham), *partis* (Mr Bingly), husbands (Mr John Knightley, Mr John Dashwood), incalculable admirers (Mr Darcy, Henry Crawford, Henry Tilney), or, though rarely, the magnetic beloved object upon whom happiness depends (Captain Wentworth and, passingly, Willoughby). Their appearance in any of these rôles she describes with an unastounded, friendly exactitude. She had a keen cool amused ear for how gentlemen talked. Sport, business and manners in love were not her province, but she did know a little about the Navy and usefully brought that in. The Army remains an occupation for officers when not busy dancing or paying calls. With her respect for the Church, Henry Tilney's charming whimsical elegance was not out of colour. It is not because Edmund Bertram is an earnest young clergyman that he does not, as a hero, entirely come off. Their cloth does not protect Mr Elton and Mr Collins. . . . In men, she honoured integrity (even stiffened at times by a touch of priggishness, as in Edmund Bertram and Mr Knightley), expected and

was amused by amiability and good address, and was agree-
ably susceptible to charm—no woman who was not could
have brought Frank Churchill, Willoughby, Henry Crawford
and Henry Tilney to life. She must have been one of those
fortunate young women who can enjoy glamour without having illusions. She writes about men with a distant confidence
that I believe to be justified. It is women who write about
men with an awful matey knowingness who give one a sad-
dening sense of the handicaps of their sex. . . . Adultery occurred but was also outside her province: "Let other pens
dwell on guilt and misery". She was, however, not squeamish:
the disgraceful affair of Willoughby and Miss Williams,
though touched in fairly lightly, is not scamped. The thought
of sexual misery both depressed and offended her: moreover
it was socially inconvenient. It is true that her characters are
preoccupied with marriage, and that the novels hinge on who
is to marry whom. But the subject, with its ramifications, is
absorbing still. And when one heard more about marriage
one heard less about sex.

Her two most imposing men are Mr Darcy in *Pride and
Prejudice* and Henry Crawford in *Mansfield Park*. . . . Mr
Darcy falls for Elizabeth Bennett, with her disconcerting
charm and impossible family, against his will: he shows the
extraordinary bends and twists a reluctant love takes. In a
crisis—and his relations with Elizabeth, up to the end of the
book, are a series of muffled crises—Mr Darcy retreats on a
violent formality. Compound of passion and snobbery, he is
a Proustian figure. Humiliated by his own inconvenient love,
he tries to put his friend Bingley off marrying Elizabeth's
sister Jane: the Bennett family simply do not do. Encounters
between Mrs Bennett and Mr Darcy, in Elizabeth's hearing,
are studies in acute mortification. He was a man of the strongest family feeling; had he not been, his own aunt, Lady
Catherine de Bourgh, would have distressed him more. Evidently he had the maximum power of embarrassing people:
why else should the dauntless Elizabeth have minded so
much when he came on her walking with her uncle and aunt
in his park? The situation was, it is true, a little embarrassing, but something about Mr Darcy made it a good deal
worse. He is a good man, a man of integrity, with the sombre

attractiveness of a wicked one. Returning again and again to
Mr Darcy, one pays Jane Austen the compliment of deciding
that there was more to him than she knew. He has that
cloudy outline important characters should have; does not
seem to have been "created" in the limited brain-bound sense
so much as observed fleetingly out of the corner of an eye,
recollected uncertainly, speculated upon. One takes him to
be a devious, constantly self-regarding and very passionate
man—but he soars out of the picture—most of him happens
off. In a woman writer's book, any man who is intended to
be either important or magnetic ought to have this quality.
. . . Henry Crawford is more energetic, dashing and un-
scrupulous. He has a certain *beauté du diable*. Though not,
like Frank Churchill, a high-spirited, rather engagingly silly
flirt, he is sardonically irresponsible where the Miss Bertrams
are concerned. He is the most sophisticated of Jane Austen's
men, and has also an excellent intellect: when he is at Mansfield Park they have good after-dinner talk (*vide* the conversation about Shakespeare). He had "moral taste"—a particular
aesthetic sensibility to innocence—which is in keeping with
his character. ("Moral taste" is interesting: only highly civilized and really rather morally neutral people have it: it is
the stuff of James and Turgeniev novels.)

Henry Crawford watches the young shy Fanny—who already so much attracts him—and her sailor brother William
together. He

saw, with lively admiration, the glow of Fanny's cheek,
the brightness of her eye, the deep interest, the absorbed
attention, while her brother was describing any of the
imminent hazards or terrific scenes, which such a period
at sea must supply.

It was a picture which Henry Crawford had moral
taste enough to value. Fanny's attractions increased—increased twofold. . . .

He enjoyed, in fact, and enjoyed morally also, this innocent
kindling of her windflower beauty. But there is a kind of
niceness about Henry Crawford; no hint of the jaded palate
about his feeling for Fanny. His susceptibility is complex.
Fanny's refusal to marry him twists him back on himself in

a mood of destructive ugliness and ill-temper. His affair, then elopement, with Maria Rushworth (*née* Bertram) is the result. One can only suppose he turned to Maria Bertram as being the type of woman he really most disliked—neither gallant nor innocent. It was one more of his "freaks of cold-blooded vanity". Had he not, already, virtually, "lost the woman he rationally as well as passionately loved"? It is impossible not to be impatient with Fanny for her refusal (if one has not, indeed, become impatient with her already). Henry Crawford was her one chance of growing up. As it is, she remains with the colourless Edmund: loyal, jejune and prim. We are told Henry Crawford regretted the injury he did to Mansfield Park in ruining Maria. But this regret in itself may have been a bitter pleasure. There are times when one feels Henry Crawford an exile from a French novel. But he remains an Englishman. Jane Austen knew an amazing amount about him, and—involuntarily—liked him a good deal. Like Mr Darcy, but more so, he towers outside the book in which he appears. Mr Darcy is part of the structure of *Pride and Prejudice*, but Henry Crawford counters the moral rhythm of *Mansfield Park*—which is at once the most intellectual and the most nearly insincere novel she wrote.

Her women—even her quieter women—have an astounding vitality. Only Fanny Price is unvital, and Fanny does not, to my mind at least, come off. Elizabeth Bennett and Emma have a Shakespearean gallant calm uncoyness. These two heroines diffuse themselves through the pages with such extraordinary brilliance that it is difficult to believe they are not in the room. Anne Eliot's is a vitality of the heart: she has Fanny's delicacy and recessiveness, but is not at any moment insipid or dim; you would always know she was there. She is essentially grown-up. At a time when to be unmarried at twenty-seven tended to be either pitiable or ridiculous, she remains assured and graceful, playing the piano for the young people to dance. . . . Marianne Dashwood, though her view of life is intended to be preposterous, is lovely and moving, with her great dark eyes. Elinor Dashwood is stodgy but has a nice humour and behaves really extraordinarily well.

Emma and Elizabeth only discover their own states of heart towards the close of the novels they animate. Elinor loves Edward and Fanny Edmund from the outset; Anne's regret for Captain Wentworth, then reawakened love for him, is the spring of her being. Emotion in Elinor, Fanny and Anne is pertinacious, patient and curiously clear-headed. Marianne, on the contrary, is not only swept off her feet by her love for Willoughby, put positively leaps into the wave. Elizabeth's and Emma's awakenings to love are excellently in character. Nothing dims Elizabeth's gallant wit: she goes on gently pulling Mr Darcy's leg. With Emma "the dread of being awakened from the happiest dream was perhaps the most prominent feeling". All the same "while he spoke, her mind was busy".

Anne Eliot's feeling for Captain Wentworth is the only love in the novels which is poetic. Elinor Dashwood and Fanny both make one feel they feel the young men in question do not really know what is good for them. In not one of the novels does the simple upright worldliness of the setting (it would never do to marry any young man who would never do) invalidate any emotion felt. Antisocial love is not necessarily stronger or purer in quality than social love.

Jane Austen's attitude to each of her women is different. Emma is seen, and felt, as divinely unconsciously funny throughout. To see one's heroine through in a comic light, without buffooning her or devaluating her for the other characters, is an achievement. (Incidentally, Emma's feeling for Frank Churchill is an excellent study of vanity in the heart.) Fanny is not Jane Austen's type at all—she is projected, too palpably "created", a *tour de force* which does not come off. Jane Austen's love of goodness impregnates all the books, but it did not do to centre this round one character: she has rather a forced tenderness for Fanny. Elinor she liked but was not interested in; Elinor is a straight line of sanity ruled through the book, serves her purpose staunchly but remains rather abstract. Marianne she deplored, but Marianne remains moving; unforgettable is her scream of agony after getting Willoughby's fatal letter (and what a model of an unforgivable letter: "the lock of hair which you so obligingly bestowed on me"). . . . . Elizabeth Bennett was clearly a joy to write about, to share vicissitudes with: Elizabeth and Jane Austen were kindred spirits; when Elizabeth came into being they were the same age, both going to balls. . . . Harriet was a sweet goose she had to like, Jane Fairfax intimidated her as much as she intimidated Emma, Mary Crawford's charm gained her in spite of herself, Lucy Steele's vulgarity and bogus emotion afflicted her as it did Elinor. . . . Anne Eliot remains the beloved grown-up friend, whose sorrows are shared, whose patience is honoured, whose beauty is seen. Jane Austen envelops her, unconsciously, in the greatness she had herself as a woman, the poeticness, the submissiveness, the courage that the younger novels had not yet brought into play. In *Persuasion*, Nature is present, and tenderly felt: up to now it has been simply a social factor—weather.

And what weather—opportune sometimes, difficult others, a saver of situations, a precipitator of crises. Snow in Highbury, rain in Bath, the June heat of the strawberry party at Donwell, through which Jane Fairfax sets out, distracted, for home, which made Frank Churchill so cross. The gay blowy day at Lyme Regis. What a glow from the fine day fixed for an outing—"Wednesday was fine, and soon after breakfast the barouche arrived. . . . Their road was through pleasant country." And, apart from the weather, what parties! Few writers' novels can hold so many, none so directly convey that (if the expression may be forgiven) a good time was had by all. She also transmits, with an extraordinary vivacity, the pleasure that people—in or out of love—take in each other's society: the charm of a new acquaintance, the surprise of a morning call, or the delight of looking at someone pretty. Here is Mary Crawford playing the harp in the rectory drawing-room:

A young woman, pretty, lively, with a harp as elegant as herself, and both placed near a window cut down to the ground and opening on a little lawn, surrounded by shrubs in the rich foliage of summer, was enough to catch any man's heart.

Elizabeth Bennett, with her colour, her grace, her vitality, is the most palpably attractive of the heroines (did she not magnetize Darcy's unwilling eyes?), Mary Crawford the most glamorous of the women. Emma must have had a lovely complexion, Elinor Dashwood had a pretty figure. None of her heroines are paragons, but they are all successes. She has a woman's regard for women who are a success, as well as the author's semi-parental pride. She knows, too, how to make the onlooker's eye add quality to its object: Emma is seen as Highbury's most important young lady, Elizabeth as she so disturbed Mr Darcy, Fanny kindling to brilliance with brother William, with Henry Crawford sitting watchfully by.

No possible shade of being bored, offended, mortified, non-plussed or flattered is overlooked by her, or not faithfully rendered. She was right: her people were young, vitally young, and when one is young these things are very important. A malaise, a regret, a reverse, what one thinks of somebody, what somebody seems to think of one, either muffle or deco-rate an entire day. The interaction of social and personal feeling was her subject, like Proust's, and her diagnosis was as correct.

The technique of the novels is beyond praise, and has been praised. Her mastery of the art she chose, or that chose her, is complete: how she achieved it no one will ever know. Though I suppose that none of her books are flawless, I can-not think of one clumsy blunder she made. Her intellect was so immediately applied, so closely related to what it fed on, so unabstract that it seems fitter to speak of it as intelligence: it was intelligence of a sublime kind. If she did speculate, this must have been in a series of photographs. She was as sensible about ideas as she was about men; she must have had a most uncloudy mind. Any wisps of reverie floating about in it got solidified into little touches in books. She was, in fact, the rightly adjusted person. . . . The kind of novel generally *called* intellectual is thin in texture, so that the anxious operation of the intellect shows. Because as a story it does not quite come off, you feel more bound to honour the author's high intention. But Jane Austen's are the truly intellectual novels because her mind impregnates the whole of their matter, functioning in every comma, add-ing colour, force, light.

Any great book strikes one as having imposed itself on its author. The element of invention, of ingenuity, is palpable only in secondary books. But no book imposes itself on a passive mind. Something other, outside, may command and mobilize the imagination, but the brain has to leap up to cope with this, like a swarm of post-office hands with an incoming mail. The greater the force and speed of what is happening imaginatively, the colder and closer scrutiny this must have from the brain. An artist, to be effective, has to be half critic. Fancy and reason ought to have equal strength: in Jane Austen they had, which is why she wrote what were almost perfect novels. Her wit worked well, allowing her fancy pleasure; her fancy, by not halting, brought her wit to no heavy and cold pause. Her style is balanced, like someone skating beautifully. Her exhilaration must have been tremendous: perhaps she only half knew what was going on. An artist can never be fully conscious. But neither can he cut ice if he is not an unremittingly conscious executant.

She wrote novels, and wished to write nothing else. "Yes, novels," she says in *Northanger Abbey*, ". . . performances which have only genius, wit and taste to recommend them." When she died she was not old, and might still have written more. She had been ill for some time before that, and *Sanditon*, which had been put away, was unfinished, which is too bad.

Scott
ON
Jane Austen:

[*Miss Austen*] *had a talent for describing the involvements and feelings and characters of ordinary life which is to me the most wonderful I ever met with. The Big Bow-wow strain I can do myself like any now going; but the exquisite touch which renders ordinary, commonplace things and characters interesting, from the truth of the description and the sentiment, is denied to me.*

CHARLOTTE BRONTË

This generation knows that Charlotte Brontë's own generation gave her too high a place in the artistic hierarchy when it exalted her above her sister Emily, but is itself tempted to place her too low because of the too easily recognizable *naïveté* of her material.

It is true that the subject-matter of all her work is, under one disguise or another, the Cinderella theme which is the stand-by of the sub-artist in fiction and the theatre, all the world over and in any age. She treats it in the form it takes in the hands of those who have moved just one degree away from complete *naïveté*: instead of it being supposed that Cinderella has the advantage of physical beauty over the Ugly Sisters, it is supposed (as an absolute and more magical compensation to the sense of inferiority which weaves and needs the story) that it is they who are beautiful, and she who is ugly, though possessed of an invisible talisman of spiritual quality which wholly annuls that disadvantage. This is the theme of *Jane Eyre* and *Villette*, and, with certain elaborations and feints, of *Shirley* also; and it cannot be denied that we have grave reason to associate it with work which is not artistic at all, which sets out not to explore reality, but to nourish the neurotic fantasies with which feebler brains defend themselves from reality.

Charlotte Brontë also uses material which many people denounce as naïve with, I think, less foundation. She records oppressions practised by the dowered on the dowerless, and by adults on children, and seems to many of her readers absurd and unpleasant when she does so; but that is perhaps not because such incidents never happen, but because we dislike admitting that they happen. There is hardly a more curious example of the gap we leave between life and literature than the surprise and incredulity recorded by successive generations of Brontëan commentators at the passages in the sisters' works which suggest that the well-to-do are sometimes uncivil to their employees. In actual fact, all of us, even today, if we were connected with a young girl who was going out into the world as a governess, would feel an anxiety that she should be with "nice people," which would imply a lively fear of what nasty people are capable of doing to governesses; but these commentators write as if Charlotte and Anne must have been the victims of hysterical morbidity when they implied that governesses were sometimes treated rudely, although the idea then prevalent, that one was divinely appointed to one's social station, cannot have improved the manners of employers. It has been the opinion of all moral teachers from the days of the Psalmist that riches lead to haughtiness and froward bearing; yet when Miss Blanch Ingram tells the footman, "Cease that chatter, blockhead," the commentators shake their heads and smile, without reflecting that she was supposed to have made that remark in the year preceding Queen Victoria's accession to the throne, when much of the eighteenth-century coarseness of manners still lingered, and that even to-day women can be found who have the tiresome habit of being rude to waiters and menservants.

We may suspect, then, that the common objection to this material is not that it has no correspondence with reality, but that it is intensely embarrassing for us to contemplate. The feeling of inferiority, under which we all labour, may find a gratifying opportunity for self-pity in the accounts of the suffering which superiors can unjustly inflict on their inferiors, but only if they are not too vivid; for if they are, then we feel terror at the quality of the universe. And if that be so when the accounts refer to the relatively remote symbolism of social matters, which we all of us can discount by reference to some other system of values which we have devised to suit our special case, how much more will it be so when they refer to the actual and agonizing experiences of our childhood! In these days one is weaker than nearly all the world. However kindly one is treated, one is frustrated and humiliated, one's natural habits are corrected, and one's free speech censored; and if one is not kindly treated, one can take no revenge, one is without means of protecting one's dignity. There must be something shameful in such a phase to an organism as much in love with the idea of its own free will as the human being. Thus the descriptions of Jane Eyre's ill-treatment at the hands of the Reeds, and the sufferings of the pupils at Lowood, revive a whole series of associations in the readers' minds which the more imaginative and intellectually developed among them will hate to recall. They will turn from Charlotte Brontë's work with the accusation that it is infantile; but what they mean is that she exposes her own and their infantilism. She lifts a curtain, and reveals what the world usually keeps hidden. In her pictures of these oppressions she demonstrates the workings of our universal sense that we are worms; as in her use of the Cinderella theme she demonstrates our universal hope that, though we are but worms, a miracle will happen, and we shall be made kings of the world. It may be objected that any hack writer of penny dreadfuls does as much; but that is untrue. The hack writer spins the consoling fantasy, and so does Charlotte Brontë; but she also depicts the hunger that goads the spinner to the task. Her work, considered as a whole, is as powerful an analysis of the working of the sense of inferiority and its part in creating romanticism as the mind of man has ever made.

But colour is lent to the suspicion that Charlotte Brontë is not an artist but a sub-artist, that she does not analyse experience, but weaves fantasies to hang between man and his painful experience, by her frequent use of the sub-artist's chosen weapon, sentimental writing. This also is a feature of her work which is specially repugnant to the present generation's hyper-sensitiveness to the superficial decorum of literature; and it remains an indefensible defect. But it adds to Charlotte Brontë's power over our attentions, because in so far as she discloses it with her unequalled ardour and honesty, she gives us a picture of the eternal artist experiencing an eternally recurrent misadventure.

For Charlotte Brontë's tendency to sentimental writing was not due to an innate inaptitude for the artistic process, but to the pressure of external circumstance. In one important respect her life was unfavourable to the practise of art. This was not loneliness and privation: Emily Brontë, suffering the same portion of these ills, was the complete artist. It was not the misconduct of her brother Branwell, though that was a contributing factor to it. It was her specially acute need to make, by separate and violent acts of the will, the place in the world for herself and her two younger sisters which should have been made for them by their elders. Her realization of this need must have been panic-stricken and desperate, for the whole of her life was ravaged by a series of progressively bitter disappointments in the protection which children expect from adults and which women expect from men.

Mrs. Brontë died of cancer when Charlotte was five years old, and for some time before her death the progress of her malady and her regular confinements prevented her from giving her children much attention. Mr. Brontë was an eccentric recluse whose capacity for parenthood seems to have been purely physical. Even before he had taken to the bottle, he took no trouble to provide his children with either his own sympathy or proper companionship, or any but the barest preparation for adult life. Mrs. Brontë's sister, who came North from Cornwall to take charge of the orphaned children, disliked Yorkshire, retired to her bedroom, and cared for none of them except Branwell. From the terrible matter-of-factness with which Emily and Charlotte Brontë draw (in Nelly Deans and in Bessie) the servant whose unimaginative cruelty changes to a not very reliable kindness, one sees that there was no steady comfort for the children in the kitchen. It was in her sister Maria, the oldest of the family, that Charlotte found a substitute for her mother; we know that from the portrait of Helen Burns in *Jane Eyre*. But Maria died at the age of twelve, when Charlotte was eight; and her only other older sister, Elizabeth, died two months later.

About the time of Charlotte's ninth birthday, then, the negligence and death of her elders left her with her own way to make in the world. But that is an understatement, for it supposes her burdenless. It would be more accurate to say that she became the head of the family, with one brother and two sisters, all deeply loved, dependent on her for everything above the bare physical necessities of life. The records of the Brontës' childhood show her eagerly answering the call to leadership; but she was not then altogether to be pitied. She was still supported by her penultimate hope. Whatever the defections of Mr. Brontë, they would not be without a man to look after them as soon as their brother grew up. It is confessed honestly and radiantly in Charlotte Brontë's books how she craved for the support that the child-bearing faculty of woman logically entitles her to expect from man, and there was a special factor in her environment to give intensity to that craving.

Victorian England was a man's country. She might well have hoped that with Branwell Brontë's fine natural endowment he would easily find a place in it, and that she would see herself and her sisters decently maintained or helped to decent employment. But she was still a girl when it became apparent that Branwell, in spite of all his brilliant promise, was growing up, not into a man, but into a pathetic nuisance, who would not even decently maintain himself. For the sixth time natural supports had failed her. She knew the terrible fear felt by the young who begin to suspect that they are going to be cheated out of the fullness of life; and she was not fearful for herself alone, but also for Anne and Emily, in whose gifts she had faith, and for whose health she had every reason to fear. She had seen her two elder sisters die, and she had probably forebodings that she was to see the other two die also. It is known that she had such forebodings about Anne.

During the years when it was becoming plain that Branwell was going to be of no help to them, but "a drain on every resource," Charlotte became more and more desperate. By this time, it is interesting to note, she was half-blind. But if no one would give her and her sisters their fair share of life, she herself would see that they got what she could snatch; and she snatched far more than one would think possible. The astounding thing about the Brontës' life is not its emptiness but—considering the bareness of Haworth Parsonage—its fullness. There were several friends; there was a good deal of employment, including the Brussels expedition; there was the literary adventure. And it was Charlotte who made the friends, Charlotte who found the teaching posts, Charlotte who wrote the letters to the publishers. Now, it is easy to sneer at these achievements, on the ground that the greatest of the three sisters, Emily, found them purely vexatious, since she was shy of strangers, loathed leaving the moors of Haworth, and would rather have kept her poems to herself. Nevertheless, Charlotte's actions followed the natural direction of sanity. Like all living things, she strove for the survival of herself and her belongings with the balance of her impulses. It was hardly to be expected that reverence for Emily's genius should oust the desire to keep her alive and any change which removed her from the rigours of the Parsonage must have at first seemed favourable to that end. There is nothing to be said against Charlotte's frenzied efforts to counter the nihilism of her surroundings, unless one is among those who would find amusement in the sight of the starving fighting for food.

In the sphere of life they were unquestionably noble; but it unfortunately happened—and here lies the disconcerting value of Charlotte as a revelation of the artist-type—that in the sphere of art they had a disintegrating effect. They committed her to a habit of activism which was the very antithesis of the quietism demanded from the artist. In her desire to make a place in the world for herself and her family against time, she could let nothing establish itself by slow growth, she had to force the pace of every intimacy and every action, which means that she had constantly to work upon people with the aim of immediately provoking them to certain emotions. Sprightly or touching letters had to be written to the friends to keep them near in spite of distance; Miss Branwell had to be induced to finance the Brussels expedition, and Mrs. Wooller had to have her interest in the new school kept warm; Southey, Wordsworth, Tennyson, Lockhart, and de Quincey had to be addressed in the vain attempt to rouse their interest in Currer, Ellis, and Acton Bell. In fact, she was forced to a passionate participation in a business of working on people's feelings exclusive of the true business of art, and the root of the evil that we call sentimentality.

This, therefore, was Charlotte's special temptation: she

was so used to manipulating people's feelings in life that she could not lose the habit in her art, and was apt to fall into sentimentality. All her novels are defaced to varying degrees by passages which have nothing to do with the organic growth of the story, and are inspired simply by guess-work as to the state of the reader's feelings. An extreme example of this is the scene where the Yorkes call on Miss Moore and find Caroline Helstone in her parlour, in the twenty-third chapter of *Shirley*. The same error is committed in an earlier scene of the book, but it is here more noteworthy and disastrous, because here there is promise of high poetic value. Caroline is sick with love for Robert Moore, and faint with despair. Mrs. Yorke looms over her like a personification of the cruelty that must govern the world if it is true that she is not to have her love; the Yorke children have the fantastic, unclassical quality that all objects not the beloved assume under the lover's eye. When Caroline's veins are flushed with quicksilver rage against that cruelty, the scene should end, and she should be left still waiting for Robert at the jessamined window. But Miss Brontë's habit of bustling was too strong for her then. She could not trust her slow magic to make the reader's interest slowly mount. She felt she must put them under a swiftly growing debt to her for entertainment. She remembered how Martha Taylor, who was the original of little Jessy Yorke, had often entertained her with her precocious tirades; so she reproduced one there and then. She also remembered what a poignant effect had been made by this child's early death; so she inserted a description of her funeral. The continuity of the scene is broken, the author's and the reader's contacts with Caroline are lost, and whatever emotion is felt is diverted from the real theme.

It would be easy to point to many other pages in Charlotte Brontë's novels where sentimental writing has been allowed to destroy the structure of the work; and there is one case where sentimentality has been allowed to plan such a structure faultily. The melodramatic plot of *Jane Eyre* is not a symbol honestly conceived by extreme *naïveté*, but was invented, in her own admission, to suit a supposed popular demand for sensationalism. That was a pity, for there are pages in the book, such as the scene where the lovers walk in the orchard under the rising moon, which deserve the best of settings. But great as is the harm done to the valuable content of Charlotte Brontë's work by her choice of certain episodes and series of episodes simply for their immediate effect on her readers, still greater is the harm done by the diffusion of sentimentality through her style. It is crammed with direct appeals to the emotions, which make it tediously repetitive, explosive, and irrelevant to the deeper themes discussed.

That this defect was not inborn in Charlotte, but was the product of her circumstances, can be proved by a reference to a letter quoted by Mrs. Gaskell from *The Little Magazine*, which the Brontës composed in their childhood. It begins: "SIR,—It is well known that the Genii have declared that unless they perform certain arduous duties every year, of a mysterious nature, all the worlds in the firmament will be burnt up and gathered together in one mighty globe," and no style could be more decorous and more sincere. But she wrote it at the age of thirteen, before she had become a panic-stricken adept in the art of negotiation. She was never to write such prose again until her passion for M. Héger made her forget all her schemes and anxieties, and changed her to the insanely honest instrument of one intention and one need.

The obviousness with which what was a virtue in Charlotte Brontë's life became a vice in her art, makes her one of the most disconcerting among great writers to contemplate. She is suspended between the two spheres of art and life, and not in a state of rest. She is torn between them. But where this generation will probably err is in supposing that her plight is unique, her helplessness before this temptation a personal defect. There is sentimentality in every age, even in our own; and we swallow it whole if its subject-matter is not of a sort that arouses suspicion. That was where Charlotte Brontë erred. All of us not actually illiterate or imbecile feel that something is wrong when a writer attempts to compel his readers' feelings by the exploitation of early deaths, handsome sinners with lunatic wives, and ecstatic dithyrambs. The march of culture has forced such knowledge on the least of us.

But let us examine the current attitude to the great Russians. A great many readers, and some of these drawn from the professionally fastidious, place Tolstoy above Turgeniev and Dostoievsky. Yet Turgeniev was, as Mr. George Moore has said in that incomparable book of criticism, *Avowals,* "a sort of Jesus of Nazareth in art," who gave himself to the artistic process with so little reservation for his personal ends, that there is no conflict in his work, only serenity; and though it is true, as Mr. Moore says in the same book, that, before we can admire Dostoievsky's novels, "modern life must wring all the Greek out of us," he also, albeit with constant cries of protest at the pain it cost him, forced himself to the honest analysis of experience. But Tolstoy is fully as sentimental a writer as Charlotte Brontë. In *War and Peace, Anna Karenina,* and *Resurrection,* he pushes his characters about with the greatest conceivable brusqueness in order to prove his thesis, and exhorts his readers to accept his interpretations of their movements. He even admits in *What is Art?* that he thinks this the proper way for the artist to behave. Nevertheless, Tolstoy arouses no repugnance in this generation, although this use of art to prove what man already knows is a shameful betrayal of the mission of art to tell man more than he knows. This is only because the subject-matter of his sentimentality is unfamiliar. He attempts to influence his readers in favour of a thesis dependent on the primitive sense of guilt, and the need for expiation by the endurance and infliction of suffering, which had been forbidden expression above a certain cultural level in the rationalist nineteenth century. We are not on our guard against it as we are against Charlotte Brontë's Cinderella theme; and we succumb to what must be an eternally recurrent temptation.

Yet if Charlotte Brontë represents an eternally recurrent defeat of the artist, she also represents his eternally recurrent triumph. She told the truth even about matters concerning which the whole civilization round her had conspired to create a fiction; and her telling of it is not an argument, but an affirmation, that comes and is, like the light of the sun and the moon. It is not only true that, as Swinburne said, again and again she shows the—

"power to make us feel in every nerve, at every step forward which our imagination is compelled to take un-

der the guidance of another's, that thus and not otherwise, but in all things altogether even as we are told
and shown, it was, and must have been, with the human
figures set before us in their action and their suffering;
that thus, and not otherwise, they absolutely must and
would have felt and thought and spoken under the proposed conditions."

It is not only true that she abounds in touches of that
kind of strange beauty which, dealing solely with the visible
world, nevertheless persuades us that the visible world is going to swing open as if it were a gate and disclose a further
view: like the description of the stable-yard in Thornfield at
dawn, with the blinds still drawn in the windows, and the
birds twittering in the blossom-laden orchard, when the mysterious stranger drives away with the surgeon after his mysterious wounding. She does more than that, she makes a
deeper revelation of the soul.

In an age which set itself to multiply the material wants
of mankind (with what results we see to-day) and to whittle
down its spiritual wants to an ethical anxiety that was often
mean, Charlotte Brontë serenely lifted up her voice, and
testified to the existence of the desires which are the buds
of all human thoughts and actions. Her candid and clair-
voyant vision of such things is displayed again and again
throughout her works, but never more notably than in the
two instances which make *Villette* one of the most interesting of English novels. The first is the description of the innocent but passionate love of the little girl Polly for the school-
boy John. The second is the description of how Lucy Snowe's
love passed without a break from John Bretton to Paul Eman-
uel; never before has there been such a frank admission of
the subtle truth that the romantic temperament writes a lover's part, and then casts an actor to play it, and that nevertheless there is more there than make-believe. To realize how
rare a spirit it required to make and record such observations
at the time one must turn to Miss Harriet Martineau's comments on the book as given in Mrs. Gaskell's *Life*; though
one should remember that Miss Martineau was herself to
suffer from the age's affectation of wantlessness. For when, as

an elderly lady, she received a present of money from her
admirers, the subscribers were greatly incensed when she proposed to spend an undue proportion of it on a silver tea
equipage; yet surely any earlier age would have understood
this belated desire for a little handsomeness.

But Charlotte Brontë did more than unconsciously correct
the error of her age; she saw as deeply as poets do. There
are surely two scenes which have the dignity and significance
of great poetry. One is the scene in *Villette*, where the fe-
vered girl wanders by night out of the silent school, with the
intention of seeking a certain stone basin that she remembers
to have seen, brimming with cool water, in a glade of the
park; and finds the city ablaze with light, thronged with a
tide of happy people, which bears up to the park that is now
fantastic with coloured lights and pasteboard palaces, a phan-
tasmagoria in which she walks and sees her friends, her foes,
her beloved, but is not seen. There has never before been
found a more vivid symbolic representation of the state of
passion in which the whole universe, lacking the condition
of union with the beloved, seems a highly coloured but in-
substantial illusion, objective counterpart to delirium. Yet
even finer is the scene in *Shirley* called "A Summer Night,"
when Shirley and Caroline creep across the moonlit fields to
warn Moore of the approach of rioters, and are too late.
There, when the two girls stand "alone with the friendly
night, the mute stars, and these whispering trees," listening
to the shouts and watching the fires of masculine dissension
(which is their opposite and what they live by), and while
what is male in woman speaks with the voice of Shirley, and
what is female speaks with the voice of Caroline, one perceives that a statement is being found for that which the intellect has not yet stated in direct terms.

Charlotte Brontë was a supreme artist; and yet she was
very nearly not an artist at all. That will make her an unsympathetic figure to many in these days, when a school of
criticism, determined to exert authority but without the intellectual power to evolve an authoritative doctrine, has im-
ported into this country its own puerile version of the debate
between romanticism and classicism which has cut up the
French world of letters into sterile sectionalism, and trots

about frivolously inventing categories on insufficient bases
rejecting works of art that do not fit into them, and attaching
certificates to those that do. But she will inspire and console
those who realize that art is a spiritual process committed to
imperfection by the flesh, which is its medium; that though
there are artists who seem to transcend the limitations of
that medium, like Bach and Mozart and Emily Brontë, they
are rare as the saints, and, like them, sublime but not final
in their achievements; and that the complete knowledge and
mastery of experience which would be attained in a perfect
world of art is like the *summum bonum* of the theologians,
the vision of God which is to reward the pure in heart, and
cannot be realized until time is changed to eternity.

Thackeray   *Since the author of* Tom Jones *was*
ON   *buried, no writer of fiction among us*
Fielding: *has been permitted to depict to his*
                   utmost power a man.

Flaubert
writing to
George Sand
ON
Dickens:

I've just read Pickwick *by Dickens. Do you know it? Some bits are magnificent; but what a defective structure! All English writers are like that. Walter Scott apart, they lack composition. This is intolerable for us Latins.*

Tolstoy
ON
Dostoevsky:

Lately I was ill, and read Dostoevsky's House of the Dead. *I have read much, and forgotten much; but I do not know in all modern literature, Pushkin included, any better book.*

. . . . .

I never saw the man, had no sort of direct relations with him; but when he died, I suddenly realized that he had been to me the most precious, the dearest, and the most necessary of beings. It never entered my head to compare myself with him. Everything that he wrote (I mean only the good, the true things) was such that the more he did like that, the more I rejoiced. Artistic accomplishment and intellect can arouse my envy; but a work from the heart—only joy.

W. M. *Thackeray* on

And now there is but one book left in the box, the smallest
one, but oh! how much the best of all. It is the work of the
master of all the English humourists now alive; the young
man who came and took his place calmly at the head of the
whole tribe, and who has kept it. Think of all we owe Mr.
Dickens since these half-dozen years, the store of happy hours
that he has made us pass, the kindly and pleasant companions whom he has introduced to us, the harmless laughter,
the generous wit, the frank, manly, human love which he has
taught us to feel! Every month of these years has brought us
some kind token from this delightful genius. His books may
have lost in art, perhaps, but could we afford to wait? Since
the days when the *Spectator* was produced by a man of kindred mind and temper, what books have appeared that have
taken so affectionate a hold of the English public as these?
They have made millions of rich and poor happy; they might
have been locked up for nine years, doubtless, and pruned
here and there, and improved (which I doubt) but where
would have been the reader's benefit all this time, while the
author was elaborating his performance? Would the communication between the writer and the public have been what
it is now—something continual, confidential, something like
personal affection? I do not know whether these stories are
written for future ages; many sage critics doubt on this head.
There are always such conjurors to tell literary fortunes; and,
to my certain knowledge, Boz, according to them, has been
sinking regularly these six years. I doubt about that mysterious writing for futurity which certain big wigs prescribe.
Snarl has a chance, certainly. His works, which have not been read
in this age, *may* be read in future; but the receipt for that
sort of writing has never as yet been clearly ascertained.

Shakespeare did not write for futurity, he wrote his plays for the same purpose which inspires the pen of Alfred Bunn, Esquire, viz., to fill his Theatre Royal. And yet we read Shakespeare now. Le Sage and Fielding wrote for their public; and though the great Dr. Johnson put his peevish protest against the fame of the latter, and voted him "a dull dog, sir, —a low fellow," yet somehow Harry Fielding has survived in spite of the critic, and Parson Adams is at this minute as real a character, as much loved by us as the old doctor himself. What a noble, divine power of genius this is, which, passing from the poet into his reader's soul, mingles with it, and there engenders, as it were, real creatures; which is as strong as history, which creates beings that take their place beside nature's own. All that we know of Don Quixote or Louis XIV we got to know in the same way—out of a book. I declare I love Sir Roger de Coverley quite as much as Izaak Walton, and have just as clear a consciousness of the looks, voice, habit, and manner of being of the one as of the other.

And so with regard to this question of futurity; if any benevolent being of the present age is imbued with a desire to know what his great-great-grandchild will think of this or that author—of Mr. Dickens especially, whose claims to fame have raised the question—the only way to settle it is by the ordinary historic method. Did not your great-great-grandfather love and delight in Don Quixote and Sancho Panza? Have they lost their vitality by their age? Don't they move laughter and awaken affection now as three hundred years ago? And so with Don Pickwick and Sancho Weller, if their gentle humours and kindly wit, and hearty benevolent natures, touch us and convince us, as it were, now, why should they not exist for our children as well as for us, and make the twenty-fifth century happy, as they have the nineteenth? Let Snarl console himself, then, as to the future.

As for the *Christmas Carol*, or any other book of a like nature which the public takes upon itself to criticise, the individual critic had quite best hold his peace. One remembers what Buonaparte replied to some Austrian critics, of much correctness and acumen, who doubted about acknowledging the French republic. I do not mean that the *Christmas Carol* is quite as brilliant or self-evident as the sun at noonday; but

it is so spread over England by this time, that no sceptic, n●
Fraser's Magazine,—no, not even the godlike and ancien●
Quarterly itself (venerable, Saturnian, big-wigged dynasty!●
could review it down. "Unhappy people! deluded race!" On●
hears the cauliflowered god exclaim, mournfully shaking th●
powder out of his ambrosial curls, "What strange new foll●
is this? What new deity do you worship? Know ye what y●
do? Know ye that your new idol hath little Latin and les●
Greek? Know ye that he has never tasted the birch at Eton●
nor trodden the flags of Carfax, nor paced the academic flat●
of Trumpington? Know ye that in mathematics, or logic, thi●
wretched ignoramus is not fit to hold a candle to a wooden●
spoon? See ye not how, from describing law humours, he now●
forsooth, will attempt the sublime? Discern ye not his faults
of taste, his deplorable propensity to write blank verse? Come
back to your ancient, venerable, and natural instructors.
Leave this new, low and intoxicating draught at which ye
rush, and let us lead you back to the old wells of classic lore.
Come and repose with us there. We are your gods; we are the
ancient oracles, and no mistake. Come listen to us once more,
and we will sing to you the mystic numbers of *as in presenti*
under the arches of the *Pons asinorum*." But the children of
the present generation hear not; for they reply, "Rush to the
Strand, and purchase five thousand more copies of the *Christmas Carol*."

In fact, one might as well detail the plot of the *Merry
Wives of Windsor* or *Robinson Crusoe*, as recapitulate here
the adventures of Scrooge the miser, and his Christmas conversion. I am not sure that the allegory is a very complete
one, and protest, with the classics, against the use of blank
verse in prose; but here all objections stop. Who can listen
to objections regarding such a book as this? It seems to me
a national benefit, and to every man or woman who reads it
a personal kindness. The last two people I heard speak of it
were women; neither knew the other, or the author, and both
said, by way of criticism, "God bless him!" A Scotch philosopher, who nationally does not keep Christmas, on reading the
book, sent out for a turkey, and asked two friends to dine—
this is a fact! Many men were known to sit down after perusing it, and write off letters to their friends, not about busi-

ness, but out of their fulness of heart, and to wish old acquaintances a happy Christmas. Had the book appeared a fortnight earlier, all the prize cattle would have been gobbled up in pure love and friendship, Epping denuded of sausages, and not a turkey left in Norfolk. His royal highness's fat stock would have fetched unheard of prices, and Alderman Bannister would have been tired of slaying. But there is a Christmas for 1844 too; the book will be as early then as now, and so let speculators look out.

As for TINY TIM, there is a certain passage in the book regarding that young gentleman, about which a man should hardly venture to speak in print or in public, any more than he would of any other affections of his private heart. There is not a reader in England but that little creature will be a bond of union between the author and him; and he will say of Charles Dickens, as the woman just now, "GOD BLESS HIM!" What a feeling is this for a writer to be able to inspire, and what a reward to reap.

Thackeray ON Sterne:	*I'm afraid—God help him—a falser and wickeder man it's difficult to read of.*
W. D. Howells ON Jane Austen:	*Jane Austen was the first and the last of the English novelists to treat material with entire truthfulness.*

Charles Dickens on

W. M. THACKERAY

In Memoriam: W. M. Thackeray

It has been desired by some of the friends of the great English writer who established this magazine,[1] that its brief record of his having been stricken from among men should be
written by the old comrade and brother in arms who pen
these lines, and of whom he often wrote himself, and always
with the warmest generosity.

I saw him first, nearly twenty-eight years ago, when he proposed to become the illustrator of my earliest book. I saw him
last, shortly before Christmas, at the Athenaeum Club, when
he told me that he had been in bed three days—that, after
these attacks, he was troubled with cold shiverings "which
quite took the power of work out of him"—and that he had it
in his mind to try a new remedy which he laughingly described. He was very cheerful, and looked very bright. In the
night of that day week, he died.

The long interval between those two periods is marked in
my remembrance of him by many occasions when he was
supremely humorous, when he was irresistibly extravagant,
when he was softened and serious, when he was charming
with children. But, by none do I recall him more tenderly
than by two or three that start out of the crowd, when he unexpectedly presented himself in my room, announcing how
that some passage in a certain book had made him cry yesterday, and how that he had come to dinner "because he
couldn't help it" and must talk such passage over. No one
can ever have seen him more genial, natural, cordial, fresh,
and honestly impulsive, than I have seen him at those times.
No one can be surer than I, of the greatness and the goodness of the heart that then disclosed itself.

[1] *The Cornhill Magazine.*

We had our differences of opinion. I thought that he too much feigned a want of earnestness, and that he made a pretence of undervaluing his art, which was not good for the art that he held in trust. But, when we fell upon these topics, it was never very gravely, and I have a lively image of him in my mind, twisting both his hands in his hair, and stamping about, laughing, to make an end of the discussion.

When we were associated in remembrance of the late Mr. Douglas Jerrold, he delivered a public lecture in London, in the course of which, he read his very best contribution to *Punch*, describing the grown-up cares of a poor family of young children. No one hearing him could have doubted his natural gentleness, or his thoroughly unaffected manly sympathy with the weak and lowly. He read the paper most pathetically, and with a simplicity of tenderness that certainly moved one of his audience to tears. This was presently after his standing for Oxford, from which place he had dispatched his agent to me, with a droll note (to which he afterwards added a verbal postscript), urging me to "come down and make a speech, and tell them who he was, for he doubted whether more than two of his electors had ever heard of him, and he thought there might be as many as six or eight who had heard of me." He introduced the lecture just mentioned, with a reference to his late electioneering failure, which was full of good sense, good spirits, and good humour.

He had a particular delight in boys, and an excellent way with them. I remember his once asking me with fantastic gravity, when he had been to Eton where my eldest son then was, whether I felt as he did in regard of never seeing a boy without wanting instantly to give him a sovereign? I thought of this when I looked down into his grave, after he was laid there, for I looked down into it over the shoulder of a boy to whom he had been kind.

These are slight remembrances; but it is to little familiar things suggestive of the voice, look, manner, never, never more to be encountered on this earth, that the mind first turns in a bereavement. And greater things that are known of him, in the way of his warm affections, his quiet endurance, his unselfish thoughtfulness for others, and his munificent hand, may not be told.

If, in the reckless vivacity of his youth, his satirical pen had ever gone astray or done amiss, he had caused it to prefer its own petition for forgiveness, long before:

> I've writ the foolish fancy of his brain;
> The aimless jest that, striking, hath caused pain;
> The idle word that he'd wish back again.

In no pages should I take it upon myself at this time to discourse of his books, of his refined knowledge of character, of his subtle acquaintance with the weaknesses of human nature, of his delightful playfulness as an essayist, of his quaint and touching ballads, of his mastery over the English language. Least of all, in these pages, enriched by his brilliant qualities from the first of the series, and beforehand accepted by the Public through the strength of his great name.

But, on the table before me, there lies all that he had written of his latest and last story. That it would be very sad to any one—that it is inexpressibly so to a writer—in its evidences of matured designs never to be accomplished, of intentions begun to be executed and destined never to be completed, of careful preparation for long roads of thought that he was never to traverse, and for shining goals that he was never to reach, will be readily believed. The pain, however, that I have felt in perusing it, has not been deeper than the conviction that he was in the healthiest vigour of his powers when he wrought on this last labour. In respect of earnest feeling, far-seeing purpose, character, incident, and a certain loving picturesqueness blending the whole, I believe it to be much the best of all his works. That he fully meant it to be so, that he had become strongly attached to it, and that he bestowed great pains upon it, I trace in almost every page. It contains one picture which must have caused him extreme distress, and which is a masterpiece. There are two children in it, touched with a hand as loving and tender as ever a father caressed his little child with. There is some young love, as pure and innocent and pretty as the truth. And it is very remarkable that, by reason of the singular construction of the story, more than one main incident usually belonging to the end of such a fiction is anticipated in the beginning, and thus there is an approach to completeness in the fragment, as to the satisfaction of the reader's mind concerning the most interesting persons, which could hardly have been better attained if the writer's breaking-off had been foreseen.

The last line he wrote, and the last proof he corrected, are among these papers through which I have so sorrowfully made my way. The condition of the little pages of manuscript where Death stopped his hand, shows that he had carried them about, and often taken them out of his pocket here and there, for patient revision and interlineation. The last words he corrected in print, were, "And my heart throbbed with an exquisite bliss." GOD grant that on that Christmas Eve when he laid his head back on his pillow and threw up his arms as he had been wont to do when very weary, some consciousness of duty done and Christian hope throughout life humbly cherished, may have caused his own heart so to throb, when he passed away to his Redeemer's rest.

He was found peacefully lying as above described, composed, undisturbed, and to all appearance asleep, on the twenty-fourth of December, 1863. He was only in his fifty-third year; so young a man, that the mother who blessed him in his first sleep, blessed him in his last. Twenty years before, he had written, after being in a white squall:

> And when, the force expended,
> The harmless storm was ended,
> And, as the sunrise splendid,
>   Came blushing o'er the sea;
> I thought, as day was breaking,
> My little girls were waking,
> And smiling, and making
>   A prayer at home for me.

Those little girls had grown to be women when the mournful day broke that saw their father lying dead. In those twenty years of companionship with him, they had learned much from him; and one of them has a literary course before her, worthy of her famous name.

On the bright wintry day, the last but one of the old year, he was laid in his grave at Kensal Green, there to mingle the dust to which the mortal part of him had returned, with that of a third child, lost in her infancy, years ago. The heads of a great concourse of his fellow-workers in the Arts, were bowed around his tomb.

Trollope
ON
Thackeray:

Thackeray sees his characters, both men and women, with a man's eye and with a woman's. He dissects with a knife and also with a needle.

Trollope
ON
Dickens:

The sale of his books here and in America is a thing of itself,—and is so great as almost to induce a belief that Pickwicks and Oliver Twists are consumed in families like legs of mutton.

ANTHONY TROLLOPE

When, a few months ago, Anthony Trollope laid down his pen for the last time, it was a sign of the complete extinction of that group of admirable writers who, in England, during the preceding half century, had done so much to elevate the art of the novelist. The author of *The Warden*, of *Barchester Towers*, of *Framley Parsonage*, does not, to our mind, stand on the very same level as Dickens, Thackeray and George Eliot; for his talent was of a quality less fine than theirs. But he belonged to the same family—he had as much to tell us about English life; he was strong, genial and abundant. He published too much; the writing of novels had ended by becoming, with him, a perceptibly mechanical process. Dickens was prolific, Thackeray produced with a freedom for which we are constantly grateful; but we feel that these writers had their periods of gestation. They took more time to look at their subject; relatively (for to-day there is not much leisure, at best, for those who undertake to entertain a hungry public), they were able to wait for inspiration. Trollope's fecundity was prodigious; there was no limit to the work he was ready to do. It is not unjust to say that he sacrificed quality to quantity. Abundance, certainly, is in itself a great merit; almost all the greatest writers have been abundant. But Trollope's fertility was gross, importunate; he himself contended, we believe, that he had given to the world a greater number of printed pages of fiction than any of his literary contemporaries. Not only did his novels follow each other without visible intermission, overlapping and treading on each other's heels, but most of these works are of extraordinary length. *Orley Farm, Can You Forgive Her? He Knew He Was Right,* are exceedingly voluminous tales. *The Way We Live Now* is one of the longest of modern novels. Trollope produced, moreover, in the intervals of larger labour a great number of short stories, many of them charming, as well as various books of travel, and two or three biographies. He was the great *improvvisatore* of these latter years. Two distinguished story-tellers of the other sex—one in France and one in England—have shown an extraordinary facility of composition; but Trollope's pace was brisker even than that of the wonderful Madame Sand and the delightful Mrs. Oliphant. He had taught himself to keep this pace, and had reduced his admirable faculty to a system. Every day of his life he wrote a certain number of pages of his current tale, a number sacramental and invariable, independent of mood and place. It was once the fortune of the author of these lines to cross the Atlantic in his company, and he has never forgotten the magnificent example of plain persistence that it was in the power of the eminent novelist to give on that occasion. The season was unpropitious, the vessel overcrowded, the voyage detestable; but Trollope shut himself up in his cabin every morning for a purpose which, on the part of a distinguished writer who was also an invulnerable sailor, could only be communion with the muse. He drove his pen as steadily on the tumbling ocean as in Montague Square; and as his voyages were many, it was his practice before sailing to come down to the ship and confer with the carpenter, who was instructed to rig up a rough writing-table in his small sea-chamber. Trollope has been accused of being deficient in imagination, but in the face of such a fact as that the charge will scarcely seem just. The power to shut one's eyes, one's ears (to say nothing of another sense), upon the scenery of a pitching Cunarder and open them upon the loves and sorrows of Lily Dale or the conjugal embarrassments of Lady Glencora Palliser, is certainly a faculty which could take to itself wings. The imagination that Trollope possessed he had at least thoroughly at his command. I speak of all this in order to explain (in part) why it was that, with his extraordinary gift, there was always in him a certain infusion of the common. He abused his gift, overworked it, rode his horse too hard. As an artist he never took himself seriously; many people will say this was why he was so delightful. The people who take themselves seriously are prigs and bores; and Trollope, with his perpetual "story," which was the only thing he cared about, his strong good sense, hearty good nature, generous appreciation of life in all its varieties, responds in perfection to a certain English ideal. According to that ideal it is rather dangerous to be explicitly or consciously an artist—to have a system, a doctrine, a form. Trollope, from the first, went in, as they say, for having as little form as possible; it is probably safe to affirm that he had no "views" whatever on the subject of novel-writing. His whole manner is that of a man who regards the practice as one of the more delicate industries, but has never troubled his head nor clogged his pen with theories about the nature of his business. Fortunately he was not obliged to do so, for he had an easy road to success; and his honest, familiar, deliberate way of treating his readers as if he were one of them, and shared their indifference to a general view, their limitations of knowledge, their love of a comfortable ending, endeared him to many persons in England and America. It is in the name of some chosen form that, of late years, things have been made most disagreeable for the novel-reader, who has been treated by several votaries of the new experiments in fiction to unwonted and bewildering sensations. With Trollope we were always safe; there were sure to be no new experiments.

His great, his inestimable merit was a complete appreciation of the usual. This gift is not rare in the annals of English fiction; it would naturally be found in a walk of literature in which the feminine mind has laboured so fruitfully. Women are delicate and patient observers; they hold their noses close, as it were, to the texture of life. They feel and perceive the real with a kind of personal tact, and their observations are recorded in a thousand delightful volumes. Trollope, therefore, with his eyes comfortably fixed on the familiar, the actual, was far from having invented a new category; his great distinction is that in resting there his vision took in so much of the field. And then he *felt* all daily and immediate things as well as saw them; felt them in a simple, direct, salubrious way, with their sadness, their gladness, their charm, their comicality, all their obvious and measurable meanings. He never wearied of the pre-established round of English customs—never needed a respite or a change—was content to go on indefinitely watching the life that surrounded him, and holding up his mirror to it. Into this mirror the public, at first especially, grew very fond of looking—for it saw itself reflected in all the most credible and supposable ways, with that curiosity that people feel to know how they look when they are represented, "just as they are," by a painter who does not desire to put them into an attitude, to drape them for an effect, to arrange his light and his accessories. This exact and on the whole becoming image, projected upon a surface without a strong intrinsic tone, constitutes mainly the entertainment that Trollope offered his readers. The striking thing to the critic was that his robust and patient mind had no particular bias, his imagination no light of its own. He saw things neither pictorially and grotesquely like Dickens; nor with that combined disposition to satire and to literary form which gives such "body," as they say of wine, to the manner of Thackeray; nor with anything of the philosophic, the transcendental cast—the desire to follow them to their remote relations—which we associate with the name of George Eliot. Trollope had his elements of fancy, of satire, of irony; but these qualities were not very highly developed, and he walked mainly by the light of his good sense, his clear, direct vision of the things that lay nearest, and his great natural kindness. There is something remarkably tender and friendly in his feeling about all human perplexities; he takes the good-natured, temperate, conciliatory view—the humorous view, perhaps, for the most part, yet without a touch of pessimistic prejudice. As he grew older, and had sometimes to go farther afield for his subjects, he acquired a savour of bitterness and reconciled himself sturdily to treating of the disagreeable. A more copious record of disagreeable matters could scarcely be imagined, for instance, than *The Way We Live Now*. But, in general, he has a wholesome mistrust of morbid analysis, an aversion to inflicting pain. He has an infinite love of detail, but his details are, for the most part, the innumerable items of the expected. When the French are disposed to pay a compliment to the English mind they are so good as to say that there is in it something remarkably *honnête*. If I might borrow this epithet without seeming to be patronising, I should apply it to the genius of Anthony

Trollope. He represents in an eminent degree this natural decorum of the English spirit, and represents it all the better that there is not in him a grain of the mawkish or the prudish. He writes, he feels, he judges like a man, talking plainly and frankly about many things, and is by no means destitute of a certain saving grace of coarseness. But he has kept the purity of his imagination and held fast to old-fashioned reverences and preferences. He thinks it a sufficient objection to several topics to say simply that they are unclean. There was nothing in his theory of the story-teller's art that tended to convert the reader's or the writer's mind into a vessel for polluting things. He recognised the right of the vessel to protest, and would have regarded such a protest as conclusive. With a considerable turn for satire, though this perhaps is more evident in his early novels than in his later ones, he had as little as possible of the quality of irony. He never played with a subject, never juggled with the sympathies or the credulity of his reader, was never in the least paradoxical or mystifying. He sat down to his theme in a serious, business-like way, with his elbows on the table and his eye occasionally wandering to the clock.

To touch successively upon these points is to attempt a portrait, which I shall perhaps not altogether have failed to produce. The source of his success in describing the life that lay nearest to him, and describing it without any of those artistic perversions that come, as we have said, from a powerful imagination, from a cynical humour or from a desire to look, as George Eliot expresses it, for the suppressed transitions that unite all contrasts, the essence of this love of reality was his extreme interest in character. This is the fine and admirable quality in Trollope, this is what will preserve his best works in spite of those flatnesses which keep him from standing on quite the same level as the masters. Indeed this quality is so much one of the finest (to my mind at least), that it makes me wonder the more that the writer who had it so abundantly and so naturally should not have just that distinction which Trollope lacks, and which we find in his three brilliant contemporaries. If he was in any degree a man of genius (and I hold that he was), it was in virtue of this happy, instinctive perception of human varieties. His knowledge of

the stuff we are made of, his observation of the common behaviour of men and women, was not reasoned nor acquired,
not even particularly studied. All human doings deeply interested him, human life, to his mind, was a perpetual story; but
he never attempted to take the so-called scientific view, the
view which has lately found ingenious advocates among the
countrymen and successors of Balzac. He had no airs of being
able to tell you *why* people in a given situation would conduct themselves in a particular way; it was enough for him
that he felt their feelings and struck the right note, because
he had, as it were, a good ear. If he was a knowing psychologist he was so by grace; he was just and true without apparatus
and without effort. He must have had a great taste for the
moral question; he evidently believed that this is the basis of
the interest of fiction. We must be careful, of course, in at-
tributing convictions and opinions to Trollope, who, as I have
said, had as little as possible of the pedantry of his art, and
whose occasional chance utterances in regard to the object of
the novelist and his means of achieving it are of an almost
startling simplicity. But we certainly do not go too far in saying that he gave his practical testimony in favour of the idea
that the interest of a work of fiction is great in proportion as
the people stand on their feet. His great effort was evidently
to make them stand so; if he achieved this result with as little
as possible of a flourish of the hand it was nevertheless the
measure of his success. If he had taken sides on the droll,
bemuddled opposition between novels of character and novels of plot, I can imagine him to have said (except that he
never expressed himself in epigrams), that he preferred the
former class, inasmuch as character in itself is plot, while plot
is by no means character. It is more safe indeed to believe
that his great good sense would have prevented him from
taking an idle controversy seriously. Character, in any sense in
which we can get at it, is action, and action is plot, and any
plot which hangs together, even if it pretend to interest us
only in the fashion of a Chinese puzzle, plays upon our emotion, our suspense, by means of personal references. We care
what happens to people only in proportion as we know what
people are. Trollope's great apprehension of the real, which
was what made him so interesting, came to him through his

desire to satisfy us on this point—to tell us what certain people were and what they did in consequence of being so. That is the purpose of each of his tales; and if these things produce an illusion it comes from the gradual abundance of his testimony as to the temper, the tone, the passions, the habits, the moral nature, of a certain number of contemporary Britons.

His stories, in spite of their great length, deal very little in the surprising, the exceptional, the complicated; as a general thing he has no great story to tell. The thing is not so much a story as a picture; if we hesitate to call it a picture it is because the idea of composition is not the controlling one and we feel that the author would regard the artistic, in general, as a kind of affectation. There is not even much description, in the sense which the present votaries of realism in France attach to that word. The painter lays his scene in a few deliberate, not especially pictorial strokes, and never dreams of finishing the piece for the sake of enabling the reader to hang it up. The finish, such as it is, comes later, from the slow and somewhat clumsy accumulation of small illustrations. These illustrations are sometimes of the commonest; Trollope turns them out inexhaustibly, repeats them freely, unfolds them without haste and without rest. But they are all of the most obvious sort, and they are none the worse for that. The point to be made is that they have no great spectacular interest (we beg pardon of the innumerable love-affairs that Trollope has described), like many of the incidents, say, of Walter Scott and of Alexandre Dumas: if we care to know about them (as repetitions of a usual case), it is because the writer has managed, in his candid, literal, somewhat lumbering way, to tell us that about the men and women concerned which has already excited on their behalf the impression of life. It is a marvel by what homely arts, by what imperturbable button-holing persistence, he contrives to excite this impression. Take, for example, such a work as *The Vicar of Bullhampton*. It would be difficult to state the idea of this slow but excellent story, which is a capital example of interest produced by the quietest conceivable means. The principal persons in it are a lively, jovial, high-tempered country clergyman, a young woman who is in love with her cousin, and a small, rather dull squire who is in love with the young woman. There is no connection between the affairs of the clergyman and those of the two other persons, save that these two are the Vicar's friends. The Vicar gives countenance, for Christian charity's sake, to a young countryman who is suspected (falsely, as it appears), of murder, and also to the lad's sister, who is more than suspected of leading an immoral life. Various people are shocked at his indiscretion, but in the end he is shown to have been no worse a clergyman because he is a good fellow. A cantankerous nobleman, who has a spite against him, causes a Methodist conventicle to be erected at the gates of the vicarage; but afterward, finding that he has no title to the land used for this obnoxious purpose, causes the conventicle to be pulled down, and is reconciled with the parson, who accepts an invitation to stay at the castle. Mary Lowther, the heroine of *The Vicar of Bullhampton*, is sought in marriage by Mr. Harry Gilmore, to whose passion she is unable to respond; she accepts him, however, making him understand that she does not love him, and that her affections are fixed upon her kinsman, Captain Marrable, whom she would marry (and who would marry her), if he were not too poor to support a wife. If Mr. Gilmore will take her on these terms she will become his spouse; but she gives him all sorts of warnings. They are not superfluous; for, as Captain Marrable presently inherits a fortune, she throws over Mr. Gilmore, who retires to foreign lands, heart-broken, inconsolable. This is the substance of *The Vicar of Bullhampton*; the reader will see that it is not a very tangled skein. But if the interest is gradual it is extreme and constant, and it comes altogether from excellent portraiture. It is essentially a moral, a social interest. There is something masterly in the large-fisted grip with which, in work of this kind, Trollope handles his brush. The Vicar's nature is thoroughly analysed and rendered, and his monotonous friend the Squire, a man with limitations, but possessed and consumed by a genuine passion, is equally near the truth.

Trollope has described again and again the ravages of love, and it is wonderful to see how well, in these delicate matters, his plain good sense and good taste serve him. His story is always primarily a love-story, and a love-story constructed on an inveterate system. There is a young lady who has two lovers, or a young man who has two sweethearts; we are treated to the innumerable forms in which this predicament may present itself and the consequences, sometimes pathetic, sometimes grotesque, which spring from such false situations. Trollope is not what is called a colourist; still less is he a poet: he is seated on the back of heavy-footed prose. But his account of those sentiments which the poets are supposed to have made their own is apt to be as touching as demonstrations more lyrical. There is something wonderfully vivid in the state of mind of the unfortunate Harry Gilmore, of whom I have just spoken; and his history, which has no more pretensions to style than if it were cut out of yesterday's newspaper, lodges itself in the imagination in all sorts of classic company. He is not handsome, nor clever, nor rich, nor romantic, nor distinguished in any way; he is simply rather a dense, narrow-minded, stiff, obstinate, common-place, conscientious modern Englishman, exceedingly in love and, from his own point of view, exceedingly ill-used. He is interesting because he suffers and because we are curious to see the form that suffering will take in that particular nature. Our good fortune, with Trollope, is that the person put before us will have, in spite of opportunities not to have it, a certain particular nature. The author has cared enough about the character of such a person to find out exactly what it is. Another particular nature in *The Vicar of Bullhampton* is the surly, sturdy, sceptical old farmer Jacob Brattle, who doesn't want to be patronised by the parson, and in his dumb, dusky, half-brutal, half-spiritual melancholy, surrounded by domestic troubles, financial embarrassments and a puzzling world, declines altogether to be won over to clerical optimism. Such a figure as Jacob Brattle, purely episodical though it be, is an excellent English portrait. As thoroughly English, and the most striking thing in the book, is the combination, in the nature of Frank Fenwick—the delightful Vicar—of the patronising, conventional, clerical element with all sorts of manliness and spontaneity; the union, or to a certain extent the contradiction, of official and personal geniality. Trollope touches these points in a way that shows that he knows his man. Delicacy is not his great sign, but when it is necessary he can be as delicate as any one else.

I alighted, just now, at a venture, upon the history of Frank Fenwick; it is far from being a conspicuous work in the immense list of Trollope's novels. But to choose an example one must choose arbitrarily, for examples of almost anything that one may wish to say are numerous to embarrassment. In speaking of a writer who produced so much and produced always in the same way, there is perhaps a certain unfairness in choosing at all. As no work has higher pretensions than any other, there may be a certain unkindness in holding an individual production up to the light. "Judge me in the lump," we can imagine the author saying; "I have only undertaken to entertain the British public. I don't pretend that each of my novels is an organic whole." Trollope had no time to give his tales a classic roundness; yet there is (in spite of an extraordinary defect), something of that quality in the thing that first revealed him. *The Warden* was published in 1855. It made a great impression; and when, in 1857, *Barchester Towers* followed it, every one saw that English literature had a novelist the more. These were not the works of a young man, for Anthony Trollope had been born in 1815. It is remarkable to reflect, by the way, that his prodigious fecundity (he had published before *The Warden* three or four novels which attracted little attention), was enclosed between his fortieth and his sixty-seventh years. Trollope had lived long enough in the world to learn a good deal about it; and his maturity of feeling and evidently large knowledge of English life were for much in the effect produced by the two clerical tales. It was easy to see that he would take up room. What he had picked up, to begin with, was a comprehensive, various impression of the clergy of the Church of England and the manners and feelings that prevail in cathedral towns. This, for a while, was his speciality, and, as always happens in such cases, the public was disposed to prescribe to him that path. He knew about bishops, archdeacons, prebendaries, precentors, and about their wives and daughters; he knew what these dignitaries say to each other when they are collected together, aloof from secular ears. He even knew what sort of talk goes on between a bishop and a bishop's lady

when the august couple are enshrouded in the privacy of the
episcopal bedroom. This knowledge, somehow, was rare and
precious. No one, as yet, had been bold enough to snatch
the illuminating torch from the very summit of the altar.
Trollope enlarged his field very speedily—there is, as I remember that work, as little as possible of the ecclesiastical in the
tale of *The Three Clerks,* which came after *Barchester Towers.* But he always retained traces of his early divination of
the clergy; he introduced them frequently, and he always did
them easily and well. There is no ecclesiastical figure, however, so good as the first—no creation of this sort so happy as
the admirable Mr. Harding. *The Warden* is a delightful tale,
and a signal instance of Trollope's habit of offering us the
spectacle of a character. A motive more delicate, more slen-
der, as well as more charming, could scarcely be conceived.
It is simply the history of an old man's conscience.

The good and gentle Mr. Harding, precentor of Barchester
Cathedral, also holds the post of warden of Hiram's Hospital,
an ancient charity where twelve old paupers are maintained
in comfort. The office is in the gift of the bishop, and its
emoluments are as handsome as the duties of the place are
small. Mr. Harding has for years drawn his salary in quiet
gratitude; but his moral repose is broken by hearing it at last
begun to be said that the wardenship is a sinecure, that the
salary is a scandal, and that a large part, at least, of his easy
income ought to go to the pensioners of the hospital. He is
sadly troubled and perplexed, and when the great London
newspapers take up the affair he is overwhelmed with confusion and shame. He thinks the newspapers are right—he perceives that the warden is an overpaid and rather a useless
functionary. The only thing he can do is to resign the place.
He has no means of his own—he is only a quiet, modest, innocent old man, with a taste, a passion, for old church-music
and the violoncello. But he determines to resign, and he does
resign in spite of the sharp opposition of his friends. He does
what he thinks right, and goes to live in lodgings over a shop
in the Barchester High Street. That is all the story, and it has
exceeding beauty. The question of Mr. Harding's resignation
becomes a drama, and we anxiously wait for the catastrophe.
Trollope never did anything happier than the picture of this

sweet and serious little old gentleman, who on most of the occasions of life has shown a lamblike softness and compliance, but in this particular matter opposes a silent, impenetrable obstinacy to the arguments of the friends who insist on his keeping his sinecure—fixing his mild, detached gaze on the distance, and making imaginary passes with his fiddle-bow while they demonstrate his pusillanimity. The subject of *The Warden*, exactly viewed, is the opposition of the two natures of Archdeacon Grantley and Mr. Harding, and there is nothing finer in all Trollope than the vividness with which this opposition is presented. The archdeacon is as happy a portrait as the precentor—an image of the full-fed, worldly churchman, taking his stand squarely upon his rich temporalities, and regarding the church frankly as a fat social pasturage. It required the greatest tact and temperance to make the picture of Archdeacon Grantley stop just where it does. The type, impartially considered, is detestable, but the individual may be full of amenity. Trollope allows his archdeacon all the virtues he was likely to possess, but he makes his spiritual grossness wonderfully natural. No charge of exaggeration is possible, for we are made to feel that he is conscientious as well as arrogant, and expansive as well as hard. He is one of those figures that spring into being all at once, solidifying in the author's grasp. These two capital portraits are what we carry away from *The Warden*, which some persons profess to regard as our writer's masterpiece. We remember, while it was still something of a novelty, to have heard a judicious critic say that it had much of the charm of *The Vicar of Wakefield*. Anthony Trollope would not have accepted the compliment, and would not have wished this little tale to pass before several of its successors. He would have said, very justly, that it gives too small a measure of his knowledge of life. It has, however, a certain classic roundness, though, as we said a moment since, there is a blemish on its fair face. The chapter on Dr. Pessimist Anticant and Mr. Sentiment would be a mistake almost inconceivable if Trollope had not in other places taken pains to show us that for certain forms of satire (the more violent, doubtless), he had absolutely no gift. Dr. Anticant is a parody of Carlyle, and Mr. Sentiment is an exposure of Dickens: and both these little *jeux d'esprit* are as infelicitous as they are misplaced. It was no less luckless an inspiration to convert Archdeacon Grantley's three sons, denominated respectively Charles James, Henry and Samuel, into little effigies of three distinguished English bishops of that period, whose well-known peculiarities are reproduced in the description of these unnatural urchins. The whole passage, as we meet it, is a sudden disillusionment; we are transported from the mellow atmosphere of an assimilated Barchester to the air of ponderous allegory.

I may take occasion to remark here upon a very curious fact—the fact that there are certain precautions in the way of producing that illusion dear to the intending novelist which Trollope not only habitually scorned to take, but really, as we may say, asking pardon for the heat of the thing, delighted wantonly to violate. He took a suicidal satisfaction in reminding the reader that the story he was telling was only, after all, a make-believe. He habitually referred to the work in hand (in the course of that work) as a novel, and to himself as a novelist, and was fond of letting the reader know that this novelist could direct the course of events according to his pleasure. Already, in *Barchester Towers,* he falls into this pernicious trick. In describing the wooing of Eleanor Bold by Mr. Arabin he has occasion to say that the lady might have acted in a much more direct and natural way than the way he attributes to her. But if she had, he adds, "where would have been my novel?" The last chapter of the same story begins with the remark, "The end of a novel, like the end of a children's dinner party, must be made up of sweetmeats and sugar-plums." These little slaps at credulity (we might give many more specimens) are very discouraging, but they are even more inexplicable; for they are deliberately inartistic, even judged from the point of view of that rather vague consideration of form which is the only canon we have a right to impose upon Trollope. It is impossible to imagine what a novelist takes himself to be unless he regard himself as an historian and his narrative as a history. It is only as an historian that he has the smallest *locus standi*. As a narrator of fictitious events he is nowhere; to insert into his attempt a back-bone of logic, he must relate events that are assumed to be real. This assumption permeates, animates all the work

of the most solid story-tellers; we need only mention (to select a single instance), the magnificent historical tone of
Balzac, who would as soon have thought of admitting to the
reader that he was deceiving him, as Garrick or John Kemble
would have thought of pulling off his disguise in front of the
foot-lights. Therefore, when Trollope suddenly winks at us
and reminds us that he is telling us an arbitrary thing, we
are startled and shocked in quite the same way as if Macaulay
or Motley were to drop the historic mask and intimate that
William of Orange was a myth or the Duke of Alva an invention.

It is a part of this same ambiguity of mind as to what
constitutes evidence that Trollope should sometimes endow
his people with such fantastic names. Dr. Pessimist Anticant
and Mr. Sentiment make, as we have seen, an awkward appearance in a modern novel; and Mr. Neversay Die, Mr.
Stickatit, Mr. Rerechild and Mr. Fillgrave (the two last the
family physicians), are scarcely more felicitous. It would be
better to go back to Bunyan at once. There is a person mentioned in *The Warden* under the name of Mr. Quiverful—a
poor clergyman, with a dozen children, who holds the living
of Puddingdale. This name is a humorous allusion to his overflowing nursery, and it matters little so long as he is not
brought to the front. But in *Barchester Towers*, which carries
on the history of Hiram's Hospital, Mr. Quiverful becomes,
as a candidate for Mr. Harding's vacant place, an important
element, and the reader is made proportionately unhappy by
the primitive character of this satiric note. A Mr. Quiverful
with fourteen children (which is the number attained in *Barchester Towers*) is too difficult to believe in. We can believe
in the name and we can believe in the children; but we cannot manage the combination. It is probably not unfair to say
that if Trollope derived half his inspiration from life, he derived the other half from Thackeray; his earlier novels, in
especial, suggest an honourable emulation of the author of
The Newcomes. Thackeray's names were perfect; they always
had a meaning, and (except in his absolutely jocose productions, where they were still admirable) we can imagine, even
when they are most figurative, that they should have been
borne by real people. But in this, as in other respects, Trol-

lope's hand was heavier than his master's; though when he is
content not to be too comical his appellations are sometimes
fortunate enough. Mrs. Proudie is excellent, for Mrs. Proudie,
and even the Duke of Omnium and Gatherum Castle rather
minister to illusion than destroy it. Indeed, the names of
houses and places, throughout Trollope, are full of colour.

I would speak in some detail of *Barchester Towers* if this
did not seem to commit me to the prodigious task of appre-
ciating each of Trollope's works in succession. Such an attempt as that is so far from being possible that I must frankly
confess to not having read everything that proceeded from
his pen. There came a moment in his vigorous career (it was
even a good many years ago) when I renounced the effort to
"keep up" with him. It ceased to seem obligatory to have
read his last story; it ceased soon to be very possible to know
which was his last. Before that, I had been punctual, devoted;
and the memories of the earlier period are delightful. It
reached, if I remember correctly, to about the publication of
He Knew He Was Right; after which, to my recollection
(oddly enough, too, for that novel was good enough to encourage a continuance of past favours, as the shopkeepers
say), the picture becomes dim and blurred. The author of
Orley Farm and *The Small House at Allington* ceased to produce individual works; his activity became a huge "serial."
Here and there, in the vast fluidity, an organic particle detached itself. *The Last Chronicle of Barset*, for instance, is
one of his most powerful things; it contains the sequel of the
terrible history of Mr. Crawley, the starving curate—an episode full of that literally truthful pathos of which Trollope
was so often a master, and which occasionally raised him quite
to the level of his two immediate predecessors in the vivid
treatment of English life—great artists whose pathetic effects
were sometimes too visibly prepared. For the most part, however, he should be judged by the productions of the first half
of his career; later the strong wine was rather too copiously
watered. His practice, his acquired facility, were such that his
hand went of itself, as it were, and the thing looked superficially like a fresh inspiration. But it was not fresh, it was
rather stale; and though there was no appearance of effort,
there was a fatal dryness of texture. It was too little of a new

story and too much of an old one. Some of these ultimate compositions—*Phineas Redux* (*Phineas Finn* is much better), *The Prime Minister, John Caldigate, The American Senator, The Duke's Children*—betray the dull, impersonal rumble of the mill-wheel. What stands Trollope always in good stead (in addition to the ripe habit of writing), is his various knowledge of the English world—to say nothing of his occasionally laying under contribution the American. His American portraits, by the way (they are several in number), are always friendly; they hit it off more happily than the attempt to depict American character from the European point of view is accustomed to do: though, indeed, as we ourselves have not yet learned to represent our types very finely—are not apparently even very sure what our types are—it is perhaps not to be wondered at that transatlantic talent should miss the mark. The weakness of transatlantic talent in this particular is apt to be want of knowledge; but Trollope's knowledge has all the air of being excellent, though not intimate. Had he indeed striven to learn the way to the American heart? No less than twice, and possibly even oftener, has he rewarded the merit of a scion of the British aristocracy with the hand of an American girl. The American girl was destined sooner or later to make her entrance into British fiction, and Trollope's treatment of this complicated being is full of good humour and of that fatherly indulgence, that almost motherly sympathy, which characterises his attitude throughout toward the youthful feminine. He has not mastered all the springs of her delicate organism nor sounded all the mysteries of her conversation. Indeed, as regards these latter phenomena, he has observed a few of which he has been the sole observer. "I got to be thinking if any one of them should ask me to marry him," words attributed to Miss Boncassen, in *The Duke's Children*, have much more the note of English American than of American English. But, on the whole, in these matters Trollope does very well. His fund of acquaintance with his own country—and indeed with the world at large—was apparently inexhaustible, and it gives his novels a spacious, geographical quality which we should not know where to look for elsewhere in the same degree, and which is the sign of an extraordinary difference between such an horizon as his and the limited world-outlook, as the Germans would say, of the brilliant writers who practise the art of realistic fiction on the other side of the Channel. Trollope was familiar with all sorts and conditions of men, with the business of life, with affairs, with the great world of sport, with every component part of the ancient fabric of English society. He had travelled more than once all over the globe, and for him, therefore, the background of the human drama was a very extensive scene. He had none of the pedantry of the cosmopolite; he remained a sturdy and sensible middle-class Englishman. But his work is full of implied reference to the whole arena of modern vagrancy. He was for many years concerned in the management of the Post-Office; and we can imagine no experience more fitted to impress a man with the diversity of human relations. It is possibly from this source that he derived his fondness for transcribing the letters of his love-lorn maidens and other embarrassed persons. No contemporary story-teller deals so much in letters; the modern English epistle (very happily imitated, for the most part), is his unfailing resource.

There is perhaps little reason in it, but I find myself comparing this tone of allusion to many lands and many things, and whatever it brings us of easier respiration, with that narrow vision of humanity which accompanies the strenuous, serious work lately offered us in such abundance by the votaries of art for art who sit so long at their desks in Parisian *quatrièmes*. The contrast is complete, and it would be interesting, had we space to do so here, to see how far it goes. On one side a wide, good-humoured, superficial glance at a good many things; on the other a gimlet-like consideration of a few. Trollope's plan, as well as Zola's, was to describe the life that lay near him; but the two writers differ immensely as to what constitutes life and what constitutes nearness. For Trollope the emotions of a nursery-governess in Australia would take precedence of the adventures of a depraved *femme du monde* in Paris or London. They both undertake to do the same thing—to depict French and English manners; but the English writer (with his unsurpassed industry) is so occasional, so accidental, so full of the echoes of voices

that are not the voice of the muse. Gustave Flaubert, Emile
Zola, Alphonse Daudet, on the other hand, are nothing if not
concentrated and sedentary. Trollope's realism is as instinctive, as inveterate as theirs; but nothing could mark more the
difference between the French and English mind than the
difference in the application, on one side and the other, of
this system. We say system, though on Trollope's part it is
none. He has no visible, certainly no explicit care for the literary part of the business; he writes easily, comfortably, and
profusely, but his style has nothing in common either with
the minute stippling of Daudet or the studied rhythms of
Flaubert. He accepted all the common restrictions, and found
that even within the barriers there was plenty of material.
He attaches a preface to one of his novels—*The Vicar of
Bullhampton*, before mentioned—for the express purpose of
explaining why he has introduced a young woman who may,
in truth, as he says, be called a "castaway"; and in relation to
this episode he remarks that it is the object of the novelist's
art to entertain the young people of both sexes. Writers of
the French school would, of course, protest indignantly
against such a formula as this, which is the only one of the
kind that I remember to have encountered in Trollope's
pages. It is meagre, assuredly; but Trollope's practice was really much larger than so poor a theory. And indeed any
theory was good which enabled him to produce the works
which he put forth between 1856 and 1869, or later. In spite
of his want of doctrinal richness I think he tells us, on the
whole, more about life than the "naturalists" in our sister
republic. I say this with a full consciousness of the opportunities an artist loses in leaving so many corners unvisited, so
many topics untouched, simply because I think his perception of character was naturally more just and liberal than that
of the naturalists. This has been from the beginning the good
fortune of our English providers of fiction, as compared with
the French. They are inferior in audacity, in neatness, in
acuteness, in intellectual vivacity, in the arrangement of material, in the art of characterising visible things. But they
have been more at home in the moral world; as people say
to-day they know their way about the conscience. This is the
value of much of the work done by the feminine wing of the

school—work which presents itself to French taste as deplorably thin and insipid. Much of it is exquisitely human, and that after all is a merit. As regards Trollope, one may perhaps characterise him best, in opposition to what I have ventured to call the sedentary school, by saying that he was a novelist who hunted the fox. Hunting was for years his most valued recreation, and I remember that when I made in his company the voyage of which I have spoken, he had timed his return from the Antipodes exactly so as to be able to avail himself of the first day on which it should be possible to ride to hounds. He "worked" the hunting-field largely; it constantly reappears in his novels; it was excellent material.

But it would be hard to say (within the circle in which he revolved) what material he neglected. I have allowed myself to be detained so long by general considerations that I have almost forfeited the opportunity to give examples. I have spoken of *The Warden* not only because it made his reputation, but because, taken in conjunction with *Barchester Towers*, it is thought by many people to be his highest flight. *Barchester Towers* is admirable; it has an almost Thackerayan richness. Archdeacon Grantley grows more and more into life, and Mr. Harding is as charming as ever. Mrs. Proudie is ushered into a world in which she was to make so great an impression. Mrs. Proudie has become classical; of all Trollope's characters she is the most often referred to. She is exceedingly true; but I do not think she is quite so good as her fame, and as several figures from the same hand that have not won so much honour. She is rather too violent, too vixenish, too sour. The truly awful female bully—the completely fatal episcopal spouse—would have, I think, a more insidious form, a greater amount of superficial padding. The Stanhope family, in *Barchester Towers*, are a real *trouvaille*, and the idea of transporting the Signora Vesey-Neroni into a cathedral-town was an inspiration. There could not be a better example of Trollope's manner of attaching himself to character than the whole picture of Bertie Stanhope. Bertie is a delightful creation; and the scene in which, at the party given by Mrs. Proudie, he puts this majestic woman to rout is one of the most amusing in all the chronicles of Barset. It is perhaps permitted to wish, by the way, that this triumph had been effected by means intellectual rather than physical; though, indeed, if Bertie had not despoiled her of her drapery we should have lost the lady's admirable "Unhand it, sir!" Mr. Arabin is charming, and the henpecked bishop has painful truth; but Mr. Slope, I think, is a little too arrant a scamp. He is rather too much the old game; he goes too coarsely to work, and his clamminess and cant are somewhat overdone. He is an interesting illustration, however, of the author's dislike (at that period at least) of the bareness of evangelical piety. In one respect *Barchester Towers* is (to the best of our recollection) unique, being the only one of Trollope's novels in which the interest does not centre more or less upon a simple maiden in her flower. The novel offers us nothing in the way of a girl; though we know that this attractive object was to lose nothing by waiting. Eleanor Bold is a charming and natural person, but Eleanor Bold is not in her flower. After this, however, Trollope settled down steadily to the English girl; he took possession of her, and turned her inside out. He never made her a subject of heartless satire, as cynical fabulists of other lands have been known to make the shining daughters of those climes; he bestowed upon her the most serious, the most patient, the most tender, the most copious consideration. He is evidently always more or less in love with her, and it is a wonder how under these circumstances he should make her so objective, plant her so well on her feet. But, as I have said, if he was a lover, he was a paternal lover; as competent as a father who has had fifty daughters. He has presented the British maiden under innumerable names, in every station and in every emergency in life, and with every combination of moral and physical qualities. She is always definite and natural. She plays her part most properly. She has always health in her cheek and gratitude in her eye. She has not a touch of the morbid, and is delightfully tender, modest and fresh. Trollope's heroines have a strong family likeness, but it is a wonder how finely he discriminates between them. One feels, as one reads him, like a man with "sets" of female cousins. Such a person is inclined at first to lump each group together; but presently he finds that even in the groups there are subtle differences. Trollope's girls, for that matter, would make delightful cous-

ins. He has scarcely drawn, that we can remember, a disagreeable damsel. Lady Alexandrina de Courcy is disagreeable, and so is Amelia Roper, and so are various provincial
(and indeed metropolitan) spinsters, who set their caps at
young clergymen and government clerks. Griselda Grantley
was a stick; and considering that she was intended to be attractive, Alice Vavasor does not commend herself particularly
to our affections. But the young women I have mentioned
had ceased to belong to the blooming season; they had entered the bristling, or else the limp, period. Not that Trollope's more mature spinsters invariably fall into these extremes. Miss Thorne of Ullathorne, Miss Dunstable, Miss
Mackenzie, Rachel Ray (if she may be called mature), Miss
Baker and Miss Todd, in *The Bertrams*, Lady Julia Guest,
who comforts poor John Eames: these and many other amiable figures rise up to contradict the idea. A gentleman who
had sojourned in many lands was once asked by a lady
(neither of these persons was English), in what country he
had found the women most to his taste. "Well, in England,"
he replied. "In England?" the lady repeated. "Oh yes," said
her interlocutor; "they are so affectionate!" The remark was
fatuous, but it has the merit of describing Trollope's heroines. They are so affectionate. Mary Thorne, Lucy Robarts,
Adela Gauntlet, Lily Dale, Nora Rowley, Grace Crawley,
have a kind of clinging tenderness, a passive sweetness, which
is quite in the old English tradition. Trollope's genius is not
the genius of Shakespeare, but his heroines have something
of the fragrance of Imogen and Desdemona. There are two
little stories to which, I believe, his name has never been
affixed, but which he is known to have written, that contain
an extraordinarily touching representation of the passion of
love in its most sensitive form. In *Linda Tressel* and *Nina
Balatka* the vehicle is plodding prose, but the effect is none
the less poignant. And in regard to this I may say that in a
hundred places in Trollope the extremity of pathos is reached
by the homeliest means. He often achieved a conspicuous
intensity of the tragical. The long, slow process of the conjugal wreck of Louis Trevelyan and his wife (in *He Knew He
Was Right*), with that rather lumbering movement which is
often characteristic of Trollope, arrives at last at an impres-

sive completeness of misery. It is the history of an accidental rupture between two stiff-necked and ungracious people—"the little rift within the lute"—which widens at last into a gulf of anguish. Touch is added to touch, one small, stupid, fatal aggravation to another; and as we gaze into the widening breach we wonder at the vulgar materials of which tragedy sometimes composes itself. I have always remembered the chapter called "Casalunga," toward the close of *He Knew He Was Right*, as a powerful picture of the insanity of stiff-neckedness. Louis Trevelyan, separated from his wife, alone, haggard, suspicious, unshaven, undressed, living in a desolate villa on a hill-top near Siena and returning doggedly to his fancied wrong, which he has nursed until it becomes an hallucination, is a picture worthy of Balzac. Here and in several other places Trollope has dared to be thoroughly logical; he has not sacrificed to conventional optimism; he has not been afraid of a misery which should be too much like life. He has had the same courage in the history of the wretched Mr. Crawley and in that of the much-to-be-pitied Lady Mason. In this latter episode he found an admirable subject. A quiet, charming, tender-souled English gentlewoman who (as I remember the story of *Orley Farm*) forges a codicil to a will in order to benefit her son, a young prig who doesn't appreciate immoral heroism, and who is suspected, accused, tried, and saved from conviction only by some turn of fortune that I forget; who is furthermore an object of high-bred, respectful, old-fashioned gallantry on the part of a neighbouring baronet, so that she sees herself dishonoured in his eyes as well as condemned in those of her boy: such a personage and such a situation would be sure to yield, under Trollope's handling, the last drop of their reality.

There are many more things to say about him than I am able to add to these very general observations, the limit of which I have already passed. It would be natural, for instance, for a critic who affirms that his principal merit is the portrayal of individual character, to enumerate several of the figures that he has produced. I have not done this, and I must ask the reader who is not acquainted with Trollope to take my assertion on trust; the reader who knows him will easily make a list for himself. No account of him is complete

in which allusion is not made to his practice of carrying certain actors from one story to another—a practice which he
may be said to have inherited from Thackeray, as Thackeray
may be said to have borrowed it from Balzac. It is a great
mistake, however, to speak of it as an artifice which would
not naturally occur to a writer proposing to himself to make
a general portrait of a society. He has to construct that society, and it adds to the illusion in any given case that certain
other cases correspond with it. Trollope constructed a great
many things—a clergy, an aristocracy, a middle-class, an ad-
ministrative class, a little replica of the political world. His
political novels are distinctly dull, and I confess I have not
been able to read them. He evidently took a good deal of
pains with his aristocracy; it makes its first appearance, if I
remember right, in *Doctor Thorne*, in the person of the Lady
Arabella de Courcy. It is difficult for us in America to measure the success of that picture, which is probably, however,
not absolutely to the life. There is in *Doctor Thorne* and
some other works a certain crudity of reference to distinctions of rank—as if people's consciousness of this matter were,
on either side, rather inflated. It suggests a general state of
tension. It is true that, if Trollope's consciousness had been
more flaccid he would perhaps not have given us Lady Lufton
and Lady Glencora Palliser. Both of these noble persons are
as living as possible, though I see Lady Lufton, with her
terror of Lucy Robarts, the best. There is a touch of poetry
in the figure of Lady Glencora, but I think there is a weak
spot in her history. The actual woman would have made a
fool of herself to the end with Burgo Fitzgerald; she would
not have discovered the merits of Plantagenet Palliser—or if
she had, she would not have cared about them. It is an illustration of the business-like way in which Trollope laid out
his work that he always provided a sort of underplot to alternate with his main story—a strain of narrative of which the
scene is usually laid in a humbler walk of life. It is to his
underplot that he generally relegates his vulgar people, his
disagreeable young women; and I have often admired the
perseverance with which he recounts these less edifying
items. Now and then, it may be said, as in *Ralph the Heir*,
the story appears to be all underplot and all vulgar people.

These, however, are details. As I have already intimated, it is difficult to specify in Trollope's work, on account of the immense quantity of it; and there is sadness in the thought that this enormous mass does not present itself in a very portable form to posterity.

Trollope did not write for posterity; he wrote for the day, the moment; but these are just the writers whom posterity is apt to put into its pocket. So much of the life of his time is reflected in his novels that we must believe a part of the record will be saved; and the best parts of them are so sound and true and genial, that readers with an eye to that sort of entertainment will always be sure, in a certain proportion, to turn to them. Trollope will remain one of the most trustworthy, though not one of the most eloquent, of the writers who have helped the heart of man to know itself. The heart of man does not always desire this knowledge; it prefers sometimes to look at history in another way—to look at the manifestations without troubling about the motives. There are two kinds of taste in the appreciation of imaginative literature: the taste for emotions of surprise and the taste for emotions of recognition. It is the latter that Trollope gratifies, and he gratifies it the more that the medium of his own mind, through which we see what he shows us, gives a confident direction to our sympathy. His natural rightness and purity are so real that the good things he projects must be real. A race is fortunate when it has a good deal of the sort of imagination—of imaginative feeling—that had fallen to the share of Anthony Trollope; and in this possession our English race is not poor.

| Trollope ON Jane Austen: | *In the comedy of folly I know no novelist who has beaten her. The letters of Mr. Collins, a clergyman in* Pride and Prejudice, *would move laughter in a low-church archbishop.* |

The familiar objection to Dickens's characters, that they are "so unreal" (a criticism common in the mouths of persons who would be the last to tolerate downright veracity in fiction), is in part explained—in part justified—by the dramatic conduct of his stories. What unreality there is, arises for the most part from necessities of "plot". This may be illustrated by a comparison between two figures wherein the master has embodied so much homely sweetness and rectitude that both are popular favourites. The boatman Peggotty and Joe Gargery the blacksmith are drawn on similar lines; in both the gentlest nature is manifest beneath a ruggedness proper to their callings. There is a certain resemblance, too, between the stories in which each plays his part; childlike in their simple virtues, both become strongly attached to a child—not their own—living under the same roof, and both suffer a grave disappointment in this affection; the boatman's niece is beguiled from him to her ruin, the blacksmith's little relative grows into a conceited youth ashamed of the old companion and the old home. To readers in general I presume that Peggotty is better known than Joe; *David Copperfield* being more frequently read than *Great Expectations*; but if we compare the two figures as to their "reality", we must decide in favour of Gargery. I think him a better piece of workmanship all round; the prime reason, however, for his standing out so much more solidly in one's mind than Little Emily's uncle is that he lives in a world, not of melodrama, but of everyday cause and effect. The convict Magwitch and his strange doings make no such demand upon one's credulity as the story of Emily and Steerforth, told as it is, with its extravagant situations and flagrantly artificial development. Pip is so thoroughly alive that we can forget his dim rela-

tions with Satis House. But who can put faith in Mr. Peggotty, when he sets forth to search for his niece over the
highways and by-ways of Europe? Who can for a moment
put faith in Emily herself after she has ceased to be the be-
trothed of Ham? As easily could one believe that David Copperfield actually overheard that wildly fantastic dialogue in
the lodging-house between the lost girl and Rosa Dartle.

Many such examples might be adduced of excellent, or
masterly, characterization spoilt by the demand for effective
intrigue. We call to mind this or that person in circumstances impossible of credit; and hastily declare that character and situation are alike unreal. And hereby hangs another
point worth touching upon. I have heard it very truly remarked that, in our day, people for the most part criticise
Dickens from a recollection of their reading in childhood;
they do not come fresh to him with mature minds; in general, they never read him at all after childish years. This is
an obvious source of much injustice. Dickens is good reading
for all times of life, as are all the great imaginative writers.
Let him be read by children together with Don Quixote. But
who can speak with authority of Cervantes who knows him
only from an acquaintance made at ten years old? To the
mind of a child Dickens is, or ought to be, fascinating—(alas
for the whole subject of children's reading nowadays!)—and
most of the fascination is due to that romantic treatment of
common life which is part, indeed, of Dickens's merit, but
has smaller value and interest to the older mind. Much of
his finest humour is lost upon children; much of his perfect
description; and all his highest achievement in characterization. Taking Dickens "as read", people inflict a loss upon
themselves and do a wrong to the author. Who, in childhood, ever cared much for *Little Dorrit*? The reason is plain;
in this book Dickens has comparatively little of his wonted
buoyancy; throughout, it is in a graver key. True, a house
falls down in a most exciting way, and this the reader will
remember; all else is to him a waste. We hear, accordingly,
that nothing good can be said for *Little Dorrit*. Whereas, a
competent judge, taking up the book as he would any other,
will find in it some of the best work Dickens ever did;
and especially in this matter of characterization; pictures so

wholly admirable, so marvellously observed and so exquisitely presented, that he is tempted to call *Little Dorrit* the best book of all.

Again, it is not unusual to seek in Dickens's characters for something he never intended to be there; in other words, his figures are often slighted because they represent a class in society which lacks many qualities desired by cultivated readers, and possesses very prominently the distasteful features such a critic could well dispense with. You lay down, for instance, Thackeray's *Pendennis*, and soon after you happen to take up *Dombey and Son*. Comparisons arise. Whilst reading of Major Bagstock, you find your thoughts wandering to Major Pendennis; when occupied (rather disdainfully) with Mr. Toots, you suddenly recall Foker. What can be the immediate outcome of such contrast? It seems impossible to deny to Thackeray a great superiority in the drawing of character; his aristocratic Major and his wealthy young jackass are so much more "real", that is to say, so much more familiar, than the promoted vulgarian Bagstock and the enriched whipper-snapper Toots. A hasty person would be capable of exclaiming that Dickens had plainly taken suggestions from Thackeray, and made but poor use of them. Observe, however, that *Dombey and Son* appeared, complete, in 1848; *Pendennis* in 1849. Observe, too, the explanation of the whole matter; that Bagstock and Toots represent quite as truthfully figures possible in a certain class, as do Thackeray's characters those to be found in a rank distinctly higher. If Thackeray (who needed no suggestions from others' books) was indeed conscious of this whimsical parallel, we can only admire the skill and finish with which he worked it out. But assuredly he dreamt of no slight to Dickens's performance. They had wrought in different material. Social distinctions are sufficiently pronounced even in our time of revolution; fifty years ago they were much more so. And precisely what estranges the cultivated reader in Bagstock and Toots, is nothing more nor less than evidence of their creator's truthfulness.

A wider question confronts one in looking steadfastly at the masterpieces of a novelist concerned with the lower, sometimes the lowest, modes of life in a great city. Among

all the names immortalized by Dickens none is more widely
familiar than that of Mrs. Gamp. It is universally admitted
that in Mrs. Gamp we have a creation such as can be met
with only in the greatest writers; a figure at once individual
and typical; a marvel of humorous presentment; vital in the
highest degree attainable by this art of fiction. From the day
of her first appearance on the stage, Mrs. Gamp has been a
delight, a wonder, a byword. She stands unique, no other
novelist can show a piece of work, in the same kind, worthy
of a place beside her; he must go to the very heights of world-
literature, to him who bodied forth Dame Quickly, and Juliet's nurse, for the suggestion of equivalent power. Granted,
then, that Mrs. Gamp has indubitable existence; who and
what is she? Well, a sick nurse, living in Kingsgate Street,
Holborn, in a filthy room somewhere upstairs, and summoned for nursing of all kinds by persons more or less
well-to-do, who are so unfortunate as to know of no less offensive substitute. We are told, and can believe, that in the
year 1844 (the date of *Martin Chuzzlewit*) few people did
know of any substitute for Mrs. Gamp; that she was an in-
stitution; that she carried her odious vices and her criminal
incompetence from house to house in decent parts in London. Dickens knew her only too well; had observed her at
moments of domestic crisis; had learnt her language and
could reproduce it (or most of it) with surprising accuracy.
In plain words, then, we are speaking of a very loathsome
creature; a sluttish, drunken, avaricious, dishonest woman.
Meeting her in the flesh, we should shrink disgusted, so well
does the foulness of her person correspond with the baseness
of her mind. Hearing her speak, we should turn away in half-
amused contempt. Yet, when we encounter her in the pages
of Dickens, we cannot have too much of Mrs. Gamp's company; her talk is an occasion of uproarious mirth, we never
dream of calling her to moral judgment, but laugh the more,
the more infamously she sees fit to behave. Now, in what
sense can this figure in literature be called a copy of the
human original?

I am perfectly aware that this inquiry goes to the roots
of the theory of Art. Here I have no space (nor would it be
the proper moment) to discuss all the issues that are in-

volved in a question so direct and natural; but if we are to talk at all about the people in Dickens, we must needs start with some understanding of what is implied when we call them true, life-like, finely presented. Is not the fact in itself very remarkable, that by dint (it seems) of *omitting* those very features which in life most strongly impress us, an artist in fiction can produce something which we applaud as an inimitable portrait? That for disgust he can give us delight, and yet leave us glorying in his verisimilitude?

Turn to another art. Open the great volume of Hogarth, and look at the several figures of women which present a fair correspondence with that of Mrs. Gamp. We admire the artist's observation, his great skill, his moral significance, even his grim humour; then—we close the book with a feeling of relief. With these faces who would spend hours of leisure? The thing has been supremely well done, and we are glad of it, and will praise the artist unreservedly; but his basely grinning and leering women must not hang upon the wall, to be looked at and talked of with all and sundry. Hogarth has copied—in the strict sense of the word. He gives us life—and we cannot bear it.

The Mrs. Gamp of our novel is a piece of the most delicate idealism. It is a sublimation of the essence of Gamp. No novelist (say what he will) ever gave us a picture of life which was not idealized; but there are degrees; degrees of purpose and of power. Juliet's Nurse is an idealized portrait, but it comes much nearer to the real thing than Mrs. Gamp; in our middle-class England we cannot altogether away with the free-spoken dame of Verona; we Bowdlerize her—of course damaging her in the process. Mrs. Berry, in *Richard Feverel*, is idealized, but she smacks too strongly of the truth for boudoir readers. Why, Moll Flanders herself is touched and softened, for all the author's illusive directness. In Mrs. Gamp, Dickens has done his own Bowdlerizing, but with a dexterity which serves only to heighten his figure's effectiveness. Vulgarity he leaves; that is of the essence of the matter; vulgarity unsurpassable is the note of Mrs. Gamp. Vileness, on the other hand, becomes grotesquerie, wonderfully converted into a subject of laughter. Her speech, the basest ever heard from human tongue, by a process of infinite subtlety, which leaves it the same yet not the same, is made an endless amusement, a source of quotation for laughing lips incapable of unclean utterance.

Idealism, then: confessed idealism. But let us take another character from another book, also a woman supposed to represent a phase of low life in London. Do you recall "good Mrs. Brown", the hag who strips little Florence Dombey of her clothes? And do you remember that this creature has a daughter, her name Alice Marlow, who—presumably having been a domestic servant, or a shop-girl, or something of the kind—was led astray by Mr. Carker of the shining teeth, and has become a wandering nondescript? Now in Alice Marlow we again have idealism; but of a different kind. This child of good Mrs. Brown, tramping into London on a bitter night, is found on the roadside and taken home for tendence by Mr. Carker's sister, neither being aware of the other's identity; and having submitted to this kindness, and having accepted money, the girl goes her way. That same night she learns who has befriended her, and forthwith rushes back a few miles, through storm and darkness, to fling the alms at the giver. Outlines of a story sufficiently theatrical; but the dialogue! One fails to understand how Dickens brought himself to pen the language—at great length—he puts into this puppet's mouth. It is doubtful whether one could pick out a single sentence, a single phrase, such as the real Alice Marlow could conceivably have used. Her passion is vehement; no impossible thing. The words in which she utters it would be appropriate to the most stagey of wronged heroines—be that who it may. A figure less life-like will not be found in any novel ever written. Yet Dickens doubtless intended it as legitimate idealization; a sort of type of the doleful multitude of betrayed women. He meant it for imagination exalting common fact. But the fact is not exalted; it has simply vanished. And the imagination is of a kind that avails nothing on any theme. In Mrs. Gamp a portion of truth is omitted; in Alice Marlow there is substitution of falsity. By the former process, true idealism *may* be reached; by the latter, one arrives at nothing but attitude and sham.

Of course omission and veiling do not suffice to create Mrs. Gamp. In his alchemy, Dickens had command of the *men-*

struum which alone is powerful enough to effect such transmutation as this; it is called humour. Humour, be it remembered, is inseparable from charity. Not only did it enable him to see this coarse creature as an amusing person; it inspired him with that large tolerance which looks through things external, gives its full weight to circumstance, and preserves a modesty, a humility, in human judgment. We can form some notion of what Mrs. Gamp would have become in the hands of a rigorous realist, with scorn and disgust (implied inevitably) taking the place of humour. We reject the photograph; it avails us nothing in art or life. Humour deals gently with fact and fate; in its smile there is forbearance, in its laugh there is kindliness. With falsehood—however well meant—it is incompatible; when it has done its work as solvent, the gross adherents are dissipated, the essential truth remains. Do you ask for the Platonic *idea* of London's monthly nurse early in Queen Victoria's reign? Dickens shows it you embodied. At such a thing as this, crawling between earth and heaven, what can one do but laugh? Its existence is a puzzle, a wonder. The class it represents shall be got rid of as speedily as possible; well and good; we cannot tolerate such a public nuisance. But the individual—so perfect a specimen—shall be preserved for all time by the magic of a great writer's deep-seeing humour, and shall be known as Mrs. Gamp.

For a moment, contrast with this masterpiece a picture in which Dickens has used his idealism on material more promising, though sought amid surroundings sufficiently like those which formed the portrait of Kingsgate Street. The most successful character in his stories written to be read at Christmas is Mrs. Lirriper. She belongs to a class distinguished then, as now, by its uncleanness, its rapacity, its knavery, its ignorance. Mrs. Lirriper keeps a London lodging-house. Here, in depicting an individual, Dickens has not typified a class. He idealizes this woman, but finds in her, ready to his hand, the qualities of goodness and tenderness and cheery honesty, so that there is no question of transmuting a subject repulsive to the senses. Mrs. Lirriper is quite possible, even in a London lodging-house; in the flesh, however, we should not exactly seek her society. Her talk (idealized with excellent adroitness) would too often jar upon the ear; her person would be, to say the least, unattractive. In the book, she has lost these accidents of position: we are first amused, then drawn on to like, to admire, to love her. An unfortunate blemish—the ever-recurring artificiality of story—threatens to make her dim; but Mrs. Lirriper triumphs over this. We bear her in memory as a person known—a person most unhappily circumstanced, set in a gloomy sphere; but of such sweet nature that we forget her inevitable defects, even as we should those of an actual acquaintance of like character.

In looking back on the events of life, do we not see them otherwise than, at the time, they appeared to us? The harsh is smoothed; the worst of everything is forgotten; things pleasant come into relief. This (a great argument for optimism) is a similitude of Dickens's art. Like Time, he obscures the unpleasing, emphasizes all we are glad to remember. Time does not falsify; neither does Dickens, whenever his art is unalloyed.

Let us turn to his literary method. It is that of all the great novelists. To set before his reader the image so vivid in his own mind, he simply describes and reports. We have, in general, a very precise and complete picture of externals—the face, the gesture, the habit. In this Dickens excels; he proves to us by sheer force of visible detail, how actual was the mental form from which he drew. We learn the tone of voice, the trick of utterance; he declared that every word spoken by his characters was audible to him. Then does the man reveal himself in colloquy; sometimes once for all, sometimes by degrees, in chapter after chapter—though this is seldom the case. We know these people because we see and hear them.

In a few instances he added deliberate analysis; it was never well done—always superfluous. Very rarely has analysis of character justified itself in fiction. To Dickens the method was alien: he could make no use whatever of it. In the early book which illustrates all his defects, *Nicholas Nickleby*, we have some dreary pages concerned with the inner man of Ralph Nickleby; seeing that the outer is but shadowy, these details cannot interest; they show, moreover, much crudity and conventionality of thought. Later, an analysis is attempted of Mr. Dombey—very laborious, very long. It does not help us in the least to understand Paul's father, himself one of the least satisfactory of Dickens's leading persons. One may surmise that the author felt something of this, and went out of his wonted way in an endeavour to give the image more life.

It results from Dickens's weakness in the devising of incident, in the planning of story, that he seldom develops character through circumstance. There are conversions, but we do not much believe in them; they smack of the stage. Possibly young Martin Chuzzlewit may be counted an exception; but there is never much life in him. From this point of view Dickens's best bit of work is Pip, in *Great Expectations*; Pip, the narrator of his own story, who exhibits very well indeed the growth of a personality, the interaction of character and event. One is not permitted to lose sight of the actual author; though so much more living than Esther Summerson, Pip is yet embarrassed, like her, with the gift of humour. We know very well whose voice comes from behind the scenes when Pip is describing Mr. Wopsle's dramatic venture. Save for this, we acknowledge a true self-revelation. What could be better than the lad's picture of his state of mind, when, after learning that he has "great expectations", he quits the country home of his childhood and goes to London? "I formed a plan in outline for bestowing a dinner of roast beef and plum-pudding, a pint of ale, and a gallon of condescension upon everybody in the village" (chap. xix.). It is one of many touches which give high value to this book.

As a rule, the more elaborate Dickens's conception of character, the smaller his success in working it out. Again and again he endeavoured to present men and women of exceptionally strong passions: the kind of persons who make such a figure on the boards, where they frown and clench their fists, and utter terrible phrases. It began in *Oliver Twist* with the man called Monk; in *Barnaby* came the murderer; in *Chuzzlewit* appears the mask known as old Martin, a thing of sawdust. Later, the efforts in this direction are more conscientious, more laboured, but rarely more successful. An exception, perhaps, may be noted in Bradley Headstone, the lover of Lizzie Hexam, whose consuming passion here and

there convinces, all the more for its well-contrived contrast
with the character of the man whom Lizzie prefers. Charley
Hexam, too, is life-like, on a lower plane. The popular voice
pleads for Sidney Carton; yes, he is well presented—but so
easy to forget. Think, on the other hand, of the long list of
women meant to be tragic, who, one and all, must be judged
failures. Edith Dombey, with her silent wrath and ludicrous
behaviour, who, intended for a strong, scornful nature,
dumbly goes to the sacrifice when bidden by her foolish
mother, and then rails at the old worldling for the miseries
needlessly brought upon herself. Rosa Dartle, at first a promising suggestion, but falling away into exaggerations of lime-
light frenzy. Lady Dedlock and her maid Hortense—which is
the more obvious waxwork? Mrs. Clennam, in *Little Dorrit*,
is wrought so patiently and placed in so picturesque a scene
that one laments over her impossibility; her so-called talk is,
perhaps, less readable than anything in Dickens. The same
book shows us, or aims at showing us, Miss Wade and Tatty-
coram, from both of whom we turn incredulous. Of Miss
Havisham one grudges to speak; her ghostly presence does
its best to spoil an admirable novel. Women, all these, only
in name; a cause of grief to the lovers of the master, a matter of scoffing to his idler critics. When we come to women
of everyday stature, then indeed it is a different thing. So
numerous are these, and so important in an estimate of Dickens's power of characterization, that I must give them a
chapter to themselves.

Neither at a black-hearted villain was he really good,
though he prided himself on his achievements in this kind.
Jonas Chuzzlewit is the earliest worth mention; and what can
be said of Jonas, save that he is a surly ruffian of whom one
knows very little? The "setting" of his part is very strong;
much powerful writing goes to narrate his history; but the
man remains mechanical. Mr. Carker hardly aims at such
completeness of scoundreldom, but he would be a fierce ras-
cal—if not so bent on exhibiting his teeth, which remind one
of the working wires. Other shapes hover in lurid vagueness.
Whether, last of all, John Jasper would have shown a great
advance, must remain doubtful. The first half of *Edwin
Drood* shows him picturesquely, and little more. We discover

no hint of real tragedy. The man seems to us a very vulgar assassin, and we care not at all what becomes of him.

Against these set the gallery of portraits in which Dickens had displayed to us the legal world of his day. Here he painted from nature, and with an artist's love of his subject. From the attorneys and barristers of *Pickwick*, sportive themselves and a cause of infinite mirth in others, to the Old Bailey practitioners so admirably grim in *Great Expectations*, one's eye passes along a row of masterpieces. Nay, it is idle to use the pictorial simile; here are men with blood in their veins—some of them with a good deal of it on their hands. They will not be forgotten; whether we watch the light comedy of Jorkins and Spenlow, or observe the grim gravity of Mr. Jaggers, it is with the same entire conviction. In this department of his work Dickens can be said to idealize only in the sense of the finest art; no praise can exaggerate his dexterity in setting forth these examples of supreme realism. As a picture of actual life in a certain small world *Bleak House* is his greatest book; from office-boy to judge, here are all who walk in "the valley of the Shadow of the Law". Impossible to run through the list, much as one would enjoy it. Think only of Mr. Vholes. In the whole range of fiction there is no character more vivid than this; exhibited so briefly yet so completely, with such rightness in every touch, such impressiveness of total effect, that the thing becomes a miracle. No strain of improbable intrigue can threaten the vitality of these dusty figures. The clerks are as much alive as their employers; the law-stationer stands for ever face to face with Mr. Tulkinghorn; Inspector Bucket has warmer flesh than that of any other detective in the library of detective literature. As for Jaggers and Wemmick, we should presume them unsurpassable had we not known their predecessors. They would make a novelist's reputation.

Among the finest examples of characterization (I postpone a review of the figures which belong more distinctly to satire) must be mentioned the Father of the Marshalsea. Should ever proof be demanded—as often it has been—that Dickens is capable of high comedy, let it be sought in the 31st chapter of book i. of *Little Dorrit*. There will be seen the old Marshalsea prisoner, the bankrupt of half a lifetime, entertaining

and patronizing his workhouse pensioner, old Mr. Nandy.
For delicacy of treatment, for fineness of observation, this
scene, I am inclined to think, is unequalled in all the novels.
Of exaggeration there is no trace; nothing raises a laugh; at
most one smiles, and may very likely be kept grave by profound interest and a certain emotion of wonder. We are in a
debtors' prison, among vulgar folk; yet the exquisite finish of
this study of human nature forbids one to judge it by any
but the highest standards. The Dorrit brothers are both well
drawn; they are characterizations in the best sense of the
word; and in this scene we have the culmination of the author's genius. That it reveals itself so quietly is but the final
assurance of consummate power.

With the normal in character, with what (all things considered) we may call wholesome normality, Dickens does not
often concern himself. Of course there are his homely-minded
"little women", of whom more in another place. And there
are his benevolent old boys (I call them so advisedly) whom
one would like to be able to class with everyday people, but
who cannot in strictness be considered here. Walking-gentle-
men appear often enough; amiable shadows, such as Tom
Pinch's friend Westlock; figures meant to be prominent, such
as Arthur Clennam. There remain a few instances of genuine
characterization within ordinary limits. I cannot fall in with
the common judgment that Dickens never shows us a gentleman. Twice, certainly, he has done so, with the interesting
distinction that in one case he depicts a gentleman of the old
school; in the other, a representative of the refined manhood
which came into existence (or became commonly observable)
in his latter years. In John Jarndyce I can detect no vulgarity;
he appears to me compact of good sense, honour, and gentle
feeling. His eccentricity does not pass bounds; the better we
know him the less observable it grows. Though we are told
nothing expressly of his intellectual acquirements, it is plain
that he had a liberal education, and that his tastes are studi-
ous. Impossible not to like and to respect Mr. Jarndyce. Compare him with Mr. Pickwick, or with the Cheerybles, and we
see at once the author's intention of social superiority, no less
than his increased skill in portraiture. The second figure, belonging to a changed time, is Mr. Crisparkle, for whose sake

especially one regrets the unfinished state of *Edwin Drood*. His breezy manner, his athletic habits, his pleasant speech, give no bad idea of the classical tutor who is neither an up-start nor a pedant. Dickens was careful in his choice of names; we see how he formed that of Crisparkle, and recognize its fitness.

Two other names occur to me, which carry with them a suggestion of true gentility—if the word is permitted; but their bearers can hardly rank with normal personages. Sir Leicester Dedlock, though by no means unsympathetically presented, belongs rather to the region of satire; he is a gen-tleman, indeed, and meant to be representative of a class, but his special characteristic overcharges the portrait. Incom-parably more of a human being than his wife, he might, with less satirical emphasis, have been a very true gentleman in-deed. Then, in *Dombey and Son*, does one not remember Cousin Feenix? The name, this time, is unfortunate; this weak-legged scion of aristocracy deserved better treatment. For he is no phantasm; has no part with the puppets of sup-posed high-birth whom Dickens occasionally set up only for the pleasure of knocking them down again. However incapa-ble of walking straight across a room, however restricted in his views of life, Cousin Feenix has the instincts of birth and breeding. I think one may say that he is Dickens's least dis-putable success in a sketch (it is only a sketch) from the aristocratic world. His talk does not seem to me exaggerated, and it is unusually interesting; his heart is right, his appre-hensions are delicate. That he should be shown as feeble in mind, no less than at the knees, is merely part of the author's scheme; and, after all, the feebleness is more apparent than real. Dickens, moreover, very often associates kindness of dis-position with lack of brains; it connects itself, I fancy, with his attitude towards liberal education, which has already been discussed, as well as with his Radicalism, still to be spoken of. No distinctly intellectual person figures in his books; David Copperfield is only a seeming exception, for who really thinks of David as a literary man? To his autobiography let all praise be given—with the reserve that we see the man himself less clearly than any other person of whom he speaks. Decidedly he is *not* "the hero of his own story". Had Dickens intended

to show us a man of letters, he would here have failed most
grievously; of course he aimed at no such thing; the attempt
would have cost him half his public. And so it is that one
never thinks of the good David as a character at all, never for
a moment credits *him*, the long-suffering youth for whom
Dora "held the pens", with that glorious endowment of genius which went to the writing of his life.

Of an average middle-class family in Dickens's earlier time
—decent, kindly, not unintelligent folk—we have the best example in the Meagles group, from *Little Dorrit*. This household may be contrasted with, say, that of the Maylies in
Oliver Twist, which is merely immature work, and with the
more familiar family circles on which Dickens lavishes his
mirth and his benevolence. The Meagles do not much interest us, which is quite right; they are thoroughly realized, and
take their place in social history. Well done, too, is the
Pocket family in *Great Expectations*, an interesting pendant
to that of the Jellybys in *Bleak House*; showing how well,
when he chose, Dickens could satirize without extravagance.
Mrs. Pocket is decidedly more credible than Mrs. Jellyby; it
might be urged, perhaps, that she belongs to the Sixties instead of to the Fifties, a point of some importance. The
likeness in dissimilitude between these ladies' husbands is
very instructive. As for the son, Herbert Pocket, he is a capital specimen of the healthy, right-minded, and fairly-edu-
cated middle-class youth. Very skilfully indeed is he placed
side by side with Pip; each throwing into relief the other's
natural and acquired characteristics. We see how long it will
take the blacksmith's foster-child (he telling the tale himself)
to reach the point of mental and moral refinement to which
Herbert Pocket has been bred.

One more illustration of the ordinary in life and character.
Evidently Dickens took much pains with Walter Gay, in
Dombey and Son, meaning to represent an average middle-
class boy, high-spirited, frank, affectionate, and full of cheerful ambition. I have already mentioned the darker design, so
quickly abandoned; we feel sure its working out would not
have carried conviction, for Walter Gay, from the first, does
not ring quite true. The note seems forced; we are not stirred
by his exuberance of jollity, and he never for a moment awak-

ens strong interest. Is it any better with Richard Carstone,—
in whom the tragic idea was, with modification, carried
through? Yes, Richard is more interesting; by necessity of his
fortunes, and by virtue of artistic effort. He has his place in a
book pervaded with the atmosphere of doom. Vivid he never
becomes; we see him as a passive victim of fate, rather than
as a struggling man; if he made a better fight, or if we were
allowed to see more of his human weakness (partly forbidden
by our proprieties), his destiny would affect us more than it
does. In truth, this kind of thing cannot be done under Dickens's restrictions. Thackeray *could* have done it magnificently;
but there was "the great, big, stupid public".

The "gentleman" Dickens loved to contemplate was—in
echo of Burns's phrase—he who derives his patent of gentility
straight from Almighty God. These he found abundantly
among the humble of estate, the poor in spirit; or indulged
his fine humanity in the belief that they abounded. A broken
squire, reduced to miserly service, but keeping through all
faults and misfortunes the better part of his honest and
kindly nature; grotesque in person, of fantastic demeanour,
but always lovable;—of this dream comes Newman Noggs. A
city clerk, grey in conscientious labour for one house, glorying
in the perfection of his ledger, taking it ill if his employers
insist on raising his salary;—the vision is christened Tim
Linkinwater. A young man of bumpkinish appearance, shy,
ungainly, who has somehow drifted into the household of a
country architect; who nourishes his soul at the church organ;
who is so good and simple and reverential that years of experience cannot teach him what everyone else sees at a glance—
the hypocritical rascality of his master; he takes shape, and is
known to us as Tom Pinch. A village blacksmith, with heart
as tender as his thews are tough; delighting above all things
in the society of a little child; so dull of brain that he gives
up in despair the effort to learn his alphabet; so sweet of
temper that he endures in silence the nagging of an out-
rageous wife; so delicate of sensibility that he perspires at the
thought of seeming to intrude upon an old friend risen in
life;—what name can be his but Joe Gargery? These, and
many another like unto them, did the master lovingly create,
and there would be something of sacrilege in a cold scrutiny

of his work. Whether or no their prototypes existed in the hurrying crowd of English life, which obscures so much good as well as evil, these figures have fixed themselves in the English imagination, and their names are part of our language. Dickens saw them, and heard them speak; to us, when we choose to enjoy without criticising, they seem no less present. Every such creation was a good deed; the results for good have been incalculable. Would he have been better occupied, had he pried into each character, revealed its vices, insisted on its sordid weaknesses, thrown bare its frequent hypocrisy, and emphasized its dreary unintelligence? Indeed, I think not. I will only permit myself the regret that he who could come so near to truth, and yet so move the affections, as in Joe Gargery, was at other times content with that inferior idealism which addresses itself only to unripe minds or to transitory moods.

The point to be kept in view regarding these ideal figures is that, however little their speech or conduct may smack of earth, their worldly surroundings are shown with marvellous fidelity. Tom Pinch worshipping at the shrine of Pecksniff may not hold our attention; but Tom Pinch walking towards Salisbury on the frosty road, or going to market in London with his sister, is unforgettable. This is what makes the difference between an impossible person in Dickens and the same kind of vision in the work of smaller writers. One cannot repeat too often that, in our literary slang, he "visualised" every character—Little Nell no less than Mr. Jaggers. Seeing *them*, he saw the house in which they lived, the table at which they ate, and all the little habits of their day-to-day life. Here is an invaluable method of illusion, if an author can adopt it. Thus fortified, Dickens's least substantial imaginings have a durability not to be hoped for the laborious accuracies of an artist uninspired.

Pass to another group in this scarcely exhaustible world—the confessed eccentrics. Here Dickens revels. An English novelist must needs be occupied to some extent with grotesque abnormalities of thought and demeanour. Dickens saw them about him even more commonly than we of to-day, and delighted in noting, selecting, combining. The result is seen in those persons of his drama who are frankly given up by many who will defend his verisimilitude in other directions. Mantalini, for example; Quilp, Captain Cuttle, Silas Wegg, and many another. For Silas Wegg, I fear, nothing can be urged, save the trifle that we know him; he becomes a bore, one of the worst instances of this form of humour weakened by extenuation. Even Dickens occasionally suffered from the necessity of filling a certain space. Think how long his novels are, and marvel that the difficulty does not more often declare itself. Of Mr. Boythorne we are accustomed to think as drawn from Landor, but then it is Landor with all the intellect left out; his roaring as gently as any sucking-dove does not greatly charm us, but his talk has good qualities. More of a character, in the proper sense of the word, is Harold Skimpole, whose portrait gave such offence to Leigh Hunt. Now Skimpole is one of the few people in Dickens whom we dislike, and so, *a priori*, demands attention. If we incline to think his eccentricity overdone, be it remembered that the man was in part an actor, and a very clever actor too. Skimpole is excellent work, and stands with fine individuality among the representatives of true unworldliness.

To which category belongs Mr. Micawber? The art of living without an income may be successfully cultivated in very different moods. It is possible for a man of the most generous instincts to achieve great things in this line of endeavour; but the fact remains that, sooner or later, somebody has the honour of discharging his liabilities. To speak severely of Mr. Micawber is beyond the power of the most conscientious critic, whether in life or art; the most rigid economist would be glad to grasp him by the hand and to pay for the bowl of punch over which this type of genial impecuniosity would dilate upon his embarrassments and his hopes; the least compromising realist has but to open at a dialogue or a letter in which Mr. Micawber's name is seen, and straightway he forgets his theories. No selfish intention can be attributed to him. His bill might *not* be provided for when he declared it *was*, and, in consequence, poor Traddles may lose the table he has purchased for "the dearest girl in the world", but Mr. Micawber had all the time been firmly assured that something would turn up; he will sympathize profoundly with Traddles, and write him an epistle which makes amends for the loss of many tables. No man ever lived who was so consistently delightful—certainly Dickens's father cannot have been so, but in this idealized portraiture we have essential truth. Men of this stamp do not abound, but they are met with, even to-day. As a rule, he who waits for something to turn up, mixing punch the while, does so with a very keen eye on his neighbour's pocket, and is recommended to us neither by Skimpole's fantastic gaiety nor by Micawber's eloquence and warmth of heart; nevertheless, one knows the irrepressibly hopeful man, full of kindliness, often distinguished by unconscious affectations of speech, who goes through life an unreluctant pensioner on the friends won by his many good and genial qualities. The one point on which experience gives no support to the imaginative figure is his conversion to practical activity. Mr. Micawber in Australia does the heart good; but he is a pious vision. We refuse to think of a wife worn out by anxieties, of children growing up in squalor; we gladly accept the flourishing colonist; but this is tribute to the author whom we love. Dickens never wrought more successfully for our pleasure and for his own fame. He is ever at his best when dealing with an amiable weakness. And in Micawber he gives us no purely national type—such men are peculiar to no country; all the characteristics of this wonderful picture can be appreciated by civilized readers throughout the world. It is not so in regard to many of his creations, though all the finest have traits of universal humanity. Should time deal hardly with him; should his emphasis of time and place begin to weigh against his wide acceptance; it is difficult to believe that the beaming visage of Wilkins Micawber will not continue to be recognized wherever men care for literary art.

This chapter must conclude with a glance at a class of human beings prominent in Dickens's earlier books, but of small artistic interest when treated in the manner peculiar to him. He was fond of characters hovering between eccentricity and madness, and in one case he depicted what he himself calls an idiot, though idiocy is not strictly speaking the form of disease exhibited. Lunatics were more often found at large in his day than in ours; perhaps that accounts for our introduction to such persons as Mrs. Nickleby's wooer and Mr.

Dick; Miss Flite, of course, had another significance. The crazy gentleman on the garden walk, who at once flatters and terrifies Mrs. Nickleby, can hardly be regarded as anything but an actor in broad farce; his talk, indeed, is midsummer madness, but is meant only to raise a laugh. At the end of the century, one does not laugh with such agreeable facility. Mrs. Nickleby commands our attention—at a respectful distance; and here, as always, behaves after her kind, illustrating the eternal feminine; but the madman we cannot accept. Betsy Trotwood's *protégé* comes nearer to the recognizable; nevertheless Mr. Dick's presence in such a book as *David Copperfield* would seem waste of space, but for certain considerations. He illustrates the formidable lady's goodness and common-sense; he served a very practical purpose, that of recommending rational treatment of the insane; and he had his place in the pages of an author whose humanity includes all that are in any way afflicted, in mind, body, or estate. Moreover, the craze about King Charles's head has been, and is likely to be, a great resource to literary persons in search of a familiar allusion. In passing to *Barnaby Rudge*, we are on different ground. Whatever else, Barnaby is a very picturesque figure, and I presume it was merely on this account that Dickens selected such a hero. In an earlier chapter, I said that this story seemed to me to bear traces of the influence of Scott; its narrative style and certain dialogues in the historical part are suggestive of this. May not the crazy Barnaby have originated in a recollection of Madge Wildfire? Crazy, I call him; an idiot he certainly is not. An idiot does not live a life of exalted imagination. But certain lunatics are of imagination all compact, and Barnaby, poetically speaking, makes a good representative of the class. Of psychology—a word unknown to Dickens—we, of course, have nothing; to ask for it is out of place. The idea, all things considered, cannot be judged a happy one. Whilst writing the latter part of the book Dickens thought for a moment of showing the rioters as led by a commanding figure, who, in the end, should prove to have escaped from Bedlam. We see his motive for this, but are not sorry he abandoned the idea. Probably *Barnaby Rudge*, good as it is, would have been still better had the suggestion of an insane central figure been also discarded.

George Eliot
ON
Thackeray:

I am not conscious of being in any way a disciple of his, unless it constitutes discipleship to think him . . . on the whole the most powerful of living novelists.

Charlotte Bronté
to George Henry
Lewes
ON
Jane Austen:

I had not seen Pride and Prejudice till I read that sentence of yours, and then I got the book. And what did I find? An accurate daguerreotyped portrait of a commonplace face; a carefully fenced, highly cultivated garden, with neat borders and delicate flowers; but no glance of a bright, vivid physiognomy, no open country, no fresh air, no blue hill, no bonny beck. . . . Now I can understand admiration of George Sand . . . she is sagacious and profound; Miss Austen is only shrewd and observant.

George Moore
ON
Sterne:

We could not have Sterne's style without his unseemly life.

George Moore
ON
Jane Austen:

Pride and Prejudice . . . tends towards the vase rather than the washtub, which is rare in English novels.

George Moore
ON
Tolstoy:

His eyesight exceeds all eyesight before or since.

Honoré de Balzac on

If I have so long delayed, in spite of its importance, in speaking of this book,[1] you must understand that it was difficult for me to acquire a sort of impartiality. Even now I am not certain that I can retain it, so extraordinary, after a third, leisurely and thoughtful reading, do I find this work.

I can imagine all the mockery which my admiration for it will provoke. There will be an outcry, of course, at my infatuation, when I am simply still filled with enthusiasm after the point at which enthusiasm should have died. Men of imagination, it will be said, conceive as promptly as they forget their affection for certain works of which the common herd arrogantly and ironically protest that they can understand nothing. Simple-minded, or even intelligent persons who with their proud gaze sweep the surface of things, will say that I amuse myself with paradox, that I have, like M. Sainte-Beuve, my *chers inconnus*. I am incapable of compromise with the truth, that is all.

M. Beyle has written a book in which sublimity glows from chapter after chapter. He has produced, at an age when men rarely *find* monumental subjects and after having written a score of extremely intelligent volumes, a work which can be appreciated only by minds and men that are truly superior. In short, he has written *The Prince up to date*, the novel that Machiavelli would write if he were living banished from Italy in the nineteenth century.

And so the chief obstacle to the renown which M. Beyle deserves lies in the fact that *La Chartreuse de Parme* can find readers fitted to enjoy it only among diplomats, ministers, observers, the leaders of society, the most distinguished artists; in a word, among the twelve or fifteen hundred per-

[1] *The Charterhouse of Parma.*

sons who are at the head of things in Europe. Do not be surprised, therefore, if, in the ten months since this surprising work was published, there has not been a single journalist who has either read, or understood, or studied it, who has announced, analysed and praised it, who has even alluded to it. I, who, I think, have some understanding of the matter, I have read it for the third time in the last few days: I have found the book finer even than before, and have felt in my heart the kind of happiness that comes from the opportunity of doing a good action.

Is it not doing a good action to try to do justice to a man of immense talent, who will appear to have genius only in the eyes of a few privileged beings and whom the transcendency of his ideas deprives of that immediate but fleeting popularity which the courtiers of the public seek and which great souls despise? If the mediocre knew that they had a chance of raising themselves to the level of the sublime by understanding them, *La Chartreuse de Parme* would have as many readers as *Clarissa Harlowe* had on its first appearance.

There are in admiration that is made legitimate by conscience ineffable delights. Therefore all that I am going to say here I address to the pure and noble hearts which, in spite of certain pessimistic declamations, exist in every country, like undiscovered pleiads, among the families of minds devoted to the worship of art. Has not humanity, from generation to generation, has it not here below its constellations of souls, its heaven, its angels, to use the favourite expression of the great Swedish prophet, Swedenborg, a chosen people for whom true artists work and whose judgments make them ready to accept privation, the insolence of upstarts and the indifference of governments?

You will pardon me, I hope, what malevolent persons will call *longueurs*. In the first place, I am firmly convinced, the analysis of so curious and so interesting a work as this will give more pleasure to the most fastidious reader than he would derive from the unpublished novel whose place it fills. Besides, any other critic would require at least three articles of the length of this, if he sought to give an adequate explanation of this novel, which often contains a whole book in a single page, and which cannot be explained save by a man to whom the North of Italy is fairly familiar. Finally, let me assure you that, with the help of M. Beyle, I am going to try to make myself instructive enough to be read with pleasure to the end.

A sister of the Marchese del Dongo, named Gina, the abbreviation of Angelina, whose early character, as a young girl, would have a certain similarity, could an Italian woman ever resemble a Frenchwoman, to the character of Madame de Lignolle in *Faublas*, marries at Milan, against the will of her brother, who wishes to marry her to an old man, noble, rich and Milanese, a certain Conte Pietranera, poor and without a penny.

The Conte and Contessa support the French party, and are the ornament of the Court of Prince Eugène. We are in the days of the Kingdom of Italy, when the story begins.

The Marchese del Dongo, a Milanese attached to Austria and her spy, spends fourteen years waiting for the fall of the Emperor Napoleon. Moreover, this Marchese, the brother of Gina Pietranera, does not live at Milan: he occupies his castle of Grianta, on the Lake of Como; he there brings up his elder son in the love of Austria and on sound principles; but he has a younger son, named Fabrizio, to whom Signora Pietranera is passionately devoted: Fabrizio is a cadet of the family; like her, he will be left without a penny in the world. Who is not familiar with the fondness of noble hearts for the disinherited? Also, she wishes to make something of him. Then, fortunately, Fabrizio is a charming boy; she obtains leave to put him to school at Milan, where, playing truant, she makes him see something of the viceregal court.

Napoleon falls for the first time. While he is on the Island of Elba, in the course of the reaction at Milan, which the Austrians have reoccupied, an insult offered to the Armies of Italy in the presence of Pietranera, who takes it up, is the cause of his death: he is killed in a duel.

A lover of the Contessa refuses to avenge her husband, Gina humiliates him by one of those acts of vengeance, magnificent south of the Alps, which would be thought stupid in Paris. This is her revenge:

Although she despises, *in petto*, this lover who has been adoring her at a distance and without reward for the last six years, she pays certain attentions to the wretch, and, when he is in a paroxysm of suspense, writes to him:

"Will you act for once like a man of spirit? Please to imagine that you have never known me. I am, with a touch of contempt, your servant,

GINA PIETRANERA."

Then, to increase still further the desperation of this rich man, with his income of two hundred thousand lire, she *ginginates* (*ginginare* is a Milanese verb meaning everything that passes at a distance between a pair of lovers before they have spoken; the verb has its noun: one is a *gingino*. It is the first stage in love). Well, she ginginates for a moment with a fool whom she soon abandons; then she retires, with a pension of fifteen hundred francs, to a third floor apartment where all Milan of the day comes to see her and admires her.

Her brother, the Marchese, invites her to return to the ancestral castle on the Lake of Como. She goes there, to see once more and to protect her charming nephew, Fabrizio, to comfort her sister-in-law and to plan her own future amid the sublime scenery of the Lake of Como, her native soil and the native soil of this nephew whom she has made her son: she has no children. Fabrizio, who loves Napoleon, learns of his landing from the Gulf of Juan and wishes to go to serve the sovereign of his uncle Pietranera. His mother, who, the wife of a rich Marchese with an income of five hundred thousand lire, has not a penny to call her own, his aunt Gina, who has nothing, give him their diamonds: Fabrizio is in their eyes a hero.

The inspired volunteer crosses Switzerland, arrives in Paris, takes part in the battle of Waterloo, then returns to Italy, where, for having dabbled in the conspiracy of 1815 against the peace of Europe, he is disowned by his father and the Austrian government place him on their index. For him, to return to Milan would be to enter the Spielberg. From this point Fabrizio, in trouble, persecuted for his heroism, this sublime boy becomes everything in the world to Gina.

The Contessa returns to Milan, she obtains a promise from Bubna and from the men of character whom Austria at this period has put in authority there, not to persecute Fabrizio, whom, following the advice of an extremely shrewd Canon, she keeps in concealment at Novara. Meanwhile, with all these things happening, no money. But Gina is of a sublime beauty, she is the type of that Lombard beauty (*bellezza folgorante*) which can be realised only at Milan and in the Scala when you see assembled there the thousand beautiful women of Lombardy. The events of this troubled life have developed in her the most magnificent Italian character: she has intellect, shrewdness, the Italian grace, the most charming conversation, an astonishing command of herself; in short, the Contessa is at one and the same time Madame de Montespan, Catherine de' Medici, Catherine II, too, if you like: the most audacious political genius and the most consummate feminine genius, hidden beneath a marvellous beauty. Having watched over her nephew, despite the hatred of the elder brother who is jealous of him, despite the hatred and indifference of the father, having snatched him from these perils, having been one of the queens of the court of the Viceroy Eugène, and then nothing; all these crises have enriched her natural forces, exercised her faculties and awakened the instincts numbed in the depths of her being by her early prosperity, by a marriage the joys of which have been rare, owing to the continual absence of Napoleon's devoted servant. Everyone sees or can divine in her the thousand treasures of passion, the resources and the refulgence of the most perfect feminine heart.

The old Canon, whom she has seduced, sends Fabrizio to Novara, a small town in Piedmont, under the tutelage of a parish priest. This priest puts a stop to the inquiries of the police by his description of Fabrizio: "a younger son who feels wronged because he is not the eldest." When Gina, who had dreamed of Fabrizio's becoming aide-de-camp to Napoleon, sees Napoleon banished to St. Helena, she realises that Fabrizio, his name inscribed in the black book of the Milanese police, is lost to her for ever.

During the uncertainties which prevailed throughout Europe at the time of the battle of Waterloo, Gina has made the acquaintance of Conte Mosca della Rovere, the Minister of the famous Prince of Parma, Ranuccio-Ernesto IV.

Let us pause at this point.

Certainly, after having read the book, it is impossible not to recognise, in Conte Mosca, the most remarkable portrait that anyone could ever make of Prince Metternich, but of a Metternich transported from the great Chancellory of the Austrian Empire to the modest State of Parma. The State of Parma and Ernesto IV seem to me similarly to be the Duke of Modena and his Duchy. M. Beyle says of Ernesto IV that he is one of the richest Princes in Europe: the wealth of the Duke of Modena is famous. In seeking to avoid personalities the author has expended more ingenuity than Walter Scott required to construct the plot of *Kenilworth*. Indeed, these two similarities are vague enough, outwardly, to be denied, and so real inwardly that the well-informed reader cannot be mistaken. M. Beyle has so exalted the sublime character of the Prime Minister of the State of Parma that it is doubtful whether Prince Metternich be so great a man as Mosca, although the heart of that celebrated statesman does offer, to those who know his life well, one or two examples of passions of a compass at least equal to that of Mosca's. It is not slandering the Austrian Minister to believe him capable of all the secret greatnesses of Mosca. As for what Mosca is throughout the book, as for the conduct of the man whom Gina regards as the greatest diplomat in Italy, it took genius to create the incidents, the events and the innumerable and recurring plots in the midst of which this immense character unfolds. All that M. de Metternich has done during his long career is not more extraordinary than what you see done by Mosca. When one comes to think that the author has invented it all, ravelled all the plot and then unravelled it, as things do ravel and unravel themselves at a court, the most daring mind, a mind to which the conception of ideas is a familiar process, is left dazed, stupefied before so huge a task. As for myself, I suspect some literary Aladdin's-lamp. To have dared to put on the stage a man of the genius and force of M. de Choiseul, Potemkin, M. de Metternich, to create him, to justify the creation by the actions of the creature himself, to make him move in an environment which is appropriate to him and in which his faculties have full play, is the work not of a man but of a fairy, a wizard. Bear in mind that the most skilfully complicated plots of Walter Scott do not arrive at the admirable simplicity which prevails in the recital of these events, so numerous, so *thickly foliaged*, to borrow the famous expression of Diderot.

Here is the portrait of Mosca. We are in 1816, remember. "He might have been forty or forty-five; he had strongly marked features, with no trace of self-importance, and a simple and light-hearted manner which told in his favour; he would have looked very well indeed, if a whim on the part of his Prince had not obliged him to wear powder on his hair as a proof of his soundness in politics."

And so the powder which M. de Metternich wears, and which softens a face already so gentle, is justified in Mosca by the will of his master. In spite of the prodigious efforts of M. Beyle, who, on page after page, naturalises in this State marvellous inventions to deceive his reader and blunt the point of his allusions, the mind is at Modena and will on no account consent to remain at Parma. Whoever has seen, known, met M. de Metternich, thinks that he hears him speaking through the mouth of Mosca, lends Mosca his voice and clothes him in his manners. Although, in the book, Ernesto IV dies, and the Duke of Modena is still living, one is often reminded of that Prince *so notorious for his severities, which the Liberals of Milan called cruelties*. Such are the expressions used by the author in speaking of the Prince of Parma.

In these two portraits, begun with a satirical intention, there is, however, nothing that can wound, nothing that reeks of vengeance. Although M. Beyle has no cause to thank M. de Metternich, who refused him his *exequatur* for the Trieste Consulate, and although the Duke of Modena has never been able to look with pleasure on the author of *Rome, Naples et Florence*, of the *Promenades en Rome*, and of certain other works, these two figures are portrayed with great taste and the utmost propriety.

This is what, no doubt, occurred during the actual work of these two creations. Carried away by the enthusiasm necessary to him who handles clay and scalpel, the brush and colours, the pen and the treasures of man's moral nature, M. Beyle, who had started out to depict a little court in Italy and a diplomat, ended with the type PRINCE and the type

PRIME MINISTER. The resemblance, begun with the fantasy of a satirical mind, ceased where the genius of the arts appeared to the artist.

This convention of masks once admitted, the reader, keenly interested, accepts the admirable Italian scene which the author paints, the town and all the buildings necessary to his story, which, in many places, has the magical quality of an Oriental tale.

This long parenthesis was indispensable. Let us continue.

Mosca is smitten with love, but with a love immense, eternal, boundless, for Gina, absolutely like M. de Metternich and his Leykam. He lets her, at the risk of compromising himself, have the latest diplomatic news before anyone else. The presence at Milan of this Minister of the State of Parma is perfectly accounted for later on.

To give you an idea of this famous Italian love, I must relate to you a distinctly curious incident. On their departure, in 1799, the Austrians saw as they left Milan, on the Bastion, a certain Contessa B——nini who was driving with a Canon, both heedless of revolutions and war: they were in love. The Bastion is a magnificent avenue which starts from the Eastern Gate (Porta Renza) and corresponds to the Champs-Elysées in Paris, with this slight difference that on the left extends the Duomo, "that mountain of gold transmuted into marble," as Francis II, who had a gift of expression, called it; and on the right the snowy fringe, the sublime chasms of the Alps. On their return in 1814 the first thing the Austrians saw was the Contessa and the Canon, sitting in the same carriage and saying, perhaps, the same things, at the same point on the Bastion. I have seen, in that city, a young man who became ill if he went more than a certain number of streets away from the house of his mistress. When a woman gives an Italian sensations, he never leaves her.

"In spite of his frivolous air and his polished manners, Mosca," says M. Beyle, "was not blessed with a soul of the French type; he could not *forget* the things that annoyed him. When there was a thorn in his pillow, he would blunt it by repeated stabbings of his throbbing limbs." This superior man guesses the superior mind of the Contessa, he falls in love with her to the point of behaving like a school-boy.

"After all," the Minister said to himself, "old age is only being incapable of indulging in these delicious timidities."

The Contessa one evening remarks the fine, benevolent gaze of Mosca. (The gaze with which M. de Metternich would deceive the Deity.)

"At Parma," she says to him, "if you were to look like that, you would give *them* the hope that they might escape hanging."

In the end the diplomat, having realised how essential this woman is to his happiness, and after three months of inward struggle, arrives with three different plans, devised to secure his happiness, and makes her agree to the wisest of them.

In Mosca's eyes, Fabrizio is a child: the excessive interest which the Contessa takes in her nephew seems to him one of those *elective maternities* which, until love comes to reign there, beguile the hearts of noble-hearted women.

Mosca, unfortunately, is married. Accordingly he brings to Milan the Duca Sanseverina-Taxis. Let me, in this analysis, introduce a few quotations which will give you examples of the vivid, free, sometimes faulty style of M. Beyle, and will enable me to make myself be read with pleasure.

The Duca is a handsome little old man of sixty-eight, dapple-grey, very polished, very neat, immensely rich, but not quite as noble as he ought to have been. Apart from this, the Duca is by no means an absolute idiot, says the Conte; "he gets his clothes and wigs from Paris. He is not the sort of man who would do anything *deliberately* mean, he seriously believes that honour consists in having a Grand Cordon, and he is ashamed of his riches. He wants an Embassy. Marry him, he will give you a hundred thousand scudi, a magnificent jointure, his *palazzo* and the most superb existence in Parma. On these conditions, I make the Prince appoint him Ambassador, he will have his Grand Cordon, and he will start the day after his marriage; you become Duchessa Sanseverina, and we live happily. Everything is settled with the Duca, who will be made the happiest man in the world by our arrangement: he will never shew his face again in Parma. If this life does not appeal to you, I have four hundred thousand francs, I hand in my resignation and we go and live at Naples."

"Do you know that what you and your Duca are proposing is highly immoral?" says the Contessa.

"No more immoral than what is done at every court," the Minister answers. "Absolute Power has this advantage, that it justifies everything. Every year we shall be afraid of a 1793, and everything that can reduce that fear will be supremely moral. You shall hear the speeches I make on the subject at my receptions. The Prince has consented, and you will have a brother in the Duca, who has not dared to hope for such a marriage, which saves his face; he thinks himself ruined because he lent twenty-five napoleons to the great Ferrante Palla, a Republican, a poet and something of a genius, whom we have sentenced to death, fortunately in his absence."

Gina accepts. We next see her Duchessa Sanseverina-Taxis, astonishing the court of Parma by her affability, by the noble serenity of her mind. Her house is the most attractive in the town, she reigns there, she is the glory of this little court.

The portrait of Ernesto IV, his reception of the Duchessa, her introduction to each member in turn of the Reigning House, all these details are marvels of wit, depth, succinctness. Never have the hearts of Princes, Ministers, courtiers and women been so depicted. The reader will find it hard to lay the book down.

When the Duchessa's nephew fled from Austrian persecution and was on his way from the Lake of Como to Novara under the protection of his confessor and the parish priest, he met Fabio Conti, General of the Armies of the State of Parma, one of the most curious figures of this court and of the book, a general who thinks of nothing but whether His Highness's soldiers ought to have seven buttons on their uniform or nine; but this comic general possesses an entrancing daughter, Clelia Conti. Fabrizio and Clelia, both trying to escape from the police, have exchanged a few words. Clelia is the most beautiful creature in Parma. As soon as the Prince sees the effect produced in his court by the Sanseverina, he thinks of counter-balancing that beauty by bringing Clelia to light. A great difficulty! Girls are not received at court: he therefore has her created a Canoness.

The Prince has of course a mistress. One of his weaknesses is to ape Louis XIV. So, to be in the picture, he has provided himself with a La Vallière, one Contessa Balbi, who dips her fingers into every money-bag, and is not forgotten when any government contract is made. Ernesto IV would be in despair if the Balbi were not slightly grasping: the scandalous fortune of his mistress is a sign of royal power. He is lucky, the Contessa is a miser!

"She received me," the Duchessa tells Mosca, "as though she expected me to give her a *buona mancia* (a tip)."

But, to the great grief of Ernesto IV, the Contessa, who has no brains, cannot be compared for a moment to the Duchessa; this humiliates him, a first source of irritation. His mistress is thirty, and a model of Italian *leggiadria*.

"She had still the finest eyes in the world and the most graceful little hands;[2] but her skin was netted with countless fine little wrinkles which made her look like a young grandmother. As she was obliged to smile at everything the Prince said, and sought to make him think, by this ironical smile, that she understood him, Conte Mosca used to say that these suppressed yawns had in course of time produced her wrinkles.

The Duchessa parries the first blow aimed at her by His Highness by making a friend of Clelia, who, fortunately, is an innocent creature. From motives of policy, the Prince allows to exist at Parma a sort of Party, called Liberal (God knows what sort of Liberals!). A Liberal is a man who has the great men of Italy, Dante, Machiavelli, Petrarch, Leo X painted welcoming Monti on a ceiling. This passes as an epigram against the power which has no longer any great men. This Liberal Party has as its chief a Marchesa Raversi, an ugly and mischievous woman, as irritating as an Opposition. Fabio Conti, the General, belongs to this Party. The

---

[2] So Balzac, reading *les petites mains les plus gracieuses*. Stendhal's words are *les petites mines*, and he makes the lady a Marchesa. Balzac's quotations are not, as a rule, textually accurate, but his analysis of the story is admirable. C. K. Scott Moncrieff.

Prince, who hangs agitators, has his reasons for allowing a Liberal Party.

Ernesto IV rejoices in a Laubardemont, his Fiscal General or Chief Justice, named Rassi. This Rassi, full of natural intelligence, is one of the most horribly comic or comically horrible personages that can be imagined: he laughs and has people hanged, he makes a game of his justice. He is necessary, indispensable to the Prince. Rassi is a blend of Fouché, Fouquier-Tinville, Merlin, Triboulet and Scapin. You call the Prince a *tyrant:* he says that this is conspiracy and he hangs you. He has already hanged two Liberals. Since this execution, notorious throughout Italy, the Prince, who is brave when on the field of battle and has led armies, the Prince, though a man of spirit, lives in fear. This Rassi becomes something terrible, he attains to gigantic proportions while still remaining grotesque: he embodies all the justice of this little State.

And now for the inevitable effects at court of the Duchessa's triumphs. The Conte and the Duchessa, that pair of eagles caged in this tiny capital, soon begin to offend the Prince. In the first place the Duchessa is sincerely attached to the Conte, the Conte is more in love every day, and this happiness irritates a bored Prince. Mosca's talents are indispensable to the Cabinet of Parma. Ranuccio-Ernesto and his Minister are attached to one another like the Siamese twins. Indeed, they have between them contrived the impossible plan ("impossible" is a rhetorical precaution on M. Beyle's part) of making a single State of Northern Italy. Beneath his mask of absolutism, the Prince is intriguing to become the Sovereign of this Constitutional Kingdom. He is dying of envy to ape Louis XVIII, to give a Charter and Two Chamber government to Northern Italy. He regards himself as a great politician, he has his ambition: he redeems in his own eyes his subordinate position by this plan with which Mosca is fully acquainted; he has control of his treasury! The more need he has of Mosca and the more he recognises his Minister's talent, the more reasons there are in the depths of this princely heart for an unconfessed jealousy. Life at court is boring, at the *palazzo* Sanseverina it is amusing. What means remain to him of demonstrating his power to himself?

The chance of tormenting his Minister. And he torments him cruelly! The Prince tries first of all, in a friendly way, to secure the Duchessa as his mistress, she refuses; there are blows to self-esteem the elements of which may easily be guessed from this brief analysis. Presently, the Prince reaches the stage of wishing to attack his Minister through the Duchessa, and he then seeks out ways of making her suffer.

All this part of the novel is of a remarkable literary solidity. This painting has the magnitude of a canvas fifty feet by thirty, and at the same time the manner, the execution is Dutch in its minuteness. We come to the drama, and to a drama the most complete, the most gripping, the strangest, the truest, the most profoundly explored in the human heart that has ever been invented, but one that has existed, undoubtedly, at many periods, and will reappear at courts where it will be enacted again, as Louis XIII and Richelieu, as Francis II and Prince Metternich, as Louis XV, the du Barry and M. de Choiseul have enacted it in the past.

The prospect which, in this new setting, has most attracted the Duchessa is that of the possibility of making a career for her hero, for this child of her heart, for Fabrizio her nephew. Fabrizio will owe his fortune to the genius of Mosca. The love which she has conceived for the child she continues to feel for the youth. I may tell you now, beforehand, that this love is to become later on, at first without Gina's knowledge, then consciously, a passion that will reach the sublime. Nevertheless she will always be the wife of the great diplomat, to whom she will never have committed any other act of infidelity than that of the passionate impulses of her heart towards this young idol; she will not deceive this man of genius, she will always make him happy and proud; she will make him aware of her least emotions, he will endure the most horrible rages of jealousy, and will never have any grounds for complaint. The Duchessa will be frank, artless, sublime, resigned, moving as a play of Shakespeare, beautiful as poetry, and the most severe reader will have no fault to find. I doubt if any poet has ever solved such a problem with as much felicity as has M. Beyle in this bold work. The Duchessa is one of those magnificent statues which make us at once admire the art that created them and inveigh against Nature which is so sparing of such models. Gina, when you have read the book, will remain before your eyes like a sublime statue: it will be neither the Venus de Milo, nor the Venus de' Medici; it will be Diana with the voluptuousness of Venus, with the suavity of Raphael's Virgins, and the movement of Italian passion. Above all, there is nothing French in the Duchessa. Yes, the Frenchman who has modelled, chiselled, wrought this marble, has left nothing on it of his native soil. *Corinne*, you must realise, is a miserable sketch compared with this living, ravishing creature. You will find her great, intellectual, passionate, always true to life, and yet the author has carefully concealed her sensual aspect. There is not in the work a single word that can make one think of the pleasures of love or can inspire them. Although the Duchessa, Mosca, Fabrizio, the Prince and his son, Clelia, although the book and its characters are, in their different ways, passion with all its furies; although it is Italy as it is, with its shrewdness, its dissimulation, its cunning, its coolness, its tenacity, its higher policy in every connexion, *La Chartreuse de Parme* is more chaste than the most puritanical of the novels of Walter Scott. To make a noble, majestic, almost irreproachable character of a duchess who makes a Mosca happy, and keeps nothing from him, is not that a masterpiece of fiction? The *Phèdre* of Racine, that sublime creation of the French stage, which Jansenism did not venture to condemn, is not so beautiful, nor so complete, nor so animated.

Well, at the moment when everything is smiling on the Duchessa, when she is amusing herself with this court life where a sudden storm is always to be feared, when she is most tenderly attached to the Conte, who, literally, is mad with happiness; when he has the patent and receives the honours of Prime Minister *which come very near to those paid to the Sovereign himself*, she says to him one day:

"And Fabrizio?"

The Conte then offers to obtain for her, from Austria, a pardon for this dear nephew.

"But, if he is somewhat superior to the young men who ride their English thoroughbreds about the streets of Milan, what a life, at eighteen, to be doing nothing with no prospect of ever having anything to do! If," says Mosca, "heaven had endowed him with a real passion, were it only for angling, I should respect it; but what is he to do at Milan, even after he has obtained his pardon?"

"I should like him to be an officer," says the Duchessa.

"Would you advise a Sovereign," says Mosca, "to entrust a post which, at a given date, may be of some importance, to a young man who has shown enthusiasm, who, from Como, has gone to join Napoleon at Waterloo? A del Dongo cannot be a merchant, nor a barrister, nor a doctor. You will cry out in protest, but you will come in the end to agree with me. If Fabrizio wishes it, he can quickly become Archbishop of Parma, one of the highest dignities in Italy, and from that Cardinal. We have had at Parma three del Dongo Archbishops, the Cardinal who wrote a book in sixteen-something, Fabrizio in 1700 and Ascanio in 1750. Only, shall I remain Minister long enough? That is the sole objection."

After two months spent in discussion, the Duchessa, defeated on every point by the Conte's observations, and rendered desperate by the precarious position of a younger son of a Milanese family, utters one day this profound Italian saying to her friend:

"Prove to me again that every other career is impossible for Fabrizio."

The Conte proves it.

The Duchessa, susceptible to the thought of fame, sees no other way of salvation, here below, for her dear Fabrizio, than the Church and its high dignities, for the future of Italy lies in Rome, and nowhere else. To anyone who has studied Italy carefully, it is clear that the unity of government in that country, that its nationality will never be reestablished save by the hand of a Sixtus V. The Pope alone has the power to stir and to reconstitute Italy. And so we see with what pains the Austrian court has watched, for the last thirty years, the elections of Popes, what aged imbeciles she has allowed to don the Triple Crown. "Perish Catholicism sooner than my domination!" seems to be her guiding motto. Miserly Austria would spend a million to prevent the election of a Pope with French ideas. And then, if some fine Italian genius employed sufficient dissimulation to put on the white cassock, he might die like Ganganelli. There perhaps is to be found the secret of the refusals of the Court of Rome, which has not chosen to accept the invigorating potion, the elixir offered to it by men of fine ecclesiastical genius from France: Borgia would not have failed to make them take their seat among his devoted Cardinals. The author of the Bull *In coena Domini* would have understood the great Gallican idea, Catholic Democracy, he would have adapted it to the circumstances. M. de Lamennais, that fallen angel, would not then, in his Breton obstinacy, have abandoned the Catholic, Apostolic and Roman Church.

So the Duchessa adopts this plan of the Conte. In this great woman there is, as in great politicians, a moment of uncertainty, of hesitation before a plan; but she never goes back upon her resolutions. The Duchessa is always right in wishing what she has wished. Her persistency, that strong quality of her imperious character, imparts an element of terror to all the scenes of this fertile drama.

Nothing could be more clever than the initiation of Fabrizio into his future destiny. The lovers display to Fabrizio the chances of his life. Fabrizio, a boy of astonishing intelligence, grasps everything at once and has a vision of the tiara. The Conte does not pretend to make a priest of him of the sort one sees everywhere in Italy. Fabrizio is a great gentleman, he can remain perfectly ignorant if it seems good to him, and will none the less become Archbishop. Fabrizio refuses to lead the life of the *caffè*, he has a horror of poverty, and realises that he cannot be a soldier. When he speaks of going and becoming an American citizen (we are in 1817), he has explained to him the dulness of life in America, without smartness, without music, without love affairs, without war, the cult of the god Dollar, and the respect due to artisans, to the masses who by their votes decide everything. Fabrizio has a horror of *mobocracy*.

At the voice of the great diplomat, who shows him life as it really is, the young man's illusions take flight. He had not understood what is incomprehensible to young people, the *"Surtout pas de zèle!"* of M. de Talleyrand.

"Remember," Mosca says to him, "that a proclamation, a

caprice of the heart flings the enthusiast into the bosom of the party opposed to his own future sympathies."

What a phrase![3]

The instructions given by the Minister to the neophyte who is to return to Parma only as a *Monsignore*, in violet stockings, and whom he sends to Naples to complete his studies with letters of recommendation to the Archbishop there, one of his clever friends; these instructions, given in the Duchessa's drawing-room, during a game of cards, are admirable. A single quotation will show you the fineness of the perceptions, the science of life which the author gives to this great character.

"Believe or not, as you choose, what they teach you, *but never raise any objection.* Imagine that they are teaching you the rules of the game of whist; would you raise any objection to the rules of whist? And once you knew and had adopted those rules, would you not wish to win? Do not fall into the vulgar habit of speaking with horror of Voltaire, Diderot, Raynal and all those harebrained Frenchmen who have brought us that foolish government by Two Chambers. Speak of them with a calm irony, they are people who have long since been refuted. You will be forgiven a little amorous intrigue, if it is done in the proper way, but they would take note of your objections: age stifles intrigue but encourages doubt. Believe everything, do not yield to the temptation to shine; be morose: discerning eyes will see your cleverness in yours and it will be time enough to be witty when you are an Archbishop!"

The astonishing and fine superiority of Mosca is never lacking, either in action or in speech; it makes this book one as profound, from page to page, as the *Maxims* of La Rochefoucauld. And observe that their passion leads the Conte and Duchessa to make mistakes, they are obliged to bring their talent into play to atone for them. To another man who had consulted him, the Conte would have explained the misfortunes that would await him at Parma after the death of

[3] What a phrase, indeed. But it is the Duchessa, not Mosca, who gives this advice to Fabrizio, at Piacenza, and it is the party "opposite to the one he has served all his life" that he is to be flung into. C. K. Scott Moncrieff.

Ernesto IV. But his passion has made him completely blind to his own interests. Talent alone can make you discover this poignant touch of comedy for yourself. Great politicians are nothing more, after all, than equilibrists who, if they do not take care, see their finest edifice come crashing to the ground. Richelieu was only saved from his peril, on the Day of the Dupes, by the broth of the Queen Mother, who refused to go to Saint-Germain without having taken the *lait de poule* which preserved her complexion. The Duchessa and Mosca live by a perpetual expenditure of all their faculties; and so the reader who follows the spectacle of their life is kept in a trance, through chapter after chapter, so well are the diffi- culties of this existence set before him, so cleverly are they explained. Finally, let us note well, these crises, these terrible scenes are woven into the substance of the book: the flowers are not stitched on, they are of the same substance as the rest.

"We must keep our love secret," the Duchessa says sadly to her lover, on the day on which she has guessed that his struggle with the Prince has begun.

When, to outact his acting, she lets Ernesto IV gather that she is only moderately in love with the Conte, she gives him a day of happiness; but the Prince is shrewd, he sees sooner or later that he has been tricked. And his disappoint- ment adds violence to the storm brought about by her ill- wishers.

This great work could not have been conceived or executed save by a man of fifty, in the full vigour of his age and in the maturity of all his talents. One sees perfection in every detail. The character of the Prince is drawn by the hand of a master, and is, as I have told you, *The Prince*. One conceives him admirably, as a man and as sovereign. This man might be at the head of the Russian Empire, he would be capable of ruling it, he would be great; but the man would remain what he is, liable to vanity, to jealousy, to passion. In the seventeenth century, at Versailles, he would be Louis XIV and would avenge himself on the Duchessa, as did Louis XIV on Fouquet. Criticism can find no fault in the greatest or in the smallest character; they are all what they ought to be. There is life and especially the life of courts, not drawn in caricature, as Hoffmann has tried to draw it, but seriously and ironically. Finally, this book explains to you admirably all that Louis XIII's *camarilla* made Richelieu suffer. This work applied to vast interests like those of the cabinet of Louis XIV, of Pitt's cabinet, of Napoleon's cabinet or of the Russian cabinet, would have been impossible owing to the prolixities and explanations which so many veiled interests would have required; whereas you get a comprehensive view of the State of Parma; and Parma enables you to understand, *mutato nomine,* the intrigues of the most exalted court. Things were like this under the Borgia Pope, at the court of Tiberius, at the court of Philip II; they must be like this also at the court of Peking!

Let us enter into the terrible Italian drama which has been slowly and logically preparing itself in a charming manner. I spare you the details of the court and its original figures; the Princess who thinks it her duty to be unhappy, because the Prince has his Pompadour; the Heir Apparent who is kept caged; the Princess Isotta, the Chamberlain, the Minister of the Interior, the Governor of the Citadel, Fabio Conti. One cannot afford to take the least thing lightly. If, like the Duchessa, Fabrizio and Mosca, you accept the court of Parma, you play your game of whist and your interests are at stake. When the Prime Minister thinks that he has fallen from power, he says quite seriously:

"When our guests have gone, we can decide on a way of barricading ourselves for the night; the best plan would be to set off while they're dancing for your place at Sacca, by the Po, from where in twenty minutes one can get into Austria."

Indeed the Duchessa, the Minister, every Parmesan subject is liable to end his days in the citadel.

When the Prince confesses his desires to the Duchessa and she in reply asks him:

"How should we ever look Mosca in the face again, that man of genius and heart?"

"I have thought of that," says the Prince: "we should never look him in the face again! The citadel waits."

The Sanseverina does not fail to repeat this saying to Mosca, who puts his affairs in order.

Four years elapse.

The Minister, who has not allowed Fabrizio to come to Parma during these four years, permits him to reappear there when the Pope has created him Monsignore, a kind of dignity which entitles him to wear violet stockings. Fabrizio has nobly answered the expectations of his political master. At Naples he has had mistresses, he has had the passion for archæology, he has sold his horses to make excavations, he has behaved well, he has aroused no jealousy, he may become Pope. What delights him most about his return to Parma is the thought of being delivered from the attentions of the charming Duchessa d'A——. His governor, who has made him an educated man, receives a Cross and a pension. Fabrizio's first appearance at Parma, his arrival, his various presentations at court, form the highest comedy of manners, character and intrigue that one can read anywhere. At more than one point, the better class of reader will lay down this book on his table to say to himself:

"Heavens! How good this is, how exquisitely arranged, how deep!"

He will meditate upon words like the following, for instance, upon which Princes ought to meditate well for their own good: *People with brains who are born on the throne or at the foot of it soon lose all fineness of touch; they proscribe, in their immediate circle, freedom of conversation which seems to them coarseness, they refuse to look at anything but masks and pretend to judge the beauty of complexions; the amusing part of it is that they imagine their touch to be of the finest.*

Here begin the Duchessa's ingenuous passion for Fabrizio, and Mosca's torments. Fabrizio is a diamond that has lost nothing by being polished. Gina, who had sent him to Naples a devil-may-care young rough-rider, whose horsewhip seemed to be an inherent part of his person, sees him now with a noble and confident bearing before strangers, and in private the same fire of youth.

"This nephew," Mosca tells his mistress, "is made to adorn all the exalted posts." But the great diplomat, attentive at first to Fabrizio, turns to look at the Duchessa and notices *a curious look in her eyes.* "I am in my fifties," he reflects.

The Duchessa is so happy that she does not give the Conte a thought. This profound effect, made on Mosca by a single glance, is irremediable.

When Ranuccio-Ernesto IV guesses that the aunt loves the nephew a little more warmly than the laws of consanguinity permit, which at Parma is incest, he is at the pinnacle of happiness. He writes his Minister an anonymous letter on the subject. When he is sure that Mosca has read it, he sends for him, without giving him time to call first on the Duchessa, and keeps him on the rack throughout a conversation full of princely friendliness and hypocrisy. Certainly the pangs of love causing a fine heart to bleed always make an effective scene; but this heart is Italian, this is the heart of a man of genius, and I know nothing that grips me so as the chapter on Mosca's jealousy.

Fabrizio does not love his aunt; he adores her as an aunt, she inspires no longing in him as a woman; nevertheless, in their conversations, a gesture, a word may make youth break out, the least thing may then make his aunt leave Parma, because riches, honours are nothing to her who, once already, before the eyes of all Milan, has managed to live on a third floor, with an income of fifteen hundred francs. The future Archbishop sees an abyss open before him. The Prince is as happy as a king, while waiting for a catastrophe to destroy the private happiness of his dear Minister. Mosca, the great Mosca, weeps like a child. The prudence of this dear Fabrizio, who understands Mosca and understands his aunt, prevents any disaster. The Monsignore makes himself fall in love with a little Marietta, an actress of the lowest grade, a columbine who has her harlequin, a certain Giletti, formerly one of Napoleon's dragoons, and a fencing master, a man horrible in mind and body, who devours Marietta, beats her, steals her blue shawls and all her earnings.

Mosca breathes again. The Prince is uneasy, his prey is escaping, he could hold the Sanseverina by her nephew, and now the nephew turns out a profound politician! In spite of Marietta, the Duchessa's passion is so artless, her familiarities are so dangerous, that Fabrizio, to restore tranquillity, proposes to the Conte, who also is an antiquarian and is engaged on excavations, to go down to the country and superintend the work. The Minister adores Fabrizio. The company which includes Marietta, her *mammaccia*—a figure drawn in four pages with an astounding truth and depth of character—and Giletti, the whole motley crew, leave Parma. This trio, Giletti, the *mammaccia* and Marietta come along the road while Fabrizio is shooting. There follows an encounter between the dragoon, who seeks, in an access of Italian vanity, to *kill the black-frock*, and Fabrizio, who is amazed at seeing Marietta on the road. This accidental duel becomes serious when Fabrizio sees that Giletti, who has only one eye, is trying to disfigure him: he kills him. Giletti was plainly the aggressor, the workmen engaged on the excavations saw everything, Fabrizio realises all the capital that the Raversi faction and the Liberals will make out of this ridiculous adventure against himself, the Ministers, his aunt; he takes flight, he crosses the Po. Thanks to the clever assistance of Lodovico, an old servant of the Sanseverina household, a fellow who writes sonnets, he finds shelter and reaches Bologna, where he sees Marietta again. Lodovico becomes fanatically attached to Fabrizio. This retired coachman is one of the most complete of the figures of the second magnitude. Fabrizio's flight, the scenery by the Po, the descriptions of famous places through which the young prelate passes, his adventures during his exile from Parma, his correspondence with the Archbishop, another character admirably drawn, the smallest details are of a literary execution that bears the hall-mark of genius. And all is so Italian as to make one take the coach and fly to Italy, there to seek this drama and this poetry. The reader becomes Fabrizio.

During this absence, Fabrizio goes to revisit his native scenes, the Lake of Como and the paternal castle, despite the dangers of his position with regard to Austria, at that time very strict. We are in 1821, a time when a passport was not to be treated lightly. The prelate recognised as Fabrizio del Dongo may be sent to the Spielberg. In this part of the book the author completes the portrait of a fine head, that of a Priore Blanès, a simple village curate, who adores Fabrizio and cultivates the study of judicial astrology. This portrait is done so seriously, there shines from it so great a faith in the occult sciences, that the satire of which those sciences—to which we shall return and which do not rest, as has been supposed, upon false foundations—might naturally be the object dies away on the lips of the incredulous. I do not know what the author's opinion may be, but he justifies that of the Priore Blanès. Priore Blanès is a character who is true in Italy. The truth of him can be felt, just as one can tell whether one of Titian's heads is the portrait of a Venetian gentleman or a fancy.

The Prince orders the preparation of the case against Fabrizio, and in this task the genius of Rassi is revealed. The Fiscal General sends the witnesses for the defence out of the country, purchases evidence for the prosecution, and, as he impudently informs the Prince, produces out of this foolish affair—the death inflicted on a Giletti by a del Dongo, in self-defence, by a del Dongo who had received the first blow! —a sentence of detention for twenty years in the fortress. The Prince would have liked a death sentence, in order to *exercise clemency* and so humiliate the Sanseverina.

"But," says Rassi, "I have done better than that, I have broken his neck, his career is barred to him for ever. The Vatican can do nothing more for a murderer."

So the Prince holds the Sanseverina in his clutches at last! Ah! It is then that the Duchessa becomes superb, that the court of Parma is agitated, that the lights go up on the drama, which assumes gigantic proportions. One of the finest scenes in modern fiction is, certainly, that in which the Sanseverina comes to pay her farewell to the Sovereign and presents him with an *ultimatum*. The scene of Elizabeth, Amy and Leicester in *Kenilworth* is no greater, more dramatic nor more terrible. The tiger is braved in his den; the serpent is caught, in vain does he writhe his coils and beg for pity, the woman crushes him. Gina desires, dictates, obtains from the Prince a rescript annulling the proceedings. She does not seek a pardon, the Prince will state that the proceedings are unjust and shall have no consequences in the future, which is an absurd thing to expect of an absolute Sovereign. This absurdity she demands, she obtains it. Mosca is magnificent in this scene where the lovers are alternately saved, lost, in peril for a gesture, a word, a glance!

In every walk of life, artists have an invincible self-respect, a sense of their art, a professional conscience which is in-eradicable from the man. One does not corrupt, one never succeeds in buying this conscience. The actor who wishes most harm to his theatre or to an author will never play a part badly. The chemist, called in to look for arsenic in a body, will find it if there is any there. The writer, the painter, are always faithful to their genius, even at the foot of the scaffold. This does not exist in woman. The universe is the stepping-stone of her passion. And so woman is greater and finer than man in this respect. Woman is passion; man is action. If this were not so, man would not adore woman. And so it is in the social circle of the court, which gives the greatest flight to her passion, that woman sheds her most brilliant radiance. Her finest stage is the world of Absolute Power. That is why there are no longer any women in France. Now Conte Mosca suppresses, from a trace of ministerial self-respect, in the Prince's rescript, the words on which the Duchessa depends. The Prince imagines that his Minister considers him before the Sanseverina, and casts a glance at him which the reader intercepts. Mosca, like a true states-man, will not countersign a stupid thing, that is all: the Prince is mistaken. In the intoxication of her triumph, re-joicing that she has saved Fabrizio, the Duchessa, who trusts in Mosca, does not peruse the rescript. She was thought to be ruined, she had made all preparations for her departure in the face of Parma, she returns from the court having effected a revolution. Mosca was thought to be in disgrace. Fabrizio's sentence was taken as an insult by the Prince to the Duchessa and Minister. Not at all, the Raversi is ban-ished. The Prince laughs, he is holding his vengeance in re-serve: this woman who has humiliated him, he is going to make die of grief.

The Marchesa Raversi, instead of composing Ovidian *Tristia*, like everyone who is banished from a court where he or she handled the reins of power, sets to work. She guesses what has happened in the Prince's cabinet, she ex-tracts his secrets from Rassi, who allows her to do so; he is aware of the Prince's intentions. The Marchesa has some let-ters written by the Duchessa, she sends her lover to the galleys at Genoa to get a letter forged from the Duchessa to

Fabrizio, telling him of her triumph, and appointing a meeting at her country house, Sacca, close to the Po, a delicious spot where the Duchessa always spends the summer. Poor Fabrizio hastens there, he is caught, they put handcuffs on him, he is shut up in the citadel, and while they are shutting him up, he recognises the daughter of the governor, Fabio Conti, the lovely and sublime Clelia, for whom he is to feel that eternal love that gives no respite.

Fabrizio del Dongo, her nephew, he whom she adores, in the most honourable fashion, in the citadel! . . . Imagine the Duchessa's feelings! She learns of Mosca's mistake. She will not see Mosca again. There is only Fabrizio now in the world! Once inside that terrible fortress, he may die there, die there by poison!

This is the Prince's system: a fortnight of terror, a fortnight of hope. And he will handle this fiery steed, this proud soul, this Sanseverina whose triumphs and happiness, though necessary to the brilliance of his court, were insulting to his inner man. Played on in this way, the Sanseverina will become thin, old and ugly: he will knead her like dough.

This terrible duel in which the Duchessa has inflicted the first wound, piercing her adversary to the heart but without killing him, in which she will receive for the next year a fresh wound daily, is the most powerful thing that the genius of the modern novel has invented.

Let us turn now to Fabrizio in prison, and so come to my analysis of that chapter, which is one of the diamonds on this crown.

The episode of the robbers in Lewis's *Monk*, his *Anaconda*, which is his best book, the interest of the last volumes by Mrs. Radcliffe, the thrilling vicissitudes in the Red Indian romances of Cooper, all the extraordinary things I know in the narratives of travels and prisoners, none of these can compare with the confinement of Fabrizio in the fortress of Parma, three hundred and something feet above the ground. This terrifying abode is a Vaucluse: he makes love there to Clelia, he is happy there, he displays the ingenuity of prisoners, and he prefers his prison to the most enchanting spot that the world has to offer. The Bay of Naples is beautiful only through the eyes of Lamartine's Elvire; but, in the eyes of a Clelia, in the trills of her voice, there are whole universes. The author depicts, as he knows how to depict, by little incidents which have the eloquence of Shakespearean action, the progress of the love between these two fair creatures, amid the dangers of an imminent death by poison. This part of the book will be read with halting breath, straining throat, avid eyes by all those readers who have imagination, or simply hearts. Everything in it is perfect, rapid, real, without any improbability or strain. There you find passion in all its glory, its rendings, its hopes, its melancholies, its returns, its abatements, its inspirations, the only ones that equal those of genius. Nothing has been forgotten. You will read there an encyclopædia of all the resources of the prisoner; his marvellous languages for which he makes use of nature, the means by which he gives life to a song and meaning to a sound. Read in prison, this book is capable of killing a prisoner, or of making him tunnel through his walls.

While Fabrizio is inspiring love and feeling it, during the most engrossing scenes of the drama inside the prison, there is, you must understand, a fight to the death going on outside the fortress. The Prince, the governor, Rassi, attempt to poison him. Fabrizio's death is determined upon at a moment when the Prince's vanity is mortally wounded. The charming Clelia, the most delicious figure you could see in a dream, then reveals the extent of her love by helping Fabrizio to escape, although his rescuers have nearly killed her father, the General.

At this crisis in the book, we understand all the incidents that have gone before. Without those adventures in which we have seen the people, in which we have watched them acting, nothing would be intelligible, everything would seem false and impossible.

Let us return to the Duchessa. The courtiers, the Raversi party triumph in the griefs of this noble woman. Her calm is killing the Prince, and no one can explain it to him. Mosca himself does not understand it. Here, we see that Mosca, great as he is, is inferior to this woman who, at this moment, seems to you to be the genius of Italy. Profound is her dissimulation, bold are her plans. As for her revenge, it will be complete. The Prince has been too greatly offended, she sees him implacable; between them, the duel is to the death; but the Duchessa's vengeance would be impotent, imperfect, if she allowed Ranuccio-Ernesto IV to take Fabrizio from her by poison. Fabrizio must be set at liberty. This attempt seems literally impossible to every reader, so carefully has *tyranny* taken its precautions, so deeply has it involved the governor, Fabio Conti, whose honour is at stake if he does not guard his prisoners.

There is in this man something of Hudson Lowe, but of a Hudson Lowe magnified to the tenth degree; he is Italian, and wishes to avenge the Raversi for the disgrace that the Duchessa has brought on her. Gina fears nothing. This is why:

"The lover thinks more often of penetrating to his mistress's chamber than the husband of guarding his wife; the prisoner thinks more often of escaping than the gaoler of shutting his door; therefore, in spite of the obstacles in their way, the lover and the prisoner must succeed in the end."

She will help him! Oh, what a fine painting of this Italian in despair, who cannot flee from this abhorrent court! "Come," she says to herself, "*forward, unhappy woman*" (we weep as we read this great feminine utterance), "do your duty, pretend to forget Fabrizio!" "*Forget him!*" the word saves her: she has not been able to shed a tear until this word. Then the Duchessa conspires, she conspires with the Prime Minister, whom she has ostensibly banished in disgrace, but who would set Parma on fire and deluge it with blood for her, who would kill everyone, the Prince even. This true lover realises that he is in the wrong, he is the most wretched of men. Alas! What a feeble excuse! He did not believe his master to be so false, so cowardly, so cruel. And so he admits that his mistress is entitled to be implacable. He finds it natural that Fabrizio should be, at this moment, everything in the world to her, he has that weakness of great men for their mistresses which leads them to understand even the infidelity which may mean their death. The enamoured veteran is sublime! He says but one word to himself, in the scene when Gina has made him come to her for their rupture. A single night has ravaged the Duchessa.

"Great God!" exclaims Mosca to himself, "she looks all her forty years to-day!"

What a book is this in which one finds these cries of passion, these profound diplomatic sayings, and on every page. Note this as well: you will not meet in this book those extra flourishes, so aptly named *tartines*. No, the characters act, reflect, feel, and always the drama sweeps on. Never does the poet, a dramatist in his ideas, stoop in his path to pick the smallest flower, everything has the rapidity of a dithyramb.

Let us proceed! The Duchessa is ravishing in her admissions to Mosca, and sublime in her despair. Finding her so changed, he supposes her to be ill, and wishes to send for Razori, the leading doctor in Parma and in Italy.

"Is that the counsel of a traitor or of a friend?" she asks. "You wish to convey to a stranger the measure of my despair!"

"I am lost," thinks the Conte, "she no longer includes me even among the common men of honour."

"Bear in mind," the Duchessa tells him with the most imperious air, "that I am not distressed by the capture of Fabrizio, that I have not the least shadow of a desire to go away, that I am full of respect for the Prince. As for yourself: I intend to have the entire control of my own behaviour, I wish to part from you as an old and good friend. Consider that I have reached sixty, the young woman is dead. With Fabrizio in prison, I am incapable of love. Finally, I should be the unhappiest woman in the world were I to compromise your future. If you see me making a show of having a young lover, do not let yourself be distressed by that. I can swear to you, by Fabrizio's future happiness, that I have never been guilty of the slightest infidelity towards you, and that in five whole years . . . that is a long time!" she says, trying to smile. "I swear to you that I have never either planned or wished such a thing. Now you understand that, leave me."

The Conte goes, he spends two days and two nights in thought.

"Great heavens!" he at length exclaims, "the Duchessa never said a word to me about an escape; can she have been wanting in sincerity for once in her life, and is the motive of her quarrel only a desire that I should betray the Prince? No sooner said than done."

Did I not tell you that this book was a masterpiece, and can you not see it for yourself, merely from this rough analysis?

The Minister, after this discovery, treads the ground as if he were a boy of fifteen, takes a new lease of life. He is going to seduce Rassi from the Prince, and make him his own creature.

"Rassi," he says to himself, "is paid by his master to carry out the sentences that disgrace us throughout Europe, but he will not refuse to let himself be paid by me to betray his master's secrets. He has a mistress and a confessor. The mistress is of so low an order that the market woman would know the whole story by to-morrow morning."

He goes to say his prayers at the cathedral and to find the Archbishop.

"What sort of man is Dugnani, the Vicar of San Paolo?" he asks him.

"A small mind with great ambition, few scruples and extreme poverty; for we too have our vices!" says the Archbishop, raising his eyes to heaven.

The Minister cannot help laughing at the analytical depth reached by true piety combined with honesty. He sends for the priest and says to him only:

"You direct the conscience of my friend the Fiscal General; are you sure he has nothing to tell me?"

The Conte is prepared to stake everything: there is only one thing that he wishes to know, the moment at which Fabrizio will be in danger of death, and he does not propose to interfere with the Duchessa's plans. His interview with Rassi is a capital scene. This is how the Conte begins, adopting the tone of the most lofty impertinence:

"What, sir, you carry off from Bologna a conspirator who is under my protection; more than that, you propose to cut off his head, and you say nothing to me about it. Do you know the name of my successor? Is it General Conti or yourself?"

The Minister and Fiscal agree upon a plan which allows them to retain their respective positions. I must leave to you the pleasure of reading the admirable details of this continuous web in which the author drives a hundred characters abreast without being more embarrassed than a skilful coachman is by the reins of a ten-horse coach. Everything is in its place, there is not the slightest confusion. You see everything, the town and the court. The drama is amazing in its skill, its execution, its clearness. The air plays over the picture, not a character is superfluous. Lodovico, who on many occasions has proved that he is an honest Figaro, is the Duchessa's right arm. He plays a fine part, he will be well rewarded.

The time has now come to speak to you of one of the subordinate characters who is shown in colossal proportions, and to whom frequent reference is made in the book, namely Ferrante Palla, a Liberal doctor under sentence of death who is wandering through Italy, where he performs his task of propaganda.

Ferrante Palla is a great poet, like Silvio Pellico, but he is what Pellico is not, a Radical Republican. Let us not concern ourselves with the faith of this man. He has faith, he is the Saint Paul of the Republic, a martyr of Young Italy, he is a sublime work of art like the *Saint Bartholomew* at Milan, like Foyatier's *Spartacus*, like Marius pondering over the ruins of Carthage. Everything that he does, everything that he says is sublime. He has the conviction, the grandeur, the passion of the believer. However high you may place, in execution, in conception, in reality, the Prince, the Minister, the Duchessa, Ferrante Palla, this superb statue, set in a corner of the picture, commands your gaze, compels your admiration. In spite of your opinions, constitutional, monarchical or religious, he subjugates you. Greater than his own misfortunes, preaching Italy from the hollow shelter of his caves, without bread for his mistress and their five children; committing highway robbery to maintain them, and keeping a note of the sums stolen and the persons robbed so as to restore to them this forced loan to the Republic *when he shall have the power to do so*; stealing moreover in order to print his pamphlets entitled: *The necessity for a budget in Italy!* Ferrante Palla is the type of a family of minds to be found in Italy, sincere but misguided, full of talent but ignorant of the fatal results of their doctrine. Send them with plenty of gold to France and to the United States, as Ministers of Absolute Princes! Instead of persecuting them, let them acquire enlightenment, these true men, full of great and exquisite qualities. They will say like Alfieri in 1793: "Little men, at work, reconcile me to the great."

I praise with all the more enthusiasm this creation of Ferrante Palla, having caressed the same figure myself. If I have the trifling advantage over M. Beyle of priority, I am inferior to him in execution. I have perceived this inward drama, so great, so powerful, of the stern and conscientious Republican in love with a Duchess who holds to Absolute Power. My Michel Chrestien, in love with the Duchesse de Maufrigneuse, could not stand out with the relief of Ferrante Palla, a lover after the style of Petrarch of the Duchessa Sanseverina. Italy and its customs, Italy and its scenery, the perils, the starvation of Ferrante Palla are far more attractive than the meagre details of Parisian civilisation. Although Michel Chrestien dies at Saint-Merry and Ferrante Palla escapes to the United States after his crimes, Italian passion is far superior to French passion, and the events of this episode add to their Apennine savour an interest with which it is useless to compete. In a period when everything is levelled more easily under the uniform of the National Guard and the *Bourgeois* law than under the steel triangle of the Republic, literature is essentially lacking, in France, in those great obstacles between lovers which used to be the source of fresh beauties, of new situations, and which made subjects dramatic. And so it was difficult for the serious paradox of the passion of a Radical for a great lady to escape trained pens.

In no book, unless it be *Old Mortality*, is there to be found a figure of an energy comparable to that which M. Beyle has given to Ferrante Palla, whose name exercises a sort of compulsion over the imagination. Between Balfour of Burley and Ferrante Palla, I have no hesitation, I choose Ferrante Palla; the design is the same; but Walter Scott, great colourist as he may be, has not the thrilling, warm colour, as of Titian, which M. Beyle has spread over his character. Ferrante Palla is a whole poem in himself, a poem superior to Lord Byron's *Corsair*. "Ah! That is how people love!" is what all M. Beyle's

feminine readers will say to themselves on reading this sublime and most reprehensible episode.

Ferrante Palla has the most impenetrable of retreats in the
neighbourhood of Sacca. He has often seen the Duchessa, he
has fallen passionately in love with her. The Duchessa has
met him, has been moved, Ferrante Palla has told her everything, as though in the presence of God. He knows that the
Duchessa loves Mosca, his own love therefore is hopeless.
There is something touching in the Italian grace with which
the Duchessa lets him give himself the pleasure of kissing
the white hands of a woman with blue blood. He has not
clasped a white hand for seven years, and this poet adores
beautiful white hands. His mistress, whom he no longer loves,
does the heavy work, makes clothes for the children, and he
cannot desert a woman who will not leave him, notwithstanding the most appalling poverty. These obligations of an honest man become apparent. The Duchessa has compassion for
everything, like a true Madonna. She has offered him his
pardon! Ah, but Ferrante Palla has, like Carl Sand, his own
little sentences to enforce; he has his preaching, his journey-
ings to rekindle the zeal of Young Italy.

"All those scoundrels, who do so much harm to the people, would live for long years," he says, "and whose fault
would that be? What would my father say when I meet him
in heaven!"

She then proposes to provide for the needs of the woman
and her children, and give him an undiscoverable hiding-
place in the *palazzo* Sanseverina.

The *palazzo* Sanseverina includes an immense reservoir,
built in the middle ages with a view to prolonged sieges, and
capable of supplying the town with water for a year. Part of
the *palazzo* is built over this immense structure. The dapple-
grey Duca spent the night after their marriage in telling his
wife the secret of the reservoir and of its hiding-place. An
enormous stone which moves on a pivot will let all the water
escape and flood the streets of Parma. In one of the thick
walls of the reservoir there is a chamber without light and
without much air, which no one would ever suspect; you
would have to pull down the reservoir to find it.

Ferrante Palla accepts the hiding-place for evil days, and

refuses the Duchessa's money; he has made a vow never to have more than a hundred francs on him. At the moment when she offers him her sequins, he has money; but he lets himself go so far as to accept one sequin.

"I take this sequin, because I love you," he says; "but I am on the wrong side of my hundred by five francs, and, if they were to hang me this minute, I should feel remorse."

"He does really love," the Duchessa says to herself.

Is not that the simplicity of Italy, taken from life? Molière, writing a novel to describe this people, the only one except the Arabs that has preserved its reverence for vows, could do nothing finer.

Ferrante Palla becomes the Duchessa's other arm in her conspiracy, and is a terrible weapon, his energy makes one shudder! Here is the scene that occurs one evening in the *palazzo* Sanseverina. The lion of the people has emerged from his retreat. He enters for the first time rooms ablaze with regal splendour. He finds there his mistress, his idol, the idol whom he has set above Young Italy, above the Republic and the welfare of humanity; he sees her distressed, tears in her eyes! The Prince has snatched from her him whom she loves best in the world, he had basely deceived her, and this *tyrant* holds the sword of Damocles over the beloved head.

"What is happening here," says this sublime Republican Don Quixote, "is an injustice of which the Tribune of the People ought to take note. On the other hand, as a private citizen, I can give the Signora Duchessa Sanseverina nothing but my life, and I lay it at her feet. The creature you see at your feet is not a puppet of the court, he is a man.—She has wept in my presence," he says to himself, "she is less unhappy."

"Think of the risk you are running," says the Duchessa.

"The Tribune will answer you: 'What is life when the voice of duty speaks?' The man will say to you: 'Here is a body of iron and a heart that fears nothing in the world but your displeasure.'"

"If you speak to me of your feelings," says the Duchessa, "I shall not see you again."

Ferrante Palla departs sadly.

Am I mistaken? Are they not as fine as Corneille, these dialogues? And, remember, such passages abound, they are

all, after their kind, at the same high level. Struck by the
beauty of this character, the Duchessa prepares a written document providing for the future of Ferrante's mistress and his
five children, without saying anything to him, for she is
afraid that he may let himself be killed on learning that his
dependents have had this provision made for them.

Finally, on the day when the whole of Parma is discussing
the probable death of Fabrizio, the Tribune braves every danger. He enters the *palazzo* at night, he arrives disguised as a
Capuchin in the Duchessa's presence; he finds her drowned
in tears and voiceless: she greets him with her hand and
points to a chair. Palla prostrates himself, prays to God, so
divine does her beauty seem to him, and breaks off his prayer
to say:

"Once again *he* offers his life."

"Think of what you are saying!" cries the Duchessa with
that haggard eye which shews more clearly than sobs that
anger is mastering affection.

"He offers his life to place an obstacle in the way of
Fabrizio's fate or to avenge it."

"If I were to accept!" she says, gazing at him.

She sees the joy of martyrdom flash in Palla's eye. She
rises, goes to look for the deed of gift prepared a month back,
for Ferrante's mistress and children.

"Read this!"

He reads it and falls on his knees, he sobs, he almost dies
of joy.

"Give me back the paper," says the Duchessa.

She burns it over a candle.

"My name," she tells him, "must not appear. If you are
taken and executed, if you are weak, I may be also, and
Fabrizio would be in danger. I wish you to sacrifice yourself."

"I will perform the task faithfully, punctually and pru-
dently."

"If I am discovered and convicted," the Duchessa goes on
proudly, "I do not wish to be accused of having corrupted
you. Do not put *him* to death until I give the signal. That
signal will be the flooding of the streets of Parma, of which
you are bound to hear."

Ferrante, delighted by the Duchessa's tone of authority,

takes his leave. When he has gone, the Duchessa calls him back.

"Ferrante, sublime man!"

He returns.

"And your children?"

"Bah! You will provide for them."

"Look, here are my diamonds."

And she gives him a little olive-wood box.

"They are worth fifty thousand francs."

"Oh! Signora!" says Ferrante with a start of horror.

"I may perhaps not see you again. Take them, it is my wish."

Ferrante leaves her. The door closes behind him, the Duchessa again calls him back. He sees her standing there, he comes back uneasily. The great Sanseverina throws herself into his arms. Ferrante is on the point of fainting. She allows him to kiss her, frees herself from his embrace when he threatens to become disrespectful, and shews him the door.

She remains standing for some time and says to herself:

"That is the one man who has understood me; Fabrizio would be like that if he could only know me."

I cannot lay too much stress on the merit of this scene. M. Beyle is not in the least a preacher. He does not urge you on to regicide, he gives you a fact, states it as it occurred. No one, not even a Republican, feels the desire to kill a tyrant on reading it. It is the play of private passions, that is all. It is a question of a duel which requires extraordinary, but equally matched arms. The Duchessa makes use of Palla to poison the Prince as the Prince makes use of one of Fabrizio's enemies to poison Fabrizio. One can avenge oneself on a king, Coriolanus avenged himself well on his country, Beaumarchais and Mirabeau avenged themselves well on their period which despised them. This is not moral, but the author has told you of it, and washes his hands of it as Tacitus washes his of the crimes of Tiberius. "I am inclined to believe," he says, "that the immoral delight in taking revenge which one finds in Italy springs from the strength of imagination of that race; other races do not forgive, they forget." Thus the moralist explains this energetic people among whom we find so many inventors, who have the richest, the finest imagination, with its accompanying drawbacks. This reflexion is more profound than it appears at a first reading, it explains the rhetorical stupidities which weigh down the Italians, the only race that is comparable to the French, a race superior to the Russians or the English, whose genius has the feminine fibre, that delicacy, that majesty which make it in many respects superior to all other races. From this point the Duchessa regains her advantage over the Prince. Hitherto, she was weak and tricked in this great duel; Mosca, prompted by his courtier's spirit, had been acting as second to the Prince. Now that her revenge is assured, Gina feels her strength. Each step that her thoughts take gives her happiness, she can play her part. The Tribune's courage heightens hers. Lodovico is electrified by her. These three conspirators, on whom Mosca shuts his eyes, while leaving his police free to act against them if they notice anything, arrive at the most extraordinary result.

The Minister has been the dupe of his mistress, he fully believed himself to be in disgrace, as he deserved. If he had not been thoroughly taken in, he could never have played the part of a forlorn lover, for happiness admits of no concealment. That fire of the heart has its smoke. But, after the fascination of Ferrante by the Duchessa, her joy enlightens the Minister, he at last guesses her purpose, without knowing how far she has gone.

Fabrizio's escape borders on the miraculous. It has required so much physical strength and such an exercise of intelligence, that the dear boy is on the point of death: the scent of his aunt's clothing and handkerchief revives him. This slight detail, which is not forgotten among a thousand other incidents, will delight those who are in love: it is placed, as might be placed in a *finale* a melody which recalls the sweetest elements of the life of love. All precautions have been carefully taken, there is no indiscretion: Conte Mosca, who is present in person at the expedition with more than two dozen spies, does not receive a single report of it as Minister.

"Now I'm committing high treason," he says to himself, blind with joy.

Everyone has understood his orders without a word said, and escapes in his own way. The business finished, each head has to think of and for itself. Lodovico is the courier, he crosses the Po. Ah! When Fabrizio is out of the reach of his crowned assassin, the Duchessa, who until then had been crouching like a jaguar, coiled like a serpent hidden in the undergrowth, flat as one of Cooper's Indians in the mud, supple as a slave and feline as a deceitful woman, rises to her full height: the panther shews her claws, the serpent is going to sting, the Indian to utter his yell of triumph, she leaps for joy, she is mad. Lodovico, who knows nothing of Ferrante Palla, who says of him in the common phrase: "He is a poor man persecuted because of Napoleon!" Lodovico is afraid that his mistress is going out of her mind. She gives him the small property of Ricciarda. He trembles on receiving this regal gift. What has he done to deserve it? "Conspire, and for Monsignore, why that is a pleasure."

It is then, the author tells us, that the Duchessa allows herself to commit an act not only horrible in the eyes of morality, but fatal to the tranquillity of her life. We suppose, of course, that in this hour of bliss, she will forgive the Prince. No.

"If you wish to acquire the property, you must do two things," she tells Lodovico, "and without exposing yourself. You must go back at once across the Po, illuminate my house at Sacca in such a way as to make people think it is on fire. I have prepared everything for this festivity, in case we succeeded. There are lamps and oil in the cellars. Here is a line to my agent. Let the whole population of Sacca drink themselves drunk, empty all my barrels and all my bottles. By the Madonna! If I find one full bottle, one barrel with two fingers of wine left in it, you lose Ricciarda! When that is done, return to Parma and let the water out of the reservoir. Wine for my dear people at Sacca, water for the town of Parma!"

This makes one shudder. It is the Italian spirit, which M. Hugo has perfectly reproduced when he makes Lucrezia Borgia say: "You have given me a ball at Venice, I offer you in return a supper at Ferrara." The two speeches are equivalent. Lodovico sees in this nothing more than a magnificent insolence and an exquisite joke. He repeats: "Wine for the people of Sacca, water for the people of Parma!" Lodovico returns after having carried out the Duchessa's orders, establishes her at Belgirate, and takes Fabrizio, who has still the Austrian police to fear, to Locarno, in Switzerland.

Fabrizio's escape, the illumination of Sacca throw the State of Parma into utter confusion. Little attention is paid to the flooding of the town. A similar event occurred at the time of the French invasion. A horrible punishment awaits the Duchessa. She sees Fabrizio dying of love for Clelia, resentful of being First Grand Vicar to the Archbishop and so unable to marry his beloved.

In the arms of his aunt and on Lake Maggiore, he dreams of his dear prison. What then are the sufferings of this woman who has ordered a crime, who has so to speak brought down the moon from the sky by taking this beloved boy out of prison, and who sees him so artless and simple, thinking of other things, refusing to perceive anything, and not allowing himself to succumb to what he had so wisely fled from in the company of his Gina, his mother, his sister, his aunt, his friend who longed to be something more than a friend to him, all this torture is unspeakable; but, in the book, it is felt, it is seen. We are pained by Fabrizio's desertion of the San-severina, although we are conscious that the gratification of her love would be criminal. Fabrizio is not even grateful. The ex-prisoner, like a Minister in retirement who dreams of coalitions which will restore him to power, thinks only of his prison; he sends for pictures of Parma, that city abhorrent to his aunt; he puts one of the fortress in his bedroom. Finally, he writes a letter of apology to General Conti for having escaped, so as to be able to say to Clelia that he finds no happiness in liberty without her, and you can imagine what effect this letter (it is taken as a masterpiece of ecclesiastical irony) produces on the General; he swears that he will be avenged. The Duchessa, terrified and brought back to a sense of self-preservation by the futility of her revenge, takes a boatman from each of the villages on Lake Maggiore; she makes them row her out to the middle of the lake; then she tells them that a search may be made for Fabrizio, who served under Napoleon at Waterloo, and bids them keep a sharp watch; she makes herself loved, and obeyed; she pays well, and so has a spy in every village; she gives each of them permission to enter her room at any hour, even at night when she is asleep. One evening, at Locarno, during a party, she hears of the death of the Prince of Parma. She looks at Fabrizio.

"I have done this for him; I would have done things a thousand times worse," she says to herself, "and look at him there, silent, indifferent, dreaming about another!"

At this thought she faints. This fainting-fit may be her ruin. The company gathers round her, Fabrizio thinks of Clelia: she sees him, she shudders, she finds herself surrounded by all these curious people, an archpriest, the local authorities, and so forth. She recovers the calm of a great lady, and says:

"He was a great Prince, who was vilely slandered; it is an immense loss for us.—Ah!" she says to herself, when she is alone, "it is now that I have to pay for the transports of happiness and childish joy that I felt in my *palazzo* at Parma when I welcomed Fabrizio there on his return from Naples. If I had said a word, all would have been over, I should have left Mosca. Once he was with me, Clelia would never have meant anything to Fabrizio. Clelia wins, she is twenty. I am almost twice her age. I must die! A *woman of forty is no longer anything save for the men who have loved her in her youth!*"

It is for this reflexion, profound in its shrewdness, suggested by grief and almost entirely true, that I quote this passage. The Duchessa's soliloquy is interrupted by a noise outside, at midnight.

"Good," she says, "they are coming to arrest me; so much the better, it will occupy my mind, fighting them for my head."

It is nothing of the sort. Conte Mosca has sent her their most faithful courier to inform her, before the rest of Europe, of recent events at Parma, and of the details of the death of Ranuccio-Ernesto IV: there has been a revolution, the Tribune Ferrante Palla has been on the verge of triumph, he has spent the fifty thousand francs, the price of the diamonds, on the cause of his dear Republic instead of giving them to his children; the rising has been suppressed by Mosca, who served under Napoleon in Spain, and who has

displayed the courage of a soldier and the coolness of a states-
man; he has saved Rassi, which he will bitterly repent; finally,
he gives details of the accession to the throne of Ranuccio-
Ernesto V, a young prince who is enamoured of Signora
Sanseverina. The Duchessa is free to return. The Princess
Dowager, who adores her for reasons which the reader knows
and has gathered from the intrigues of the court at the time
when the Duchessa reigned there, writes her a charming letter, creates her Duchessa in her own right, and Grand Mistress. It would not, however, be prudent for Fabrizio to return at present, the sentence must be quashed by a retrial of
the case.

The Duchessa conceals Fabrizio at Sacca, and returns to
Parma triumphant. Thus the subject revives of its own accord without effort, without monotony. There is not the
slightest resemblance between the early favour enjoyed by the
innocent Sanseverina, under Ranuccio-Ernesto IV, and the
favour enjoyed by the Duchessa who has had him poisoned,
under Ranuccio-Ernesto V. The young twenty-year-old Prince
is madly in love with her, the peril incurred by the criminal
is balanced by the boundless power enjoyed by the Dowager's
Grand Mistress. This Louis XIII on a small scale finds his
Richelieu in Mosca. The great Minister, during the riots, carried away by *a lingering trace of zeal*, of enthusiasm, has
called him a boy. The word has remained in the Prince's
heart, it has hurt him. Mosca is useful to him; but the Prince,
who is only twenty years old in politics, is fifty in self-esteem.
Rassi is working in secret, he searches among the people and
through all Italy, and learns that Ferrante Palla, who is as
poor as Job, has sold nine or ten diamonds at Genoa. During
the underground burrowings of the Fiscal General joy reigns
at court. The Prince, a shy young man like all shy young
men, attacks the woman of forty, grows frenzied in his pursuit of her; it is true that Gina, more beautiful than ever,
does not look more than thirty, she is happy, she is making
Mosca thoroughly happy, Fabrizio is saved, he is to be tried
again, acquitted, and will be, when his sentence is quashed,
Coadjutor to the Archbishop, who is seventy-eight years old,
with the right of eventual succession.

Clelia alone causes the Duchessa any misgivings. As for the

Prince, she is amused by him. They act plays at court (those *commedie dell' arte* in which each character invents the dialogue as he goes on, the outline of the plot being posted up in the wings—a sort of glorified charade). The Prince takes the lovers' parts, and Gina is always the leading lady. Literally, the Grand Mistress is dancing upon a volcano. This part of the work is charming. In the very middle of one of these plays, this is what happens. Rassi has said to the Prince: "Does Your Highness choose to pay a hundred thousand francs to find out the exact manner of His august father's death?" He has had the hundred thousand francs, because the Prince is a boy. Rassi has tried to corrupt the Duchessa's head maid, this maid has told Mosca everything. Mosca has told her to let herself be corrupted. Rassi requires one thing only, to have the Duchessa's diamonds examined by two jewellers. Mosca posts counter-spies and learns that one of these inquisitive jewellers is Rassi's brother. Mosca appears, between the acts of the play, to warn the Duchessa, whom he finds in the highest spirits.

"I have very little time," she says to Mosca, "but let us go into the guard-room."

There she says with a laugh to her friend the Minister:

"You always scold me when I tell you unnecessary secrets; very well, it was I who called Ernesto V to the throne; it was a case of avenging Fabrizio, whom I loved far more than I love him to-day, though always quite innocently. You will scarcely believe in my innocence, but that does not matter, since you love me in spite of my crimes! Very well, there is one crime in my life: Ferrante Palla had my diamonds. I did worse, I let myself be kissed by him so that he should poison the man who wished to poison our Fabrizio. Where is the harm?"

"And you tell me this in the guard-room?" says the Conte, *slightly taken aback!*

This last expression is charming.

"It is because I am in a hurry," she says, "Rassi is on the track; but I have never spoken of insurrection, I abhor Jacobins. Think it over, and give me your advice after the play."

"I will give it you now," replies Mosca without hesitation. "You will buttonhole the Prince behind the scenes, make him lose his head, but without doing anything dishonourable, you understand."

The Duchessa is called to go on the stage, and returns behind the scenes.

Ferrante Palla's farewell to his idol is one of the finest things in this book, where there are so many fine things; but we come now to the capital scene, to the scene which crowns the work, to the burning of the papers in the case drawn up by Rassi, which the Grand Mistress obtains from Ranuccio-Ernesto V and the Princess Dowager, a terrible scene, in which she is now lost, now saved, at the whim of the mother and son who feel themselves overpowered by the force of character of this sort of Princesse des Ursins. This scene occupies only eight pages, but it is without parallel in the art of literature. There is nothing analogous to which it can be compared, it is unique. I say nothing of it, it is sufficient to draw attention to it. The Duchessa triumphs, she destroys the proofs and even carries away one of the documents for Mosca, who takes note of the names of some of the witnesses and cries: "It was high time, they were getting warm!" Rassi is in despair: the Prince has given orders for a retrial of Fabrizio's case. Fabrizio, instead of making himself a prisoner, as Mosca wishes, in the town prison, which is under the Prime Minister's orders, returns at once to his beloved citadel, where the General, who thought that his honour had been tarnished by the escape, rigorously confines him with the intention of getting rid of him. Mosca would have answered for him, with his life, in the town prison; but in the citadel Fabrizio is helpless.

This news comes as a bolt from the blue to the Duchessa: she remains speechless and unhearing. Fabrizio's love for Clelia bringing him back to the place where death lies in wait for him and where the girl will give him a moment's happiness for which he must pay with his life—the thought of this crushes her, and Fabrizio's imminent danger is the last straw.

This danger exists already, it is not created to fit the scene, it is the result of the passions aroused by Fabrizio during his former imprisonment, by his escape, by the fury of Rassi who has been forced to sign the order for a fresh trial. And so, even in the most minute details, the author loyally obeys the laws of the poetry of the novel. This exact observation of the rules, whether it come from the calculation, meditation, and natural deduction of a well chosen, well developed and fruitful subject, or from the instinct peculiar to talent, produces this powerful and permanent interest which we find in great, in fine works of art.

Mosca, in despair, makes the Duchessa understand the impossibility of getting a young Prince to believe that a prisoner can be poisoned in his State, and offers to get rid of Rassi.

"But," he tells her, "you know how squeamish I am about that sort of thing. Sometimes, at the end of the day, I still think of those two spies whom I had shot in Spain."

"Rassi owes his life, then," replies the Duchessa, "to the fact that I care more for you than for Fabrizio; I do not wish to poison the evenings of the old age which we shall have to spend together."

The Duchessa hastens to the fortress, and is there convinced of Fabrizio's peril; she goes to the Prince. The Prince is a boy who, as the Minister has foreseen, does not understand the danger that can threaten an innocent person in *his* State Prison. He declines to dishonour himself, to pass judgment on his own justice. Finally, in view of the imminence of the peril (the poison has been given), the Duchessa wrests from him the order to set Fabrizio at liberty in exchange for a promise to yield to this young Prince's desires. This scene has an originality of its own after that of the burning of the papers. At that time, Gina's only thought was for herself, now it is for Fabrizio. Fabrizio once acquitted and appointed Coadjutor to the Archbishop with the right of eventual succession, which is tantamount to being made Archbishop, the Duchessa finds a way to elude the consequences of her promise by one of those dilemmas which women who are not in love can always find with a maddening coolness. She is to the end the woman of great character whose career started as you have read. There follows a change in the Ministry. Mosca leaves Parma with his wife, for the Duchessa and he, both widowed, have now married. But nothing goes well, and at the end of a year the Prince recalls Conte and Contessa Mosca. Fabrizio is Archbishop and in high favour. There follows the love of Clelia and Archbishop Fabrizio, which ends in the death of Clelia, in that of a beloved child, and in the resignation and withdrawal of the Archbishop, who dies, doubtless after a long expiation, in the Charterhouse of Parma.

I explain this ending to you in a few words, since, in spite of beautiful details, it is sketched rather than finished. If the author had had to develop the romance of the end like that of the beginning, it would have been difficult to know where to stop. Is there not a whole drama in the love of a celibate priest? So there is a whole drama in the love of the Coadjutor and Clelia. Book upon book!

Had M. Beyle some woman in his mind when he drew his Sanseverina? I fancy so. For this statue, as for the Prince and the Prime Minister, there must necessarily have been some model. Is she at Milan? Is she at Rome, at Naples, at Florence? I cannot say. Although I am quite convinced that there do exist women like the Sanseverina, though in very small numbers, and that I know some myself, I believe also that the author has perhaps enlarged the model and has completely idealised her. In spite of this labour, which removes all similarity, one may find in the Princesse B—— certain traits of the Sanseverina. Is she not Milanese? Has she not passed through good and adverse fortune? Is she not shrewd and witty?

You know now the framework of this immense edifice, and I have taken you round it. My hasty analysis, bold, believe me, for it requires boldness to undertake to give you an idea of a novel constructed out of incidents as closely compressed as are those of *La Chartreuse de Parme*; my analysis, dry as it may be, has outlined the masses for you, and you can judge whether my praise is exaggerated. But it is difficult to enumerate to you in detail the fine and delicate sculptures that enrich this solid structure, to stop before the statuettes, the paintings, the landscapes, the bas-reliefs which decorate it. This is what happened to me. At the first reading, which took me quite by surprise, I found faults in the book. On my reading it again, the *longueurs* vanished, I saw the necessity for the detail which, at first, had seemed to me too long or too diffuse. To give you a good account of it, I ran through the book once more. Captivated then by the execution, I spent more time than I had intended in the contemplation of this fine book, and everything struck me as most harmonious, connected naturally or by artifice but concordantly.

Here, however, are the errors which I pick out, not so much from the point of view of art as in view of the sacrifices which every author must learn to make to the majority.

If I found confusion on first reading the book, my impression will be that of the public, and therefore evidently this book is lacking in method. M. Beyle has indeed disposed the events as they happened, or as they ought to have happened; but he has committed, in his arrangement of the facts, a mistake which many authors commit, by taking a subject true in nature which is not true in art. When he sees a landscape, a great painter takes care not to copy it slavishly, he has to give us not so much its letter as its spirit. So, in his simple, artless and unstudied manner of telling his story, M. Beyle has run the risk of appearing confused. Merit which requires to be studied is in danger of remaining unperceived. And so I could wish, in the interest of the book, that the author had begun with his magnificent sketch of the battle of Waterloo, that he had reduced everything which precedes it to some account given by Fabrizio or about Fabrizio while he is lying in the village in Flanders where he arrives wounded. Certainly, the work would gain in lightness. The del Dongo father and son, the details about Milan, all these things are not part of the book: the drama is at Parma, the principal characters are the Prince and his son, Mosca, Rassi, the Duchessa, Ferrante Palla, Lodovico, Clelia, her father, the Raversi, Giletti, Marietta. Skilled advisers or friends endowed with simple common sense might have procured the development of certain portions which the author has not supposed to be as interesting as they are, and would have called for the excision of several details, superfluous in spite of their fineness. For instance, the work would lose nothing if the Priore Blanès were to disappear entirely.

I will go farther, and will make no compromise, in favour of this fine work, over the true principles of art. The law which governs everything is that of unity in composition; whether you place this unity in the central idea or in the plan of the book, without it there can be only confusion. So, in spite of its title, the work is ended when Conte and Contessa Mosca return to Parma and Fabrizio is Archbishop. The great comedy of the court is finished. It is so well finished, and the author has so clearly felt this, that it is in this place that he sets his Moral, as our forerunners used to do at the end of their fables.

"One can conclude with this moral," he says: "the man who comes to a court risks his happiness, if he is happy; and in any case makes his future depend upon the intrigues of a chambermaid.

"On the other hand, in America, in the Republic, one has to waste one's whole time paying serious court to the shopkeepers in the street and becoming as stupid as themselves; and there, there is no Opera."

If, beneath the Roman purple and with a mitre on his head, Fabrizio loves Clelia, become Marchesa Crescenzi, and if you were telling us about it, you would then wish to make the life of this young man the subject of your book. But if you wished to describe the whole of Fabrizio's life, you ought, being a man of such sagacity, to call your book *Fabrizio, or the Italian in the Nineteenth Century*. In launching himself upon such a career, Fabrizio ought not to have found himself outshone by figures so typical, so poetical as are those of the two Princes, the Sanseverina, Mosca, Ferrante Palla. Fabrizio ought to have represented the young Italian of to-day. In making this young man the principal figure of the drama, the author was under an obligation to give him a large mind, to endow him with a feeling which would make him superior to the men of genius who surround him, and which he lacks. Feeling, in short, is equivalent to talent. *To feel* is the rival of *to understand* as *to act* is the opposite of *to think*. The friend of a man of genius can raise himself to his level by affection, by understanding. In matters of the heart, an inferior man may prevail over the greatest artist. There lies the justification of those women who fall in love with imbeciles. So, in a drama, one of the most ingenious resources of the artist is (in the case in which we suppose M. Beyle to be) to make a hero superior by his feeling when he cannot by genius compete with the people among whom he is placed. In this respect, Fabrizio's part requires recasting. The genius of Catholicism ought to urge him with its divine hand towards the *Charterhouse of Parma,* and that genius ought from time to time to overwhelm him with the tidings of heavenly grace. But then the Priore Blanès could not perform this part, for it is impossible to cultivate judicial astrology and to be a saint according to the Church. The book ought therefore to be either shorter or longer.

Possibly the slowness of the beginning, possibly that ending which begins a new book and in which the subject is abruptly strangled, will damage its success, possibly they have already damaged it. M. Bcylc has moreover allowed himself certain repetitions, perceptible only to those who know his earlier books; but such readers themselves are necessarily connoisseurs, and so fastidious. M. Beyle, keeping in mind that great principle: "Unlucky in love, as in the arts, who says too much!" ought not to repeat himself, he, always concise and leaving much to be guessed. In spite of his sphinx-like habit, he is less enigmatic here than in his other works, and his true friends will congratulate him on this.

The portraits are brief. A few words are enough for M. Beyle, who paints his characters both by action and by dialogue; he does not weary one with descriptions, he hastens to the drama and arrives at it by a word, by a thought. His landscapes, traced with a somewhat dry touch which, however, is suited to the country, are lightly done. He takes his stand by a tree, on the spot where he happens to be; he shews you the lines of the Alps which on all sides enclose the scene of action, and the landscape is complete. The book is particularly valuable to travellers who have strolled by the Lake of Como, over the Brianza, who have passed under the outermost bastions of the Alps and crossed the plains of Lombardy. The spirit of those scenes is finely revealed, their beauty is well felt. One can see them.

The weak part of this book is the style, in so far as the arrangement of the words goes, for the thought, which is eminently French, sustains the sentences. The mistakes that M. Beyle makes are purely grammatical; he is careless, incorrect, after the manner of seventeenth-century writers. The quotations I have made shew what sort of faults he lets himself commit. In one place, a discord of tenses between verbs,

—

sometimes the absence of a verb; here, again, sequences of *c'est*, of *ce que*, of *que*, which weary the reader, and have the effect on his mind of a journey in a badly hung carriage over a French road. These quite glaring faults indicate a scamping of work. But, if the French language is a varnish spread over thought, we ought to be as indulgent towards those in whom it covers fine paintings as we are severe to those who shew nothing but the varnish. If, in M. Beyle, this vanish is a little yellow in places and inclined to scale off in others, he does at least let us see a sequence of thoughts which are derived from one another according to the laws of logic. His long sentence is ill constructed, his short sentence lacks polish. He writes more or less in the style of Diderot, who was not a writer; but the conception is great and strong; the thought is original, and often well rendered. This system is not one to be imitated. It would be too dangerous to allow authors to imagine themselves to be profound thinkers.

M. Beyle is saved by the deep feeling that animates his thought. All those to whom Italy is dear, who have studied or understood her, will read *La Chartreuse de Parme* with delight. The spirit, the genius, the customs, the soul of that beautiful country live in this long drama that is always engaging, in this vast fresco so well painted, so strongly coloured, which moves the heart profoundly and satisfies the most difficult, the most exacting mind. The Sanseverina is the Italian woman, a figure as happily portrayed as Carlo Dolci's famous head of *Poetry*, Allori's *Judith*, or Guercino's *Sibyl* in the Manfredini gallery. In Mosca he paints the man of genius in politics at grips with love. It is indeed love without speech (the speeches are the weak point in *Clarisse*), active love, always true to its own type, love stronger than the call of duty, love, such as women dream of, such as gives an additional interest to the least things in life. Fabrizio is quite the young Italian of to-day at grips with the distinctly clumsy despotism which suppresses the imagination of that fine country; but, as I have said above, the dominant thought or the feeling which urges him to lay aside his dignities and to end his life in a Charterhouse needs development. This book is admirably expressive of love as it is felt in the South. Obviously, the North does not love in this way. All these characters have a heat, a fever of the blood, a vivacity of hand, a rapidity of mind which is not to be found in the English nor in the Germans nor in the Russians, who arrive at the same results only by processes of revery, by the reasonings of a smitten heart, by the slow rising of their sap. M. Beyle has in this respect given this book the profound meaning, the feeling which guarantees the survival of a literary conception. But unfortunately it is almost a secret doctrine, which requires laborious study. *La Chartreuse de Parme* is placed at such a height, it requires in the reader so perfect a knowledge of the court, the place, the people that I am by no means astonished at the absolute silence with which such a book has been greeted. That is the lot that awaits all books in which there is nothing vulgar. The secret ballot in which vote one by one and slowly the superior minds who make the name of such works, is not counted until long afterwards. Besides, M. Beyle is not a courtier, he has the most profound horror of the press. From largeness of character or from the sensitiveness of his self-esteem, as soon as his book appears, he takes flight, leaves Paris, travels two hundred and fifty leagues in order not to hear it spoken of. He demands no articles, he does not haunt the footsteps of the reviewers. He has behaved thus after the publication of each of his books. I admire this pride of character or this sensitiveness of self-esteem. Excuses there may be for mendicity, there can be none for that quest for praise and articles on which modern authors go begging. It is the mendicity, the pauperism of the mind. There are no great works of art that have fallen into oblivion. The lies, the complacencies of the pen cannot give life to a worthless book.

After the courage to criticise comes the courage to praise. Certainly it is time someone did justice to M. Beyle's merit. Our age owes him much: was it not he who first revealed to us Rossini, the finest genius in music? He has pleaded constantly for that glory which France had not the intelligence to make her own. Let us in turn plead for the writer who knows Italy best, who avenges her for the calumnies of her conquerors, who has so well explained her spirit and her genius.

I had met M. Beyle twice in society, in twelve years, be-

fore the day when I took the liberty of congratulating him
on La Chartreuse de Parme on meeting him in the Boulevard
des Italiens. On each occasion, his conversation has fully
maintained the opinion I had formed of him from his works.
He tells stories with the spirit and grace which M. Charles
Nodier and M. de Latouche possess in a high degree. Indeed
he recalls the latter gentleman by the irresistible charm of
his speech, although his physique—for he is extremely stout
—seems at first sight to preclude refinement, elegance of
manners; but he instantly disproves this suspicion, like Dr.
Koreff, the friend of Hoffmann. He has a fine forehead, a
keen and piercing eye, a sardonic mouth; in short, he has
altogether the physiognomy of his talent. He retains in conversation that enigmatic turn, that eccentricity which leads
him never to sign the already illustrious name of Beyle, to call
himself one day Cotonnet, another Frédéric. He is, I am told,
the nephew of the famous and industrious Daru, one of the
strong arms of Napoleon. M. Beyle was naturally in the Emperor's service; 1815 tore him, necessarily, from his career,
he passed from Berlin to Milan, and it is to the contrast between the life of the North and that of the South, which
impressed him, that we are indebted for this writer. M.
Beyle is one of the superior men of our time. It is difficult
to explain how this observer of the first order, this profound
diplomat who, whether in his writings or in his speech, has
furnished so many proofs of the loftiness of his ideas and
the extent of his practical knowledge should find himself
nothing more than Consul at Civita-vecchia. No one could
be better qualified to represent France at Rome. M. Méri-
mée knew M. Beyle early and takes after him; but the master is more elegant and has more ease. M. Beyle's works are
many in number and are remarkable for fineness of observation and for the abundance of their ideas. Almost all of them
deal with Italy. He was the first to give us exact information
about the terrible case of the Cenci; but he has not sufficiently explained the causes of the execution, which was independent of the trial, and due to factional clamour, to the
demands of avarice. His book De l'amour is superior to M.
de Sénancour's, he shews affinity to the great doctrines of
Cabanis and the School of Paris; but he fails by the lack of

method which, as I have already said, spoils *La Chartreuse de Parme.* He has ventured, in this treatise, upon the word *crystallisation* to explain the phenomenon of the birth of this sentiment, a word which has been taken as a joke, but will survive on account of its profound accuracy. M. Beyle has been writing since 1817. He began with a certain show of Liberalism; but I doubt whether this great calculator can have let himself be taken in by the stupidities of Dual Chamber government. *La Chartreuse de Parme* has an underlying bias which is certainly not against Monarchy. He finds fault with what he admires, he is a Frenchman.

M. de Chateaubriand said, in a preface to the eleventh edition of *Atala,* that his book in no way resembled the previous editions, so thoroughly had he revised it. M. le Comte de Maistre admits having rewritten *Le Lépreux de la vallée d'Aoste* seventeen times. I hope that M. Beyle also will set to work going over, polishing *La Chartreuse de Parme,* and will stamp it with the imprint of perfection, the emblem of irreproachable beauty which MM. de Chateaubriand and de Maistre have given to their precious books.

R. L. Stevenson
ON
Zola:

A man of the unquestionable force of M. Zola spends himself on technical successes. To afford a popular flavour and attract the mob, he adds a steady current of what I may be allowed to call the rancid.

Joseph Conrad
ON
Stendhal:

Stendhal's mind was of the first order. His spirit above must be raging with a peculiarly Stendhalesque scorn and indignation. For the truth is that more than one kind of intellectual cowardice hides behind the literary formulas. And Stendhal was pre-eminently courageous. He wrote his two great novels, which so few people have read, in a spirit of fearless liberty.

Flaubert
ON
Stendhal:

As for Beyle, after reading Le rouge et le noir *I fail completely to understand Balzac's enthusiasm for such a writer.*

Ford Madox Hueffer
ON
Balzac:

Balzac . . . pretended to be at once a realist and a philosopher. Had he done what he pretended to do he would have been the most immense— as he was certainly the most industrious—figure of the modern world. But the fact is that, though he had got hold of a tremendous idea—an idea as tremendous as that of the railway, the electric telegraph, the Crystal Palace or the aeroplane—he was utterly without either the technical knowledge or the knowledge of humanity that would have carried it out. He knew less of either than Dickens, less than Fielding, much less than Thackeray, and he knew infinitely less than Smollett whom in many ways he resembled. But . . . he was of this inestimable service to humanity: he handed on to later writers that one great idea of their functions, the aspiration to faire concurrence a l'état civil—to beat the Blue Book out of the field.

Angus Wilson on

There has, in the last twenty years, been a rehabilitation or, at any rate, a serious defence of most of the nineteenth-century novelists, whose pretensions—in their own day—were to the highest rank. Zola, however, has continued to lie neg-lected in the dusty cupboard[1] to which he had already been assigned by many younger French writers in his own lifetime. His work has had considerable direct influence, but this very influence has militated against the survival of his reputation, since it was, in general, exercised upon writers who were al-ways estimable yet always of the second rank. To be largely responsible for George Moore and Arnold Bennett in Eng-land, Frank Norris and Dreiser in America, Heinrich Mann in Germany, Jules Romains in France, is an equivocal hon-our. His reputation would have been happier without the well-meant partisanship of minor followers, happier without a school from which as usual the more remarkable disciples seceded, more particularly, happier without the complicated and fourth-rate cultural superstructure of Naturalism which his fear of the personal foundations of his work and his deep intellectual sense of inferiority caused him to erect. With-out followers, without the embarrassingly naïve theories of *Le Roman Expérimental*, he might have been judged as an individual, as one of the great cumbrous, magnificent pithe-canthropi of nineteenth-century literature. Viewed in such a light Zola can be seen as the close companion of Balzac,

[1] The decline into which the nineteenth century fell at one period may be well illustrated by the critic H. L. Mencken's remarks in *A Book of Prefaces*, 1917. "Wells, Bennett, Benson, Walpole, Beres-ford, Galsworthy, Hichens, De Morgan, Miss Sinclair, Hewlett . . . even the least of them is, at all events, a more complete artist than, say, Dickens, or Bulwer Lytton, or Sienkiewicz, or Zola."

Dickens, and Dostoevsky, a little less than them, for certain defects which I shall try to analyse, but offering, nevertheless, a wonderful, enveloping world as they do, and having, in certain respects, both social and personal, a strange clarity of direct vision which their great fusions of the dream kingdom and the waking world obliterated. It is probable that the deserved re-estimation of his work may not be far distant. It must be remembered that he was nearly thirty years younger than Dickens, the deeper patterns of whose work— both social and personal—have only begun to be recognized in the last decade, and that he was identified in his lifetime with literary and social battles the last rumblings of whose cannons are still faintly audible today. The full battery of the shocked and prurient combined was turned upon Zola's work because if he spoke crudely, he also spoke morally. As usual, one of the most successful weapons of the prude and the libertine—and they are always found in alliance in the face of social honesty—has been the old philistine club— surely once Goliath's—of self-satisfied laughter. Zola has been declared not only obscene, but childishly so, and worse still, old-fashioned in his obscenity. To read his work seriously has been like facing the imputation of telling an old dirty joke. It is a charge which few have cared to incur. If we add to this the fact that the Rougon-Macquart has the misfortune to appear as a long family chronicle, although it is in fact a series of separate novels covered by the slenderest links, we can understand the oblivion to which it has been assigned. If the present small work does no more than encourage a few readers to unlock the rusty cupboard which contains so much delight it will have served its purpose.

It is interesting to speculate at what date Zola began to imagine the vast scheme which was to occupy some twenty-five or more years of his life. We know that, even in his early poetic projects, he always inclined towards the epic; but the Creation and the Fall[2] are not unusual subjects upon which young poets centre vague ambitions with ideas as vague concerning their realization. Such inchoate hopes can hardly be

[2] We shall see, however, that for personal, psychological reasons the Fall and Paradise inevitably played some part even in the final realistic work.

regarded seriously as pointers to what Zola was actually to achieve. It may well be that, though *Thérèse Raquin* had shown him his powers of creation and formal organization, both it and *Madeleine Férat* had proved that the violent conflicts within him could not be happily satisfied by transference to paper on a purely personal level. It is notable that the psychological approach, the result of his admiration for Stendhal and the most immediate avenue of escape from his overturned Romantic idols, was thereafter only to be resumed partially in the deep despair of *La Joie de Vivre* of 1884, but not entirely until 1890. Determination to put the years of failure behind him was now his overruling passion.

Nothing perhaps can have seemed so serious a bar to achievement as his comparative lack of education. Education and taste were the two things he lacked to place him on a level with the classes he envied and despised. It is an ironic fact that it was ultimately to be in exactly these two spheres that the society he conquered was to be revenged upon him. Energy and riches can give a man control over these two citadels of the governing classes at a comparatively late stage in life, but if they are to be well founded, if good taste and learning are to be worn with the ease and confidence which are indispensable in the eyes of those to whom they are second nature, they can only be acquired by an adult person if he is endowed with humility as well as imitative powers. Humility was the least of Zola's qualities, though he had more than enough of the related but less helpful characteristic of lack of self-confidence beneath his enormous will to power. It is not therefore surprising that the somewhat correspondence-course nature of his self-acquired education, with its cocksure dogmatism and patent-leather up-to-dateness, should have been a target for his critics both in his lifetime and after; while the nouveau riche vulgarity of taste exemplified so well in the over-lavish, expensive junk-shop furnishing of his villa at Médan, which advertised the huge financial success of his work, was a perpetual source of amusement and ridicule to his detractors. In an age when intellectual materialist dogmatism was giving place to modish "croyances" and a sceptical approach to science, Zola clung to his hard-won materialist knowledge with a provincial assumption of modernity, partly it is true from a crudity of intellect, but partly also from a deep and thoughtful distrust of the ultimate social implications of the new spirit of faith. In an age, too, when ostentatious splendour was being rejected as vulgar by those who favoured an etiolated elegance of taste perhaps no less vulgar, Zola still clung to an eclectic display of riches that surpassed the Second Empire at its own game. It is easy to say that such determinations do more credit to his heart than to his head or eye, but the socialism which he built upon his crude materialism was a more meaningful reaction to the contemporary social structure than fin-de-siècle despair; while against the decorative horrors of Médan must be set the great understanding of Impressionism which is implicit in his own work and the strength which his very vulgarity gave to his writing.

The mistake, in fact, which most critics have made is to extend the ridicule which they express for his superficial materialist philosophy and the vulgarity of his home from his life to his works. Vulgarity and excess do exist in his novels, a surface lack of subtlety, at times an irksome over-sureness, but these less happy features are integrally woven into a pattern of great complexity, modified by a descriptive power that proceeds from a very subtle sense of atmosphere, and invested with a dramatic force which springs from personal despairs and doubts as deep and complex as those of the greatest of the nineteenth-century novelists.

There is, however, a certain logic in the fate which made the hard-won fortresses of education and taste the weak defence-posts against which "informed critics" have directed their successful attacks upon his work—how successful may be seen from the smiles which greet his name at most literary functions even today. For it was Médan, with its profusion of Japanese prints, Greco-Roman statues, ormolu clocks, Sèvres vases and medieval missals, which was the culminating expression of his material victory. With his vulgar taste he cocked a snook at the forces he had conquered, though in his naïveté he thought he was making a salon entry. It was under the cover of the scientific arguments from the works of Dr. Prosper Lucas on heredity and atavism and from Letourneau's *Physiology of the Passions*—a whole mischmasch of somewhat outdated materialist psychology and retailed Darwinism[3]—that he found courage to launch the work which was to be the artistic crown of his existence. It is easy to understand that, after the humiliations of his early manhood, he should feel the need of "serious" and respectable intellectual parentage for the birth of his child, especially when one knows how deeply suppressed were the personal motivations of his work, and that he must have realized what hostility and outcry the violence of his social attacks would inevitably unleash. We may be thankful to M. Letourneau and Dr. Lucas for providing the justification which his feelings of inferiority required, but we need not take very seriously the array of medico-psychological jargon with which the notebooks for the early Rougon-Macquart novels are filled, for as we shall see the hereditary aspect of the novels was never allowed to get in the way of Zola's creative genius. Indeed, this somewhat pathetic aspect of the inception of his great work might well have been forgotten, had not his disciple Céard later introduced him to the works of the materialist psychologist Claude Bernard, and so led him to publish in 1880, at the most controversial moment of his career, following the publication of *L'Assommoir* and *Nana,* a theoretical defence of his work—*Le Roman Expérimental,* in which he attempted to transfer the scientific views of Bernard to the sphere of literature. Few of the theoretical manifestos of great artists have been adequate to their works but it has to be said that *Le Roman Expérimental* is peculiarly silly. It is not surprising that, drawing attention as it must have done to the démodé scientific and philosophical theories which were the jumping-off point of the Rougon-Macquart novels, it should have done immeasurable harm to Zola's claims to be regarded as a serious artist.

However impoverished and outdated the scientific material on which Zola worked so hard in the Bibliothèque Nationale during the years immediately before the Franco-Prussian War, it did provide a framework, cavalierly though it was later to be treated, within which his overflowing emotions

[3] Darwin, however, was translated into French in 1862, and published with a preface by Bernard in 1866.

and creative powers could be confined. Without the careful
genealogical tables of the Rougon-Macquart family with their
pompous notes of inherited characteristics, regressions to maternal grandmothers on the intellectual side and dormant
physical paralysis derived from the paternal great-uncle, without the atavism and the heredity, there could have been no
Rougon-Macquart family. Without the Rougon-Macquart
family, with its three branches each stretching into a different
social sphere, the total picture of Second Empire society could
not have been presented. So rigid an initial arrangement
might have petrified in the hands of a lesser artist, but for
Zola, often unconsciously, "the history of a family under the
Second Empire" was an organic creation, amidst whose
changes and growths both the family of the Rougon-Macquart
and the Second Empire itself were often to be pushed from
the scene. This organic nature of the great work, I shall hope
to show, derived from the fact that under all the scientific
ideas of heredity, even beneath the fierce attack on society,
the novels had their roots in deep personal aspects of the
author's life—aspects which could find their answer in social
analysis, because his own inner conflicts were directly related
to the social conflicts of the time.

There was, however, one immediate and powerful influence, far greater and more penetrating, that directed the
form which his work was to take. We have seen that one
of the great discoveries during his impoverished life on the
Left Bank had been the works of Balzac, and his admiration
for the *Comédie Humaine* grew steadily, outweighing that of
Stendhal, forming a ground of dissension with Flaubert during the early days of their friendship. A caricature by André
Gill, made when Zola became famous, shows the bust of
Balzac returning the later novelist's salute, and Zola was both
proud and pleased with the tribute. Comparisons between
the *Comédie Humaine* and the *Rougon-Macquart* are not
very fruitful; the whole social outlook of the two writers is so
completely different, their views of the mainsprings of human conduct so remote from one another, their conceptions
of the purpose of existence so alien. But there remains in
each, for all the differences of their thought, a striking likeness in their passionate interest in power and energy—qualities

which they both possessed in abnormal degree—and this gives to their work a common quality of force and violence, of giant proportion, always under control, yet always, it would seem, on the point of breaking loose from its creator. In any case, Zola's admiration for Balzac was probably decisive in determining the vast scope of the Rougon-Macquart series.

It is impossible not to be impressed by the conviction of ultimate achievement with which Zola presented his original scheme for the ten novels, eventually to increase and grow into twenty, to his publisher Lacroix in 1868. Henry James' tribute is an apt expression of awe: "No finer act of courage and confidence is recorded in the history of letters. The critic . . . returns again and again to the great wonder of it, in which something so strange is mixed with something so august. Entertained and carried out almost from the threshold of manhood, the high project announces beforehand its inevitable weakness and yet speaks in the same voice for its admirable, its almost unimaginable strength."[4]

In the ninety volumes of manuscript notes for the Rougon-Macquart deposited by Madame Zola in the Bibliothèque Nationale we have an unique opportunity of seeing a great literary work in formation. Only fragments of these notes have been printed, partly by Zola's son-in-law Maurice Le Blond in his prefaces to the standard editions, partly by M. Henri Massis in his *Comment Zola composait ses romans*, itself a remarkable work written when its author was only a youth. What does emerge, apart from the immensely painstaking documentation and the brilliant formal planning of the novels, are the many changes which inevitably took place over the years, though the original grandeur of conception was increased rather than diminished. These became more than ever necessary after the fall of the Empire in 1870. History contributed the final dramatic ending to Zola's epic, but the epic had, of course, to be replanned. As a result many events were telescoped and this accounts for the over-

---

[4] Barbusse's tribute is less elegant but more exact: "There is hardly an example in the history of intellectual creations of a man seeing in advance with so much precision the concrete contours of a multiform work."

crowded canvas of many of the novels.[5] Even before the composition of the introductory novel *La Fortune des Rougon* we find many changes of name for both the Rougon and the Macquart branches of the family, and the Mouret branch does not appear in the first notes.

The emergence of these three rivers is important, for with them the broad class structure of the analysis of Second Empire society is determined. From the legitimate Rougon heirs of the crazy source of the family, Tante Dide, sprang the hard, ambitious, intellectually brilliant set of adventurers who descend like hungry dogs upon the bleeding quarry of rich Imperial Paris, tearing it to pieces, until in its final death throes they emerge themselves exhausted, effete and vicious as the original aristocracy that they have despoiled. Zola's habitual ambivalence in relation to society is illustrated very clearly in the novels which deal with this ruling-class branch of the family. Pierre and Félicité Rougon, the parents who achieve local power in Plassans, the original Provençal home town of the family, by backing the Bonapartist horse in 1851, come in for his most fierce exposure as representatives of the local Aix-en-Provence families who had ignored the Zolas in their time of poverty. Eugène Rougon, their son, however, who rises to be a principal minister of Napoleon III, is the very representative of the powerful, ruthless man that Zola with his ambition and strength of purpose might have been in the sphere of action,[6] and it is most notable that Eugène's success is attained through a hard-won battle for sexual supremacy, which is made to give him an almost magical access of force.

The Mourets, in whom are depicted the bourgeoisie, though illegitimate, are significantly a female line, for Zola's chief hatred of the bourgeoisie was directed against its "mollesse" and "souplesse." From the marriage of Ursule

---

[5] *La Débâcle*, for example, the novel of the Franco-Prussian War, was originally planned to deal with the Franco-Italian campaign of 1859.

[6] Paul Alexis, Zola's chief disciple, took this view. But Zola's son-in-law Le Blond disagreed and thought the character founded on the minister Rouher. Zola in his notes calls Eugène "un Mornay au petit pied."

Macquart to a Marseilles tradesman spring the small bourgeois of Plassans, and from them, in turn, comes Octave Mouret, like his cousin Eugène an adventurer, who with quick Midi wits and ruthless use of his sexual charms, preys upon the small tradesmen of Paris, and founds the first great monopoly store "Au Bonheur des Dames" upon the ruin of the very class from which he is sprung. Once again Zola's attitude is somewhat ambiguous. For the central core of the bourgeoisie he has nothing but hatred; mean or spendthrift, pious or adulterous, they either fade out of life in a devitalized miasma of prudery, are swallowed up in the fatty richness of a complacent gluttony, or are torn to pieces in a hysterical effort to break free from their domestic prison. But for Octave Mouret, who dares to tread upon his own kind, his admiration is direct. He even attempts, in the unsatisfactory Christian Socialist ending of *Au Bonheur des Dames*, to resolve the contradiction between his belief in the survival of the fittest with his hatred of cut-throat morality.

From the main illegitimate branch of the Macquart come the proletariat, the submerged section of this fierce competitive society—vicious, ignorant, pathetic in their small but hopeless ambition only to survive—they are yet shown as the most productive of ultimate diversity because of the very formlessness which marks them as a class. Gervaise, for example, the tragic heroine of *L'Assommoir* and the type of the slum-dweller, is the mother of Étienne, the growing revolutionary, Claude, the artist, Nana, the high-class tart, and Jacques, the criminal. Though Zola's lack of illusion about the poor made him an object of radical attack in his own day, and of censure from Communist writers like Barbusse in ours, his loathing for their degradation is accompanied by a certain pity. For the independent workers, and their numbers were not large at that time, he has an admiration as great as that for successful men, and less uneasy. No nineteenth-century novelist, perhaps, succeeded so well in depicting the courage and honesty of the individual, aspiring workman of the century, and he does so with a lack of sentimentalism and a real understanding of the necessary limitations of such a life that is quite unique.

Such an exact class analysis if it had been rigidly adhered

to, might well have produced novels that were text-books of political economy or social sermons rather than works of art. Zola, however, was too great an artist and too determinedly objective a writer to fall into this error more than occasionally. In the first place, though one may speak of his "pity," his "admiration," his "hatred," these are seldom stated explicitly. Zola gave up a psychological approach to character after *Thérèse Raquin* until the deliberate reversion of *La Bête Humaine*—one of the few examples of his scheme controlling him, rather than he the scheme, for it had been planned from the start, and in order to write it he had to introduce a completely new figure as late as 1890. Nor are his occasional personal homilies very important. Such moral judgments as appear are implicit in the descriptive narrative and the speech of the characters. But more important than this artistic objectivity, to which he adhered so earnestly, is his disregard of the total formal structure of the series if an individual novel seemed to demand it. Important divergences exist even in the basic class construction of the Rougon-Macquart. The supreme example of the bourgeoise, the handsome, sleek, treacherous Lisa Quenu, the central character of *Le Ventre de Paris*, is the eldest of the proletarian Macquart line. Angélique, the idealized symbol of true love in *Le Rêve*, is the daughter of the political informer and procuress, Sidonie Rougon. The important fact is that, though Zola needed the formal scheme of the series to liberate his vast energies, and though he was often unaware himself of its secondary nature, most of the novels of the series, and, certainly, the best, were carefully planned as separate units, and if they interfered with the whole, the whole had to be remoulded. Frequently the members of the Rougon-Macquart are only formally the central characters, the real emphasis of the novels being placed upon other social groups, of whom the adventurers and outcasts from Plassans form useful observers. Étienne Lantier, the son of Gervaise Macquart, for example, who finds employment in a mining town, is able to observe his new surroundings with an exactitude which would be absurd in a local inhabitant, and so it is with Jean Macquart, freshly arrived among the peasants of *La Terre*, or Nana, as she rises to the heights of the demi-monde. Such

Rougons and Macquarts are useful eyes—Zola's eyes. He made little attempt, beyond an occasional explanatory reference which almost always appears forced, to connect the members of the family in one book with those in another. Such characters as do reappear have little consistency, except for Nana whose future had probably already been planned in detail when she appeared as the vicious little girl of *L'Assommoir*. Jacques Lantier, the central character of *La Bête Humaine*, was simply invented after the novels, in which his branch of the family appeared, had been published, and what evidence they give of the general family background clearly precludes his existence. It was not the family heredity, nor even the theoretical class analysis that the family provided, with which Zola was concerned, however he may have wished to think so, but particular patterns of life which made immediate appeal to him. Nevertheless by establishing a broad general scheme and fulfilling it equally broadly, he insured that his artistic powers should be exercised over the widest possible field.

Zola's view of society as a whole was conditioned by the dichotomy which was the subject of the first chapter. His sense of personal social humiliation in childhood and adolescence gave him a hatred for all sections of society, though for the poorest he retained an emotional compassion as great as his physical disgust. This general pessimism inclined him to a despairing, almost anarchic view of society. On the other hand, his natural ambition, energy and personal success in the material sphere could not allow him to remain content with such pessimism. On this side of his nature, he was more suited to be an optimistic radical, and indeed his reverence for the scientific advance of the century made him a staunch adherent of Progress. His reading of materialist philosophy, however, led him into the realm of scientific determinism and this, in general, supported the generally pessimistic side of his nature—so that his eventual picture of society in the Rougon-Macquart was of an organism so complex, that unless like the nihilists one was prepared to destroy it all in one holocaust, there was no alternative but to wait for the effects of education and scientific invention to take their appointed course.

Zola's approach to knowledge was analytical, as the note-books show. His method of work was to collect as much in-formation as possible and then to extract an analysed scheme. The final result of his selection often appears as too great a simplification of the material he was studying, but, neverthe-less, the effects of the complexity of the subject he studied in such detail are implicit in his books: his awareness of the great multiplicity of interdependent strands that lay beneath the apparent simplicity only served to emphasize his deter-ministic attitude towards society and added to the natural disinclination of his compassionate heart to judge the be-haviour of individuals. The objective analysis which he gives of the corrupt, putrescent society of the Second Empire is filled with burning indignation, but only rarely does this find relief in attacks upon particular characters. For many years, almost throughout the publication of the Rougon-Macquart novels, he defended this objectivity on the aesthetic grounds of the Naturalist creed, though his personal identification with the misery which he described was always pushing him towards some more positive attitude. There is a very close affinity between his view of contemporary French society and that of Karl Marx—the same brilliant simplification, the same puritanical horror, the same disgust at human waste, not only among the poor, but in all classes. For Zola, however, no manifesto call to arms was possible, he felt too keenly the individual lives he described, their circumscribed wills, their despairing unhappiness, their intense if short-lived pleasures, to be confident of the cleansing power of action. Only in Germinal (1885) did he evidence any faith in the possibility of mass action as the necessary solution. From that time, it is true, his novels showed society more and more in its group aspects and less in individuals, but he did not again suggest any sympathy for the idea of socialism brought about by the masses themselves.[7] He was not by nature a man who could easily accept the idea of violence, against which the whole of his luxury-loving, bourgeois taste and the great gentleness of his character revolted. However violent his own inner emo-

[7] In L'Argent, however, one of the more sympathetic characters is shown as actuated by Marx's writings.

tions, physical and external violence, which is a constant feature of his novels, always appears as a symbol of the self-destructive, corrupt elements in life.

In this mistrust of mass action, he resembles Dickens, whose early life and education led him to a similar view of society, veering from a vague political radicalism to a sort of pessimistic anarchism. But, whereas Dickens' pessimism increased as a result of the progressive deterioration of his domestic life, Zola's was eventually dissolved by his fruitful liaison with Jeanne Rozerat; in both cases, however, the pessimism of their works was in direct contrast with the external success and bonhomie of their lives. Not a little of the violence of their novels originates from this split in their personalities.

Zola, like Dickens, mistrusted all the political parties. But whereas Dickens' political scepticism came from his view that all power was a corrupting influence on the will, Zola's contempt came largely from a general disbelief in the strength of the human will either for good or for evil. With his own abnormally developed will and energy, Zola was, perhaps, over-inclined to regard humanity as shifting, windswept sand whose apparent stability or direction was liable at any minute to be changed by some chance desire or momentary difficulty. For the ruling classes and bourgeoisie there were the varying shades of Legitimist, Orléanist, Ultramontane, Bonapartist or Republican which were worn either for some immediate gain, from prejudice or from social snobbery. Ministers, deputies, judges and bureaucrats alike are twitched on the ends of the golden wires of the great money adventurers who had made the Empire, and who, like Aristide Rougon, rushed to and fro to patch the breaks in the rotting nets of their vast, speculative fishing for gold. The events of 1848 and 1851 had certainly lent colour to the view that, for large numbers of men and women, political ideals were coats to be worn according to the weather. Zola believed that the components of the social organism were decaying and would in their time die, as the whole edifice of the Second Empire crumbled in the course of the Rougon-Macquart, or as the small shops decayed and eventually fell prey to the monopolist competition of "Au Bonheur des Dames." Occasionally the pressure of hunger upon the workers might cause a sudden revolt in the course of which the unadaptable bourgeois might suffer. Étienne, the defeated strike leader of *Germinal*, hears the picks of the miners beneath the ground as he leaves the village and reflects that they sound like an ever-growing army stretching into the future. This ending suggests that Zola did consider the possibility of the decay being arrested by mass class action. But it is a momentary mood. In the main, he regarded revolutionaries as dreamers like Souvarov, the Russian anarchist of *Germinal*, or Florent, the duped hero of *Le Ventre de Paris*, or as a particular variation of the prevailing selfish knave who had assumed such opinions because too many were already sharing the pickings of the orthodox parties. The opinions of 1848 he particularly despised. The plotters who gather round Florent are sincere, but their group is riddled with police spies, and their whole conspiracy is treated as a farce. As a rule, however, '48 men are merely workers who are too lazy and cunning to work for independence—tramps like Jésus Christ in *La Terre*, rogues like old Antoine Macquart, or "flâneurs" and "maquereaux" like Lantier, the lover of Gervaise. Pity is reserved only for the youth Silvère Mouret and his girl companion who, in the Plassans rising of 1851, fell as duped sacrifices to the roguery of those who had encouraged their enthusiasm. But the love of Silvère and his vivandière has a special symbolic significance for Zola as we shall see in the analysis of the sexual motives of the Rougon-Macquart novels. Equally futile are most purely individual revolts against social convention, for they are usually made without consideration of their consequences and the human will is not strong enough to endure. Hélène Mouret with her married lover in the garden of *Une Page d'Amour*, Serge Mouret, the priest with the half-wild girl Albine in the garden of Paradou, Renée with her stepson in the tropical gardens of *La Curée* are doomed to failure. The knot, social or personal, is too hard for the individual to untie.

Nevertheless, for Zola, as for Dickens, the picture of society which his analysis produced was too horrible to be passed over without some attempted solution. When the radical newspapers objected to his picture of the working classes in *L'Assommoir*, Zola declared that as an artist he was concerned only with truth, not with opinions. This aesthetic creed of the naturalists was his constant sermon; but, nevertheless, it is possible to see a series of attempted solutions in the Rougon-Macquart novels which taken in conjunction with changes in his private life bridge the apparent gap between the objective novels of the family chronicle and the "romans à thèse" and the propaganda novels of 1894 onwards. The first faint positive note is struck in *Son Excellence Eugène Rougon*, published in 1876. This eldest son of the eldest branch gambles for success by helping Louis Napoléon to power in 1851, and, as a reward, becomes a chief minister. At the opening of the book, however, he has fallen from power through court intrigues. But not only is Eugène ruthless in his control of others of weaker will, he is also resolute and patient in the control of his own will, and, by waiting and using events, he returns to power. An important element in his success is his mastery of his lust for the adventuress Clorinde, and his refusal to use sex except as part of the general scheme of his life. Eugène is the first character for whom Zola expresses a certain social approval—not the fool who attempts to alter events, but the man who directs his own advantage in "the direction in which society is moving." Such Zola seems to suggest may be the only kind of enlightened behaviour in a deterministic, complex world. It is interesting to contrast this attitude with that of Dickens, for whom ruthless people are almost always villains. Since both writers were ambitious, successful men, the contrast is a curious one. The explanation, I believe, lies in the fact that Zola was able to face the ruthless element in his own campaign for success, because he was a naturally kindly man, whilst Dickens could not do so without acknowledging the deep sadistic element in his emotions.

Eugène Rougon's ride on the crest of the social wave is later repeated in the career of Octave Mouret, who, after using his charm and good looks to conquer the depraved bourgeois world of *Pot-Bouille*, turns the shop "Au Bonheur des Dames," left to him by his first wife, into the first great Parisian multiple store. But here a different element enters in the person of the heroine Denise, a sort of Pamela, a sweet young shop-assistant whose battle for her virtue eventually wins for her a marriage with her boss. Her charitable impulses and knowledge of the sufferings of shop-assistants make her demand from Octave a co-operative Fourierist organization of the store as the price of her hand. This is a solution more akin to those which Dickens attempted and never found satisfactory. Though there is nothing objectionable in the ending, the mixture of the calculating virginity of Denise and the calculating promiscuity of Octave make it one of the least pleasant of Zola's books.

Something of this he must have felt himself, for *La Joie de Vivre* (1884), the next novel, presents charity in a very different light. Pauline, one of the most attractive of Zola's heroines, is possibly a tribute to his wife, who was famous for her good works and to whom he had been particularly closely drawn during their common harrowing experiences at the time of his mother's death in 1880, an episode which also appears in the book. But however fine the character of Pauline, the futility of the medical and educational help she organizes for the ignorant, brutal poor of the seaside village in which she lives, is clearly a culminating irony in a book of such pessimism and despair that its title is one of the most bitter ever bestowed.

We have already seen that, for a moment, in *Germinal*, published in the following year, Zola came down in support of workers' action, and there can be little doubt that the countless tributes from working men did much to fix his steps in the path of Socialism, though it was not ultimately to be of the strike-action type portrayed in the book.

It is not, indeed, until the last two novels of the Rougon-Macquart that a note of genuine hope for society is struck. In *La Débâcle*, Jean Macquart, the simple peasant, with an emotional understanding greater than his powers of expression, ready and sure in emergency, is contrasted with the doubt-ridden, impulsive intellectual Maurice. Zola comes down against the revolutionary ideas of the Communards and in favour of a peaceful, constructive future in the hands of the working community. In *Le Docteur Pascal* religious superstition and bourgeois pride destroy the great scientific work of the hero, but an heir is born, the work has not been wasted, hope lies in the future. These somewhat naïve conclusions, expressed even more directly in the trilogy of the three cities, look directly forward to the busy, hivelike, loving, co-operative, fecund Fourierist communities of the novels of Zola's last years. To explain this change by his association with Jeanne Rozerat and the birth of his two children would seem too simple. Nevertheless, for Zola, society and sex were closely connected concepts, sexual sterility, social corruption and death, which he so feared, intricately entwined.

To understand fully, then, the change in the social patterns of his work, we must now examine the sexual patterns in the Rougon-Macquart novels and their relation to his own life. For Zola, sex is the Achilles' heel of humanity, responsible parenthood its crowning glory. Sex was a temptation into which a man might be led without the full use of his will, habitual promiscuity was the negation of the will. The sexually promiscuous, in his books, are the indolent, the slipshod, the weak. The sexual act was a loss of energy, a further emphasis of the random futility of humanity in a determined, cruel world. Work—regular hours of writing, regular numbers of words written—was Zola's recipe for success and self-respect. Promiscuity was a sin against work.

Adultery was the besetting sin of the upper classes and the grande bourgeoisie. Zola opposed most strongly the whole system of arranged marriages, their lovelessness, their calculation, their loneliness. *Pot-Bouille* is the story of a community of outwardly respectable bourgeois whose inner life is a continual interchange of partners for the bed, where the husbands frequent high-class prostitutes, and the wives await the sound of the front door closing behind their husbands to open the back door to their waiting lovers, where the servants mimic and mock their masters' infidelities in crude and filthy language that matches the "ordures" which they throw out in the mornings. Octave Mouret, alone, can be forgiven, for he calculatingly uses sex for his advancement. Entertaining, powerful though it is, the whole book is a little like a "witty French farce" scrawled on a lavatory wall. The protests of the bourgeoisie, those who had thought *L'Assommoir* so impressive a book, were shrill. But Zola persisted that his picture was just.[8] From very early in his career he had attacked the emptiness and sentimental emotionalism of the Catholic girls' school, to which even non-practising bourgeois sent their daughters. A rapid, romantic education and an arranged marriage led, he suspected, straight to the adultery of the bored young wife.

The atmosphere of adultery and wasteful promiscuity reigns also in Zola's upper-class novels—differing only from the bourgeois world by its modish frankness, its bored explorations into sexual bypaths, its greater recognition of the cicisbeo. Only in certain devout, Legitimist households is moral laxity frowned upon, and these dark, chilling salons, where the old marquises and generals scorn Imperial vulgarity and Orléanist treachery, seem to wear chastity only as another dried wreath of immortelles upon the tomb of the political and social death of their inhabitants. For the new moneyed barons, the bankers, the financiers, the very centre of the great "pourriture" of Second Empire society, sex has its particular and deadly peril. Muffat, the Catholic puritan minister, the Baron Deneuilly, whose vast enterprises control all Paris in the book of that name, all the great money lords become the prey of some guttersnipe actress-prostitute who drains the money-blood from them. The naked, middle-aged Muffat, beaten by Nana, as he crawls on all fours like a dog, may come from Otway's *Venice Preserved*, but he is the symbol of all that Zola believed that sexual passion could do to degrade the powerful will and the adult intellect. Only Eugène Rougon spurning Clorinde, whom he longed to possess, is saved. For the rest, Nana, with her "belles cuisses," her "hanches roulantes," her "gorge superbe," arises from the filth of the slums to be avenged for the degradation of the poor.[9]

If the energies of the rich were spent and wasted in fruitless, tiring sexual exploits, the poor turned to sex as the only pleasure they could afford—"le petit plaisir des pauvres." But they paid for it in further degradation and misery. Ostensibly

[8] It must be admitted that Huysmans who helped him with architectural information said that the bourgeois language "was pitched a tone too low. It is more jesuitical, more shrill."

[9] Zola's own note for Nana is to the point: "a gang after a bitch, who is not on heat and who mocks the dogs that follow her."

L'Assommoir, the bistro with its fatal yellow goddess of absinthe, was a sermon against drink, one of the greatest temperance tracts Vizetelly, Zola's English translator, naïvely called it; but it is not really through drink that Coupeau and Gervaise, the good-natured, deserving working-class couple, come to ruin. The false turnings, which Zola clearly marks in the roads that lead Coupeau to the strait-jacket and Gervaise to die in filth and rags, are sexual. It is weakness and desire that make Gervaise forgive Coupeau when he returns drunk to the laundry in mid-afternoon. It is the kiss "en pleine bouche" that he gives her and her easy acceptance of fuddled lovemaking that spell squalor and ruin. It is Coupeau's "bon copain" acceptance of his wife's ex-lover as lodger that completes the process. "Faire dodo" is the fatality of the poor.

Throughout his career Zola was attacked as a pornographic writer—a view which has since been increased in America by large numbers of illicit, hotted-up translations sold by book pedlars and in "dirty" book shops. Nothing, in fact, could be less attractive than the squalor and disease which surround the sex life of his poor, the boredom and anxiety that beset his rich in their lovemaking. There are, however, certain romantic love episodes in Zola's work—though they are never cited by the smut salesmen—about which an atmosphere of sensuality and excitement hangs that might be charged with the accusation of pornography. They are all of a very special kind: the innocent love of the very young, a sort of natural lovemaking of Adam and Eve before the fall. This is the declared symbol of *La Faute de l'Abbé Mouret* in which the young priest Serge is nursed back from fever by a wild, natural girl Albine in a ruined garden of an eighteenth-century château. But the avenging angel in the person of the savage, puritanical friar drives them out and the end is death and sterility. For Angélique, the girl-heroine of the "roman bleu," *Le Rêve,* the first kiss of marriage is followed by death. For Sylvère and his girl companion there is only death from the enemy firing squad. On occasion the more sophisticated, even the depraved, may seek to return to this Paradise in a desperate attempt to get free of the horror of existence, but the end for them is the same. Renée, the young, consumptive society woman, tries to recreate childish happiness in an affaire with her seventeen-year-old depraved stepson Maxime in the tropical gardens of their Paris mansion. Nana's only genuine innocent happiness comes with Zézé, the young boy, in the garden of the country house which Count Muffat has rented for her. Not only are all these idyllic, sensual love affairs sterile and deadly, but their childlike aspect is marked in a peculiar form. They are essentially adolescent, and this in a very pathological way, they have a curious intersexual appearance—Maxime, Zézé, even Serge are pretty youths, and for Nana and Renée excitement comes originally when they are seen decked in women's clothes. Paradise then is not only illusory, it is a very hot-house land.[10]

The answer to this sexual despair, the very core of his social pessimism, lies in Zola's own life. Nothing in Zola's early days in Paris had helped him to escape from his retrospective view of happiness, and his marriage seems to have proved to be no solution. Alexandrine was a good wife, ambitious, thoughtful for his needs, strong in character, emotionally profound. But she appears to have been only a supplement to his already deep mother-fixation. Had they been able to have children, all this might have been changed, but, unfortunately, this was not to be so. It was a tragedy that weighed upon them as the years passed, until they would lie side by side at night in terror, each knowing what was in the other's mind —the thought of final extinction, of death. *La Joie de Vivre*, conceived during the breakdown which followed his mother's death, recounts this in horrifying terms. Sterility and death, then, mark sexual union for Zola, and the "natural" childlike mating which appears as an escape turns out to be an etiolated union of Narcissus and Circe amidst the poisonous tendrils of some tropical cactus. Here surely lies the key to the horror and despair of Zola's world, and it is only after his fruitful union with Jeanne Rozerat—a union which caused such misery to poor Alexandrine—that the picture changes. Already in *La Débâcle*, more openly in *Le Docteur Pascal*, and finally in *Paris*, the end of the long trilogy of Abbé Fro-

[10] In the latter part of his life, in attacks on Puvis de Chavannes and Burne-Jones, and in *Paris* Zola was particularly violent against their sexless epicene representations of human beauty.

ment's road to a new faith,[11] a note of hope appears—fecundity, work no longer as a drug but in happy knowledge that it will be carried on by posterity, a socialism gradual but sure because there is all the future in which to complete it—this was the faith which Jeanne Rozerat gave to Zola. It saved him from morbidity, and it ended his career as a great writer. The "black poet" changed to a naïve propagandist, repeating the old characters and themes of the Rougon-Macquart, but with a discursiveness, a lifelessness and a stilted preaching which are the negation of his art.

[11] It is notable that the family life which won the Abbé from despair was that of a high-minded union not blessed by any ceremony religious or civil.

Maupassant
ON
Zola:

For Zola, then, truth alone can produce works of art. We are not to use our imagination, we are to observe and describe meticulously what we have seen. . . . However, child of romanticism that he is, and himself a romantic in method, he has a tendency to the lyrical, a need to exalt, to enlarge. . . . His theory and his practice are perpetually in conflict.

Joseph Conrad on

IVAN TURGENEV

Dear Edward:

I am glad to hear that you are about to publish a study of Turgenev,[1] that fortunate artist who has found so much in life for us and no doubt for himself, with the exception of bare justice. Perhaps that will come to him, too, in time. Your study may help the consummation. For his luck persists after his death. What greater luck an artist like Turgenev could wish for than to find in the English-speaking world a translator who has missed none of the most delicate, most simple beauties of his work, and a critic who has known how to analyse and point out its high qualities with perfect sympathy and insight.

After twenty odd years of friendship (and my first literary friendship too) I may well permit myself to make that statement, while thinking of your wonderful Prefaces as they appeared from time to time in the volumes of Turgenev's complete edition, the last of which came into the light of public indifference in the ninety-ninth year of the nineteenth century.

With that year one may say, with some justice, that the age of Turgenev had come to an end too; yet work so simple and human, so independent of the transitory formulas and theories of art, belongs as you point out in the Preface to "Smoke" "to all time."

Turgenev's creative activity covers about thirty years. Since it came to an end the social and political events in Russia have moved at an accelerated pace, but the deep origins of them, in the moral and intellectual unrest of the souls, are recorded in the whole body of his work with the unerring

[1] *Turgenev: A Study.* By Edward Garnett.

lucidity of a great national writer. The first stirrings, the first gleams of the great forces can be seen almost in every page of the novels, of the short stories and of "A Sportsman's Sketches"—those marvellous landscapes peopled by unforgettable figures.

Those will never grow old. Fashions in monsters do change, but the truth of humanity goes on for ever, unchangeable and inexhaustible in the variety of its disclosures. Whether Turgenev's art, which has captured it with such mastery and such gentleness, is for "all time" it is hard to say. Since, as you say yourself, he brings all his problems and characters to the test of love we may hope that it will endure at least till the infinite emotions of love are replaced by the exact simplicity of perfected Eugenics. But even by then, I think, women would not have changed much; and the women of Turgenev who understood them so tenderly, so reverently and so passionately—they, at least, are certainly for all time.

Women are, one may say, the foundation of his art. They are Russian of course. Never was a writer so profoundly, so whole-souledly national. But for non-Russian readers, Turgenev's Russia is but a canvas on which the incomparable artist of humanity lays his colours and his forms in the great light and the free air of the world. Had he invented them all and also every stick and stone, brook and hill and field in which they move, his personages would have been just as true and as poignant in their perplexed lives. They are his own and also universal. Any one can accept them with no more question than one accepts the Italians of Shakespeare.

In the larger, non-Russian view, what should make Turgenev sympathetic and welcome to the English-speaking world, is his essential humanity. All his creations, fortunate and unfortunate, oppressed and oppressors are human beings, not strange beasts in a menagerie or damned souls knocking themselves to pieces in the stuffy darkness of mystical contradictions. They are human beings, fit to live, fit to suffer, fit to struggle, fit to win, fit to lose, in the endless and inspiring game of pursuing from day to day the ever-receding future.

I began by calling him lucky, and he was, in a sense. But one ends by having some doubts. To be so great without the slightest parade and so fine without any tricks of "cleverness" must be fatal to any man's influence with his contemporaries.

Frankly, I don't want to appear as qualified to judge of things Russian. It wouldn't be true. I know nothing of them. But I am aware of a few general truths, such as, for instance, that no man, whatever may be the loftiness of his character, the purity of his motives and the peace of his conscience —no man, I say, likes to be beaten with sticks during the greater part of his existence. From what one knows of his history it appears clearly that in Russia almost any stick was good enough to beat Turgenev with in his latter years. When he died the characteristically chicken-hearted Autocracy hastened to stuff his mortal envelope into the tomb it refused to honour, while the sensitive Revolutionists went on for a time flinging after his shade those jeers and curses from which that impartial lover of *all* his countrymen had suffered so much in his lifetime. For he, too, was sensitive. Every page of his writing bears its testimony to the fatal absence of callousness in the man.

And now he suffers a little from other things. In truth it is not the convulsed terror-haunted Dostoevski but the serene Turgenev who is under a curse. For only think! Every gift has been heaped on his cradle: absolute sanity and the deepest sensibility, the clearest vision and the quickest responsiveness, penetrating insight and unfailing generosity of judgment, an exquisite perception of the visible world and an unerring instinct for the significant, for the essential in the life of men and women, the clearest mind, the warmest heart, the largest sympathy—and all that in perfect measure. There's enough there to ruin the prospects of any writer. For you know very well, my dear Edward, that if you had Antinous himself in a booth of the world's fair, and killed yourself in protesting that his soul was as perfect as his body, you wouldn't get one per cent of the crowd struggling next door for a sight of the Double-headed Nightingale or of some weak-kneed giant grinning through a horse collar.

LEO TOLSTOI AND FYODOR DOSTOIEVSKI

TOLSTOI

Nowadays people set Balzac above Tolstoi. This is lunacy. Balzac's books are repulsive, posturing, full of absurdities; in them, humanity is judged by a literary man anxious to write a great book; in Tolstoi, by a serene god. Balzac succeeds in giving the impression of greatness; in Tolstoi everything is great by nature—the droppings of an elephant beside those of a goat. Those great harvest scenes in *Anna Karenina*, the hunting scenes, the skating scenes, etc., are like vast unbroken surfaces that space out the rest, and make everything seem on an ampler scale. It seems as though there were the whole meadow of standing hay, the whole summer, between two conversations of Levine's. One loves different things by turns in this great world, and scenes that are like nothing else —the emotion of the man riding a race (O my beauty, my beauty!), of the man who has laid a wager, sitting on the window-sill, the gaiety of life under canvas, of the life of the little hunting squire, of old Prince Stsherbatski at the German Spa when he talks about the good old days of feudal Russia (getting up late, in the chapter about taking the waters, etc.), of the aristocratic spendthrift (Natasha's brother) in *War and Peace*, of old Prince Bolkonski. This is not the work of an observing eye but of a thinking mind. Every so-called stroke of observation is simply the clothing, the proof, the instance, of a law, a law of reason or of unreason, which the novelist has laid bare. And our impression of breadth and life is due precisely to the fact that none of this is the fruit of observation, but that every deed, every action, being no other than an expression of a law, one feels oneself moving amid a throng of laws—only, since the truth of these laws is established for Tolstoi by the inward authority they have exercised over his thinking, there are some which we are still baffled by. It is not easy to understand what he means when he speaks of Kitty's sly look when she talked about religion, nor when he speaks of Anna's delight at humbling Vronsky's pride.

We are pleased to see how the man of splendid intellect really draws on much the same kind of wit we often draw on ourselves (Ruskin's witticisms about his dog Vizir and his servant Anne, Tolstoi's witticisms setting the tone of the opening of *Anna Karenina*). And for all that, in this apparently inexhaustible fund of creation it seems as though Tolstoi were repeating himself, as though he had no more than a few themes at his disposal, disguised and reshaped, but the same in both novels. The stars, and the sky that Levine rivets his gaze on are pretty much the same as the comet that Peter saw, as Prince Andrew's wide blue sky. What is more, Levine, first discarded by Kitty in favour of Vronsky, then loved by her, reminds one of Natasha leaving Prince Andrew for Peter's brother-in-law, then going back to him. And might not the same memory have "sat" for Kitty passing by in the carriage and Natasha in the carriage following the army?

DOSTOIEVSKI

Dostoievski mentions among the worst miseries of his convict-life never, during the space of four years, being able to be by himself. But it would seem that even when continually exposed to the presence of others one should be able to isolate or abstract oneself. That is in everyone's power, and should have been more so, one would suppose, for Dostoievski than for any, he who ought to have known so well how to abolish what was around him by the hallucinating power of imagination. Anyhow, there are more incommoding presences to put aside than human ones, which at least are exterior to you and who, though able to incommode the process of thought, cannot prevent it. These presences are inmates. A man who has a disease lodged in him, who during these same four years (and often for much longer) has experienced frightful suffering and is never free from the stupefying discomfort that attends an incessant fever, so that it is an effort for him to turn over in bed, that man, always at the mercy of his disease, is much less alone than Dostoievski among the convicts, to whom, besides, he paid no attention and who paid no attention to him. But pain and fever compel you to attend to them.

For Dostoievski, forced labour was probably the stroke of good fortune which set free his inner life. It is strange how from that time on his letters resemble Balzac's: request for money, promises, based on hopes of fame, to repay at a hundred per cent. "*The Idiot* will be a fine book" (like *Le Lys dans la Vallée*) because he feels a new man awakening in him. Whatever Gide may say, there are dissertations interpolated in the narrative, those long reflections on capital punishment in *The Idiot,* for instance.

Crime and Punishment could be the title of all Dostoievski's novels (as all Flaubert's, *Madame Bovary* above all, could be called *L'Education sentimentale*). But probably he makes two persons by dividing what really appertained to one. There was certainly a crime in his life, and a punishment (which perhaps had no connection with the crime), but he has preferred to allot them severally, to attribute in case of need the impressions of punishment to himself (*The House of the Dead*), and the crime to others. His genius—contrary to what Rivière says—was for construction.

Dostoevsky ON Tolstoy:	*. . . An artist is bound to make himself acquainted, down to the smallest detail, not only with the technique of writing, but with everything . . . relating to that reality which he designs to show forth. We have only one writer who is really remarkable in that respect: it is Count Leo Tolstoy.*

André Gide on

The few psychological and moral truths Dostoevsky's works will permit us to touch upon are in my estimation so important that I am all eagerness to reach them. By their very boldness and originality they would seem paradoxical to you if I approached them directly. I needs must proceed warily.

In our last talk I spoke to you of the figure of the man himself. The moment is favourable, I think, for presenting it in its own atmosphere the better to bring its particular features into relief.

I have been on intimate terms with some Russians, but I have never been in Russia; hence, without help, my task would be extremely difficult. I shall first of all submit a few observations on the Russian people that I found in a German monograph on Dostoevsky. Mme Hoffmann, in her excellent biography, insists first and foremost on the solidarity, the common brotherhood between all classes of Russian society, which end in sweeping away social barriers and facilitate naturally the freedom of intercourse we find in all Dostoevsky's novels. An introduction, a sudden feeling of sympathetic understanding; and we have at once what one of his heroes so expressively describes as "chance relationships." Homes are transformed into hostelries, the stranger of yesterday becomes the honoured guest of to-day: a friend's friend visits you, and immediately everything between you is on a footing of intimacy.

Another observation of Mme Hoffmann's concerning the Russian people. It is inherently incapable of leading a strict and methodical existence, of being punctual even. It would seem as if the Russian did not suffer much in consequence of his own improvidence, for he makes no great effort to free himself from it. And if I may be permitted to seek an excuse for the lack of order in my causeries, I shall find it in the very confusion of Dostoevsky's ideas, in their extreme entanglement and in the peculiar difficulties experienced in trying to hold them to a plan which satisfies our Western logic. This wavering and indecision Mme Hoffmann ascribes partly to the weakening of time sense due to the endless summer days and interminable winter nights, when the rhythm of the passing hours is lost. In a short address delivered at the *Vieux Colombier* I already quoted Mme Hoffmann's illustration of the Russian who met reproaches on account of his unpunctuality with "Yes, life is difficult! There are moments which must be lived well, and this is more important than the punctual keeping of any engagement!"—a sentence full of significance, for it reveals at the same time the strange consciousness a Russian has of his inner life, more important to him than all social connections.

I should like to point out, with Mme Hoffmann, the propensity to pity and suffering, *Leiden und Mitleiden*, to compassion extending even to the criminal. In Russia there exists but one word to designate the poor and the criminal, but one to cover actual crime and ordinary offences. Add to this an almost religious contrition and we shall the better understand the Russian's ineradicable mistrustfulness in all his relations with strangers, with foreigners in particular. Westerners often complain of this mistrustfulness, which proceeds, so Mme Hoffmann maintains, from the uneasy consciousness of his own insufficiency and proneness to sin, rather than from any feeling that other people are of no account: it is a mistrust that springs from humility of spirit.

Nothing could better throw light on this strange religiosity of the Russian, which persists even when belief is long since dead, than the four conversations of Prince Myshkin, the hero of *The Idiot*. These I shall now read to you.

"'As to the question of faith,' he began, smiling, . . . 'I had four different conversations in two days last week. I came in the morning by the new railway and talked for four hours with a man in the train. We made friends on the spot. I had heard a great deal about him beforehand and had heard he was an atheist, among other things. He really is a very learned man. What's more, he's an unusually well-bred man,

so that he talked to me quite as if I were his equal in ideas
and attainments. He doesn't believe in God. Only, one thing
struck me: that he seemed not to be talking about that at
all the whole time; and it struck me, just because whenever
I have met unbelievers before, or read their books, it always
seemed to me that they were speaking and writing in their
books about something quite different, although it seemed to
me about that on the surface. I said so to him at the time,
but I suppose I didn't say so clearly, or did not know how
to express it, for he didn't understand. In the evening, I
stopped for the night at a provincial hotel, and a murder had
just been committed there the night before, so that every one
was talking about it when I arrived. Two peasants, middle-
aged men, friends who had known each other for a long time,
and were not drunk, had had tea and were meaning to go to
bed in the same room. But one had noticed during those
last two days that the other was wearing a silver watch on a
yellow bead chain, which he seems not to have seen on him
before. The man was not a thief: he was an honest man, in
fact, and by a peasant's standard by no means poor. But he
was so taken by the watch, and so fascinated by it, that at
last he could not restrain himself. He took a knife and when
his friend had turned away, he approached him cautiously
from behind, and praying fervently, "God forgive me for
Christ's sake!" he cut his friend's throat at one stroke like a
sheep and took his watch.'

"Rogozhin went off into peals of laughter; he laughed as
though he were in a sort of fit. It was positively strange to
see such laughter after the gloomy mood that had preceded it.

"'I do like that! Yes, that beats everything!' he cried convulsively, gasping for breath. 'One man doesn't believe in
God at all, while the other believes in him so thoroughly
that he prays as he murders men! . . . You could never have
invented that, brother! Ha!—ha!—ha! That beats everything!'

"'Next morning I went out to walk about the town,'
Myshkin went on, as soon as Rogozhin was quiet again,
though his lips still quivered with spasmodic convulsive
laughter. 'I saw a drunken soldier in a terribly disorderly
state staggering about the wooden pavement. He came up to
me. "Buy a silver cross, sir!" said he. "I'll let you have it for

twenty kopecks. It's silver." I saw in his hand a cross—he must have just taken it off—on a very dirty blue ribbon; but one could see at once it was only tin. It was a big one with eight corners, of a regular Byzantine pattern. I took out twenty kopecks and gave them to him, and at once put the cross round my neck; and I could see from his face how glad he was that he had cheated a stupid gentleman, and he went off immediately to drink what he had got for it, there was no doubt about that. At that time, brother, I was quite carried away by the rush of impressions that burst upon me in Russia; I had understood nothing about Russia before. I had grown up, as it were, inarticulate, and my memories of my country were somehow fantastic during those five years abroad. Well, I walked on, thinking, "Yes, I'll put off judging that man who sold his Christ. God only knows what's hidden in these weak drunken beasts." An hour later, when I was going back to the hotel, I came upon a peasant woman with a tiny baby in her arms. She was quite a young woman, and the baby was about six weeks old. The baby smiled at her for the first time in its life. "What are you doing, my dear?" (I was always asking questions in those days.) "God has just such gladness every time He sees from heaven that a sinner is praying to him with all his heart, as a mother has when she sees the first smile on her baby's face." That was what the woman said to me almost in those words, this deep, subtle, and truly religious thought—a thought in which all the essence of Christianity finds expression; that is the whole conception of God as our Father and of God's gladness in man, like a father's in his own child—the fundamental idea of Christ! A simple peasant woman! It's true she was a mother . . . and who knows, very likely that woman was the wife of that soldier. Listen, Parfyon! You asked me a question just now; here is my answer. The essence of religious feeling does not come under any sort of reasoning or atheism, and has nothing to do with any crimes or misdemeanours. There is something else here, and there will always be something else—something that the atheists will for ever slur over; they will always be talking of something else. But the chief thing is that you will notice it more clearly and quickly in the Russian heart than anywhere else. And this is my conclusion. It's one of the chief convictions I've gathered from our Russia. There is work to be done, Parfyon! There is work to be done in our Russian world, believe me.'"

And we see at the end of this story another characteristic reveal itself: the belief in the special mission of the Russian people.

This belief we find in several Russian writers: in Dostoevsky it becomes an active and painful conviction, and his chief grievance against Turgeniev was simply that he could not trace in him this national feeling, his opinion being that Turgeniev was too westernized.

In his speech at the Pushkin celebrations, Dostoevsky declared that Pushkin, still in full flush of imitating Byron and Chénier, suddenly found what Dostoevsky calls the "Russian note," a note "fresh and sincere." Replying to the question (which he describes as "accursed") "What faith can we have in the Russian people and in its worth?" Pushkin exclaimed, "Humble thyself, thou son of arrogance, and first conquer thy pride. Humble thyself and before the people, bend thy neck towards thy mother earth."

Never perhaps are ethnic differences more clearly marked than when the manner of interpreting *honour* is involved. The hidden mainspring of civilized man's conduct seems to me to be less a matter of amour-propre, as La Rochefoucauld would have said, than a feeling for what we call the "point of honour." This feeling for personal honour, this sensitive spot, is not exactly alike for Frenchman, Englishman, Italian, and Spaniard. But contrasted with the Russian conception, the codes of honour of all Western nations seem to fuse practically into one. When we appreciate the Russians' idea of honour, we see at once how often the code of the Western world is opposed to the teaching of the Gospels. And the Russian idea of honour is as much closer to the Gospels by virtue of its remoteness from Western nations; in other words, Christian feeling is predominant in the Russians, and often takes precedence of "honour" as we Westerners interpret the idea.

Faced with the choice of seeking revenge or asking pardon by admitting himself in the wrong, the Westerner will often consider the second alternative lacking in dignity, the attitude of a coward or a nonentity. The Westerner tends to esteem unwillingness to forgive, forget, or remit offences a mark of strength of character, and certainly he tries never to put himself in the wrong; but, should he have done so, it would appear that the most unpleasant thing that could befall him would be the necessity for admitting the fact! The Russian, on the other hand, is ever ready to admit himself in the wrong—and even before his enemies—equally willing to humble himself and seek forgiveness.

The Greek Orthodox religion, no doubt, is only encouraging a national inclination by tolerating, nay, approving, public confession. The notion of confession, not murmured low into priestly ears, but made openly, before any and all, comes up again and again, almost with the quality of an obsession, in Dostoevsky's novels. When Raskolnikhov has confessed his crime to Sonia, in *Crime and Punishment*, she advises him, as the one means of unburdening his soul, at once to prostrate himself in the public street and cry aloud, "I have the blood of a fellow-being on my hands." Most of Dostoevsky's characters are seized at certain moments—and almost in invariably unexpected and ill-advised fashion—with the urgent desire to make confession, to ask pardon of some fellow-creature who often has not a notion what it is all about, the desire to place themselves in a posture of inferiority to the person addressed.

You remember, I am sure, the extraordinary scene in *The Idiot*, in the course of an evening party at Nastasya Filippovna's house. To pass the time someone suggested in place of parlour games or charades that each guest should confess the vilest act he ever committed; and the wonderful part is that the suggestion was not scouted, and that each one present commenced his or her confession, with varying degree of sincerity, no doubt, but almost without a vestige of shame.

And more curious still, an anecdote from Dostoevsky's own life, which I have from a Russian in his intimate circle. I was imprudent enough to tell it to several individuals and already it has been made use of; but in the form I found it retailed, it was fast approaching unrecognizability. Hence my anxiety to give the exact facts here.

There are, in Dostoevsky's life, certain extremely obscure

episodes. One, in particular, already alluded to in *Crime and Punishment* and which seems to have served as theme for a certain chapter in *The Possessed*. This chapter does not figure in the novel, having been so far withheld in Russia even. It has, I believe, been printed in Germany, but in an edition for private circulation only.[1] It deals with the rape of a young girl. The child victim hangs herself, and in the next room, Stavrogin, the guilty man, knowing that she is hanging herself waits until life has left her little body. What measure of truth is there in this sinister tale? For the moment, it is not for me to say. The fact remains that Dostoevsky, after an adventure of this nature, was moved to what one must needs describe as remorse. This remorse preyed upon him for a while, and doubtless he said to himself what Sonia said to Raskolnikov. The need for confession became urgent, but confession not merely to a priest. He sought to find the person before whom confession would cause him the acutest suffering. Turgeniev, without the shadow of a doubt! Dostoevsky had not seen him for long, and was on uncommonly bad terms with him. M. Turgeniev was a respectable man, rich, famous, and held in wide esteem. Dostoevsky summoned up all his courage, or rather, he succumbed to a kind of giddiness, to a mysterious and awful attraction. Picture Turgeniev's comfortable study: the author himself at his desk.—The bell rings.—A manservant announces Fyodor Dostoevsky.—What is his business?—He is shown in, and at once begins to tell his tale.—Turgeniev listens, dumb with stupefaction. What business of his is all this? No doubt the other man is mad!—After the confession, a great silence. Dostoevsky waits for some word or sign from Turgeniev, believing no doubt that like in his own novels, Turgeniev will take him in his arms, kiss him and weep over him, and be reconciled . . . but nothing happens:

"Monsieur Turgeniev, I must tell you how deeply I despise myself. . . ."

He pauses again. . . . The silence remains unbroken until Dostoevsky, unable to contain himself any longer, bursts out

[1] See *Nouvelle Revue Française*, June–July, 1922, and *Stavrogin's Confession*, translated, with introductory and explanatory notes, by S. S. Koteliansky and Virginia Woolf, 1922. (*Translator's note.*)

in wrath: "But *you* I despise even more! That's all I wanted to say to you," and off he goes, slamming the door behind him.

Here we see how humility is suddenly displaced by a very different feeling. The man who in his humility was abasing himself, draws up in revolt at the humiliation. Humility opens the gates of Heaven: humiliation the gates of Hell. Humility implies a measure of free-will submission; it is accepted without constraint and proves the truth of the Gospel teaching: "*For whosoever exalteth himself shall be abased: and he that humbleth himself shall be exalted.*" Humiliation, on the other hand, degrades the soul, warping and deforming it; it irritates, impoverishes, and blights, inflicting a moral hurt most ill to heal.

There is not, I believe, one single deformation or deviation of character—these kinks that make so many of Dostoevsky's characters so strangely morbid and disturbing—but which has its beginning in some humiliation.

The Insulted and Injured is the title of one of his first books, and his work as a whole is obsessed without ceasing by the idea that humiliation damns, whereas humility sanctifies. Heaven, as Alyosha Karamazov dreams and describes it to us, is a world where there will be no injured, neither insulted.

The strangest, most disturbing figure of these novels, the terrible Stavrogin in *The Possessed*, whose character at first is so different from all others, is explained, and his demoniac nature accounted for, by certain passages in the book:

"Nikolay Vsyevolodovitch Stavrogin," says one of the other characters, "was leading at that time in Petersburg a life, so to say, of mockery. I can't find another word to describe it, because he is not a man who falls into disillusionment, and he disdained to be occupied with work at that time."

And Stavrogin's mother, to whom these remarks were addressed, says a little farther on:

"No, it was something more than eccentricity, and I assure you, something sacred even! A proud man who has suffered humiliation early in life and reached the stage of 'mockery,' as you so subtly called it."

And later:

"And if Nikolay had always had at his side (Varvara Petrovna almost shouted) a gentle Horatio, great in his humility—another excellent expression of yours, Stephan Trofimovitch!—he might long ago have been saved from the sad and sudden demon of irony, which has tormented him all his life."

It happens that some of Dostoevsky's characters, whose natures have been profoundly warped by humiliation, find as it were delight and satisfaction in the resultant degradation, loathsome though it be.

"Was there resentment in my heart?" says the hero of A Raw Youth just when his amour-propre had been cruelly wounded, "I don't know. Perhaps there was. Strange to say, I always had, perhaps from my earliest childhood, one characteristic; if I were ill-treated, absolutely wronged and insulted to the last degree, I always showed at once an irresistible desire to submit passively to the insult, and even to accept more than my assailant wanted to inflict on me, as though I would say: 'All right, you have humiliated me, so I will humiliate myself even more; look and enjoy it.'"

For if humility be a surrender of pride, humiliation, on the other hand, but serves to strengthen it.

Listen to the tale told by the wretched hero of the Notes from Underground:

"One night, as I was passing a tavern, I saw through a lighted window some gentlemen fighting with billiard cues, and saw one of them thrown out of the window. At other times, I should have felt very much disgusted, but I was in such a mood at the time, that I actually envied the gentleman thrown out of the window—and I envied him so much that I even went into the tavern and into the billiard-room. 'Perhaps,' I thought, 'I'll have a fight, too, and they'll throw me out of the window.'

"I was not drunk—but what is one to do?—depression will drive a man to such a pitch of hysteria! But nothing happened. It seemed that I was not even equal to being thrown out of the window, and I went away without having my fight.

"An officer put me in my place from the first moment. I was standing by the billiard-room tables and in my ignorance blocking up the way, and he wanted to pass; he took me by the shoulders and without a word, without warning or explanation, moved me from where I was standing to another spot and passed by as though he had not noticed me. I could have forgiven blows, but I could not forgive his having moved me without noticing me.

"Devil knows what I would have given for a real, regular quarrel—a more decent, a more literary one, so to speak. I had been treated like a fly. This officer was over six foot, while I was a spindly little fellow. But the quarrel was in my hands. I had only to protest and I certainly would have been thrown out of the window. But I changed my mind, and preferred to beat a resentful retreat."

But if we carry the story further, we shall soon see the excess of hatred to be nothing other than love inverted.

". . . I often met that officer afterwards in the street, and noticed him very carefully. I am not quite sure whether he recognized me: I imagine not, I judge from certain signs. But I—I stared at him with spite and hatred, and so it went on —for several years! My resentment grew even deeper with years. At first I began making stealthy inquiries about this officer. It was difficult for me to do so, for I knew no one. But one day I heard one shout his name in the street as I was following him at a distance, as though I was tied to him, —and so I learned his surname. Another time I followed him to his flat, and for ten kopecks learned from the porter where he lived, on which storey, whether he lived alone or with others, and so on—in fact, everything one could learn from a porter. One morning, though I had never tried my hand with the pen, it suddenly occurred to me to write a satire on this officer in the form of a novel which would unmask his villainy; I even exaggerated it; at first I so altered his surname that it could not easily be recognized, but on second thoughts I changed it, and sent the story to the O.Z.

"But at that time such attacks were not the fashion and my story was not printed. That was a great vexation to me. Sometimes I positively choked with resentment. At last I determined to challenge my enemy to a duel. I composed a splendid, charming little letter to him, imploring him to apologize to me, and hinting rather plainly at a duel in case of refusal. The letter was so composed that if the officer had

had the least understanding of the good and beautiful, he would certainly have flung himself on my neck and offered his friendship. And how fine that would have been! How we should have got on together!"

So often in Dostoevsky one particular feeling is suddenly supplanted in this way by its direct opposite! We can find example after example of it. For instance, that unhappy child (in *The Karamazovs*) biting with hatred into Alyosha's finger when the latter holds out his hand to him, just at the time when the child, though he does not recognize it, is developing for the same Alyosha a shy, wild affection.

And what, in this young child, could have caused such a warping of affection?

He had seen Dmitri Karamazov, Alyosha's brother, come drunk out of an inn, thrash his father, and pull him insolently by the beard: "Papa, papa, how he humiliated you!" he cried later.

Thus, over against humility—on the same moral plane, if I may be permitted to say so, but at the other extreme of the scale—there is pride, which humiliation exaggerates, exasperates, and deforms, sometimes hideously.

Certainly, psychological axioms appear to Dostoevsky for what they really are: special definitions of truth. As novelist (for Dostoevsky is no mere theoretician, he is an explorer) he steers clear of introduction and realizes how imprudent (on his part, at least) any attempts to formulate general laws would be.[2] It is for us to discover these laws in his books, by cutting, as it were, paths through the thicket. Here is one of the laws we can establish: the man who has suffered humiliation seeks to inflict humiliation in his turn.[3]

Despite the extraordinarily rich diversity of his *Comédie Humaine*, Dostoevsky's characters group and arrange them-

[2] "However adventurous the Russian genius," wrote Boris de Schloezer in the *Nouvelle Revue Française*, February 1922, "it characteristically chooses a firm foundation in concrete fact and living reality: this basis once assured, it launches out into speculation of the most abstract and daring nature, returning in the end, rich with the gathered spoils of thought, to the fact and reality from which it started and in which it is perfected."

[3] E.g., Lebedyev in *The Idiot*. See Appendix (2), the admirable chapter describing Lebedyev's enjoyment in torturing General Ivolgin.

selves always on one plane only, that of humility and pride. This system of grouping discomfits us; indeed, at first, it appears far from clear, for the very simple reason that we do not usually approach the problem of making a diversion at such an angle and that we distribute mankind in hierarchies. Let me explain my idea: in Dickens's wonderful novels, for instance, I am often uneasy at the conventionality, childishness even, of his *hierarchy*, or to use Nietzsche's phrase, *scale of values*. While reading him I have the impression that I am contemplating one of Fra Angelico's *Last Judgements* where you have the redeemed, the damned, and the indeterminate (not too numerous!) over whom angel and demon struggle. The balance that weighs them all, as in an Egyptian bas-relief, reckons only the positive or negative quality of their virtue. Heaven for the just: for the wicked, Hell. Herein Dickens is true to the opinion of his countrymen and of his time. It does happen that the evil prosper, while the just are sacrificed—to the great shame of this earthly existence and of society as we have organized it. All his novels endeavour to show us and make us realize the shining superiority of qualities of heart over qualities of head. I have selected Dickens as a type because of all the great novelists we know he uses this classification in its simplest form: which—if I may say in conclusion—is the secret of his popularity.

Now, after reading in close succession practically all Dostoevsky's works, I have the impression that there exists in them, too, a similar classification: less apparent, no doubt, although almost as simple, and, in my estimation, much more significant. For it is not according to the positive or negative quality of their virtue that one can *hierarchize* (forgive me this horrible word!) his characters: not according to their goodness of heart, but by their degree of pride.

Dostoevsky presents on one side the humble (some of these are humble to an abject degree, and seem to enjoy their abasement); on the other, the proud (some to the point of crime). The latter are usually the more intelligent. We shall see them, tormented by the demon of pride, ever striving after something higher still:

"There, I'll bet anything—that you've been sitting side by side in the drawing-room all night wasting your precious time discussing something lofty and elevated," says Stavrogin to the abominable Pyotr Stepanovitch in *The Possessed*. Or again:

"In spite of the terror which I detected in her myself, Katerina Nikolaevna has always from the first cherished a certain reverence and admiration for the nobility of Andrey Petrovitch's principles and the loftiness of his mind. . . . In his letter he gave her the most solemn and chivalrous promises that she should have nothing to fear—she responding with the same heroic feelings. There may have been a sort of chivalrous rivalry on both sides."[4]

"There is nothing in it to fret your vanity," said Elizabeth to Stavrogin: "The day before yesterday when I 'insulted' you before everyone and you answered me so chivalrously, I went home and guessed at once that you were running away from me because you were married, and not from contempt for me, which, as a fashionable young lady, I dreaded more than anything," adding by way of conclusion, "Anyhow, it eases our vanity."[5]

His women, even more so than his characters of the other sex, are ever moved and determined by considerations of pride. Look at Raskolnikov's sister, Nastasya Filippovna and Anglaïa Epantchin in *The Idiot*, Elizabeth Nikolaïevna in *The Possessed*, and Katerina Ivanovna in *The Karamazovs!*

But, by an inversion which I make bold to describe as inspired by the New Testament, the most abject characters are nearer the Kingdom of Heaven than the noblest. To such a degree is Dostoevsky's work dominated by these profound truths. *"God resisteth the proud, but giveth grace to the humble."*—*"For the Son of man is come to save that which was lost."*

On the one hand, denial and surrender of the self; on the other, affirmation of the personality, the *will to power*, an exaggerated loftiness of sentiment. And take due note of this fact; in Dostoevsky's novels, the *will to power* leads inevitably to ruin.

M. Souday recently accused me of sacrificing, indeed, of

4 *A Raw Youth.*
5 *The Possessed.*

immolating Balzac to Dostoevsky. Need I protest? My admiration of Dostoevsky is certainly fervent, but I do not think I am blinded by it. I readily agree that Balzac's creations surpass the Russian novelist's in their diversity, and that his *Comédie Humaine* is the more varied. Dostoevsky certainly goes deeper and touches more important points than any other author, but we can admit that his characters are one and all cut from the same cloth. Pride and humility! these hidden reagents never change, although by graduating the doses of them, we obtain reactions that are infinitely rich and minutely varied in colour.

With Balzac (as invariably in Western society, in French especially, to which his novels hold a mirror) two factors are active which in Dostoevsky's work practically do not exist: first, the intellect, second, the will. I do not pretend that in Balzac will-power always urges a man towards what is good, and that his strong-willed characters are never but virtuous. But at least consider how many of his characters attain to what is of good repute by effort of will and open up a glorious career by dint of perseverance, cleverness, and determination. Think of his David Séchards, his Bianchons, Joseph Brideaus, and Daniel d'Arthez—and there are twenty such I could name!

In all Dostoevsky we have not a single great man. "But what about that splendid Father Zossima in *The Karamazovs?*" you may say. Yes, he is certainly the noblest figure the Russian novelist had drawn; he far and away dominates the whole tragedy, and once we have entered into possession of the promised complete version of *The Karamazovs*, we shall understand still better his importance. At the same time we shall realize what in Dostoevsky's eyes constitutes his real greatness. Father Zossima is not of the great as the world reckons them. He is a saint—no hero! And he has reached saintliness by surrender of will and abdication of intellect.

If I examine along with Balzac's the resolute characters that Dostoevsky presents, I suddenly realize what terrible creatures they are, one and all. Look at Raskolnikov, heading the list; in his beginnings, a miserable worm—with ambitions, who would like to be a Napoleon, and only attains to being the murderer of an old broker-woman and of an innocent girl. Look at Stavrogin, Pyotr Stepanovitch, Ivan Karamazov, the hero of *A Raw Youth* (the only one of Dostoevsky's characters who, from his earliest days, at least since consciousness dawned, lived with a fixed determination, to wit, in this case, of becoming a Rothschild, and, by mockery as it were, in all the books of Dostoevsky nowhere is there a more pithless creature, at the mercy of his fellow-beings, individually and collectively). His heroes' determination, every particle of cleverness and will-power they possess, seem but to hurry them onward to perdition, and if I seek to know what part mind plays in Dostoevsky's novels, I realize that its power is demonic.

His most dangerous characters are the strongest intellectually, and not only do I maintain that the mind and the will of Dostoevsky's characters are active solely for evil, but that, when urged and guided towards good, the virtue to which they attain is rotten with pride and leads to destruction. Dostoevsky's heroes inherit the Kingdom of God only by the denial of mind and will and the surrender of personality.

We can without hesitation affirm that Balzac, too, is, to a certain degree, a Christian author. But only by confronting the two ethical points of view, the French author's and the Russian's, can we realize the chasm between the former's Catholicism and the latter's purely evangelical doctrine, and how widely the Catholic spirit can differ from the purely Christian. Or, to offend none, let me express myself thus: Balzac's *Comédie Humaine* sprang from the contact between the Gospels and the Latin mind: Dostoevsky's from the contact between the Gospels and Buddhism, the Asiatic mind.

These are merely preliminary considerations which will help us at our next meeting to probe deeper into the souls of these strange creations.

Today high tide is at ten. The waters rush up the narrowing strand, carrying foam-bubbles and jelly-fish—primitive children of an unnatural mother, who will abandon them on the sands to death by evaporation. The waves run up, almost to the foot of my beach-chair; sometimes I must lift away my plaid-wrapped legs as the waters encroach and threaten to cover them. My heart responds blithely, though also with utter respect, to these sportive little tricks the mighty ocean plays me; my sympathy, a deep and tender, primitive, soul-extending stirring, is far indeed from any annoyance.

No bathers yet. They await the midday warmth to wade out into the ebbing tide, little flutters and shrieks escaping them as they begin their pert yet fearful toying with the vast. Coast-guards in cork jackets, lynx-eyed, tooting their horns, watch over all this amateurish frivolity. My "workshop" here surpasses any I know. It is lonely; but even were it livelier, the tumultuous surf so shuts me in, and the sides of my admirable beach-chair, seat and cabin in one, familiar from my youth up, is so peculiarly protective that there can be no distraction. Beloved, incomparably soothing and suitable situation—it recurs in my life again and again, as by a law. Beneath a sky where gently shifting continents of cloud link the blue depths, rolls the sea, a darkening green against the clear horizon, oncoming in seven or eight foaming white rows of surf that reach out of sight in both directions. There is superb activity farther out, where the advancing waves hurl themselves first and highest against the bar. The bottle-green wall gleams metallic as it mounts and halts and curls over, then shatters with a roar and an explosion of foam down, down, in ever recurrent crash, whose dull thunder forms the deep ground-bass to the higher key of the boiling and hissing waves as they break nearer in. Never does the eye tire of this sight nor the ear of this music.

A more fitting spot could not be for my purpose: which is to recall and to reflect upon the great book whose title stands at the head of my paper. And here by the sea there comes to mind inevitably an old, I might almost say an innate association of ideas: the spiritual identity of two elementary experiences, one of which is a parable of the other. I mean the ocean and the epic. The epic, with its rolling breadth, its breath of the beginnings and the roots of life, its broad and sweeping rhythm, its all-consuming monotony—how like it is to the sea, how like to it is the sea! It is the Homeric element I mean, the story going on and on, art and nature at once, naïve, magnificent, material, objective, immortally healthy, immortally realistic! All this was strong in Tolstoy, stronger than in any other modern creator of epic art; it distinguishes his genius, if not in rank, yet in essence, from the morbid manifestation, the ecstatic and highly distorted phenomenon, that was Dostoyevsky. Tolstoy himself said of his early work *Childhood* and *Boyhood*: "Without false modesty, it is something like the Iliad." That is the merest statement of fact; only on exterior grounds does it fit still better the giant work of his maturity, *War and Peace.* It fits everything he wrote. The pure narrative power of his work is unequalled. Every contact with it, even when he wished no longer to be an artist, when he scorned and reviled art and only employed it as a means of communicating moral lessons; every contact with it, I say, rewards the talent that knows how to receive (for there is no other) with rich streams of power and refreshment, of creative primeval lustiness and health. Seldom did art work so much like nature; its immediate, natural power is only another manifestation of nature itself; and to read him again, to be played upon by the animal keenness of this eye, the sheer power of this creative attack, the entirely clear and true greatness, unclouded by any mysticism, of this epic, is to find one's way home, safe from every danger of affectation and morbid trifling; home to originality and health, to everything within us that is fundamental and sane.

Turgenyev once said: "We have all come out from under

Gogol's *Mantle*"—a fiendishly clever pun which puts in a phrase the extraordinary uniformity and unity, the thick traditionalism of Russian literature as a whole. Actually, they are all there simultaneously, its masters and geniuses, they can put out their hands to each other, their life-spans in great part overlap. Nikolai Gogol read aloud some of *Dead Souls* to the great Pushkin, and the author of *Yevgeny Onyegin* shook with laughter—and then suddenly grew sad. Lermontov was the contemporary of both. Turgenyev, as one may easily forget, for his frame, like Dostoyevsky's, Lieskov's, and Tolstoy's, belongs to the second half of the nineteenth century, came only four years later than Lermontov into the world and ten before Tolstoy, whom he adjured in a touching letter expressing his faith in humanistic art, "to go back to literature." What I mean by thick traditionalism is illustrated by an anecdote that most significantly connects Tolstoy's artistically finest work, *Anna Karenina*, with Pushkin.

One evening in the spring of 1873, Count Leo Nikolayevich entered the room of his eldest son, who was reading aloud to his old aunt Pushkin's *Stories of Byelkin*; the father took the book and read: "The guests assembled in the country house." "That's the way to begin," he said; went into his study and wrote: "In the Oblonsky house great confusion reigned." That was the original first sentence from *Anna Karenina*. The present beginning, the *aperçu* about happy and unhappy families, was introduced later. That is a marvellously pretty little anecdote. He had already begun much and brought much to triumphant conclusion. He was the fêted creator of the Russian national epos, in the form of a modern novel, the giant panorama *War and Peace*. And he was about to excel both formally and artistically this chef-d'œuvre of his thirty-five years in the work he had now in hand, which one may with an easy mind pronounce the greatest society novel of world literature. And here he was, restlessly prowling about the house, searching, searching, not knowing how to begin. Pushkin taught him, tradition taught him, Pushkin the classic master, from whose world his own was so remote, both personally and generally speaking. Pushkin rescued him, as he hesitated on the brink; showed him how one sets to, takes a firm grip, and plumps the reader *in medias res*. Unity is achieved, the continuity of that astonishing family of intellects which one calls Russian literature is preserved in this little piece of historical evidence.

Merezhkovsky points out that historically and premodernly only Pushkin among these writers really possesses charm. He inhabits a sphere by himself, a sensuously radiant, naïve, and blithely poetic one. But with Gogol there begins what Merezhkovsky calls critique: "the transition from unconscious creation to creative consciousness"; for him that means the end of poetry in the Pushkin sense, but at the same time the beginning of something new. The remark is true and perceptive. Thus did Heine speak of the age of Goethe, an æsthetic age, an epoch of art, an objective-ironic point of view. Its representative and dominant figure had been the Olympian; it died with his death. What then began was a time of taking sides, of conflicting opinions, of social consolidation, yes, of politics and, in short, of morals—a morality that branded as frivolous every purely æsthetic and universal point of view.

In Heine's comments, as in Merezhkovsky's, there is feeling for temporal change, together with feeling for its opposite, the timeless and perpetual. Schiller, in his immortal essay, reduced it to the formula of the sentimental and the naïve. What Merezhkovsky calls "critique" or "creative consciousness," what seems to him like contrast with the unconscious creation of Pushkin, as the more modern element, the future on the way, is precisely what Schiller means by the sentimental in contrast to the naïve. He too brings in the temporal, the evolutional, and—"*pro domo*," as we know—declares the sentimental, the creativeness of conscious critique, in short the moralistic, to be the newer, more modern stage of development.

There are now two things to say: first, Tolstoy's original convictions were definitely on the side of the æsthetic, of pure art, the objectively shaping, anti-moralistic principle; and second, in him took place that very cultural and historical change which Merezhkovsky speaks of, that move away from Pushkin's simplicity towards critical responsibility and morality. Within his own being it took such a radical and tragic form that he went through the severest crises and much anguish and even so could not utterly repudiate his own mighty creativeness. What he finally arrived at was a rejection and negation of art itself as an idle, voluptuous, and immoral luxury, admissible only in order to make moral teachings acceptable to men, even though dressed in the mantle of art.

But to return to the first position: we have his own unequivocal declarations to the effect that a purely artistic gift stands higher than one with social significance. In 1859, when he was thirty-one years old, he gave, as a member of the Moscow society of Friends of Russian Literature, an address in which he so sharply emphasized the advantages of the purely art element in literature over all the fashions of the day that the president of the society, Khomyakov, felt constrained to rejoin that a servant of pure art might quite easily become a social reformer even without knowing or willing it. Contemporary criticism saw in the author of *Anna Karenina* the protagonist of the art-for-art's-sake position, the representative of free creativeness apart from all tendentiousness or doctrine. Indeed, it considered this naturalism the characteristically new thing; the public must in time grow up to it, though at present they had got used, in the works of others, to the presentation of political and social ideas in the form of art. In point of fact, all this was only one side of the business. As an artist and son of his time, the nineteenth century, Tolstoy was a naturalist, and in this connection he represented—in the sense of a trend—the new. But as an intellectual he was beyond (or rather, he struggled amid torments to arrive beyond) the new, to something further still, on the other side of his, the naturalistic century. He was reaching after conceptions of art which approached much nearer to "mind" (*Geist*), to knowledge, to "critique" than to nature. The commentators of 1875, impressed by the first chapters of *Anna Karenina* as they appeared in a Russian magazine, the *Messenger*, seeking benevolently to prepare the way with the public for the naturalism of the work, did not dream that the author was in full flight towards an anti-art position, which was already hampering his work on his masterpiece and even endangering its completion.

This development was to go very far, the vehemence of its

consistency shrank from nothing: neither from the anti-cultural nor even from the absurd. Before long, he was to regret in public having written *Childhood and Youth*, the work of his freshest youthful hours—so poor, so insincere, so literary, so sinful was this book. He was to condemn root and branch the "artist twaddle" with which the twelve volumes of his works were filled, to which "the people of our day ascribe an undeserved significance." It was the same undeserved significance that they ascribed to art itself—for instance, to Shakespeare's plays. He went so far—one must set it down with respect and a sober face, or at least with the smallest, most non-committal smile—as to put Mrs. Harriet Beecher Stowe, the author of *Uncle Tom's Cabin*, far above Shakespeare.

We must be at pains to understand this. Tolstoy's hatred for Shakespeare dated from much earlier than is usually supposed. It signified rebellion against nature, the universal, the all-affirming. It was jealousy of the morally tormented for the irony of the absolute creator, it meant the straining away from nature, naïveté, moral indifference, towards "*Geist*" in the moralistically critical sense of the word; towards moral valuations and edifying doctrine. Tolstoy hated himself in Shakespeare, hated his own vital bearish strength, which was originally like Shakespeare's, natural and creatively a-moral; though his struggles for the good, the true and right, the meaning of life, the doctrine of salvation, were after all only the same thing in another and self-denying form. The immensity of his writings sometimes resulted in a gigantic clumsiness which forces a respectful smile. And yet it is precisely the paradoxically ascetic application of a titanic helplessness arising from a primeval force that, viewed as art, gives his work that huge moral *élan*, that Atlas-like moral muscle-tensing and flexing which reminds one of the agonized figures of Michelangelo's sculpture.

I said that Tolstoy's hatred of Shakespeare belongs to an earlier period than is generally thought. But all that which later made his friends and admirers like Turgenyev weep, his denial of art and culture, his radical moralism, his highly questionable pose of prophet and confessor in his last period —all that begins much further back, it is quite wrong to imagine this process as something suddenly occurring in a crisis of conversion in later life, coincident with Tolstoy's old age. The same kind of mistake occurs in the popular opinion that Richard Wagner suddenly got religion—whereas the matter was one of a development vastly and fatally consistent and inevitable, the direction of which is clearly and unmistakably traceable in *The Flying Dutchman* and in *Tannhäuser*. The judgment of the Frenchman, Vogüé, was entirely correct when, on the news that the great Russian writer was now "as though paralysed by a sort of mystic madness," Vogüé declared that he had long ago seen it coming. The course of Tolstoy's intellectual development had been present in the seed in *Childhood* and *Boyhood* and the psychology of Levin in *Anna Karenina* had marked out the path it would take.

So much is true, that Levin is Tolstoy, the real hero of the mighty novel, which is a glorious, indestructible signpost on the woeful Way of the Cross the poet was taking; a monument of an elemental and creative bear-strength, which was first heightened and then destroyed by the inner ferment of his subtilizing conscience and his fear of God. Yes, Levin is Tolstoy—almost altogether Tolstoy, this side Tolstoy the artist. To this character Tolstoy transferred not only the important facts and dates of his own life: his experiences as a farmer, his romance and betrothal (which are completely autobiographic), the sacred, beautiful, and awe-full experiences of the birth of his first child, and the death of his brother—which forms a pendant of equal and boundless significance—not only there but in his whole inner life, his crises of conscience, his groping after the whole duty of man and the meaning of life, his painful wrestling over the good life, which so decisively estranged him from the doings of urban society; his gnawing doubts about culture itself or that which his society called culture, doubts of all this brought him close to the anchorite and nihilist type. What Levin lacks of Tolstoy is only just that he is not a great artist besides. But to estimate *Anna Karenina* not only artistically but also humanly, the reader must saturate himself with the thesis that Constantin Levin himself wrote the novel. Insead of being the man with the pointer, indicating the incomparable beauty of the painting as a whole, I shall do better to speak of the conditions of difficulty and stress under which the work came to birth.

That is the right word: it came to birth; but there did not lack much for it not to be born. A work of this kind, so all of one piece and that piece so absorbing, so complete in the large and in the small, makes us suppose that its creator gave himself utterly to it with entire and devoted heart and, like one driven to self-expression, committed it, so to speak, in one gush to paper. That is a misapprehension; although, even so, the origin of *Anna Karenina* does in fact lie in the happiest, most harmonious period of Tolstoy's life. The years in which he worked on it belong to the first decade and a half of his marriage with the woman whose literary image is Kitty Shtcherbatsky and who later suffered so much from her Lievotshka—until at last just before his death the old man broke away and ran. It is she who, in addition to her constant pregnancies, and her abundant activities as mistress of the farm, as mother and housewife, copies *War and Peace* seven times with her own hand—that first colossal intellectual harvest of the period that brought the doubting, brooding man relative peace in the patriarchal animalism of marriage and family life in the country. It was the period at which the poor Countess looked so yearningly back when Leochen had become "the prophet of Yasnaya Polyana" and succeeded under self-torture, and even so up to the end never quite succeeded, in brooding to death all his sensual and instinctive passions: family, nation, state, church, club, and chase, at bottom the whole life of the body, but most particularly art, which for him quite essentially meant sensuality and the body's life.

Well, those fifteen years were a good, happy time, though from a later, higher point of view, good only in a low and animal sense. *War and Peace* had made Tolstoy the "great writer of Russia," and as such he went to work to write a new historical and national epos. He had in mind a novel about Peter the Great and his times. And for months he carried on conscientious and comprehensive studies for it in the libraries and archives of Moscow. "Lievotshka reads and reads," it says in the Countess's letters. Did he read too much? Did he take in too much, did he spoil his appetite? Oddly enough, it turned out that the Czar reformer, the imperial compeller of civilization, was at bottom an unsympathetic figure to Tolstoy. To hold the position he had achieved as the national epic-writer, he had wanted to repeat his performance in *War and Peace*. It would not come off; the material unexpectedly resisted him. After endless preparatory labour he flung the whole thing away, sacrificed his whole investment of time and study, and turned to something quite different: the passion and stumbling of *Anna Karenina*, the modern novel of St. Petersburg and Moscow high society.

The first onset, by dint of Pushkin's help, was fresh and blithe. But before long Tolstoy got stuck, though the reader in his untrammelled enjoyment would never guess it. For weeks and months the work only dragged on or did not go at all. What was the trouble? Household cares, children's illnesses, fluctuations in his own health—oh, no, these were all nothing compared with a piece of work like *Anna Karenina*—or they ought to be. What is really disturbing is doubt of the importance and personal urgency of what we are doing. Might we not do better to learn Greek, to get some fundamental knowledge of the New Testament? Then the schools for the children of peasants we have founded. Should they not claim more of our time and thought? Is not the whole of belles-lettres folly? And is it not our duty or even much more consistent with our deepest need to bury ourselves in theological and philosophical studies in order to find at last the meaning of life? That contact with the mystery of death which he had had when his older brother died had made a strong impression on Tolstoy's own vitality, powerful to the point of mysticism, which demanded spiritual wrestling, not in a literary way but in something confessional on the pattern of Saint Augustine and Rousseau. Such a book, sincere as far as human power could make it, weighed on his mind and gave him increasing distaste for writing novels. Actually, he would never have finished *Anna Karenina* if it had not begun appearing in the *Rusky Vyestnik* (*Russian Messenger*) of Katkov. The fact made him responsible to the publisher and the reading public. In January 1875 and the following three months successive numbers of the novel appeared in the magazine. Then they left off, because the author had no more to deliver. The first months of the next year produced a few fragments, then seven months' pause. Then in December one more number. What we find simply enchanting, what we cannot imagine as originating in anything except a state of prolonged inspiration—Tolstoy groaned over. "My tiresome, horrible *Anna Karenina*," he wrote from Samara, where he was drinking mares' milk. *Sic!* Literally. "At last," he wrote in March 1876, "I was driven to finish my novel, of which I am sick to death." Of course in the process the enthusiasm and eagerness came back by fits and starts. But it was just at such times that the writing was prone to go more slowly—owing to fastidious artistry that caused endless filing and remodelling and improving out of a stylistic perfectionism which still shows through the most inadequate translation. This amazing saint took his art the more seriously the less he believed in it.

The publication dragged on, with constant interruptions, as far as the eighth book. Then it stopped, for now the thing had become political and the national epic-writer of Russia had in the latest number expressed himself so heretically about Slavophilism, the current enthusiasm for the Bulgarian, Serbian, Bosnian brothers in their fight for freedom against the Turks, the much ado over the volunteers and the patriotic nonsense uttered by Russian society, that Katkov dared not print it. He demanded cuts and changes, which the author in high dudgeon refused to make. Tolstoy had the final numbers printed separately with a note on the disagreement.

What I have boldly called the greatest society novel in all literature is an anti-society novel. The Bible text: "Vengeance is mine, I will repay, saith the Lord," stands at its head. The moral momentum of the work was certainly the desire to lash society for the cold, cruel rebuff inflicted by it on a woman who goes astray through passion but is fundamentally proud and high-minded, instead of leaving to God the punishment for her sins. Indeed, society might well do just that, for after all it is society and its irrevocable laws that God too avails Himself of to exact the payment. It shows the fatal and inevitable character of Anna's doom that it proceeds inscrutably, step by step, up to the frightful end out of her affront to the moral law. So there is a certain contradiction in the author's original moral motive, in the complaint he lodges against society. One asks oneself in what way would God punish if society did not behave as it does? Custom and morality, how far are they distinguishable, how far are they—in effect—one and the same, how far do they coincide in the heart of the socially circumscribed human being? The question hovers unanswered over the whole novel. But such a work is not compelled to answer questions. Its task is to bring them out, to enrich the emotions, to give them the highest and most painful degree of questionableness. Thus it will have performed its task, and in this case the story-teller's love for his creature leaves no doubt at all, no matter how much suffering he painfully and relentlessly visits on her.

Tolstoy loves Anna very much, one feels that. The book bears her name; it could bear no other. But its hero is not Anna's lover, the strong, decent, chivalrous, and somewhat limited officer of the Guards, Count Vronsky. Nor is it Alexander Alexandrovich, Anna's husband, with whatever profound skill Tolstoy has modelled this incomparable, at once repellent and superior, comic and touching cuckold. No, the hero is another person altogether, who has as good as nothing to do with Anna's lot, and whose introduction in a way twists the theme of the novel and almost pushes its first motive into second place. It is Constantin Levin, the introspective man, the author's image—he, no other, with his brooding and scrutinizing, with the peculiar force and obstinate resistance of his critical conscience, that makes the great society novel into an anti-society novel.

What an extraordinary fellow he is, this surrogate of the author! What in the French *pièce à thèse* is called the *raisonneur*—Levin is that in Tolstoy's society world. Yet how un-French! To amount to something as a critic of society, one must, I suppose, be in society oneself; but precisely that he is not in the least, this tortured, radically remote *raisonneur*, despite his native right to move in the highest circles. Strong and shy, defiant and dubious, with an intelligence of great anti-logical, natural, even helpless abundance, Levin is at bottom convinced that decency, uprightness, seriousness, and sincerity are possible only in singleness, in dumb isolation, each for himself; and that all social life turns him into a chatterer, a liar, and a fool. Observe him in the salons of Moscow, or on cultural occasions when he has to make conversation, play a social part, express "views." Such a coming-together of people seems to him banal, he sees himself a blushing fool, a prattler, a parrot. This Rousseauian quite sincerely considers all urban civilization, with the intellectual and cultural goings-on bound up in it, a sink of iniquity. Only life in the country is worthy of a man—though not the country life that the city man in sentimental relaxation finds "charming." Levin's learned brother, for instance, even boasts in a way that he enjoyed such an unintellectual occupation as fishing. No, what Levin means is the real, serious life on the land, where you have to work hard, where the human being dwells truly and perforce at the heart of that nature whose "beauty" the guest from civilization sentimentally admires from outside.

Levin's morality and conscientiousness are strongly physical, having reference to the body and bound up with it. "I need physical exercise," he says to himself, "otherwise my character suffers." He resolves to help the peasants with the mowing and it gives him the highest moral and physical pleasure (a splendid and Tolstoyan chapter). His scorn of the "intellectual" or, better, his disbelief in it, estranging him as a product of civilization, involving him in contradictions, is radical. It leads him, when he has to come right down to it, into paradoxes, into opinions hard to express among civilized beings. Take for instance popular education—or, worse still, any education at all. Levin's position towards it is the same as his position towards nature: "The same people whom you say you love."—"I never said that," thought Constantin Levin. —"Why should I bother my head about schools where I shall never send my own children and where the peasants will never send theirs either? And on top of that, I am not even convinced that it is necessary to send them!"—"You can make better use of a peasant and labourer who can read and write than of one who cannot."—"No, ask anybody you like," countered Constantin Levin decisively; "a worker with some schooling is distinctly worse."—"Do you admit that education is a blessing for the people?"—"Yes, that I admit," responded Levin thoughtlessly, and saw at once that what he had said was not really just what he thought.—Very bad! A difficult, dangerous case! He recognizes the blessings of "education," because what he "really" thinks about it, in the nineteenth century, cannot be put into words and for that reason may even be unthinkable.

Of course he moves in the thought-channels of his century, and they in a certain way are scientific. He "observes humanity, not as something standing outside of zoological law but as something dependent on its environment, and he proceeds from this dependence in order to discover the laws lying at the base of its development." So at least the scholar understands him; and it is no other than Taine to whom he there makes acknowledgment, good, great, nineteenth-century. But there is something in him that either goes back behind the scientific spirit of his epoch or goes on beyond it, something desperately bold, inadmissible, impossible in conversation. He lies on his back and looks up at the high and cloudless sky. "Do I not know that that is infinite space and not a round vault? But however I screw up my eyes and strain my sight I cannot see it not round and not bounded; and in spite of my knowledge about infinite space I am incontestably right when I see a solid blue dome, and more right than when I strain my eyes to see beyond it. . . . Can this be faith?"

But whether faith or the new realism, it is no longer the scientific spirit of the nineteenth century. In a sort of way it recalls Goethe. And Levin-Tolstoy's sceptical, realistic, rebellious attitude towards patriotism, towards the Slavic brethren and the war volunteers, does the same. He declines to share in the enthusiasm, he is solitary in the midst of it, precisely as Goethe was at the time of the Freiheitskrieg—although in both cases something new, the democratic, joined the national movement and for the first time the popular will conditioned the conduct of the government. That too is nineteenth-century; and Levin, or Lievotshka, as the poor Countess called him, could simply not do with the truths of his time. He called them comfortless. He is a step further on; I cannot help calling it a very dangerous step, which, if not safeguarded by the profoundest love of truth and human sympathy, can quite easily lead to black reaction and barbarism. Today it takes no forlorn, single-handed courage to throw overboard the scientific discipline of the nineteenth century and surrender to the "mythus," the "faith"—in other words, to a paltry and culture-destroying vulgarity. Masses of people do it today; but it is not a step forward, it is a hundred miles backwards. Such a step will be in a forward direction only when it is taken for humanity's sake, only if another step follows it straightway, moving from the new realism of the solid blue vault to the neither old nor new but humanly eternal idealism of truth, freedom, and knowledge. Today there are some desperately stupid ideas about reaction in the air.

A digression—but a necessary one. Levin, then, cannot do with the ideals of his epoch, he cannot live with them. What I call his physical morality and conscientiousness is shaken to the depths by the experience of the physically transcendent and transparent mysteries of birth and death; and all that the times teach him about organisms and their destruction, about the indestructibility of matter and the laws of conservation of energy, about evolution, and so forth, all that looks to him not only like utter ignorance of the whole problem of the meaning of life but also like a kind of thinking that makes it impossible for him to get the knowledge he needs. That in infinite time, infinite space, infinite matter, and organism, a cell frees itself; that it persists for a while and then bursts and that this bubble is he himself, Levin; that seems to him like the malicious mockery of some demon. It cannot indeed be refuted; it must be overcome some other way, that one may not be driven to shoot oneself.

What to his profounder necessities looks like a mortal lie and a kind of thinking which is no sort of instrument for the apprehension of truth—that actually is the naturalistic materialism of the nineteenth century, whose inspiration is honest love of truth, despite the comfortless pessimism that is its necessary aura. The honesty must be preserved; but a little illumination is required in order to do justice to life and its deeper concerns. So there is real humour in the fact that in *Anna Karenina* a simple little peasant shows the brooding man the way out of his despair. This little peasant teaches him, or recalls to his mind, something he has always known: true, he says, living for our physical well-being and in order to fill our bellies is natural and inborn and laid upon us all. But even so, it is not righteous or even important. What we have to do is to live for the "truth," "for our souls," "as God wills," for "the Good." How wonderful that this necessity is laid upon us just as naturally inborn and imposed as the need to fill our bellies! Wonderful indeed; for the sure conviction common to all men that it is shameful to live only for the belly, and that one must rather live for God, for the true and the good, has nothing to do with reason, but quite the contrary. It is reason that makes us care for the body and in its interest to exploit our neighbours all we can. Knowledge of the good, asserts Levin, does not lie in the realm of reason; the good stands outside the scientific chain of cause and effect. The good is a miracle, because it is contrary to reason and yet everyone understands it.

There is something outside of and beyond the melancholy science of the nineteenth century, which resigned all attempt to give meaning to life. There is a spiritual factor, a spiritual need. And Levin is enchanted and soothed by this absurdly simple statement of the human being's supra-reasonable obligation to be good. In his joy he forgets that also that melancholy materialistic naturalistic science of the nineteenth century had, after all, as motive power, human striving for the good. He forgot that it was stern and bitter love of truth that made it deny meaning to life. It too, denying God, lived for God. That, too, is possible, and Levin forgets it. Art he does not need even to forget; he knows, it seems, nothing about it, obviously thinking of it only as the society prattle of the "cultured" about painting, the Luccas, Wagner, and so on. Here is the difference between him and Leo Tolstoy. Tolstoy knew art; he has suffered frightfully from and for it, achieved mightier things in it than the rest of us can hope to achieve. Perhaps it was just the violence of his artist personality that made him fail to see that knowledge of the good is just the opposite of a reason to deny art. Art is the most beautiful, austerest, blithest, most sacred symbol of all supra-reasonable human striving for good above and beyond reason, for truth and fullness. The breath of the rolling sea of epic would not so expand our lungs with living air if it did not bring with it the astringent quickening spice of the spiritual and the divine.

IVAN TURGÉNIEFF

When the mortal remains of Ivan Turgénieff were about to be transported from Paris for interment in his own country, a short commemorative service was held at the Gare du Nord. Ernest Renan and Edmond About, standing beside the train in which his coffin had been placed, bade farewell in the name of the French people to the illustrious stranger who for so many years had been their honoured and grateful guest. M. Renan made a beautiful speech, and M. About a very clever one, and each of them characterised, with ingenuity, the genius and the moral nature of the most touching of writers, the most lovable of men. "Turgénieff," said M. Renan, "received by the mysterious decree which marks out human vocations the gift which is noble beyond all others: he was born essentially impersonal." The passage is so eloquent that one must repeat the whole of it. "His conscience was not that of an individual to whom nature had been more or less generous: it was in some sort the conscience of a people. Before he was born he had lived for thousands of years; infinite successions of reveries had amassed themselves in the depths of his heart. No man has been as much as he the incarnation of a whole race: generations of ancestors, lost in the sleep of centuries, speechless, came through him to life and utterance."

I quote these lines for the pleasure of quoting them; for while I see what M. Renan means by calling Turgénieff impersonal, it has been my wish to devote to his delightful memory a few pages written under the impression of contact and intercourse. He seems to us impersonal, because it is from his writings almost alone that we of English, French and German speech have derived our notions—even yet, I fear, rather meagre and erroneous—of the Russian people. His genius for us is the Slav genius; his voice the voice of those vaguely-imagined multitudes whom we think of more and more to-day as waiting their turn, in the arena of civilisation, in the grey expanses of the North. There is much in his writings to encourage this view, and it is certain that he interpreted with wonderful vividness the temperament of his fellow-countrymen. Cosmopolite that he had become by the force of circumstances, his roots had never been loosened in his native soil. The ignorance with regard to Russia and the Russians which he found in abundance in the rest of Europe—and not least in the country he inhabited for ten years before his death—had indeed the effect, to a certain degree, to throw him back upon the deep feelings which so many of his companions were unable to share with him, the memories of his early years, the sense of wide Russian horizons, the joy and pride of his mother-tongue. In the collection of short pieces, so deeply interesting, written during the last few years of his life, and translated into German under the name of *Senilia*, I find a passage—it is the last in the little book—which illustrates perfectly this reactionary impulse: "In days of doubt, in days of anxious thought on the destiny of my native land, thou alone art my support and my staff, O great powerful Russian tongue, truthful and free! If it were not for thee how should man not despair at the sight of what is going on at home? But it is inconceivable that such a language has not been given to a great people." This Muscovite, home-loving note pervades his productions, though it is between the lines, as it were, that we must listen for it. None the less does it remain true that he was not a simple conduit or mouthpiece; the inspiration was his own as well as the voice. He was an individual, in other words, of the most unmistakable kind, and those who had the happiness to know him have no difficulty to-day in thinking of him as an eminent, responsible figure. This pleasure, for the writer of these lines, was as great as the pleasure of reading the admirable tales into which he put such a world of life and feeling: it was perhaps even greater, for it was not only with the pen that nature had given Turgénieff the power to express himself. He was the richest, the most delightful, of talkers, and his face, his person, his temper, the thoroughness with which he had been equipped for human intercourse, make in the memory of his friends an image which is completed, but not thrown into the shade, by his literary distinction. The whole image is tinted with sadness: partly because the element of melancholy in his nature was deep and constant—readers of his novels have no need to be told of that; and partly because, during the last years of his life, he had been condemned to suffer atrociously. Intolerable pain had been his portion for too many months before he died; his end was not a soft decline, but a deepening distress. But of brightness, of the faculty of enjoyment, he had also the large allowance usually made to first-rate men, and he was a singularly complete human being. The author of these pages had greatly admired his writings before having the fortune to make his acquaintance, and this privilege, when it presented itself, was highly illuminating. The man and the writer together occupied from that moment a very high place in his affection. Some time before knowing him I committed to print certain reflections which his tales had led me to make; and I may perhaps, therefore, without impropriety give them a supplement which shall have a more vivifying reference. It is almost irresistible to attempt to say, from one's own point of view, what manner of man he was.

It was in consequence of the article I just mentioned that I found reason to meet him, in Paris, where he was then living, in 1875. I shall never forget the impression he made upon me at that first interview. I found him adorable; I could scarcely believe that he would prove—that any man could prove—on nearer acquaintance so delightful as that. Nearer acquaintance only confirmed my hope, and he remained the most approachable, the most practicable, the least unsafe man of genius it has been my fortune to meet. He was so simple, so natural, so modest, so destitute of personal pretension and of what is called the consciousness of powers, that one almost doubted at moments whether he were a man of genius after all. Everything good and fruitful lay near to him; he was interested in everything; and he was absolutely without that eagerness of self-reference which sometimes accompanies great, and even small, reputations. He had not a particle of vanity; nothing whatever of the air of having a part to play or a reputation to keep up. His humour exercised itself as freely upon himself as upon other subjects, and he told stories at his own expense with a sweetness of hilarity which made his peculiarities really sacred in the eyes of a friend. I remember vividly the smile and tone of voice with which he once repeated to me a figurative epithet which Gustave Flaubert (of whom he was extremely fond) had applied to him— an epithet intended to characterise a certain expansive softness, a comprehensive indecision, which pervaded his nature, just as it pervades so many of the characters he has painted. He enjoyed Flaubert's use of this term, good-naturedly opprobrious, more even than Flaubert himself, and recognised perfectly the element of truth in it. He was natural to an extraordinary degree; I do not think I have ever seen his match in this respect, certainly not among people who bear, as he did, at the same time, the stamp of the highest cultivation. Like all men of a large pattern, he was composed of many different pieces; and what was always striking in him was the mixture of simplicity with the fruit of the most various observation. In the little article in which I had attempted to express my admiration for his works, I had been moved to say of him that he had the aristocratic temperament: a remark which in the light of further knowledge seemed to me singularly inane. He was not subject to any definition of that sort, and to say that he was democratic would be (though his political ideal was a democracy), to give an equally superficial account of him. He felt and understood the opposite sides of life; he was imaginative, speculative, anything but literal. He had not in his mind a grain of prejudice as large as the point of a needle, and people (there are many) who think this a defect would have missed it immensely in Ivan Serguéitch. (I give his name, without attempting the Russian orthography, as it was uttered by his friends when they addressed him in French.) Our Anglo-Saxon, Protestant, moralistic, conventional standards were far away from him, and he judged things with a freedom and spontaneity in which I found a perpetual refreshment. His sense of beauty, his love of truth and right, were the foundation of his nature; but half the charm of conversation with him was that one breathed an air in which cant phrases and arbitrary measurements simply sounded ridiculous.

I may add that it was not because I had written a laudatory article about his books that he gave me a friendly welcome; for in the first place my article could have very little importance for him, and in the second it had never been either his habit or his hope to bask in the light of criticism. Supremely modest as he was, I think he attached no great weight to what might happen to be said about him; for he felt that he was destined to encounter a very small amount of intelligent appreciation, especially in foreign countries. I never heard him even allude to any judgment which might have been passed upon his productions in England. In France he knew that he was read very moderately; the "demand" for his volumes was small, and he had no illusions whatever on the subject of his popularity. He had heard with pleasure that many intelligent persons in the United States were impatient for everything that might come from his pen; but I think he was never convinced, as one or two of the more zealous of these persons had endeavoured to convince him, that he could boast of a "public" in America. He gave me the impression of thinking of criticism as most serious workers think of it—that it is the amusement, the exercise, the subsistence of the critic (and, so far as this goes, of immense use); but that though it may often concern other readers, it does not much concern the artist himself. In comparison with all those things which the production of a considered work forces the artist little by little to say to himself, the remarks of the critic are vague and of the moment; and yet, owing to the large publicity of the proceeding, they have a power to irritate or discourage which is quite out of proportion to their use to the person criticised. It was not, moreover (if this explanation be not more gross than the spectre it is meant to conjure away), on account of any esteem which he accorded to my own productions (I used regularly to send them to him) that I found him so agreeable, for to the best of my belief he was unable to read them. As regards one of the first that I had offered him he wrote me a little note to tell me that a distinguished friend, who was his constant companion, had read three or four chapters aloud to him the evening before and that one of them was written *de main de maître!* This gave me great pleasure, but it was my first and last pleasure of the kind. I continued, as I say, to send him my fictions, because they were the only thing I had to give; but he never alluded to the rest of the work in question, which he evidently did not finish, and never gave any sign of having read its successors. Presently I quite ceased to expect this, and saw why it was (it interested me much), that my writings could not appeal to him. He cared, more than anything else, for the air of reality, and my reality was not to the purpose. I do not think my stories struck him as quite meat for men. The manner was more apparent than the matter; they were too *tarabiscoté*, as I once heard him say of the style of a book—had on the surface too many little flowers and knots of ribbon. He had read a great deal of English, and knew the language remarkably well—too well, I used often to think, for he liked to speak it with those to whom it was native, and, successful as the effort always was, it deprived him of the facility and raciness with which he expressed himself in French.

I have said that he had no prejudices, but perhaps after all he had one. I think he imagined it to be impossible to a person of English speech to converse in French with complete correctness. He knew Shakespeare thoroughly, and at one time had wandered far and wide in English literature. His opportunities for speaking English were not at all frequent, so that when the necessity (or at least the occasion) presented itself, he remembered the phrases he had encountered in books. This often gave a charming quaintness and an unexpected literary turn to what he said. "In Russia, in spring, if you enter a beechen grove"—those words come back to me from the last time I saw him. He continued to read English books and was not incapable of attacking the usual Tauchnitz novel. The English writer (of our day) of whom I remember to have heard him speak with most admiration was Dickens, of whose faults he was conscious, but whose power of presenting to the eye a vivid, salient figure he rated very high. In the young French school he was much interested; I mean, in the new votaries of realism, the grandsons of Balzac. He was a good friend of most of them, and with Gustave Flaubert, the most singular and most original of the group, he was altogether intimate. He had his reservations and discriminations, and he had, above all, the great back-garden of his Slav imagination and his Germanic culture, into which the door constantly stood open, and the grandsons of Balzac were not, I think, particularly free to accompany him. But he had much sympathy with their experiment, their general movement, and it was on the side of the careful study of life as the best line of the novelist that, as may easily be supposed, he ranged himself. For some of the manifestations of the opposite tradition he had a great contempt. This was a kind of emotion he rarely expressed, save in regard to certain public wrongs and iniquities; bitterness and denunciation seldom passed his mild lips. But I remember well the little flush of conviction, the seriousness, with which he once said, in allusion to a novel which had just been running through the *Revue des Deux Mondes*, "If I had written anything so bad as that, I should blush for it all my life."

His was not, I should say, predominantly, or even in a high degree, the artistic nature, though it was deeply, if I may make the distinction, the poetic. But during the last twelve years of his life he lived much with artists and men of letters, and he was eminently capable of kindling in the glow of discussion. He cared for questions of form, though not in the degree in which Flaubert and Edmond de Goncourt cared for them, and he had very lively sympathies. He had a great regard for Madame George Sand, the head and front of the old romantic tradition; but this was on general grounds, quite independent of her novels, which he never read, and which she never expected him, or apparently any one else, to read. He thought her character remarkably noble and sincere. He had, as I have said, a great affection for Gustave Flaubert, who returned it; and he was much interested in Flaubert's extraordinary attempts at bravery of form and of matter, knowing perfectly well when they failed. During those months which it was Flaubert's habit to spend in Paris, Turgénieff went almost regularly to see him on Sunday afternoon, and was so good as to introduce me to the author of *Madame Bovary*, in whom I saw many reasons for Turgénieff's regard. It was on these Sundays, in Flaubert's little salon, which, at the top of a house at the end of the Faubourg Saint-Honoré, looked rather bare and provisional, that, in the company of the other familiars of the spot, more than one of whom[1] have commemorated these occasions, Turgénieff's beautiful faculty of talk showed at its best. He was easy, natural, abundant, more than I can describe, and everything that he said was touched with the exquisite quality of his imagination. What was discussed in that little smoke-clouded room was chiefly questions of taste, questions of art and form; and the speakers, for the most part, were in æsthetic matters, radicals of the deepest dye. It would have been late in the day to propose among them any discussion of the relation of art to morality, any question as to the degree in which a novel might or might not concern itself with the teaching of a lesson. They had settled these preliminaries long ago, and it would have been primitive and incongruous to recur to them. The conviction that held them together was the conviction that art and morality are two perfectly different things, and that the former has no more to do with the latter than it has with astronomy or embryology. The only duty of a novel was to be well written; that merit included every other of which it was capable. This state of mind was never more apparent than one afternoon when *ces messieurs* delivered themselves on the subject of an incident which had just befallen one of them. *L'Assommoir* of Emile Zola had been discontinued in the journal through which it was running as a serial, in consequence of repeated protests from the subscribers. The subscriber, as a type of human imbecility, received a wonderful dressing, and the Philistine in general was roughly handled. There were gulfs of difference between Turgénieff and Zola, but Turgénieff, who, as I say, understood everything, understood Zola too, and rendered perfect justice to the high solidity of much of his work. His attitude, at such times, was admirable, and I could imagine nothing more genial or more fitted to give an idea of light, easy, human intelligence. No one could desire more than he that art should be art; always, ever, incorruptibly, art. To him this proposition would have seemed as little in need of proof, or susceptible of refutation, as the axiom that law should always be law or medicine always medicine. As much as any one he was prepared to take note of the fact

[1] Maxime Du Camp, Alphonse Daudet, Emile Zola.

that the demand for abdications and concessions never comes
from artists themselves, but always from purchasers, editors,
subscribers. I am pretty sure that his word about all this
would have been that he could not quite see what was meant
by the talk about novels being moral or the reverse; that a
novel could no more propose to itself to be moral than a painting or a symphony, and that it was arbitrary to lay down a
distinction between the numerous forms of art. He was the
last man to be blind to their unity. I suspect that he would
have said, in short, that distinctions were demanded in the
interest of the moralists, and that the demand was indelicate,
owing to their want of jurisdiction. Yet at the same time that
I make this suggestion as to his state of mind I remember
how little he struck me as bound by mere neatness of formula,
how little there was in him of the partisan or the pleader.
What he thought of the relation of art to life his stories,
after all, show better than anything else. The immense variety of life was ever present to his mind, and he would never
have argued the question I have just hinted at in the interest
of particular liberties—the liberties that were apparently the
dearest to his French *confrères*. It was this air that he carried
about with him of feeling all the variety of life, of knowing
strange and far-off things, of having an horizon in which the
Parisian horizon—so familiar, so wanting in mystery, so perpetually *exploité*—easily lost itself, that distinguished him
from these companions. He was not all there, as the phrase is;
he had something behind, in reserve. It was Russia, of course,
in a large measure; and, especially before the spectacle of
what is going on there to-day, that was a large quantity. But
so far as he was on the spot, he was an element of pure
sociability.

I did not intend to go into these details immediately, for
I had only begun to say what an impression of magnificent
manhood he made upon me when I first knew him. That
impression, indeed, always remained with me, even after it
had been brought home to me how much there was in him
of the quality of genius. He was a beautiful intellect, of
course, but above all he was a delightful, mild, masculine
figure. The combination of his deep, soft, lovable spirit, in
which one felt all the tender parts of genius, with his im-

mense, fair Russian physique, was one of the most attractive things conceivable. He had a frame which would have made it perfectly lawful, and even becoming, for him to be brutal; but there was not a grain of brutality in his composition. He had always been a passionate sportsman; to wander in the woods or the steppes, with his dog and gun, was the pleasure of his heart. Late in life he continued to shoot, and he had a friend in Cambridgeshire for the sake of whose partridges, which were famous, he used sometimes to cross the Channel. It would have been impossible to imagine a better representation of a Nimrod of the north. He was exceedingly tall, and broad and robust in proportion. His head was one of the finest, and though the line of his features was irregular, there was a great deal of beauty in his face. It was eminently of the Russian type—almost everything in it was wide. His expression had a singular sweetness, with a touch of Slav languor, and his eye, the kindest of eyes, was deep and melancholy. His hair, abundant and straight, was as white as silver, and his beard, which he wore trimmed rather short, was of the colour of his hair. In all his tall person, which was very striking wherever it appeared, there was an air of neglected strength, as if it had been a part of his modesty never to remind himself that he was strong. He used sometimes to blush like a boy of sixteen. He had very few forms and ceremonies, and almost as little manner as was possible to a man of his natural *prestance*. His noble appearance was in itself a manner; but whatever he did he did very simply, and he had not the slightest pretension to not being subject to rectification. I never saw any one receive it with less irritation. Friendly, candid, unaffectedly benignant, the impression that he produced most strongly and most generally was, I think, simply that of goodness.

When I made his acquaintance he had been living, since his removal from Baden-Baden, which took place in consequence of the Franco-Prussian war, in a large detached house on the hill of Montmartre, with his friends of many years, Madame Pauline Viardot and her husband, as his fellow-tenants. He occupied the upper floor, and I like to recall, for the sake of certain delightful talks, the aspect of his little green sitting-room, which has, in memory, the consecration of irrecoverable hours. It was almost entirely green, and the walls were not covered with paper, but draped in stuff. The *portières* were green, and there was one of those immense divans, so indispensable to Russians, which had apparently been fashioned for the great person of the master, so that smaller folk had to lie upon it rather than sit. I remember the white light of the Paris street, which came in through windows more or less blinded in their lower part, like those of a studio. It rested, during the first years that I went to see Turgénieff, upon several choice pictures of the modern French school, especially upon a very fine specimen of Théodore Rousseau, which he valued exceedingly. He had a great love of painting, and was an excellent critic of a picture. The last time I saw him—it was at his house in the country—he showed me half a dozen large copies of Italian works, made by a young Russian in whom he was interested, which he had, with characteristic kindness, taken into his own apartments in order that he might bring them to the knowledge of his friends. He thought them, as copies, remarkable; and they were so, indeed, especially when one perceived that the original work of the artist had little value. Turgénieff warmed to the work of praising them, as he was very apt to do; like all men of imagination he had frequent and zealous admirations. As a matter of course there was almost always some young Russian in whom he was interested, and refugees and pilgrims of both sexes were his natural clients. I have heard it said by persons who had known him long and well that these enthusiasms sometimes led him into error, that he was apt to *se monter la tête* on behalf of his protégés. He was prone to believe that he had discovered the coming Russian genius; he talked about his discovery for a month, and then suddenly one heard no more of it. I remember his once telling me of a young woman who had come to see him on her return from America, where she had been studying obstetrics at some medical college, and who, without means and without friends, was in want of help and of work. He accidentally learned that she had written something, and asked her to let him see it. She sent it to him, and it proved to be a tale in which certain phases of rural life were described with striking truthfulness. He perceived in the young lady a great natural talent; he sent her story off to Russia to be printed, with the conviction that it would make a great impression, and he expressed the hope of being able to introduce her to French readers. When I mentioned this to an old friend of Turgénieff he smiled, and said that we should not hear of her again, that Ivan Serguéitch had already discovered a great many surprising talents, which, as a general thing, had not borne the test. There was apparently some truth in this, and Turgénieff's liability to be deceived was too generous a weakness for me to hesitate to allude to it, even after I have insisted on the usual certainty of his taste. He was deeply interested in his young Russians; they were what interested him most in the world. They were almost always unhappy, in want and in rebellion against an order of things which he himself detested. The study of the Russian character absorbed and fascinated him, as all readers of his stories know. Rich, unformed, undeveloped, with all sorts of adumbrations, of qualities in a state of fusion, it stretched itself out as a mysterious expanse in which it was impossible as yet to perceive the relation between gifts and weaknesses. Of its weaknesses he was keenly conscious, and I once heard him express himself with an energy that did him honour and a frankness that even surprised me (considering that it was of his countrymen that he spoke), in regard to a weakness which he deemed the greatest of all—a weakness for which a man whose love of veracity was his strongest feeling would have least toleration. His young compatriots, seeking their fortune in foreign lands, touched his imagination and his pity, and it is easy to conceive that under the circumstances the impression they often made upon him may have had great intensity. The Parisian background, with its brilliant sameness, its absence of surprises (for those who have known it long), threw them into relief and made him see them as he saw the figures in his tales, in relations, in situations which brought them out. There passed before him in the course of time many wonderful Russian types. He told me once of his having been visited by a religious sect. The sect consisted of but two persons, one of whom was the object of worship and the other the worshipper. The divinity apparently was travelling about Europe in company with his prophet. They were intensely serious but it was very handy, as the term is, for each. The god had always his altar and the altar had (unlike some altars) always its god.

In his little green salon nothing was out of place; there were none of the odds and ends of the usual man of letters, which indeed Turgénieff was not; and the case was the same in his library at Bougival, of which I shall presently speak. Few books even were visible; it was as if everything had been put away. The traces of work had been carefully removed. An air of great comfort, an immeasurable divan and several valuable pictures—that was the effect of the place. I know not exactly at what hours Turgénieff did his work; I think he had no regular times and seasons, being in this respect as different as possible from Anthony Trollope, whose autobiography, with its candid revelation of intellectual economies, is so curious. It is my impression that in Paris Turgénieff wrote little; his times of production being rather those weeks of the summer that he spent at Bougival, and the period of that visit to Russia which he supposed himself to make every year. I say "supposed himself," because it was impossible to see much of him without discovering that he was a man of delays. As on the part of some other Russians whom I have known, there was something Asiatic in his faculty of procrastination. But even if one suffered from it a little one thought of it with kindness, as a part of his general mildness and want of rigidity. He went to Russia, at any rate, at intervals not infrequent, and he spoke of these visits as his best time for production. He had an estate far in the interior, and here, amid the stillness of the country and the scenes and figures which give such a charm to the *Memoirs of a Sportsman*, he drove his pen without interruption.

It is not out of place to allude to the fact that he possessed considerable fortune; this is too important in the life of a man of letters. It had been of great value to Turgénieff, and I think that much of the fine quality of his work is owing to it. He could write according to his taste and his mood; he was never pressed nor checked (putting the Russian censorship aside) by considerations foreign to his plan, and never was in danger of becoming a hack. Indeed, taking into consideration the absence of a pecuniary spur and that complicated indolence from which he was not exempt, his industry is surprising, for his tales are a long list. In Paris, at all events, he was always open to proposals for the midday breakfast. He liked to breakfast *au cabaret*, and freely consented to an appointment. It is not unkind to add that, at first, he never kept it. I may mention without reserve this idiosyncrasy of Turgénieff's, because in the first place it was so inveterate as to be very amusing—it amused not only his friends but himself; and in the second, he was as sure to come in the end as he was sure not to come in the beginning. After the appointment had been made or the invitation accepted, when the occasion was at hand, there arrived a note or a telegram in which Ivan Serguéitch excused himself, and begged that the meeting might be deferred to another date, which he usually himself proposed. For this second date still another was sometimes substituted; but if I remember no appointment that he exactly kept, I remember none that he completely missed. His friends waited for him frequently, but they never lost him. He was very fond of that wonderful Parisian *déjeûner*—fond of it I mean as a feast of reason. He was extremely temperate, and often ate no breakfast at all; but he found it a good hour for talk, and little, on general grounds, as one might be prepared to agree with him, if he was at the table one was speedily convinced. I call it wonderful, the *déjeûner* of Paris, on account of the assurance with which it plants itself in the very middle of the morning. It divides the day between rising and dinner so unequally, and opposes such barriers of repletion to any prospect of ulterior labours, that the unacclimated stranger wonders when the fertile French people do their work. Not the least wonderful part of it is that the stranger himself likes it, at last, and manages to piece together his day with the shattered fragments that survive. It was not, at any rate, when one had the good fortune to breakfast at twelve o'clock with Turgénieff that one was struck with its being an inconvenient hour. Any hour was convenient for meeting a human being who conformed so completely to one's idea of the best that human nature is capable of. There are places in Paris which I can think of only in relation to some occasion on which he was present, and when I pass them the particular things I

heard him say there come back to me. There is a café in the
Avenue de l'Opéra—a new, sumptuous establishment, with
very deep settees, on the right as you leave the Boulevard
—where I once had a talk with him, over an order singularly
moderate, which was prolonged far into the afternoon, and
in the course of which he was extraordinarily suggestive and
interesting, so that my memory now reverts affectionately to
all the circumstances. It evokes the grey damp of a Parisian
December, which made the dark interior of the café look
more and more rich and hospitable, while the light faded,
the lamps were lit, the habitués came in to drink absinthe
and play their afternoon game of dominoes, and we still lingered over our morning meal. Turgénieff talked almost exclusively about Russia, the nihilists, the remarkable figures
that came to light among them, the curious visits he received,
the dark prospects of his native land. When he was in the
vein, no man could speak more to the imagination of his
auditor. For myself, at least, at such times, there was something extraordinarily vivifying and stimulating in his talk, and
I always left him in a state of "intimate" excitement, with
a feeling that all sorts of valuable things had been suggested
to me; the condition in which a man swings his cane as he
walks, leaps lightly over gutters, and then stops, for no reason
at all, to look, with an air of being struck, into a shop window where he sees nothing. I remember another symposium,
at a restaurant on one of the corners of the little *place* in
front of the Opéra Comique, where we were four, including
Ivan Serguéitch, and the two other guests were also Russian,
one of them uniting to the charm of this nationality the
merit of a sex that makes the combination irresistible. The
establishment had been a discovery of Turgénieff's—a discovery, at least, as far as our particular needs were concerned—
and I remember that we hardly congratulated him on it. The
dinner, in a low entresol, was not what it had been intended
to be, but the talk was better even than our expectations. It
was not about nihilism but about some more agreeable features of life, and I have no recollection of Turgénieff in a
mood more spontaneous and charming. One of our friends
had, when he spoke French, a peculiar way of sounding the
word *adorable*, which was frequently on his lips, and I re-

member well his expressive prolongation of the *a* when, in speaking of the occasion afterwards, he applied this term to Ivan Serguéitch. I scarcely know, however, why I should drop into the detail of such reminiscences, and my excuse is but the desire that we all have, when a human relationship is closed, to save a little of it from the past—to make a mark which may stand for some of the happy moments of it.

Nothing that Turgénieff had to say could be more interesting than his talk about his own work, his manner of writing. What I have heard him tell of these things was worthy of the beautiful results he produced; of the deep purpose, pervading them all, to show us life itself. The germ of a story, with him, was never an affair of plot—that was the last thing he thought of: it was the representation of certain persons. The first form in which a tale appeared to him was as the figure of an individual, or a combination of individuals, whom he wished to see in action, being sure that such people must do something very special and interesting. They stood before him definite, vivid, and he wished to know, and to show, as much as possible of their nature. The first thing was to make clear to himself what he did know, to begin with; and to this end, he wrote out a sort of biography of each of his characters, and everything that they had done and that had happened to them up to the opening of the story. He had their *dossier*, as the French say, and as the police has of that of every conspicuous criminal. With this material in his hand he was able to proceed; the story all lay in the question, What shall I make them do? He always made them do things that showed them completely; but, as he said, the defect of his manner and the reproach that was made him was his want of "architecture"—in other words, of composition. The great thing, of course, is to have architecture as well as precious material, as Walter Scott had them, as Balzac had them. If one reads Turgénieff's stories with the knowledge that they were composed—or rather that they came into being—in this way, one can trace the process in every line. Story, in the conventional sense of the word—a fable constructed, like Wordsworth's phantom, "to startle and waylay"—there is as little as possible. The thing consists of the motions of a group of selected creatures, which are not

the result of a preconceived action, but a consequence of the
qualities of the actors. Works of art are produced from every
possible point of view, and stories, and very good ones, will
continue to be written in which the evolution is that of a
dance—a series of steps the more complicated and lively the
better, of course, determined from without and forming a
figure. This figure will always, probably, find favour with
many readers, because it reminds them enough, without reminding them too much, of life. On this opposition many
young talents in France are ready to rend each other, for
there is a numerous school on either side. We have not yet
in England and America arrived at the point of treating such
questions with passion, for we have not yet arrived at the
point of feeling them intensely, or indeed, for that matter, of
understanding them very well. It is not open to us as yet to
discuss whether a novel had better be an excision from life
or a structure built up of picture-cards, for we have not made
up our mind as to whether life in general may be described.
There is evidence of a good deal of shyness on this point—
a tendency rather to put up fences than to jump over them.
Among us, therefore, even a certain ridicule attaches to the
consideration of such alternatives. But individuals may feel
their way, and perhaps even pass unchallenged, if they remark that for them the manner in which Turgénieff worked
will always seem the most fruitful. It has the immense recommendation that in relation to any human occurrence it begins, as it were, further back. It lies in its power to tell us
the most about men and women. Of course it will but slen-
derly satisfy those numerous readers among whom the answer to this would be, "Hang it, we don't care a straw about
men and women: we want a good story!"

And yet, after all, *Elena* is a good story, and *Lisa* and
Virgin Soil are good stories. Reading over lately several of
Turgénieff's novels and tales, I was struck afresh with their
combination of beauty and reality. One must never forget,
in speaking of him, that he was both an observer and a poet.
The poetic element was constant, and it had great strangeness and power. It inspired most of the short things that he
wrote during the last few years of his life, since the publication of *Virgin Soil*, things that are in the highest degree fanci-

ful and exotic. It pervades the frequent little reveries, visions, epigrams of the *Senilia*. It was no part of my intention, here, to criticise his writings, having said my say about them, so far as possible, some years ago. But I may mention that in re-reading them I find in them all that I formerly found of two other elements—their richness and their sadness. They give one the impression of life itself, and not of an arrangement, a *réchauffé* of life. I remember Turgénieff's once saying in regard to Homais, the little Norman country apothecary, with his pedantry of "enlightened opinions," in *Madame Bovary*, that the great strength of such a portrait consisted in its being at once an individual, of the most concrete sort, and a type. This is the great strength of his own representations of character; they are so strangely, fascinatingly particular, and yet they are so recognisably general. Such a remark as that about Homais makes me wonder why it was that Turgénieff should have rated Dickens so high, the weakness of Dickens being in regard to just that point. If Dickens fail to live long, it will be because his figures are particular without being general; because they are individuals without being types; because we do not feel their continuity with the rest of humanity—see the matching of the pattern with the piece out of which all the creations of the novelist and the dramatist are cut. I often meant, but accidentally neglected, to put Turgénieff on the subject of Dickens again, and ask him to explain his opinion. I suspect that his opinion was in a large measure merely that Dickens diverted him, as well he might. That complexity of the pattern was in itself fascinating. I have mentioned Flaubert, and I will return to him simply to say that there was something very touching in the nature of the friendship that united these two men. It is much to the honour of Flaubert, to my sense, that he appreciated Ivan Turgénieff. There was a partial similarity between them. Both were large, massive men, though the Russian reached to a greater height than the Norman; both were completely honest and sincere, and both had the pessimistic element in their composition. Each had a tender regard for the other, and I think that I am neither incorrect nor indiscreet in saying that on Turgénieff's part this regard had in it a strain of compassion. There was something in Gustave

Flaubert that appealed to such a feeling. He had failed, on the whole, more than he had succeeded, and the great machinery of erudition,—the great polishing process,—which he brought to bear upon his productions, was not accompanied with proportionate results. He had talent without having cleverness, and imagination without having fancy. His effort was heroic, but except in the case of *Madame Bovary*, a masterpiece, he imparted something to his works (it was as if he had covered them with metallic plates) which made them sink rather than sail. He had a passion for perfection of form and for a certain splendid suggestiveness of style. He wished to produce perfect phrases, perfectly interrelated, and as closely woven together as a suit of chain-mail. He looked at life altogether as an artist, and took his work with a seriousness that never belied itself. To write an admirable page— and his idea of what constituted an admirable page was transcendent—seemed to him something to live for. He tried it again and again, and he came very near it; more than once he touched it, for *Madame Bovary* surely will live. But there was something ungenerous in his genius. He was cold, and he would have given everything he had to be able to glow. There is nothing in his novels like the passion of Elena for Inssaroff, like the purity of Lisa, like the anguish of the parents of Bazaroff, like the hidden wound of Tatiana; and yet Flaubert yearned, with all the accumulations of his vocabulary, to touch the chord of pathos. There were some parts of his mind that did not "give," that did not render a sound. He had had too much of some sorts of experience and not enough of others. And yet this failure of an organ, as I may call it, inspired those who knew him with a kindness. If Flaubert was powerful and limited, there is something human, after all, and even rather august in a strong man who has not been able completely to express himself.

After the first year of my acquaintance with Turgénieff I saw him much less often. I was seldom in Paris, and sometimes when I was there he was absent. But I neglected no opportunity of seeing him, and fortune frequently assisted me. He came two or three times to London, for visits provokingly brief. He went to shoot in Cambridgeshire, and he passed through town in arriving and departing. He liked the

English, but I am not sure that he liked London, where he had passed a lugubrious winter in 1870–71. I remember some of his impressions of that period, especially a visit that he had paid to a "bishopess" surrounded by her daughters, and a description of the cookery at the lodgings which he occupied. After 1876 I frequently saw him as an invalid. He was tormented by gout, and sometimes terribly besieged; but his account of what he suffered was as charming—I can apply no other word to it—as his description of everything else. He had so the habit of observation, that he perceived in excruciating sensations all sorts of curious images and analogies, and analysed them to an extraordinary fineness. Several times I found him at Bougival, above the Seine, in a very spacious and handsome chalet—a little unsunned, it is true—which he had built alongside of the villa occupied by the family to which, for years, his life had been devoted. The place is delightful; the two houses are midway up a long slope, which descends, with the softest inclination, to the river, and behind them the hill rises to a wooded crest. On the left, in the distance, high up and above an horizon of woods, stretches the romantic aqueduct of Marly. It is a very pretty domain. The last time I saw him, in November 1882, it was at Bougival. He had been very ill, with strange, intolerable symptoms, but he was better, and he had good hopes. They were not justified by the event. He got worse again, and the months that followed were cruel. His beautiful serene mind should not have been darkened and made acquainted with violence; it should have been able to the last to take part, as it had always done, in the decrees and mysteries of fate. At the moment I saw him, however, he was, as they say in London, in very good form, and my last impression of him was almost bright. He was to drive into Paris, not being able to bear the railway, and he gave me a seat in the carriage. For an hour and a half he constantly talked, and never better. When we got into the city I alighted on the boulevard extérieur, as we were to go in different directions. I bade him good-bye at the carriage window, and never saw him again. There was a kind of fair going on, near by, in the chill November air, beneath the denuded little trees of the Boulevard, and a Punch and Judy show, from which nasal sounds proceeded.

I almost regret having accidentally to mix up so much of Paris with this perhaps too complacent enumeration of occasions, for the effect of it may be to suggest that Ivan Turgénieff had been Gallicised. But this was not the case; the French capital was an accident for him, not a necessity. It touched him at many points, but it let him alone at many others, and he had, with that great tradition of ventilation of the Russian mind, windows open into distances which stretched far beyond the *banlieue*. I have spoken of him from the limited point of view of my own acquaintance with him, and unfortunately left myself little space to allude to a matter which filled his existence a good deal more than the consideration of how a story should be written—his hopes and fears on behalf of his native land. He wrote fictions and dramas, but the great drama of his life was the struggle for a better state of things in Russia. In this drama he played a distinguished part, and the splendid obsequies that, simple and modest as he was, have unfolded themselves over his grave, sufficiently attest the recognition of it by his countrymen. His funeral, restricted and officialised, was none the less a magnificent "manifestation." I have read the accounts of it, however, with a kind of chill, a feeling in which assent to the honours paid him bore less part than it ought. All this pomp and ceremony seemed to lift him out of the range of familiar recollection, of valued reciprocity, into the majestic position of a national glory. And yet it is in the presence of this obstacle to social contact that those who knew and loved him must address their farewell to him now. After all, it is difficult to see how the obstacle can be removed. He was the most generous, the most tender, the most delightful, of men; his large nature overflowed with the love of justice: but he also was of the stuff of which glories are made.

Turgenev TO AND OF Flaubert:	*Cheer up, old fellow! After all, you are Flaubert!*

HENRY JAMES AND THE RUSSIAN
NOVELISTS

James usually spoke of Tolstoy in terms of guarded respect. His attitude was like that of Delacroix, who said to his students as they passed Ingres' Odalisque in the Louvre: *Messieurs, le châpeau dans la main, mais les yeux fixés à terre*. Neither Tolstoy nor Dostoyevsky was very much to his taste, and he regarded their effect on other writers as little short of disastrous. Turgenev, on the other hand, he loved and admired, both as a friend and a writer, but then Turgenev was a sort of Russian Henry James, an expatriate who cultivated the French novelists and was regarded as an equal by Flaubert himself. His concern, like James's, was with the fine details of craftsmanship; he was, in the latter's phrase, the novelist's novelist, "an artistic influence extraordinarily valuable and ineradicably established." Too many of Turgenev's rivals, James complained, "appear to hold us in comparison by violent means, and introduce us in comparison to vulgar things."

Did he mean to include Tolstoy among these rivals? It seems likely. For observe how he contrasts him with Turgenev:

The perusal of Tolstoy—a wonderful mass of life—is an immense event, a kind of splendid accident, for each of us: his name represents nevertheless no such eternal spell of method, no such quiet irresistibility of presentation, as shines, close to us and lighting our possible steps, in that of his precursor. Tolstoy is a reflector as vast as a natural lake; a monster harnessed to his great subject—all human life!—as an elephant might be harnessed, for purposes of traction, not to a carriage, but to a coach house. His own case is prodigious, but his example for others dire: disciples not elephantine he can only mislead and betray.

The compliment, if one was intended, fades under the words "monster" and "elephant." Later James became more candid. When Hugh Walpole wrote to ask him if he did not feel that Dostoyevsky's "mad jumble that flings things down in a heap" was nearer truth than the "picking and composing" of Stevenson, James seized the occasion to state his credo in organ tones:

> Form alone *takes*, and holds and preserves, substance —saves it from the welter of helpless verbiage that we swim in as in a sea of tasteless tepid pudding, and that makes one ashamed of an art capable of such degradations. Tolstoy and Dostoyevsky are fluid pudding, though not tasteless, because the amount of their own minds and souls in solution in the broth gives it savour and flavour, thanks to the strong, rank quality of their genius and their experience. But there are all sorts of things to be said of them, and in particular that we see how great a vice is their lack of composition, their defiance of economy and architecture, directly they are emulated and imitated; *then*, as subjects of emulation, models, they quite give themselves away.

Leon Edel maintains that the now famous term "fluid pudding" has been misunderstood and that James meant so to characterize the novels of the two Russian authors only insofar as they are used as models. But I question this. A fluid pudding is a fluid pudding, whether one eats it or paints it. James evidently considered the process of imitation as a peculiarly revealing one, for it is precisely here, in his opinion, that Tolstoy and Dostoyevsky "quite give themselves away" i.e., expose their essential fluidity. But surely these imitators, whoever they were, failed because they saw only formlessness where there was form, just as so many Jamesian imitators have seen only form where there was substance. If we are to rate novelists by the efforts of those who copy them, James will fare quite as badly as Tolstoy or Dostoyevsky.

A year later James wrote another letter to Walpole in

which he dropped the last pretense of admiration for Tolstoy. If his term "fluid pudding" has been misunderstood, surely there is no misunderstanding the following:

> I have been reading over Tolstoy's interminable *Peace and War*, and am struck with the fact that I now protest as much as I admire. He doesn't *do* to read over, and that exactly is the answer to those who idiotically proclaim the impunity of such formless shape, such flopping looseness and such a denial of composition, selection and style. He has a mighty fund of life, but the *waste*, and the ugliness and vice of waste, the vice of a not finer *doing* are sickening. For me he makes "composition" throne, by contrast, in effulgent lustre!

It was unfortunate that Walpole should have been the person to invite James to consider the Russians. For he did it in such a way as to raise the master's ire against a straw man; he must have known perfectly well that to ask a lover of Stevenson to admire a "mad jumble" was like asking the Pope to admire Luther. He wanted a strong reaction, and he got it. James's explosion has provided a perfect text for extremists to fight over through the years. On one side we can line up all who excuse their clumsy craftsmanship by greatness of purpose, their fudged details by the scope of their panorama, those who profess to deal in raw chunks of life salted with "compassion." On the other we can line up those attenuated scribblers who seek with polished phrases to conceal that they have nothing to write about. It is all great fun, and everybody gets very heated, but we must remember that it is only a parlor game. It has nothing to do with literature, and it has nothing to do with art.

For James's impatience with the formlessness that he unfairly attributed to the Russian novelists leads him to make a false distinction between a work of art and a "mass of life." Tolstoy, according to him, is not an artist but a "reflector of life." Tolstoy and Dostoyevsky fail in composition, but are saved by the "strong, rank quality of their genius and their experience." Now this, I submit, is meaningless. Tolstoy could only reflect life through his art. If life is reflected, it is because art succeeds, and if art succeeds, it is because the

form is right. Life is only a subject; it cannot rub off onto
a book any more than a bowl of fruit can rub off onto a
canvas. There is only one process for James as for Tolstoy,
and that process is art. There they fail or there they succeed.
"Life" will not help either in the least bit.

Because *War and Peace* is a long book and has many characters, it has been said to "sprawl." Yet actually it is unified
by the Napoleonic invasion of Russia which directly affects
the outward and inner life of every character. It is true that
Tolstoy continually shifts the point of view from character
to character, but how else could he succeed in re-creating a
war? James can confine *The Ambassadors* to Strether's point
of view because Strether's point of view is the subject of the
novel, but if he had set himself Tolstoy's job, he would have
needed not one, but a hundred pairs of eyes. In any event, I
agree with E. M. Forster that the question of the point of
view is one more interesting to writers than readers. It was
vital to the construction of James's novels, but it is not vital
to that of all others.

To me there is "flopping looseness" in *War and Peace* only
in Tolstoy's essays on military and historical theory. I find
these as intrusive and boring as commercials in a television
play, but they are easily skipped, so long as one is careful not
to skip with them the chapters dealing with the personalities
of the war leaders and the battle scenes, which are of the
essence of Tolstoy's scheme. The pictures of Kutuzov at the
front and of Napoleon watching the drowning of the over-
eager cavalry, of the battlefield of Borodino and of the burning of Moscow, give us the historical perspective against
which the individuals must be seen. The form of the novel
is the same that was used by Margaret Mitchell in *Gone With
the Wind*: the principal character, Armageddon, unites the
other characters and changes their lives. But form can be
obvious and still be form. And is there a better fictional
device for a war?

It is fashionable to describe *War and Peace* as a great,
crowded canvas, and to think of Tolstoy as daubing at it with
broad strokes. But the more I look at it, the more I am astonished (outside of the essay sections) at the amount of meticu-
lous craftsmanship involved. As Max Reinhardt was able to

create the illusion of a vast army with a few soldiers, so does Tolstoy create a mighty conflict with a whiff of smoke, a bit of snow and a handful of aristocrats from Russian court society. Think of our own war novelists and how carefully they delineate the assorted backgrounds of the soldiers of a squadron. Think of those flashbacks that show the lieutenant at Groton and the Negro private in an overcrowded Southern school. Imagine Norman Mailer limited in *The Naked and the Dead* to the Lowells and Cabots of Boston! Yet Tolstoy's characters are not only from the same social milieu; they are almost all related to each other. I suppose it is true that the great landlords and serf owners of an obsolute monarchy were more representative of their nation than capitalists are of a democracy, but even so, Tolstoy is telling the story of Russia's agony from the viewpoint of a very tiny class of sufferers. What he understands is that if a human being is described completely, his class makes little difference. He becomes a human being on the printed page, and other humans, of whatever class, can recognize themselves in his portrait. The lesson of Tolstoy is precisely how little of life, not how much, the artist needs.

The only moral classifications into which Tolstoy divides his characters are those of serious and nonserious. If one is trivial-minded about the great questions of life, if one is bent on playing games, like Pierre's first wife, one is condemned. But as long as one cares about one's role in the universe, then, regardless of one's ineffectiveness, all is forgiven. Pierre, for example, makes a mess of everything that he touches, his estates, his marriage, even his social career. When war comes, he wanders, a useless civilian, about the battlefield at Borodino like a sleepwalker, concerned only with his own doubts about the purpose of life. He is arrested by the French in Moscow and suffers great hardships, but he still accomplishes nothing. Nobody but himself is helped by his agony. Prince André, on the other hand, looks after his serfs conscientiously, manages his estates economically and is a brilliant officer in the war. Yet there is no feeling in the novel that André is a "better" man than Pierre. They are both serious men and, as such, appreciate and understand each other. That one is effectively and the other ineffectively good is a mere detail. What concern has God with such details?

In *Anna Karenina* I find only Levin's agricultural theories "floppingly loose." They are as irrelevant to the story as the historical asides in *War and Peace*, and much more difficult to skip, being more deeply imbedded in the plot. But a graver fault in the structure of the novel is Tolstoy's failure to prepare us for Anna's adultery. We meet her first as a charming and deeply understanding sister-in-law who, by consummate tact, saves her brother's crumbling marriage, but we pass with a dizzy speed over the year which elapses between her meeting Vronsky and her succumbing to him. We grasp Anna's character at last—or a good deal of it—but the hole in this part of the book is never quite filled. We never know why such a woman should have married a man like her husband or why, having done so, she should have been unfaithful to him. But aside from being occasionally bored by Levin and occasionally confused by the early Anna, I find no other looseness in the novel. It is like a well-organized English novel of its period: it has two plots, constantly interwoven and always in dramatic contrast, and in the end married love brings happiness and adultery despair. Even James could not have said that it contained the vice of waste.

Tolstoy liked to accomplish a great many obvious as well as a great many subtle things, and he was not afraid of old and well-worn formulas. What he needed for war was a burning capital and what he needed for a drama of love was a married and an unmarried couple. He never hesitated to hammer in his contrasts with heavy strokes. On the side of Kitty and Levin and lawful love are the rolling acres of a well-managed farm, and Moscow, no longer the capital, but still the center of the oldest, truest Russian values. On the side of Anna and Vronsky and illicit passion are the superficial court society of St. Petersburg and a motley pile of borrowed notions from Paris and London. The great columns of the two plots stand up before us, massive, conventional, imposing and trite, but on closer examination we find that the bas-reliefs that gird them have been carved with the greatest delicacy and skill. Whatever assumptions we make as we go along, we will find that we must qualify, until we begin to wonder if the two columns are twins or opposites.

Levin and Kitty, for example, may be depicted as the young couple on whose love we may properly smile, but in contrast to Anna and Vronsky they are frequently ridiculous. Levin is absurdly and irrationally jealous, and his nervousness on the birth of his child seems almost a caricature of the traditionally nervous father. He is violent, rude and ill-tempered, and Kitty is excitable and possessive. It is true that Tolstoy obviously likes Levin and considers his faults as rather lovably Russian, but he is careful at the same time to show us that the other characters consider him a bull in a china shop. Vronsky, on the other hand, leads a St. Petersburg society life of which his creator disapproves to such an extent that it has become traditional to regard him as a shallow gadabout who is unworthy of the passion that he has inspired in Anna. But consider him more closely. Vronsky may be irresponsible in seducing Anna, but after that he behaves with the greatest possible style. He is never unfaithful to her, never deserts her, always tries to spare her pain, does everything he can to legalize their relationship and even attempts suicide when none of his plans for her happiness work out. There are moments in the book when he and Anna seem a couple unjustly condemned by a censorious and hypocritical society, while Kitty and Levin seem like spoiled youngsters who cannot find happiness in a veritable flood of good fortune.

For Tolstoy is not really condemning Anna, any more than he is praising Kitty. Anna is, indeed, the more high-minded of the two. He is rather proving that for women of their background and position (Levin's brother's mistress is quite happy as such), cohabitation outside of marriage is impossible. Kitty and Anna are both intensely female in their possessiveness. Levin feels, when Kitty wishes to accompany him to his brother's deathbed, that it is intolerable to be so shackled. Yet she comes and is a great help. Within the framework of a happy marriage such matters can always be adjusted. Kitty becomes absorbed in her babies, and Levin can then attend all the agricultural conventions that he wants. But no such adjustment is possible for Anna. She destroys her life with Vronsky by her mad jealousy and her need to be with him every moment. Anna turns into a kind of monster, making scenes over everything, crazed by the thought that her lover should have any life or interest outside the dull and lonely house where she rants at him. Vronsky is a model of patience and restraint, but he is helpless to arrest her insane course of self-destruction. Anna has been idle and restless in St. Petersburg society, but she is utterly shattered when its doors are closed to her but not to him. It is ridiculous; it is pathetic; it is nineteenth century but it is very feminine. Kitty would have been just as bad.

James in the letters to Walpole deals specifically with Tolstoy, but Dostoyevsky is included at least by implication. Certainly James does nothing to rebut Walpole's assertion that the author of Crime and Punishment created his effects by "flinging things down in heaps." It is illuminating and also rather pathetic to contrast Walpole's fanciful picture with the actual one of Dostoyevsky, impoverished and epileptic, at work in Dresden on the manuscript of The Idiot. His notebooks show eight different proposed treatments of the central theme, and even when he had settled on the outline, the execution was agonizingly slow. He wrote to the poet Maykov:

All this time I literally worked day and night in spite of my fits. But, alas, I notice with despair that for some reason I am not able to work as quickly as I did a short while ago. I crawl like a crab, and then I begin to count the sheets—three and a half or four in a whole month. This is terrible, and I don't know what will happen to me.

Surely the confusion that Walpole finds on the surface of the novels results from the magnitude of the author's task rather than from a failure in artistry. For, as is now commonly recognized, Dostoyevsky wanted to show man not only in relation to his fellow creatures but in his relation to God. Most of nineteenth century fiction was concerned with character; Dostoyevsky was concerned with soul. His subject required a new dimension and an immense amount of planning. It seems to me that even a cursory review of his books shows a love of craftsmanship as deep as that of James himself.

Dostoyevsky uses three principal techniques in the construction of his novels. The first is the dialogue, or general conversation, usually at a social gathering, where the characters argue with each other about themselves, social conditions in Russia, liberalism and religion. The talks are marked by irrelevancies, low comedy, testiness, self-pity and sudden violent fits of temper. Just when the action seems about to take a step forward, someone inevitably enters or changes the subject to arrest it, so that these sections of the novels have some of the static, frustrating quality of Ivy Compton-Burnett's dialogues. But the comedy, or at times farce, is always hilarious; the lies and antics of General Ivolgin and of old Karamazov have a Falstaffian richness. Farce and tragedy stand up boldly side by side in Dostoyevsky; together they make up the dreamlike quality of a mortal existence where we are separated from God.

The author, however, realizes that he cannot tell the whole story by such discussions, and at regular intervals he interrupts, with a firm editorial hand, to move his plot forward or to fill in the biographies of his characters. In these parts he is smooth, sharply analytical and brilliant. The passages in *The Idiot* that describe Madame Yepanchin's concern about her unmarried daughters are as vivid and clever as any of their counterparts in Jane Austen. Sometimes Dostoyevsky uses his editorial hand to tell a seemingly irrelevant story or legend like the famous "Grand Inquisitor" in *The Brothers Karamazov*. Certainly it absorbs us to a point where we forget the very novel of which it is a part. But as soon as we return to Ivan who has related it, we realize that it is the perfect parable of his own agnosticism, and the parable and Ivan are henceforth inseparable in our minds.

Finally, Dostoyevsky uses the method of dramatic, violent scenes that illuminate the dusky landscape with a sudden shocking light. He may use them as preludes, to foreshadow what is going to happen, or as crises, to explain what already has. In *The Brothers Karamazov* the great scene where the father and sons go to the monastery contains in it the germs of everything that happens afterward, whereas the scene in *The Idiot* where Nastasya at her birthday party, elopes with Rogozhin, gives us the final key to a character who has hitherto baffled us. It is only when we read such a scene that we realize to the full how necessary the previous chapters have been.

What in all of this becomes of James's "point of view"? It is lost, of course. But it was vital for Dostoyevsky, in his psychic probing, to be able to move in and out of the mind of each of his characters, to substitute himself as narrator or as observer, or even to have the characters create other observers by telling stories. In the massive job that he set for himself he needed every trick in the novelist's bag, and he used them all. To have limited him to one would have been like limiting a playwright to the classic unities. Racine was content to contain his action to a single day and place, but what would have become of Shakespeare? I cannot imagine two novels more different than *The Brothers Karamazov* and *The Ambassadors*, nor can I imagine two novels more admirable. It is idle to choose between them, for one always has both.

Tolstoy ON Gogol:	*. . . Take Gogol's* Dead Souls. *What is it? Neither a novel nor a story. It is something entirely original.*
George Moore ON Dickens:	*If Dickens had not come into our literature we should lose more than a certain number of books, something of ourselves, for Dickens has become part of our perceptions, and, as the world exists in our perceptions, he has enlarged the world for us.*
Turgenev to Flaubert ON Tolstoy and Flaubert:	*I consider* [Tolstoy] *the foremost living writer. You know who, in my opinion, could contest his place.*

Flaubert
ON
Zola:

In my opinion Nana contains wonderful things. . . . It is a colossus with dirty feet, but it is a colossus.

Flaubert
ON
Turgenev:

I dined with Turgenev. That man's imagery is so powerful, even in conversation, that he showed me G. Sand leaning on her elbow on the balcony of Madame Viardot's château.

D. H. Lawrence
ON
Flaubert:

The trouble with realism . . . is that the writer, when he is a truly exceptional man like Flaubert . . . tries to read his own sense of tragedy into people much smaller than himself. I think it is a final criticism against Madame Bovary that people such as Emma Bovary and her husband Charles simply are too insignificant to carry the full weight of Gustave Flaubert's sense of tragedy. Emma and Charles Bovary are a couple of little people. Gustave Flaubert is not a little person. But, because he is a realist and does not believe in "heroes," Flaubert insists on pouring his own deep and bitter tragic consciousness into the little skins of the country doctor and his uneasy wife. The result is a discrepancy. Madame Bovary is a great book and a very wonderful picture of life. But we cannot help resenting the fact that the great tragic soul of Gustave Flaubert is, so to speak, given only the rather commonplace bodies of Emma and Charles Bovary.

Mr. Scott Moncrieff's monumental translation of Proust's *A la Recherche du Temps perdu* is both sensitive and accurate; it has been unreservedly praised by the best judges, and if I do not altogether concur it is because I was hoping to find Proust easier in English than in French, and do not. All the difficulties of the original are here faithfully reproduced. A sentence begins quite simply, then it undulates and expands, parentheses intervene like quick-set hedges, the flowers of comparison bloom, and three fields off, like a wounded partridge, crouches the principal verb, making one wonder as one picks it up, poor little thing, whether after all it was worth such a tramp, so many guns, and such expensive dogs, and what, after all, is its relation to the main subject, potted so gaily half a page back, and proving finally to have been in the accusative case. These, however, are the disciplines of Proust. No earnest sportsman would forgo them. And perhaps Mr. Scott Moncrieff is right in insisting that the English audience shall also participate, and shall train, through the ardours of each single sentence, for the mastery of the work as a whole.

The work as a whole! Ten times as long as an ordinary novel! And as baffling as life itself—life when apprehended by the modern cultivated man. "Life" and "Proust" are not identical, it is true; as we shall see, there are notable differences between them, all in life's favour. But the main features correspond, and it is possible to say that the work, more than any other, expresses the spirit of our age. As a contemporary document, it is invaluable. Just as the historian of the early Roman Empire turns to Virgil and finds in his sensitive verse not the exploits of Aeneas but the semi-content and the half-expressed regrets of a generation that had escaped the republican storms and abandoned the risks of liberty: just as the historian of the late Middle Ages turns to Dante and finds there described not a personal fantasy but the last and the greatest of the crusades that were supposed to end in heaven; so, reading Proust, the historian of the early twentieth century will see not the dallyings of the insignificant hero, not the local snobberies of the Faubourg Saint-Germain, but— you and me! He will say, "This work, whatever its qualities as art, is an epic, for it expresses the spirit of its age." And he will add (perhaps rather to our surprise if we still take notice of the remarks of wise men): "It was pre-eminently an age of adventure."

There is, of course, nothing of the swashbuckler about Proust, me, or you. There is no question of adventure of that sort; the laurels of the House of Guermantes have faded long before the action starts; the martial ardours of Saint Loup are slightly *démodé* and absurd, like the caperings of a heraldic lion; there is no true summons to battle when the bugles of Doncières blow and its fortifications take shape in the mists. And when the Great War does come it is a monster, indecent and imbecile, shaggy with dispatches, in whose fœtid darkness M. de Charlus waddles about seeking pleasure and Madame Verdurin personates Joan of Arc. Of adventure in the chivalrous or romantic sense there is nothing, nothing. But the characters want to live, the author wants to write about them, and when we ask why, in a world so obviously unsatisfactory, we get an answer which will be echoed in our own private diary, namely, "We want to know what will happen to-morrow." To-morrow may not be better than to-day, and may well be worse, but it has one unique attraction: it has not yet come. Proust, though introspective, and unhappy, was full of vitality—he could not have written a million words if he was not—he was inquisitive about to-morrow, he and his characters cling to existence though logic indicates suicide, and though disease drags them down still keep one eye open, half an eye, and scan the bitter unremunerative levels of the sea. *A la Recherche du Temps perdu* is an epic of curiosity and of despair. It is an adventure in the modern mode where the nerves and brain as well as the blood take part, and the whole man moves forward to encounter he does not know what; certainly not to any goal.

His despair is fundamental. It is not a theory in him, but an assumption, so that the wreckage of his creation evolves as naturally as the music of the spheres. Consider his insistence on illness. Disease and death await every individual, but it is only when we are ill ourselves, or are nursing a friend or passing through a hospital ward that we realize this vividly. To Proust it was always vivid, at garden parties and dinners the germs continue to work and disintegrate the bodies of the guests, Swann trails about with dotlets of prussian blue on his face, a cuirass of diamonds heaves above Princesse d'Orvillers's cancer, the grandmother poses coquettishly for her photograph after a stroke. The cumulative effect (and this is an important point) is *not* macabre. He was too great an artist to indulge in the facile jiggle of a Dance of Death. They are living beings, not masked skeletons or physiological transparencies who climb the height of La Raspelière or talk against the music of Vinteuil. But they are doomed more obviously than ourselves to decay. Avoiding tragic horror, which perhaps he mistrusted, and pity, which he could seldom supply, he has achieved a new view of the impermanence of the human race, and it is instructive to compare him here for a moment with Tolstoy.

The epilogue at the close of *War and Peace* is disheartening enough; it is sad to see what time has done to Nicolay and Natasha. But there the rhythmic rise, fall, rise, of the generations offers an alternative vision, whereas Proust, at the close of *Le Temps retrouvé*, is tethered to his selected personages, and cannot supply their wastage by new births. He introduces a new generation it is true; Madame de Saint-Euverte is a girl instead of the anxious harridan whom we have hitherto connected with the title. But he only introduces it to slap the old in the face. The upwelling of fresh lives did not interest him, and as to babies, they were quite outside his imaginative scope. His vision of humanity is (in this sense) limited, and perhaps he was assisted in it by his unusual conception of time. Tolstoy conceived of time as something regular, against which a chronicle could be stretched; to Proust it is almost as intermittent as memory and affection, and it is easier in such a cosmogony to picture the human race as always decaying and never being renovated. But his actual belief in decay—that lies deeper than any fancy or theory, that rests direct upon his equipment of despair.

Despair underlies all his view of personal relationships. How he emphasizes the element of gratuitous cruelty that exists in us, shows Françoise, apparently such a dear old family servant, torturing the scullery-maid with the unexpected weapon of asparagus, and inserts at the very end of the epic, like a full-stop of blood, the virtual murder of Berma! And—apart from cruelty—what repulsive defects he discovers in us! The worst of them is our inability to love or be loved. Let A and B be two people (for one can put his view in algebraic form) who do not love one another, but have some slight social relationship. They get on quite well. Then let A fall in love with B. Instantly their understanding vanishes, because A's affection has transformed B into a non-existing quantity called X. B has never heard of X, cannot behave like X, is accused of inconsistency and duplicity, retorts with similar charges, and it ends in a quarrel. And if love happens to be mutual the situation is even worse, for now not one mind but two are engaged on the falsification, and while A transforms B into X, B transforms A into Y. The charges of cruelty and deceit are now doubled, nay, quadrupled, for in their mutual excitement the lovers, like two flawed mirrors, reflect and distort each other's misunderstandings into infinity. Mutual love, fortunately for the human race, is uncommon, but when it comes such tortures arise that love unrequited seems like heaven.

Thus Proust's general theory of human intercourse is that the fonder we are of people the less we understand them— the theory of the complete pessimist. Dante took a different view. And it is worth while stopping a moment in this maelstrom of the modern and, looking back six hundred years, reminding ourselves what that other view of love was, and why Dante took it. Dante believed that the fonder we are of people the better we understand them—the theory of the complete optimist. To him, knowledge was love, love knowledge, and Beatrice not Beatrice until he could meet her in heaven. On earth, an imperfect place, he, too, had made the mistake

of turning her into X and of expecting a response from he
that she could no more supply than Odette could supply it t
Swann. But in the empyrean these illusions fade, the fact o
love is disengaged from the accidents of loving, and by th
time the triple rainbow is reached the mind and the hear
are completely reconciled and begin their real existence. His
view is the complete antithesis of Proust's, not because of a
different temperament, but because he lived in the age o
Faith.

To myself, a child of unbelief, Proust seems more likely to
be right, yet does he make enough allowance for a certain
good sense that persists in the human organism even when it
is heated by passion? Does he not lay too much stress on
jealousy? He regards it as the very food of love. When the
hero is tired of Albertine and about to leave her, the suspicion that she loves another renders her suddenly desirable,
there is nothing he will not do to own her, no lengths of
tyranny, self-abnegation, or ridiculousness, and the same idea
runs through the other two big affairs in the book, and makes
his world more uncomfortable than our own. We, too, are
jealous, but not all of us, all the time, partly because we have
our livings to get, whereas Proust's people taste the sweets
and attendant bitternesses of leisure. He and "life" are not
identical here, life being the more amiable of the two, and
future historians will find that his epic of curiosity and despair almost sums up you and me, but not quite.

A word in conclusion on his curiosity. It was indefatigable.
Never looking upward, and seldom down, it advances like
some rare insect across the floors of France, waving its antennæ
and exploring both the realm of social conduct and the realm
of art. He is not sure which realm is the more tolerable, he
varies, as every sensitive creature must. But on the whole he
votes for art. Bergotte, Elstir, Vinteuil, Berma, even the dilet-
tante Swann, are superior to the smart hostesses, the politicians, the lift-boys, the lovers; they, too, will die, their work
will be misunderstood, . . . but on the whole . . . one cannot put it more strongly than that: on the whole art is best,
and at the close we leave the hero starting out to be an author,
rummaging in his past, disinterring forgotten facts, facts
which exist again for an instant before they crumble and are

lost for ever. That instant is the artist's instant; he must simultaneously recollect and create, and Mr. Clive Bell, in an interesting essay, gives us an account of Proust's method here, and of the memory-snatching habits that have produced a masterpiece. His book is the product of a double curiosity. The initial curiosity was social; he went to all those awful parties and had those barren relationships and expensive illnesses, and knew in his own person what it is to be a snob, a jealous lover, an orphan, and an invalid with a red nose. And then came the second curiosity, the artistic. He recollected the parties, and robbed them of their stings; they hurt him no longer, and were for the first time useful. Even love, that most distressing of all illusions, can be useful, and A and B, subjected to analysis, can be seen functioning like bacteria in a test-tube, innocuous at last, and suitable as characters for a book. The curiosity of Proust was not quite the same as yours and mine, but then he was not as nice as you and me and he was also infinitely more sensitive and intelligent. His curiosity belongs to our age; we can say that of it, just as his despair is akin to ours, although we sometimes hope. Almost, though not entirely, does he represent us; to the historian the similarity will be sufficient, and the epic quality of the work will be acknowledged.

GEORGE MEREDITH

Twenty years ago[1] the reputation of George Meredith was at its height. His novels had won their way to celebrity through all sorts of difficulties, and their fame was all the brighter and the more singular for what it had subdued. Then, too, it was generally discovered that the maker of these splendid books was himself a splendid old man. Visitors who went down to Box Hill reported that they were thrilled as they walked up the drive of the little suburban house by the sound of a voice booming and reverberating within. The novelist, seated among the usual knickknacks of the drawing-room, was like the bust of Euripides to look at. Age had worn and sharpened the fine features, but the nose was still acute, the blue eyes still keen and ironical. Though he had sunk immobile into an arm-chair, his aspect was still vigorous and alert. It was true that he was almost stone-deaf, but this was the least of afflictions to one who was scarcely able to keep pace with the rapidity of his own ideas. Since he could not hear what was said to him, he could give himself whole-heartedly to the delights of soliloquy. It did not much matter, perhaps, whether his audience was cultivated or simple. Compliments that would have flattered a duchess were presented with equal ceremony to a child. To neither could he speak the simple language of daily life. But all the time this highly wrought, artificial conversation, with its crystallised phrases and its high-piled metaphors, moved and tossed on a current of laughter. His laugh curled round his sentences as if he himself enjoyed their humorous exaggeration. The master of language was splashing and diving in his element of words. So the legend grew; and the fame of George Meredith, who

[1] Written in January 1928.

sat with the head of a Greek poet on his shoulders in a suburban villa beneath Box Hill, pouring out poetry and sarcasm and wisdom in a voice that could be heard almost on
the high road, made his fascinating and brilliant books seem
more fascinating and brilliant still.

But that is twenty years ago. His fame as a talker is necessarily dimmed, and his fame as a writer seems also under a
cloud. On none of his successors is his influence now marked.
When one of them whose own work has given him the right
to be heard with respect chances to speak his mind on the
subject, it is not flattering.

> Meredith [writes Mr. Forster in his *Aspects of the
> Novel*] is not the great name he was twenty years ago.
> . . . His philosophy has not worn well. His heavy at-
> tacks on sentimentality—they bore the present genera-
> tion. . . . When he gets serious and noble-minded there
> is a strident overtone, a bullying that becomes distress-
> ing. . . . What with the faking, what with the preach-
> ing, which was never agreeable and is now said to be
> hollow, and what with the home countries posing as the
> universe, it is no wonder Meredith now lies in the
> trough.

The criticism is not, of course, intended to be a finished estimate; but in its conversational sincerity it condenses accurately enough what is in the air when Meredith is mentioned.
No, the general conclusion would seem to be, Meredith has
not worn well. But the value of centenaries lies in the occasion they offer us for solidifying such airy impressions. Talk,
mixed with half-rubbed-out memories, forms a mist by degrees through which we scarcely see plain. To open the books
again, to try to read them as if for the first time, to try to
free them from the rubbish of reputation and accident—that,
perhaps, is the most acceptable present we can offer to a
writer on his hundredth birthday.

And since the first novel is always apt to be an unguarded
one, where the author displays his gifts without knowing how
to dispose of them to the best advantage, we may do well to
open *Richard Feverel* first. It needs no great sagacity to see
that the writer is a novice at his task. The style is extremely

uneven. Now he twists himself into iron knots; now he lies
flat as a pancake. He seems to be of two minds as to his
intention. Ironic comment alternates with long-winded narrative. He vacillates from one attitude to another. Indeed, the
whole fabric seems to rock a little insecurely. The baronet
wrapped in a cloak; the county family; the ancestral home;
the uncles mouthing epigrams in the dining-room; the great
ladies flaunting and swimming; the jolly farmers slapping
their thighs: all liberally if spasmodically sprinkled with
dried aphorisms from a pepper-pot called the Pilgrim's Scrip
—what an odd conglomeration it is! But the oddity is not
on the surface; it is not merely that whiskers and bonnets
have gone out of fashion: it lies deeper, in Meredith's intention, in what he wishes to bring to pass. He has been, it is
plain, at great pains to destroy the conventional form of the
novel. He makes no attempt to preserve the sober reality of
Trollope and Jane Austen; he has destroyed all the usual stair-
cases by which we have learnt to climb. And what is done so
deliberately is done with a purpose. This defiance of the ordinary, these airs and graces, the formality of the dialogue with
its Sirs and Madams are all there to create an atmosphere
that is unlike that of daily life, to prepare the way for a new
and an original sense of the human scene. Peacock, from
whom Meredith learnt so much, is equally arbitrary, but the
virtue of the assumptions he asks us to make is proved by
the fact that we accept Mr. Skionar and the rest with natural
delight. Meredith's characters in *Richard Feverel*, on the
other hand, are at odds with their surroundings. We at once
exclaim how unreal they are, how artificial, how impossible.
The baronet and the butler, the hero and the heroine, the
good woman and the bad woman are mere types of baronets
and butler, good women and bad. For what reason, then, has
he sacrificed the substantial advantages of realistic common
sense—the staircase and the stucco? Because, it becomes clear
as we read, he possessed a keen sense not of the complexity
of character, but of the splendour of a scene. One after another in this first book he creates a scene to which we can
attach abstract names—Youth, The Birth of Love, The Power
of Nature. We are galloped to them over every obstacle on
the pounding hoofs of rhapsodical prose.

Away with Systems! Away with a corrupt World! Let us breathe the air of the Enchanted Island! Golden lie the meadows; golden run the streams; red gold is on the pine stems.

We forget that Richard is Richard and that Lucy is Lucy; they are youth; the world runs molten gold. The writer is a rhapsodist, a poet then; but we have not yet exhausted all the elements in this first novel. We have to reckon with the author himself. He has a mind stuffed with ideas, hungry for argument. His boys and girls may spend their time picking daisies in the meadows, but they breathe, however unconsciously, an air bristling with intellectual question and comment. On a dozen occasions these incongruous elements strain and threaten to break apart. The book is cracked through and through with those fissures which come when the author seems to be of twenty minds at the same time. Yet it succeeds in holding miraculously together, not certainly by the depths and originality of its character drawing but by the vigour of its intellectual power and by its lyrical intensity.

We are left, then, with our curiosity aroused. Let him write another book or two; get into his stride; control his crudities: and we will open *Harry Richmond* and see what has happened now. Of all the things that might have happened this surely is the strangest. All trace of immaturity is gone; but with it every trace of the uneasy adventurous mind has gone too. The story bowls smoothly along the road which Dickens has already trodden of autobiographical narrative. It is a boy speaking, a boy thinking, a boy adventuring. For that reason, no doubt, the author has curbed his redundance and pruned his speech. The style is the most rapid possible. It runs smooth, without a kink in it. Stevenson, one feels, must have learnt much from this supple narrative, with its precise adroit phrases, its exact quick glance at visible things.

Plunged among dark green leaves, smelling woodsmoke, at night; at morning waking up, and the world alight, and you standing high, and marking the hills where you will see the next morning and the next, morning after morning, and one morning the dearest person in the world surprising you just before you wake: I thought this a heavenly pleasure.

It goes gallantly, but a little self-consciously. He hears himself talking. Doubts begin to rise and hover and settle at last (as in *Richard Feverel*) upon the human figures. These boys are no more real boys than the sample apple which is laid on top of the basket is a real apple. They are too simple, too gallant, too adventurous to be of the same unequal breed as David Copperfield, for example. They are sample boys, novelist's specimens; and again we encounter the extreme conventionality of Meredith's mind where we found it, to our surprise, before. With all his boldness (and there is no risk that he will not run with probability) there are a dozen occasions on which a reach-me-down character will satisfy him well enough. But just as we are thinking that the young gentlemen are altogether too pat, and the adventures which befall them altogether too slick, the shallow bath of illusion closes over our heads and we sink with Richmond Roy and the Princess Ottilia into the world of fantasy and romance, where all holds together and we are able to put our imagination at the writer's service without reserve. That such surrender is above all things delightful: that it adds spring-heels to our boots: that it fires the cold scepticism out of us and makes the world glow in lucid transparency before our eyes, needs no showing, as it certainly submits to no analysis. That Meredith can induce such moments proves him possessed of an extraordinary power. Yet it is a capricious power and highly intermittent. For pages all is effort and agony; phrase after phrase is struck and no light comes. Then, just as we are about to drop the book, the rocket roars into the air; the whole scene flashes into light; and the book, years after, is recalled by that sudden splendour.

If, then, this intermittent brilliancy is Meredith's characteristic excellence it is worth while to look into it more closely. And perhaps the first thing that we shall discover is that the scenes which catch the eye and remain in memory are static; they are illuminations, not discoveries; they do not improve our knowledge of the characters. It is significant that Richard and Lucy, Harry and Ottilia, Clara and Vernon,

Beauchamp and Renée are presented in carefully appropriate surroundings—on board a yacht, under a flowering cherry tree, upon some river-bank, so that the landscape always makes part of the emotion. The sea or the sky or the wood is brought forward to symbolise what the human beings are feeling or looking.

> The sky was bronze, a vast furnace dome. The folds of light and shadow everywhere were satin rich. That afternoon the bee hummed of thunder and refreshed the ear.

That is a description of a state of mind.

> These winter mornings are divine. They move on noiselessly. The earth is still as if waiting. A wren warbles, and flits through the lank, drenched branches; hillside opens green; everywhere is mist, everywhere expectancy.

That is a description of a woman's face. But only some states of mind and some expressions of face can be described in imagery—only those which are so highly wrought as to be simple and, for that reason, will not submit to analysis. This is a limitation; for though we may be able to see these people, very brilliantly, in a moment of illumination, they do not change or grow; the light sinks and leaves us in darkness. We have no such intuitive knowledge of Meredith's characters as we have of Stendhal's, Tchehov's, Jane Austen's. Indeed, our knowledge of such characters is so intimate that we can almost dispense with "great scenes" altogether. Some of the most emotional scenes in fiction are the quietest. We have been wrought upon by nine hundred and ninety-nine little touches; the thousandth, when it comes, is as slight as the others, but the effect is prodigious. But with Meredith there are no touches; there are hammer-strokes only, so that our knowledge of his characters is partial, spasmodic, and intermittent.

Meredith, then, is not among the great psychologists who feel their way, anonymously and patiently, in and out of the fibres of the mind and make one character differ minutely and completely from another. He is among the poets who identify the character with the passion or with the idea; who symbolise and make abstract. And yet—here lay his difficulty perhaps—he was not a poet-novelist wholly and completely as Emily Brontë was a poet-novelist. He did not steep the world in one mood. His mind was too self-conscious, and too sophisticated to remain lyrical for long. He does not sing only; he dissects. Even in his most lyrical scenes a sneer curls its lash round the phrases and laughs at their extravagance. And as we read on, we shall find that the comic spirit, when it is allowed to dominate the scene, licked the world to a very different shape. *The Egoist* at once modifies our theory that Meredith is pre-eminently the master of great scenes. Here there is none of that precipitate hurry that has rushed us over obstacles to the summit of one emotional peak after another. The case is one that needs argument; argument needs logic; Sir Willoughby, "our original male in giant form," is turned slowly round before a steady fire of scrutiny and criticism which allows no twitch on the victim's part to escape it. That the victim is a wax model and not entirely living flesh and blood is perhaps true. At the same time Meredith pays us a supreme compliment to which as novel-readers we are little accustomed. We are civilised people, he seems to say, watching the comedy of human relations together. Human relations are of profound interest. Men and women are not cats and monkeys, but beings of a larger growth and of a greater range. He imagines us capable of disinterested curiosity in the behaviour of our kind. This is so rare a compliment from a novelist to his reader that we are at first bewildered and then delighted. Indeed his comic spirit is a far more penetrating goddess than his lyrical. It is she who cuts a clear path through the brambles of his manner; she who surprises us again and again by the depth of her observations; she who creates the dignity, the seriousness, and the vitality of Meredith's world. Had Meredith, one is tempted to reflect, lived in an age or in a country where comedy was the rule, he might never have contracted those airs of intellectual superiority, that manner of oracular solemnity which it is, as he points out, the use of the comic spirit to correct.

But in many ways the age—if we can judge so amorphous a shape—was hostile to Meredith, or, to speak more accurately, was hostile to his success with the age we now live in—the year 1928. His teaching seems now too strident and too optimistic and too shallow. It obtrudes; and when philosophy is not consumed in a novel, when we can underline this phrase with a pencil, and cut out that exhortation with a pair of scissors and paste the whole into a system, it is safe to say that there is something wrong with the philosophy or with the novel or with both. Above all, his teaching is too insistent. He cannot, even to hear the profoundest secret, suppress his own opinion. And there is nothing that characters in fiction resent more. If, they seem to argue, we have been called into existence merely to express Mr. Meredith's views upon the universe, we would rather not exist at all. Thereupon they die; and a novel that is full of dead characters, even though it is also full of profound wisdom and exalted teaching, is not achieving its aim as a novel. But here we reach another point upon which the present age may be inclined to have more sympathy with Meredith. When he wrote, in the seventies and eighties of the last century, the novel had reached a stage where it could only exist by moving onward. It is a possible contention that after those two perfect novels, *Pride and Prejudice* and *The Small House at Allington*, English fiction had to escape from the dominion of that perfection, as English poetry had to escape from the perfection of Tennyson. George Eliot, Meredith, and Hardy were all imperfect novelists largely because they insisted upon introducing qualities, of thought and of poetry, that are perhaps incompatible with fiction at its most perfect. On the other hand, if fiction had remained what it was to Jane Austen and Trollope, fiction would by this time be dead. Thus Meredith deserves our gratitude and excites our interest as a great innovator. Many of our doubts about him and much of our inability to frame any definite opinion of his work comes from the fact that it is experimental and thus contains elements that do not fuse harmoniously—the qualities are at odds: the one quality which binds and concentrates has been omitted. To read Meredith, then, to our greatest advantage we must make certain allowances and relax certain standards. We must not expect the perfect quietude of a traditional style nor the triumphs of a patient and pedestrian psychology. On the other hand, his claim, "My method has been to prepare my readers for a crucial exhibition of the personae, and then to give the scene in the fullest of their blood and brain under stress of a fierce situation," is frequently justified. Scene after scene rises on the mind's eye with a flare of fiery intensity. If we are irritated by the dancing-master dandyism which made him write "gave his lungs full play" instead of laughed, or "tasted the swift intricacies of the needle" instead of sewed, we must remember that such phrases prepare the way for the "fierce situations." Meredith is creating the atmosphere from which we shall pass naturally into a highly pitched state of emotion. Where the realistic novelist, like Trollope, lapses into flatness and dullness, the lyrical novelist, like Meredith, becomes meretricious and false; and such falsity is, of course, not only much more glaring than flatness, but it is a greater crime against the phlegmatic nature of prose fiction. Perhaps Meredith had been well advised if he had abjured the novel altogether and kept himself wholly to poetry. Yet we have to remind ourselves that the fault may be ours. Our prolonged diet upon Russian fiction, rendered neutral and negative in translation, our absorption in the convolutions of psychological Frenchmen, may have led us to forget that the English language is naturally exuberant, and the English character full of humours and eccentricities. Meredith's flamboyancy has a great ancestry behind it; we cannot avoid all memory of Shakespeare.

When such questions and qualifications crowd upon us as we read, the fact may be taken to prove that we are neither near enough to be under his spell nor far enough to see him in proportion. Thus the attempt to pronounce a finished estimate is even more illusive than usual. But we can testify even now that to read Meredith is to be conscious of a packed and muscular mind; of a voice booming and reverberating with its own unmistakable accent even though the partition between us is too thick for us to hear what he says distinctly. Still, as we read we feel that we are in the presence of a Greek god though he is surrounded by the innumerable ornaments of a suburban drawing-room; who talks brilliantly, even if he is deaf to the lower tones of the human voice;

who, if he is rigid and immobile, is yet marvellously alive
and on the alert. This brilliant and uneasy figure has his
place with the great eccentrics rather than with the great
masters. He will be read, one may guess, by fits and starts;
he will be forgotten and discovered and again discovered and
forgotten like Donne, and Peacock, and Gerard Hopkins. But
if English fiction continues to be read, the novels of Meredith
must inevitably rise from time to time into view; his work
must inevitably be disputed and discussed.

Meredith ON Dickens:	*Dickens was the incarnation of cock- neydom, a caricaturist who aped the moralist; he should have kept to short stories. If his novels are read at all in the future, people will wonder what we saw in him.*

E. M. Forster on

When I was appointed to this lectureship the work of Virginia Woolf was much in my mind, and I asked to be allowed to speak on it. To speak on it, rather than to sum it up. There are two obstacles to a summing up. The first is the work's richness and complexity. As soon as we dismiss the legend of the Invalid Lady of Bloomsbury, so guilelessly accepted by Arnold Bennett, we find ourselves in a bewildering world where there are few headlines. We think of *The Waves* and say "Yes—that is Virginia Woolf"; then we think of *The Common Reader*, where she is different, of *A Room of One's Own* or of the preface to *Life As We Have Known It:* different again. She is like a plant which is supposed to grow in a well-prepared garden bed—the bed of esoteric literature—and then pushes up suckers all over the place, through the gravel of the front drive, and even through the flagstones of the kitchen yard. She was full of interests, and their number increased as she grew older, she was curious about life, and she was tough, sensitive but tough. How can her achievement be summed up in an hour? A headline sometimes serves a lecturer as a life-line on these occasions, and brings him safely into the haven where he would be. Shall I find one today?

The second obstacle is that the present year is not a good date on which to sum up anything. Our judgements, to put it mildly, are not at their prime. We are all of us upon the Leaning Tower, as she called it, even those of us who date from the nineteenth century, when the earth was still horizontal and the buildings perpendicular. We cannot judge the landscape properly as we look down, for everything is tilted. Isolated objects are not so puzzling; a tree, a wave, a hat, a jewel, an old gentleman's bald head look much as they always did. But the relation between objects—that we cannot estimate, and that is why the verdict must be left to another generation. I have not the least faith that anything which we now value will survive historically (something which we should have valued may evolve, but that is a different proposition); and maybe another generation will dismiss Virginia Woolf as worthless and tiresome. However this is not my opinion, nor I think yours; we still have the word, and when you conferred the Rede Lectureship on me—the greatest honour I have ever received—I wondered whether I could not transmit some honour to her from the university she so admired, and from the central building of that university. She would receive the homage a little mockingly, for she was somewhat astringent over the academic position of women. "What? I in the Senate House?" she might say; "are you sure that is quite proper? And why, if you want to discuss my books, need you first disguise yourselves in caps and gowns?" But I think she would be pleased. She loved Cambridge. Indeed, I cherish a private fancy that she once took her degree here. She, who could disguise herself as a member of the suite of the Sultan of Zanzibar, or black her face to go aboard a Dreadnought as an Ethiopian[1]—she could surely have hoaxed our innocent praelectors, and, kneeling in this very spot, have presented to the Vice-Chancellor the exquisite but dubious head of Orlando.

There is after all one little life-line to catch hold of: she liked writing.

These words, which usually mean so little, must be applied to her with all possible intensity. She liked receiving sensations—sights, sounds, tastes—passing them through her mind, where they encountered theories and memories, and then bringing them out again, through a pen, on to a bit of paper. Now began the higher delights of authorship. For these pen-marks on paper were only the prelude to writing, little more than marks on a wall. They had to be combined, arranged, emphasised here, eliminated there, new relationships had to be generated, new pen-marks born, until out of

---

[1] See Adrian Stephen, *The Dreadnought Hoax*. See, still more, an unpublished paper which she herself once wrote for a Women's Institute, leaving it helpless with laughter.

the interactions, something, one thing, one, arose. This one thing, whether it was a novel or an essay or a short story or a biography or a private paper to be read to her friends, was, if it was successful, itself analogous to a sensation. Although it was so complex and intellectual, although it might be large and heavy with facts, it was akin to the very simple things which had started it off, to the sights, sounds, tastes. It could be best described as we describe them. For it was not about something. It was something. This is obvious in "esthetic" works, like *Kew Gardens* and *Mrs. Dalloway*; it is less obvious in a work of learning, like the *Roger Fry*, yet here too the analogy holds. We know, from an article by Mr. R. C. Trevelyan,[2] that she had, when writing it, a notion corresponding to the notion of a musical composition. In the first chapter she stated the themes, in the subsequent chapters she developed them separately, and she tried to bring them all in again at the end. The biography is duly about Fry. But it is something else too; it is one thing, one.

She liked writing with an intensity which few writers have attained, or even desired. Most of them write with half an eye on their royalties, half an eye on their critics, and a third half eye on improving the world, which leaves them with only half an eye for the task on which she concentrated her entire vision. She would not look elsewhere, and her circumstances combined with her temperament to focus her. Money she had not to consider, because she possessed a private income, and though financial independence is not always a safeguard against commercialism, it was in her case. Critics she never considered while she was writing, although she could be attentive to them and even humble afterwards. Improving the world she would not consider, on the ground that the world is man-made, and that she, a woman, had no responsibility for the mess. This last opinion is a curious one, and I shall be returning to it; still, she held it, it completed the circle of her defences, and neither the desire for money nor the desire for reputation nor philanthropy could influence her. She had a singleness of purpose which will not recur in this country for many years, and writers who have

[2] *The Abinger Chronicle*, April 1941.

liked writing as she liked it have not indeed been common in any age.

Now the pitfall for such an author is obvious. It is the Palace of Art, it is that bottomless chasm of dulness which pretends to be a palace, all glorious with corridors and domes, but which is really a dreadful hole into which the unwary aesthete may tumble, to be seen no more. She has all the aesthete's characteristics: selects and manipulates her impressions; is not a great creator of character; enforces patterns on her books; has no great cause at heart. So how did she avoid her appropriate pitfall and remain up in the fresh air, where we can hear the sound of the stable boy's boots, or boats bumping, or Big Ben; where we can taste really new bread, and touch real dahlias?

She had a sense of humour, no doubt, but our answer must go a little deeper than that hoary nostrum. She escaped, I think, because she liked writing for fun. Her pen amused her, and in the midst of writing seriously this other delight would spurt through. A little essay, called *On Being Ill*, exemplifies this. It starts with the thesis that illness in literature is seldom handled properly (de Quincey and Proust were exceptional), that the body is treated by novelists as if it were a sheet of glass through which the soul gazes, and that this is contrary to experience. There are possibilities in the thesis, but she soon wearies of exploring them. Off she goes amusing herself, and after half a dozen pages she is writing entirely for fun, caricaturing the type of people who visit sickrooms, insisting that Augustus Hare's *Two Noble Lives* is the book an invalid most demands, and so on. She could describe illness if she chose—for instance, in *The Voyage Out*—but she gaily forgets it in *On Being Ill*. The essay is slight, and was not offered for public sale, still it does neatly illustrate the habit of her mind. Literature was her merry-go-round as well as her study. This makes her amusing to read, and it also saves her from the Palace of Art. For you cannot enter the Palace of Art, therein to dwell, if you are tempted from time to time to play the fool. Lord Tennyson did not consider that. His remedy, you remember, was that the Palace would be purified when it was inhabited by all mankind, all behaving seriously at once. Virginia Woolf found a simpler and a sounder solution.

No doubt there is a danger here—there is danger everywhere. She might have become a glorified diseuse, who frittered away her broader effects by mischievousness, and she did give that impression to some who met her in the flesh; there were moments when she could scarcely see the busts for the moustaches she pencilled on them, and when the bust was a modern one, whether of a gentleman in a top hat or of a youth on a pylon, it had no chance of remaining sublime. But in her writing, even in her light writing, central control entered. She was master of her complicated equipment, and though most of us like to write sometimes seriously and sometimes in fun, few of us can so manage the two impulses that they speed each other up, as hers did.

The above remarks are more or less introductory. It seems convenient now to recall what she did write, and to say a little about her development. She began back in 1915 with *The Voyage Out*—a strange tragic inspired novel about English tourists in an impossible South American hotel; her passion for truth is here already, mainly in the form of atheism, and her passion for wisdom is here in the form of music. The book made a deep impression upon the few people who read it. Its successor, *Night and Day*, disappointed them. This is an exercise in classical realism, and contains all that has characterised English fiction, for good and evil, during the last two hundred years: faith in personal relations, recourse to humorous side-shows, geographical exactitude, insistence on petty social differences: indeed most of the devices she so gaily derides in *Mr. Bennett and Mrs. Brown*. The style has been normalised and dulled. But at the same time she published two short stories, *Kew Gardens* and *The Mark on the Wall*. These are neither dull nor normal; lovely little things; her style trails after her as she walks and talks, catching up dust and grass in its folds, and instead of the precision of the earlier writing we have something more elusive than had yet been achieved in English. Lovely little things, but they seemed to lead nowhere, they were all tiny dots and coloured blobs, they were an inspired breathlessness, they were a beautiful droning or gasping which trusted to luck. They were perfect as far as they went, but that was not far, and none of us guessed that out of the pollen of those flowers would come the trees of the future. Consequently when *Jacob's Room* appeared in 1922 we were tremendously surprised. The style and sensitiveness of *Kew Gardens* remained, but they were applied to human relationships, and to the structure of society. The blobs of colour continue to drift past, but in their midst, interrupting their course like a closely sealed jar, stands the solid figure of a young man. The improbable has occurred; a method essentially poetic and apparently trifling has been applied to fiction. She was still uncertain of the possibilities of the new technique, and *Jacob's Room* is an uneven little book, but it represents her great departure, and her abandonment of the false start of *Night and Day*. It leads on to her genius in its fulness; to *Mrs. Dalloway* (1925), *To the Lighthouse* (1927), and *The Waves* (1931). These successful works are all suffused with poetry and enclosed in it. *Mrs. Dalloway* has the framework of a London summer's day, down which go spiralling two fates: the fate of the sensitive worldly hostess, and the fate of the sensitive obscure maniac; though they never touch they are closely connected, and at the same moment we lose sight of them both. It is a civilised book, and it was written from personal experience. In her work, as in her private problems, she was always civilised and sane on the subject of madness. She pared the edges off this particular malady, she tied it down to being a malady, and robbed it of the evil magic it has acquired through timid or careless thinking; here is one of the gifts we have to thank her for. *To the Lighthouse* is, however, a much greater achievement, partly because the chief characters in it, Mr. and Mrs. Ramsay, are so interesting. They hold us, we think of them away from their surroundings, and yet they are in accord with those surroundings, with the poetic scheme. *To the Lighthouse* is in three movements. It has been called a novel in sonata form, and certainly the slow central section, conveying the passing of time, does demand a musical analogy. We have, when reading it, the rare pleasure of inhabiting two worlds at once, a pleasure only art can give: the world where a little boy wants to go to a lighthouse but never manages it until, with changed emotions, he goes there as a young man; and the world where there is pattern, and this world is emphasised by passing much of the observation through the mind of Lily Briscoe, who is a painter. Then comes *The Waves*. Pattern here is supreme—indeed it is italicised. And between the motions of the sun and the waters, which preface each section, stretch, without interruption, conversation, words in inverted commas. It is a strange conversation, for the six characters, Bernard, Neville, Louis, Susan, Jinny, Rhoda, seldom address one another, and it is even possible to regard them (like Mrs. Dalloway and Septimus) as different facets of one single person. Yet they do not conduct internal monologues, they are in touch amongst themselves, and they all touch the character who never speaks, Percival. At the end, most perfectly balancing their scheme, Bernard, the would-be novelist, sums up, and the pattern fades out. *The Waves* is an extraordinary achievement, an immense extension of the possibilities of *Kew Gardens* and *Jacob's Room*. It is trembling on the edge. A little less—and it would lose its poetry. A little more—and it would be over into the abyss, and be dull and arty. It is her greatest book, though *To the Lighthouse* is my favourite.

It was followed by *The Years*. This is another experiment in the realistic tradition. It chronicles the fortunes of a family through a documented period. As in *Night and Day*, she deserts poetry, and again she fails. But in her posthumous novel *Between the Acts* (1941) she returns to the method she understood. Its theme is a village pageant, which presents the entire history of England, and into which, at the close, the audience is itself drawn, to continue that history; "The curtain rose" is its concluding phrase. The conception is poetic, and the text of the pageant is mostly written in verse. She loved her country—her country that is "the country," and emerges from the unfathomable past. She takes us back in this exquisite final tribute, and she points us on, and she shows us through her poetic vagueness something more solid than patriotic history, and something better worth dying for.

Amongst all this fiction, nourishing it and nourished by it, grow other works. Two volumes of *The Common Reader* show the breadth of her knowledge and the depth of her literary sympathy; let anyone who thinks her an exquisite recluse read what she says on Jack Mytton the foxhunter, for instance. As a critic she could enter into anything—anything lodged in the past, that is to say; with her contemporaries she sometimes had difficulties. Then there are the biographies, fanciful and actual. *Orlando* is, I need hardly say, an original book, and the first part of it is splendidly written: the description of the Great Frost is already received as a "passage" in English literature, whatever a passage may be. After the transformation of sex things do not go so well; the authoress seems unconvinced by her own magic and somewhat fatigued by it, and the biography finishes competently rather than brilliantly; it has been a fancy on too large a scale, and we can see her getting bored. But *Flush* is a complete success, and exactly what it sets out to be; the material, the method, the length, accord perfectly, it is doggie without being silly, and it does give us, from the altitude of the carpet or the sofa-foot, a peep at high poetic personages, and a new angle on their ways. The biography of Roger Fry—one should not proceed direct from a spaniel to a Slade Professor, but Fry would not have minded and spaniels mind nothing—reveals a new aspect of her powers, the power to suppress herself. She indulges in a pattern, but she never intrudes her personality or over-handles her English; respect for her subject dominates her, and only occasionally—as in her description of the divinely ordered chaos of Fry's studio with its still-life of apples and eggs labelled "please do not touch" —does she allow her fancy to play. Biographies are too often described as "labours of love," but the *Roger Fry* really is in this class; one artist is writing with affection of another, so that he may be remembered and may be justified.

Finally, there are the feminist books—*A Room of One's Own* and *Three Guineas*—and several short essays, etc., some of them significant. It is as a novelist that she will be judged. But the rest of her work must be remembered, partly on its merits, partly because (as Mr. William Plomer has pointed out[3]) she is sometimes more of a novelist in it than in her novels.

After this survey, we can state her problem. Like most

[3] *Horizon,* May 1941.

novelists worth reading, she strays from the fictional norm. She dreams, designs, jokes, invokes, observes details, but she does not tell a story or weave a plot, and—can she create character? That is her problem's centre. That is the point where she felt herself open to criticism—to the criticisms, for instance, of her friend Hugh Walpole. Plot and story could be set aside in favour of some other unity, but if one is writing about human beings, one does want them to seem alive. Did she get her people to live?

Now there seem to be two sorts of life in fiction, life on the page and life eternal. Life on the page she could give; her characters never seem unreal, however slight or fantastic their lineaments, and they can be trusted to behave appropriately. Life eternal she could seldom give; she could seldom so portray a character that it was remembered afterwards on its own account, as Emma is remembered, for instance, or Dorothea Casaubon, or Sophia and Constance in *The Old Wives' Tale*. What wraiths, apart from their context, are the wind-sextet from *The Waves*, or Jacob away from *Jacob's Room!* They speak no more to us or to one another as soon as the page is turned. And this is her great difficulty. Holding on with one hand to poetry, she stretches and stretches to grasp things which are best gained by letting go of poetry. She would not let go, and I think she was quite right, though critics who like a novel to be a novel will disagree. She was quite right to cling to her specific gift, even if this entailed sacrificing something else vital to her art. And she did not always have to sacrifice; Mr. and Mrs. Ramsay do remain with the reader afterwards, and so perhaps do Rachel from *The Voyage Out*, and Clarissa Dalloway. For the rest—it is impossible to maintain that here is an immortal portrait gallery. Socially she is limited to the upper-middle professional classes, and she does not even employ many types. There is the bleakly honest intellectual (St. John Hirst, Charles Tansley, Louis, William Dodge), the monumental majestic hero (Jacob, Percival), the pompous amorous pillar of society (Richard Dalloway as he appears in *The Voyage Out*, Hugh Whitbread), the scholar who cares only for young men (Bonamy, Neville), the pernickety independent (Mr. Pepper, Mr. Banks); even the Ramsays are tried out first as the Ambroses. As soon as we understand the nature of her equipment, we shall see that as regards human beings she did as well as she could. Belonging to the world of poetry, but fascinated by another world, she is always stretching out from her enchanted tree and snatching bits from the flux of daily life as they float past, and out of these bits she builds novels. She would not plunge. And she should not have plunged. She might have stayed folded up in her tree singing little songs like *Blue-Green* in the *Monday or Tuesday* volume, but fortunately for English literature she did not do this either.

So that is her problem. She is a poet, who wants to write something as near to a novel as possible.

I must pass on to say a little—it ought to be much—about her interests. I have emphasised her fondness for writing both seriously and in fun, and have tried to indicate how she wrote: how she gathered up her material and digested it without damaging its freshness, how she rearranged it to form unities, how she was a poet who wanted to write novels, how these novels bear upon them the marks of their strange gestation—some might say the scars. What concerns me now is the material itself, her interests, her opinions. And not to be too vague, I will begin with food.

It is always helpful, when reading her, to look out for the passages which describe eating. They are invariably good. They are a sharp reminder that here is a woman who is alert sensuously. She had an enlightened greediness which gentlemen themselves might envy, and which few masculine writers have expressed. There is a little too much lamp oil in George Meredith's wine, a little too much paper crackling on Charles Lamb's pork, and no savour whatever in any dish of Henry James', but when Virginia Woolf mentions nice things they get right into our mouths, so far as the edibility of print permits. We taste their deliciousness. And when they are not nice, we taste them equally, our mouths awry now with laughter. I will not torture this great university of Oxbridge by reminding it of the exquisite lunch which she ate in a don's room here in the year 1920; such memories are now too painful. Nor will I insult the noble college of women in this same university—Fernham is its name—by reminding

it of the deplorable dinner which she ate that same evening
in its Hall—a dinner so lowering that she had to go to a cupboard afterwards and drink something out of a bottle; such
memories may still be all too true to fact. But I may without
offence refer to the great dish of Bœuf en Daube which
forms the centre of the dinner of union in *To the Lighthouse*,
the dinner round which all that section of the book coheres,
the dinner which exhales affection and poetry and loveliness,
so that all the characters see the best in one another at last
and for a moment, and one of them, Lily Briscoe, carries
away a recollection of reality. Such a dinner cannot be built
on a statement beneath a dish-cover which the novelist is too
indifferent or incompetent to remove. Real food is necessary,
and this, in fiction as in her home, she knew how to provide.
The Bœuf en Daube, which had taken the cook three days
to make and had worried Mrs. Ramsay as she did her hair,
stands before us "with its confusion of savoury brown and
yellow meats and its bay leaves and its wine"; we peer down
the shiny walls of the great casserole and get one of the best
bits, and like William Banks, generally so hard to please, we
are satisfied. Food with her was not a literary device put in
to make the book seem real. She put it in because she tasted
it, because she saw pictures, because she smelt flowers, because she heard Bach, because her senses were both exquisite
and catholic, and were always bringing her first-hand news of
the outside world. Our debt to her is in part this: she reminds us of the importance of sensation in an age which
practises brutality and recommends ideals. I could have illustrated sensation more reputably by quoting the charming
passage about the florists' shop in *Mrs. Dalloway*, or the passage where Rachel plays upon the cabin piano. Flowers and
music are conventional literary adjuncts. A good feed isn't,
and that is why I preferred it and chose it to represent her
reactions. Let me add that she smokes, and now let the
Bœuf en Daube be carried away. It will never come back in
our lifetime. It is not for us. But the power to appreciate it
remains, and the power to appreciate all distinction.

After the senses, the intellect. She respected knowledge,
she believed in wisdom. Though she could not be called an
optimist, she had, very profoundly, the conviction that mind

is in action against matter, and is winning new footholds in the void. That anything would be accomplished by her or in her generation, she did not suppose, but the noble blood from which she sprang encouraged her to hope. Mr. Ramsay, standing by the geraniums and trying to think, is not a figure of fun. Nor is this university, despite its customs and costumes: "So that if at night, far out at sea over the tumbling waves, one saw a haze on the waters, a city illuminated, a whiteness in the sky, such as that now over the hall of Trinity where they're still dining or washing up plates: that would be the light shining there—the light of Cambridge."

No light shines now from Cambridge visibly, and this prompts the comment that her books were conditioned by her period. She could not assimilate this latest threat to our civilisation. The submarine perhaps. But not the flying fortress or the land mine. The idea that all stone is like grass, and like all flesh may vanish in a twinkling, did not enter into her consciousness, and indeed it will be some time before it can be assimilated by literature.[4] She belonged to an age which distinguished sharply between the impermanency of man and the durability of his monuments, and for whom the dome of the British Museum Reading Room was almost eternal. Decay she admitted: the delicate grey churches in the Strand would not stand for ever; but she supposed, as we all did, that decay would be gradual. The younger generation —the Auden-Isherwood generation as it is convenient to call it—saw more clearly here than could she, and she did not quite do justice to its vision, any more than she did justice to its experiments in technique—she who had been in her time such an experimenter. Still, to belong to one's period is a common failing, and she made the most of hers. She respected and acquired knowledge, she believed in wisdom. Intellectually, no one can do more; and since she was a poet, not a philosopher or a historian or a prophetess, she had not to consider whether wisdom will prevail and whether the square upon the oblong, which Rhoda built out of the music of Mozart, will ever stand firm upon this distracted earth.

[4] Elizabeth Bowen is, so far as I know, the only novelist who has assimilated the bombed areas of London into her art; descriptions of them are of course frequent.

The square upon the oblong. Order. Justice. Truth. She cared for these abstractions, and tried to express them through symbols, as an artist must, though she realised the inadequacy of symbols.

They come with their violins, said Rhoda; they wait; count; nod; down come their bows. And there is ripples and laughter like the dance of olive trees. . . .

"Like" and "like" and "like"—but what is the thing that lies beneath the semblance of the thing? Now that lightning has gashed the tree and the flowering branch has fallen . . . let me see the thing. There is a square. There is an oblong. The players take the square and place it upon the oblong. They place it very accurately; they make a perfect dwelling-place. Very little is left outside. The structure is now visible; what is inchoate is here stated; we are not so various or so mean; we have made oblongs and stood them upon squares. This is our triumph; this is our consolation.

The consolation, that is to say, of catching sight of abstractions. They have to be symbolised, and "the square upon the oblong" is as much a symbol as the dancing olive trees, but because of its starkness it comes nearer to conveying what she seeks. Seeking it, "we are not so various or so mean"; we have added to the human heritage and reaffirmed wisdom.

The next of her interests which has to be considered is society. She was not confined to sensations and intellectualism. She was a social creature, with an outlook both warm and shrewd. But it was a peculiar outlook, and we can best get at it by looking at a very peculiar side of her: her Feminism.

Feminism inspired one of the most brilliant of her books —the charming and persuasive A Room of One's Own; it contains the Oxbridge lunch and the Fernham dinner, also the immortal encounter with the beadle when she tried to walk on the college grass, and the touching reconstruction of Shakespeare's sister—Shakespeare's equal in genius, but she perished because she had no position or money, and that has been the fate of women through the ages. But Feminism is also responsible for the worst of her books—the cantankerous

Three Guineas—and for the less successful streaks in *Orlando*. There are spots of it all over her work, and it was constantly in her mind. She was convinced that society is man-made, that the chief occupations of men are the shedding of blood, the making of money, the giving of orders, and the wearing of uniforms, and that none of these occupations is admirable. Women dress up for fun or prettiness, men for pomposity, and she had no mercy on the judge in his wig, the general in his bits and bobs of ribbon, the bishop in his robes, or even on the harmless don in his gown. She felt that all these mummers were putting something across over which women had never been consulted, and which she at any rate disliked. She declined to co-operate, in theory, and sometimes in fact. She refused to sit on committees or to sign appeals, on the ground that women must not condone this tragic male-made mess, or accept the crumbs of power which men throw them occasionally from their hideous feast. Like Lysistrata, she withdrew.

In my judgement there is something old-fashioned about this extreme Feminism; it dates back to her suffragette youth of the 1910's, when men kissed girls to distract them from wanting the vote, and very properly provoked her wrath. By the 1930's she had much less to complain of, and seems to keep on grumbling from habit. She complained, and rightly, that though women today have won admission into the professions and trades they usually encounter a male conspiracy when they try to get to the top. But she did not appreciate that the conspiracy is weakening yearly, and that before long women will be quite as powerful for good or evil as men. She was sensible about the past; about the present she was sometimes unreasonable. However, I speak as a man here, and as an elderly one. The best judges of her Feminism are neither elderly men nor even elderly women, but young women. If they, if the students of Fernham, think that it expresses an existent grievance, they are right.

She felt herself to be not only a woman but a lady, and this gives a further twist to her social outlook. She made no bones about it. She was a lady, by birth and upbringing, and it was no use being cowardly about it, and pretending that her mother had turned a mangle, or that Sir Leslie had been a plasterer's mate. Working-class writers often mentioned their origins, and were respected for doing so. Very well; she would mention hers. And her snobbery—for she was a snob—has more courage in it than arrogance. It is connected with her insatiable honesty, and is not, like the snobbery of Clarissa Dalloway, bland and frilled and unconsciously sinking into the best armchair. It is more like the snobbery of Kitty when she goes to tea with the Robsons; it stands up like a target for anyone to aim at who wants to. In her introduction to *Life As We Have Known It* (a collection of biographies of working-class women edited by Margaret Llewellyn Davies) she faces the fire. "One could not be Mrs. Giles of Durham, because one's body had never stood at the wash-tub; one's hands had never wrung and scrubbed and chopped up whatever the meat is that makes a miner's supper." This is not disarming, and it is not intended to disarm. And if one said to her that she could after all find out what meat a miner does have for his supper if she took a little trouble, she would retort that this wouldn't help her to chop it up, and that it is not by knowing things but by doing things that one enters into the lives of people who do things. And she was not going to chop up meat. She would chop it badly, and waste her time. She was not going to wring and scrub when what she liked doing and could do was write. To murmurs of "Lucky lady you!" she replied, "I am a lady," and went on writing. "There aren't going to be no more ladies. 'Ear that?" She heard. Without rancour or surprise or alarm, she heard, and drove her pen the faster. For if, as seems probable, these particular creatures are to be extinguished, how important that the last of them should get down her impressions of the world and unify them into a book! If she didn't, no one else would. Mrs. Giles of Durham wouldn't. Mrs. Giles would write differently, and might write better, but she could not produce *The Waves*, or a life of Roger Fry.

There is an admirable hardness here, so far as hardness can be admirable. There is not much sympathy, and I do not think she was sympathetic. She could be charming to individuals, working-class and otherwise, but it was her curiosity and her honesty that motivated her. And we must remember that sympathy, for her, entailed a tremendous and exhausting process, not lightly to be entered on. It was not a half-crown or a kind word or a good deed or a philanthropic sermon or a godlike gesture; it was adding the sorrows of another to one's own. Half fancifully, but wholly seriously, she writes:

> But sympathy we cannot have. Wisest Fate says no. If her children, weighted as they already are with sorrow, were to take on them that burden too, adding in imagination other pains to their own, buildings would cease to rise; roads would peter out into grassy tracks: there would be an end of music and of painting; one great sigh alone would rise to Heaven, and the only attitudes for men and women would be those of horror and despair.

Here perhaps is the reason why she cannot be warmer and more human about Mrs. Giles of Durham.

This detachment from the working-classes and Labour reinforces the detachment caused by her Feminism, and her attitude to society was in consequence aloof and angular. She was fascinated, she was unafraid, but she detested mateyness, and she would make no concessions to popular journalism, and the "let's all be friendly together" stunt. To the crowd—so far as such an entity exists—she was very jolly, but she handed out no bouquets to the middlemen who have arrogated to themselves the right of interpreting the crowd, and get paid for doing so in the daily press and on the wireless. These middlemen form after all a very small clique—larger than the Bloomsbury they so tirelessly denounce, but a mere drop in the ocean of humanity. And since it was a drop whose distinction was proportionate to its size, she saw no reason to conciliate it.

"And now to sum up," says Bernard in the last section of *The Waves*. That I cannot do, for reasons already given; the material is so rich and contradictory, and ours is not a good vintage year for judgements. I have gone from point to point as best I could, from her method of writing to her books, from her problems as a poet-novelist to her problems as a woman and as a lady. And I have tried to speak of her with the directness which she would wish, and which could alone honour her. But how are all the points to be combined?

What is the pattern resultant? The best I can do is to quote Bernard again. "The illusion is upon me," he says, "that something adheres for a moment, has roundness, weight, depth, is completed. This, for the moment, seems to be her life." Bernard puts it well. But, as Rhoda indicated in that earlier quotation, these words are only similes, comparisons with physical substances, and what one wants is the thing that lies beneath the semblance of the thing; that alone satisfies, that alone makes the full statement.

Whatever the final pattern, I am sure it will not be a depressing one. Like all her friends, I miss her greatly—I knew her ever since she started writing. But this is a personal matter, and I am sure that there is no case for lamentation here, or for the obituary note. Virginia Woolf got through an immense amount of work, she gave acute pleasure in new ways, she pushed the light of the English language a little further against darkness. Those are facts. The epitaph of such an artist cannot be written by the vulgar-minded or by the lugubrious. They will try, indeed they have already tried, but their words make no sense. It is wiser, it is safer, to regard her career as a triumphant one. She triumphed over what are primly called "difficulties," and she also triumphed in the positive sense: she brought in the spoils. And sometimes it is as a row of little silver cups that I see her work gleaming. "These trophies," the inscription runs, "were won by the mind from matter, its enemy and its friend."

One of the most enduring memories of my literary life is the sensation produced by the appearance in 1895 of Crane's "Red Badge of Courage" in a small volume belonging to Mr. Heinemann's Pioneer Series of Modern Fiction—very modern fiction of that time, and upon the whole not devoid of merit. I have an idea the series was meant to give us shocks, and as far as my recollection goes there were, to use a term made familiar to all by another war, no "duds" in that small and lively bombardment. But Crane's work detonated on the mild din of that attack on our literary sensibilities with the impact and force of a twelve-inch shell charged with a very high explosive. Unexpected it fell amongst us; and its fall was followed by a great outcry.

Not of consternation, however. The energy of that projectile hurt nothing and no one (such was its good fortune), and delighted a good many. It delighted soldiers, men of letters, men in the street; it was welcomed by all lovers of personal expression as a genuine revelation, satisfying the curiosity of a world in which war and love have been subjects of song and story ever since the beginning of articulate speech.

Here we had an artist, a man not of experience but a man inspired, a seer with a gift for rendering the significant on the surface of things and with an incomparable insight into primitive emotions, who, in order to give us the image of war, had looked profoundly into his own breast. We welcomed him. As if the whole vocabulary of praise had been blown up sky-high by this missile from across the Atlantic, a rain of words descended on our heads, words well or ill chosen, chunks of pedantic praise and warm appreciation, clever words, and words of real understanding, platitudes, and felicities of criticism, but all as sincere in their response as the striking piece of work which set so many critical pens scurrying over the paper.

One of the most interesting, if not the most valuable, of printed criticisms was perhaps that of Mr. George Wyndham, soldier, man of the world, and in a sense a man of letters. He went into the whole question of war literature, at any rate during the nineteenth century, evoking comparisons with the *Mémoires* of General Marbot and the famous *Diary of a Cavalry Officer* as records of a personal experience. He rendered justice to the interest of what soldiers themselves could tell us, but confessed that to gratify the curiosity of the potential combatant who lurks in most men as to the picturesque aspects and emotional reactions of a battle we must go to the artist with his Heaven-given faculty of words at the service of his divination as to what the truth of things is and must be. He comes to the conclusion that:

"Mr. Crane has contrived a masterpiece."

"Contrived"—that word of disparaging sound is the last word I would have used in connection with any piece of work by Stephen Crane, who in his art (as indeed in his private life) was the least "contriving" of men. But as to "masterpiece," there is no doubt that "The Red Badge of Courage" is that, if only because of the marvellous accord of the vivid impressionistic description of action on that woodland battlefield, and the imaged style of the analysis of the emotions in the inward moral struggle going on in the breast of one individual—the Young Soldier of the book, the protagonist of the monodrama presented to us in an effortless succession of graphic and coloured phrases.

Stephen Crane places his Young Soldier in an untried regiment. And this is well contrived—if any contrivance there be in a spontaneous piece of work which seems to spurt and flow like a tapped stream from the depths of the writer's being. In order that the revelation should be complete, the Young Soldier has to be deprived of the moral support which he would have found in a tried body of men matured in achievement to the consciousness of its worth. His regiment had been tried by nothing but days of waiting for the order to move; so many days that it and the Youth within it have come to think of themselves as merely "a part of a vast blue demonstration." The army had been lying camped near a river, idle and fretting, till the moment when Stephen Crane lays hold of it at dawn with masterly simplicity: "The cold passed reluctantly from the earth. . . ." These are the first words of the war book which was to give him his crumb of fame.

The whole of that opening paragraph is wonderful in the homely dignity of the indicated lines of the landscape, and the shivering awakening of the army at the break of the day before the battle. In the next, with a most effective change to racy colloquialism of narrative, the action which motivates, sustains and feeds the inner drama forming the subject of the book, begins with the Tall Soldier going down to the river to wash his shirt. He returns waving his garment above his head. He had heard at fifth-hand from somebody that the army is going to move to-morrow. The only immediate effect of this piece of news is that a Negro teamster, who had been dancing a jig on a wooden box in a ring of laughing soldiers, finds himself suddenly deserted. He sits down mournfully. For the rest, the Tall Soldier's excitement is met by blank disbelief, profane grumbling, an invincible incredulity. But the regiment is somehow sobered. One feels it, though no symptoms can be noticed. It does not know what a battle is, neither does the Young Soldier. He retires from the babbling throng into what seems a rather comfortable dugout and lies down with his hands over his eyes to think. Thus the drama begins.

He perceives suddenly that he had looked upon wars as historical phenomenons of the past. He had never believed in war in his own country. It had been a sort of play affair. He had been drilled, inspected, marched for months, till he has despaired "of ever seeing a Greek-like struggle. Such were no more. Men were better or more timid. Secular and religious education had effaced the throat-grappling instinct, or else firm finance held in check the passions."

Very modern this touch. We can remember thoughts like these round about the year 1914. That Young Soldier is representative of mankind in more ways than one, and first of all in his ignorance. His regiment had listened to the tales of veterans, "tales of gray bewhiskered hordes chewing tobacco with unspeakable valour and sweeping along like the Huns." Still, he cannot put his faith in veterans' tales. Recruits were their prey. They talked of blood, fire, and sudden death, but much of it might have been lies. They were in no wise to be trusted. And the question arises before him whether he will or will not "run from a battle"? He does not know. He cannot know. A little panic fear enters his mind. He jumps up and asks himself aloud, "Good Lord, what's the matter with me?" This is the first time his words are quoted, on this day before the battle. He dreads not danger, but fear itself. He stands before the unknown. He would like to prove to himself by some reasoning process that he will not "run from the battle." And in his unblooded regiment he can find no help. He is alone with the problem of courage.

In this he stands for the symbol of all untried men.

Some critics have estimated him a morbid case. I cannot agree to that. The abnormal cases are of the extremes; of those who crumple up at the first sight of danger, and of those of whom their fellows say "He doesn't know what fear is." Neither will I forget the rare favourites of the gods whose fiery spirit is only soothed by the fury and clamour of a battle. Of such was General Picton of Peninsular fame. But the lot of the mass of mankind is to know fear, the decent fear of disgrace. Of such is the Young Soldier of "The Red Badge of Courage." He only seems exceptional because he has got inside of him Stephen Crane's imagination, and is presented to us with the insight and the power of expression of an artist whom a just and severe critic, on a review of all his work, has called the foremost impressionist of his time; as Sterne was the greatest impressionist, but in a different way, of his age.

This is a generalized, fundamental judgment. More superficially both Zola's "La Débâcle" and Tolstoi's "War and Peace" were mentioned by critics in connection with Crane's war book. But Zola's main concern was with the downfall of the imperial régime he fancied he was portraying; and in Tolstoi's book the subtle presentation of Rostov's squadron under fire for the first time is a mere episode lost in a mass of other matter, like a handful of pebbles in a heap of sand.

I could not see the relevancy. Crane was concerned with elemental truth only; and in any case I think that as an artist he is non-comparable. He dealt with what is enduring, and was the most detached of men.

That is why his book is short. Not quite two hundred pages. Gems are small. This monodrama, which happy inspiration or unerring instinct has led him to put before us in narrative form, is contained between the opening words I have already quoted and a phrase on page 194 of the English edition, which runs: "He had been to touch the great death, and found that, after all, it was but the great death. He was a man."

On these words the action ends. We are only given one glimpse of the victorious army at dusk, under the falling rain, "a procession of weary soldiers became a bedraggled train, despondent and muttering, marching with churning effort in a trough of liquid brown mud under a low wretched sky . . .", while the last ray of the sun falls on the river through a break in the leaden clouds.

This war book, so virile and so full of gentle sympathy, in which not a single declamatory sentiment defaces the genuine verbal felicity, welding analysis and description in a continuous fascination of individual style, had been hailed by the critics as the herald of a brilliant career. Crane himself very seldom alluded to it, and always with a wistful smile. Perhaps he was conscious that, like the mortally wounded Tall Soldier of his book, who, snatching at the air, staggers out into a field to meet his appointed death on the first day of battle—while the terrified Youth and the kind Tattered Soldier stand by silent, watching with awe "these ceremonies at the place of meeting"—it was his fate, too, to fall early in the fray.

D. H. Lawrence on

HERMAN MELVILLE

Moby Dick, or the White Whale.

A hunt. The last great hunt.

For what?

For Moby Dick, the huge white sperm whale: who is old, hoary, monstrous, and swims alone; who is unspeakably terrible in his wrath, having so often been attacked; and snow-white.

Of course he is a symbol.

Of what?

I doubt if even Melville knew exactly. That's the best of it.

He is warm-blooded, he is lovable. He is lonely Leviathan, not a Hobbes sort. Or is he?

But he is warm-blooded and lovable. The South Sea Islanders, and Polynesians, and Malays, who worship shark, or crocodile, or weave endless frigate-bird distortions, why did they never worship the whale? So big!

Because the whale is not wicked. He doesn't bite. And their gods had to bite.

He's not a dragon. He is Leviathan. He never coils like the Chinese dragon of the sun. He's not a serpent of the waters. He is warm-blooded, a mammal. And hunted, hunted down.

It is a great book.

At first you are put off by the style. It reads like journalism. It seems spurious. You feel Melville is trying to put something over you. It won't do.

And Melville really is a bit sententious: aware of himself, self-conscious, putting something over even himself. But then it's not easy to get into the swing of a piece of deep mysticism when you just set out with a story.

Nobody can be more clownish, more clumsy and sententiously in bad taste, than Herman Melville, even in a great book like *Moby Dick*. He preaches and holds forth because he's not sure of himself. And he holds forth, often, so amateurishly.

The artist was so *much* greater than the man. The man is rather a tiresome New Englander of the ethical mystical-transcendentalist sort: Emerson, Longfellow, Hawthorne, etc. So unrelieved, the solemn ass even in humour. So hopelessly *au grand sérieux*, you feel like saying: Good God, what does it matter? If life is a tragedy, or a farce, or a disaster, or anything else, what do I care! Let life be what it likes. Give me a drink, that's what I want just now.

For my part, life is so many things I don't care what it is. It's not my affair to sum it up. Just now it's a cup of tea. This morning it was wormwood and gall. Hand me the sugar.

One wearies of the *grand sérieux*. There's something false about it. And that's Melville. Oh, dear, when the solemn ass brays! brays! brays!

But he was a deep, great artist, even if he was rather a sentential man. He was a real American in that he always felt his audience in front of him. But when he ceases to be American, when he forgets all audience, and gives us his sheer apprehension of the world, then he is wonderful, his book commands a stillness in the soul, an awe.

In his "human" self, Melville is almost dead. That is, he hardly reacts to human contacts any more; or only ideally: or just for a moment. His human-emotional self is almost played out. He is abstract, self-analytical and abstracted. And he is more spellbound by the strange slidings and collidings of Matter than by the things men do. In this he is like Dana. It is the material elements he really has to do with. His drama is with them. He was a futurist long before futurism found paint. The sheer naked slidings of the elements. And the human soul experiencing it all. So often, it is almost over the border: psychiatry. Almost spurious. Yet so great.

It is the same old thing as in all Americans. They keep their old-fashioned ideal frock-coat on, and an old-fashioned silk hat, while they do the most impossible things. There you are: you see Melville hugged in bed by a huge tattooed South Sea Islander, and solemnly offering burnt offering to this savage's little idol, and his ideal frock-coat just hides his shirt-tails and prevents us from seeing his bare posterior as he salaams, while his ethical silk hat sits correctly over his brow the while. That is so typically American: doing the most impossible things without taking off their spiritual get-up. Their ideals are like armour which has rusted in, and will never more come off. And meanwhile in Melville his bodily knowledge moves naked, a living quick among the stark elements. For with sheer physical vibrational sensitiveness, like a marvellous wireless-station, he registers the effects of the outer world. And he records also, almost beyond pain or pleasure, the extreme transitions of the isolated, far-driven soul, the soul which is now alone, without any real human contact.

The first days in New Bedford introduce the only human being who really enters into the book, namely, Ishmael, the "I" of the book. And then the moment's hearts-brother, Queequeg, the tattooed, powerful South Sea harpooner, whom Melville loves as Dana loves "Hope". The advent of Ishmael's bedmate is amusing and unforgettable. But later the two swear "marriage", in the language of the savages. For Queequeg has opened again the flood-gates of love and human connexion in Ishmael.

"As I sat there in that now lonely room, the fire burning low, in that mild stage when, after its first intensity has warmed the air, it then only glows to be looked at; the evening shades and phantoms gathering round the casements, and peering in upon us silent, solitary twain: I began to be sensible of strange feelings. I felt a melting in me. No more my splintered hand and maddened heart was turned against the wolfish world. This soothing savage had redeemed it. There he sat, his very indifference speaking a nature in which there lurked no civilised hypocrisies and bland deceits. Wild he was; a very sight of sights to see; yet I began to feel myself mysteriously drawn towards him."—So they smoked together and are clasped in each other's arms. The friendship is finally sealed when Ishmael offers sacrifice to Queequeg's little idol, Gogo.

"I was a good Christian, born and bred in the bosom of the infallible Presbyterian Church. How then could I unite with the idolater in worshipping his piece of wood? But what is worship?—to do the will of God—*that* is worship. And what is the will of God?—to do to my fellow-man what I would have my fellow-man do to me—*that* is the will of God."— Which sounds like Benjamin Franklin, and is hopelessly bad theology. But it is real American logic. "Now Queequeg is my fellow-man. And what do I wish that this Queequeg would do to me? Why, unite with me in my particular Presbyterian form of worship. Consequently, I must unite with him; ergo, I must turn idolater. So I kindled the shavings; helped prop up the innocent little idol; offered him burnt biscuit with Queequeg, salaamed before him twice or thrice; kissed his nose; and that done, we undressed and went to bed, at peace with our own consciences and all the world. But we did not go to sleep without some little chat. How it is I know not; but there is no place like bed for confidential disclosures between friends. Man and wife, they say, open the very bottom of their souls to each other; and some old couples often lie and chat over old times till nearly morning. Thus, then, lay I and Queequeg—a cosy, loving pair——"

You would think this relation with Queequeg meant something to Ishmael. But no. Queequeg is forgotten like yesterday's newspaper. Human things are only momentary excitements or amusements to the American Ishmael. Ishmael, the hunted. But much more Ishmael the hunter. What's a Queequeg? What's a wife? The white whale must be hunted down. Queequeg must be just "KNOWN", then dropped into oblivion.

And what in the name of fortune is the white whale?

Elsewhere Ishmael says he loved Queequeg's eyes: "large, deep eyes, fiery black and bold." No doubt like Poe, he wanted to get the "clue" to them. That was all.

The two men go over from New Bedford to Nantucket, and there sign on to the Quaker whaling ship, the *Pequod*. It is all strangely fantastic, phantasmagoric. The voyage of the soul. Yet curiously a real whaling voyage, too. We pass on into the midst of the sea with this strange ship and its incredible crew. The Argonauts were mild lambs in comparison. And Ulysses went *defeating* the Circes and overcoming the wicked hussies of the isles. But the *Pequod*'s crew is a collection of maniacs fanatically hunting down a lonely, harmless white whale.

As a soul history, it makes one angry. As a sea yarn, it is marvellous: there is always something a bit over the mark, in sea yarns. Should be. Then again the masking up of actual seaman's experience with sonorous mysticism sometimes gets on one's nerves. And again, as a revelation of destiny the book is too deep even for sorrow. Profound beyond feeling.

You are some time before you are allowed to see the captain, Ahab: the mysterious Quaker. Oh, it is a God-fearing Quaker ship.

Ahab, the captain. The captain of the soul.

> I am the master of my fate,
> I am the captain of my soul!

Ahab!

"Oh, captain, my captain, our fearful trip is done."

The gaunt Ahab, Quaker, mysterious person, only shows himself after some days at sea. There's a secret about him! What?

Oh, he's a portentous person. He stumps about on an ivory stump, made from sea-ivory. Moby Dick, the great white whale tore off Ahab's leg at the knee, when Ahab was attacking him.

Quite right, too. Should have torn off both his legs, and a bit more besides.

But Ahab doesn't think so. Ahab is now a monomaniac. Moby Dick is his monomania. Moby Dick must DIE, or Ahab can't live any longer. Ahab is atheist by this.

All right.

This *Pequod*, ship of the American soul, has three mates.

1. Starbuck: Quaker, Nantucketer, a good responsible man of reason, forethought, intrepidity, what is called a dependable man. At the bottom, *afraid*.

2. Stubb: "Fearless as fire, and as mechanical." Insists on being reckless and jolly on every occasion. Must be afraid too, really.

3. Flask: Stubborn, obstinate, without imagination. To him "the wondrous whale was but a species of magnified mouse or water-rat——"

There you have them: a maniac captain and his three mates, three splendid seamen, admirable whalemen, first-class men at their job.

America!

It is rather like Mr. Wilson and his admirable, "efficient" crew, at the Peace Conference. Except that none of the Pequodders took their wives along.

A maniac captain of the soul, and three eminently practical mates.

America!

Then such a crew. Renegades, castaways, cannibals: Ishmael, Quakers.

America!

Three giant harpooners, to spear the great white whale.

1. Queequeg, the South Sea Islander, all tattooed, big and powerful.

2. Tashtego, the Red Indian of the sea-coast, where the Indian meets the sea.

3. Daggoo, the huge black negro.

There you have them, three savage races, under the American flag, the maniac captain, with their great keen harpoons, ready to spear the white whale.

And only after many days at sea does Ahab's own boat-crew appear on deck. Strange, silent, secret, black-garbed Malays, fire-worshipping Parsees. These are to man Ahab's boat, when it leaps in pursuit of that whale.

What do you think of the ship *Pequod*, the ship of the soul of an American?

Many races, many peoples, many nations, under the Stars and Stripes. Beaten with many stripes.

Seeing stars sometimes.

And in a mad ship, under a mad captain, in a mad, fanatic's hunt.

For what?

For Moby Dick, the great white whale.

But splendidly handled. Three splendid mates. The whole thing practical, eminently practical in its working. American industry!

And all this practicality in the service of a mad, mad chase.

Melville manages to keep it a real whaling ship, on a real cruise, in spite of all fantastics. A wonderful, wonderful voyage. And a beauty that is so surpassing only because of the author's awful flounderings in mystical waters. He wanted to get metaphysically deep. And he got deeper than metaphysics. It is a surpassingly beautiful book, with an awful meaning, and bad jolts.

It is interesting to compare Melville with Dana, about the albatross—Melville a bit sententious. "I remember the first albatross I ever saw. It was during a prolonged gale in waters hard upon the Antarctic seas. From my forenoon watch below I ascended to the overcrowded deck, and there, lashed upon the main hatches, I saw a regal feathered thing of unspotted whiteness, and with a hooked Roman bill sublime. At intervals it arched forth its vast, archangel wings—wondrous throbbings and flutterings shook it. Though bodily unharmed, it uttered cries, as some King's ghost in supernatural distress. Through its inexpressible strange eyes methought I peeped to secrets not below the heavens—the white thing was so white, its wings so wide, and in those for ever exiled waters, I had lost the miserable warping memories of traditions and of towns. I assert then, that in the wondrous bodily whiteness of the bird chiefly lurks the secret of the spell——"

Melville's albatross is a prisoner, caught by a bait on a hook.

Well, I have seen an albatross, too: following us in waters hard upon the Antarctic, too, south of Australia. And in the Southern winter. And the ship, a P. and O. boat, nearly empty. And the lascar crew shivering.

The bird with its long, long wings following, then leaving us. No one knows till they have tried, how lost, how lonely those Southern waters are. And glimpses of the Australian coast.

It makes one feel that our day is only a day. That in the dark of the night ahead other days stir fecund, when we have lapsed from existence.

Who knows how utterly we shall lapse.

But Melville keeps up his disquisition about "whiteness". The great abstract fascinated him. The abstract where we end, and cease to be. White or black. Our white, abstract end!

Then again it is lovely to be at sea on the *Pequod*, with never a grain of earth to us.

"It was a cloudy, sultry afternoon; the seamen were lazily lounging about the decks, or vacantly gazing over into the lead-coloured waters. Queequeg and I were mildly employed weaving what is called a sword-mat, for an additional lashing to our boat. So still and subdued, and yet somehow preluding was all the scene, and such an incantation of reverie lurked in the air that each silent sailor seemed resolved into his own invisible self——"

In the midst of this preluding silence came the first cry: "There she blows! there! there! there! She blows!" And then comes the first chase, a marvellous piece of true sea-writing, the sea, and sheer sea-beings on the chase, sea-creatures chased. There is scarcely a taint of earth—pure sea-motion.

" 'Give way men,' whispered Starbuck, drawing still further aft the sheet of his sail; 'there is time to kill fish yet before the squall comes. There's white water again!—Close to!—Spring!' Soon after, two cries in quick succession on each side of us denoted that the other boats had got fast; but hardly were they overboard when with a lightning-like hurtling whisper Starbuck said: 'Stand up!' and Queequeg, harpoon in hand, sprang to his feet.—Though not one of the oarsmen was then facing the life and death peril so close to them ahead, yet their eyes on the intense countenance of the mate in the stern of the boat, they knew that the imminent instant had come; they heard, too, an enormous wallowing sound, as of fifty elephants stirring in their litter. Meanwhile the boat was still booming through the mist, the waves curbing and hissing around us like the erected crests of enraged serpents.

" 'That's his hump. *There! There*, give it to him!' whispered Starbuck.—A short rushing sound leapt out of the boat; it was the darted iron of Queequeg. Then all in one welded motion came a push from astern, while forward the boat seemed striking on a ledge; the sail collapsed and exploded; a gush of scalding vapour shot up near by; something rolled and tumbled like an earthquake beneath us. The whole crew were half-suffocated as they were tossed helter-skelter into the white curling cream of the squall. Squall, whale, and harpoon had all blended together; and the whale, merely grazed by the iron, escaped——"

Melville is a master of violent, chaotic physical motion; he can keep up a whole wild chase without a flaw. He is as perfect at creating stillness. The ship is cruising on the Carrol Ground, south of St. Helena.—"It was while gliding through these latter waters that one serene and moonlight night, when all the waves rolled by like scrolls of silver; and by their soft, suffusing seethings, made what seemed a silvery silence, not a solitude; on such a silent night a silvery jet was seen far in advance of the white bubbles at the bow——"

Then there is the description of brit. "Steering northeastward from the Crozello we fell in with vast meadows of brit, the minute, yellow substance upon which the right whale largely feeds. For leagues and leagues it undulated round us, so that we seemed to be sailing through boundless fields of ripe and golden wheat. On the second day, numbers of right whales were seen, secure from the attack of a sperm whaler like the *Pequod*. With open jaws they sluggishly swam through the brit, which, adhering to the fringed fibres of that wondrous Venetian blind in their mouths, was in that manner separated from the water that escaped at the lip. As moving mowers who, side by side, slowly and seethingly advanced their scythes through the long wet grass of the marshy meads; even so these monsters swam, making a strange, grassy, cutting sound; and leaving behind them endless swaths of blue on the yellow sea. But it was only the sound they made as they parted the brit which at all reminded one of mowers. Seen from the mastheads, especially when they paused and were stationary for a while, their vast black forms looked more like masses of rock than anything else——"

This beautiful passage brings us to the apparition of the squid.

"Slowly wading through the meadows of brit, the *Pequod* still held her way northeastward towards the island of Java; a gentle air impelling her keel, so that in the surrounding serenity her three tall, tapering masts mildly waved to that languid breeze, as three mild palms on a plain. And still, at wide intervals, in the silvery night, that lonely, alluring jet would be seen.

"But one transparent-blue morning, when a stillness almost preternatural spread over the sea, however unattended with any stagnant calm; when the long burnished sunglade on the waters seemed a golden finger laid across them, enjoining secrecy; when all the slippered waves whispered together as they softly ran on; in this profound hush of the visible sphere a strange spectre was seen by Daggoo from the mainmast head.

"In the distance, a great white mass lazily rose, and rising higher and higher, and disentangling itself from the azure, at last gleamed before our prow like a snow-slide, new slid from the hills. Thus glistening for a moment, as slowly it subsided, and sank. Then once more arose, and silently gleamed. It seemed not a whale; and yet, is this Moby Dick? thought Daggoo——"

The boats were lowered and pulled to the scene.

"In the same spot where it sank, once more it slowly rose. Almost forgetting for the moment all thoughts of Moby Dick, we now gazed at the most wondrous phenomenon which the secret seas have hitherto revealed to mankind. A vast pulpy mass, furlongs in length and breadth, of a glancing cream-colour, lay floating on the water, innumerable long arms radiating from its centre, and curling and twisting like a nest of anacondas, as if blindly to clutch at any hapless object within reach. No perceptible face or front did it have; no conceivable token of either sensation or instinct; but undulated there on the billows, an unearthly, formless, chance-like apparition of life. And with a low sucking it slowly disappeared again."

The following chapters, with their account of whale-hunts, the killing, the stripping, the cutting up, are magnificent records of actual happening. Then comes the queer tale of the meeting of the *Jeroboam*, a whaler met at sea, all of whose men were under the domination of a religious maniac, one of the ship's hands. There are detailed descriptions of the actual taking of the sperm oil from a whale's head. Dilating on the smallness of the brain of a sperm whale, Melville significantly remarks—"for I believe that much of a man's character will be found betokened in his backbone. I would rather feel your spine than your skull, whoever you are——" And of the whale, he adds:

"For, viewed in this light, the wonderful comparative smallness of his brain proper is more than compensated by the wonderful comparative magnitude of his spinal cord."

In among the rush of terrible, awful hunts, come touches of pure beauty.

"As the three boats lay there on that gently rolling sea, gazing down into its eternal blue noon; and as not a single groan or cry of any sort, nay not so much as a ripple or a thought, came up from its depths; what landsman would have thought that beneath all that silence and placidity the utmost monster of the seas was writhing and wrenching in agony!"

Perhaps the most stupendous chapter is the one called "The Grand Armada", at the beginning of Volume III. The *Pequod* was drawing through the Sunda Straits towards Java when she came upon a vast host of sperm whales. "Broad on both bows, at a distance of two or three miles, and forming a great semicircle embracing one-half of the level horizon, a continuous chain of whale-jets were up-playing and sparkling in the noonday air." Chasing this great herd, past the Straits of Sunda, themselves chased by Javan pirates, the whalers race on. Then the boats are lowered. At last that curious state of inert irresolution came over the whales, when they were, as the seamen say, gallied. Instead of forging ahead in huge martial array they swam violently hither and thither, a surging sea of whales, no longer moving on. Starbuck's boat, made fast to a whale, is towed in amongst this howling Leviathan chaos. In mad career it cockles through the boiling surge of monsters, till it is brought into a clear lagoon in the very centre of the vast, mad, terrified herd. There a sleek, pure calm reigns. There the females swam in peace, and the young whales came snuffing tamely at the boat, like dogs. And there the astonished seamen watched the love-making of these amazing monsters, mammals, now in rut far down in the sea —"But far beneath this wondrous world upon the surface, another and still stranger world met our eyes, as we gazed over the side. For, suspended in these watery vaults, floated the forms of the nursing mothers of the whales, and those that by their enormous girth seemed shortly to become mothers. The lake, as I have hinted, was to a considerable depth exceedingly transparent; and as human infants while sucking will calmly and fixedly gaze away from the breast, as if leading two different lives at a time; and while yet drawing moral nourishment, be still spiritually feasting upon some unearthly reminiscence, even so did the young of these whales seem looking up towards us, but not at us, as if we were but a bit of gulf-weed in their newborn sight. Floating on their sides, the mothers also seemed quietly eyeing us.—Some of the subtlest secrets of the seas seemed divulged to us in this enchanted pond. We saw young Leviathan amours in the deep. And thus, though surrounded by circle upon circle of consternation and affrights, did these inscrutable creatures at the centre freely and fearlessly indulge in all peaceful concernments; yea, serenely revelled in dalliance and delight——"

There is something really overwhelming in these whale-hunts, almost superhuman or inhuman, bigger than life, more terrific than human activity. The same with the chapter on ambergris: it is so curious, so real, yet so unearthly. And again in the chapter called "The Cassock"—surely the oddest piece of phallicism in all the world's literature.

After this comes the amazing account of the Try-works, when the ship is turned into the sooty, oily factory in mid-ocean, and the oil is extracted from the blubber. In the night of the red furnace burning on deck, at sea, Melville has his startling experience of reversion. He is at the helm, but has turned to watch the fire: when suddenly he feels the ship rushing backward from him, in mystic reversion—"Uppermost was the impression, that whatever swift, rushing thing I stood on was not so much bound to any haven ahead, as rushing from all havens astern. A stark bewildering feeling, as of death, came over me. Convulsively my hands grasped the tiller, but with the crazy conceit that the tiller was, somehow, in some enchanted way, inverted. My God! What is the matter with me, I thought!"

This dream-experience is a real soul-experience. He ends with an injunction to all men, not to gaze on the red fire when its redness makes all things look ghastly. It seems to

him that his gazing on fire has evoked this horror of reversion, undoing.

Perhaps it had. He was water-born.

After some unhealthy work on the ship, Queequeg caught
a fever and was like to die. "How he wasted and wasted in
those few, long-lingering days, till there seemed but little left
of him but his frame and tattooing. But as all else in him
thinned, and his cheek-bones grew sharper, his eyes, nevertheless, seemed growing fuller and fuller; they took on a
strangeness of lustre; and mildly but deeply looked out at you
there from his sickness, a wondrous testimony to that immortal health in him which could not die, or be weakened.
And like circles on the water, which as they grow fainter,
expand; so his eyes seemed rounding and rounding, like the
circles of Eternity. An awe that cannot be named would steal
over you as you sat by the side of this waning savage——"

But Queequeg did not die—and the *Pequod* emerges from
the Eastern Straits, into the full Pacific. "To my meditative
Magian rover, this serene Pacific once beheld, must ever after
be the sea of his adoption. It rolls the utmost waters of the
world——"

In this Pacific the fights go on: "It was far down the afternoon, and when all the spearings of the crimson fight were
done, and floating in the lovely sunset sea and sky, sun and
whale both died stilly together; then such a sweetness and
such a plaintiveness, such inwreathing orisons curled up in
that rosy air, that it almost seemed as if far over from the
deep green convent valleys of the Manila Isles, the Spanish
land-breeze had gone to sea, freighted with these vesper
hymns. Soothed again, but only soothed to deeper gloom,
Ahab, who has steered off from the whale, sat intently watching his final wanings from the now tranquil boat. For that
strange spectacle, observable in all sperm whales dying—the
turning of the head sunwards, and so expiring—that strange
spectacle, beheld of such a placid evening, somehow to Ahab
conveyed wondrousness unknown before, 'He turns and turns
him to it; how slowly, but how steadfastly, his home-ren-
dering and invoking brow, with his last dying motions. He
too worships fire . . .'"

So Ahab soliloquises: and so the warm-blooded whale turns

for the last time to the sun, which begot him in the waters.

But as we see in the next chapter, it is the Thunder-fire which Ahab really worships: that living sundering fire of which he bears the brand, from head to foot; it is storm, the electric storm of the *Pequod*, when the corposants burn in high, tapering flames of supernatural pallor upon the mast-head, and when the compass is reversed. After this all is fatality. Life itself seems mystically reversed. In these hunters of Moby Dick there is nothing but madness and possession. The captain, Ahab, moves hand in hand with the poor imbecile negro boy, Pip, who has been so cruelly demented, left swimming alone in the vast sea. It is the imbecile child of the sun hand in hand with the northern monomaniac, captain and master.

The voyage surges on. They meet one ship, then another. It is all ordinary day-routine, and yet all is a tension of pure madness and horror, the approaching horror of the last fight. "Hither and thither, on high, glided the snow-white wings of small unspecked birds; these were the gentle thoughts of the feminine air; but to and fro in the deeps, far down in the bottomless blue, rushed mighty leviathans, sword-fish and sharks; and these were the strong, troubled, murderous things of the masculine sea——" On this day Ahab confesses his weariness, the weariness of his burden. "But do I look very old, so very, very old, Starbuck? I feel deadly faint, and bowed, and humped, as though I were Adam staggering beneath the piled centuries since Paradise——" It is the Gethsemane of Ahab, before the last fight: the Gethsemane of the human soul seeking the last self-conquest, the last attainment of extended consciousness—infinite consciousness.

At last they sight the whale. Ahab sees him from his hoisted perch at the masthead—"From this height the whale was now seen some mile or so ahead, at every roll of the sea revealing his high, sparkling hump, and regularly jetting his silent spout into the air."

The boats are lowered, to draw near the white whale. "At length the breathless hunter came so nigh his seemingly unsuspectful prey that his entire dazzling hump was distinctly visible, sliding along the sea as if an isolated thing, and continually set in a revolving ring of finest, fleecy, greenish foam.

He saw the vast involved wrinkles of the slightly projecting head, beyond. Before it, far out on the soft, Turkish-rugged waters, went the glistening white shadow from his broad, milky forehead, a musical rippling playfully accompanying the shade; and behind, the blue waters interchangeably flowed over the moving valley of his steady wake; and on either side bright bubbles arose and danced by his side. But these were broken again by the light toes of hundreds of gay fowl softly feathering the sea, alternate with their fitful flight; and like to some flagstaff rising from the pointed hull of an argosy, the tall but shattered pole of a recent lance projected from the white whale's back; and at intervals one of the clouds of soft-toed fowls hovering, and to and fro shimmering like a canopy over the fish, silently perched and rocked on this pole, the long tail-feathers streaming like pennons.

"A gentle joyousness—a mighty mildness of repose in swiftness, invested the gliding whale——"

The fight with the whale is too wonderful, and too awful, to be quoted apart from the book. It lasted three days. The fearful sight, on the third day, of the torn body of the Parsee harpooner, lost on the previous day, now seen lashed on to the flanks of the white whale by the tangle of harpoon lines, has a mystic dream-horror. The awful and infuriated whale turns upon the ship, symbol of this civilised world of ours. He smites her with a fearful shock. And a few minutes later, from the last of the fighting whale-boats comes the cry: "'The ship! Great God, where is the ship?' Soon they, through the dim, bewildering mediums, saw her sidelong fading phantom, as in the gaseous *fata Morgana*; only the uppermost masts out of the water; while fixed by infatuation, or fidelity, or fate, to their once lofty perches, the pagan harpooners still maintained their sinking lookouts on the sea. And now concentric circles seized the lone boat itself, and all its crew, and each floating oar, and every lance-pole, and spinning, animate and inanimate, all round and round in one vortex, carried the smallest chip of the *Pequod* out of sight——"

The bird of heaven, the eagle, St. John's bird, the Red Indian bird, the American, goes down with the ship, nailed by Tastego's hammer, the hammer of the American Indian. The eagle of the spirit. Sunk!

"Now small fowls flew screaming over the yet yawning gulf; a sullen white surf beat against its steep sides; then all collapsed; and then the great shroud of the sea rolled on as it rolled five thousand years ago."

So ends one of the strangest and most wonderful books in the world, closing up its mystery and its tortured symbolism. It is an epic of the sea such as no man has equalled; and it is a book of exoteric symbolism of profound significance, and of considerable tiresomeness.

But it is a great book, a very great book, the greatest book of the sea ever written. It moves awe in the soul.

The terrible fatality.

Fatality.

Doom.

Doom! Doom! Doom! Something seems to whisper it in the very dark trees of America. Doom!

Doom of what?

Doom of our white day. We are doomed, doomed. And the doom is in America. The doom of our white day.

Ah, well, if my day is doomed, and I am doomed with my day, it is something greater than I which dooms me, so I accept my doom as a sign of the greatness which is more than I am.

Melville knew. He knew his race was doomed. His white soul, doomed. His great white epoch, doomed. Himself, doomed. The idealist, doomed. The spirit, doomed.

The reversion. "Not so much bound to any haven ahead, as rushing from all havens astern."

That great horror of ours! It is our civilisation rushing from all havens astern.

The last ghastly hunt. The White Whale.

What then is Moby Dick? He is the deepest blood-being of the white race; he is our deepest blood-nature.

And he is hunted, hunted, hunted by the maniacal fanaticism of our white mental consciousness. We want to hunt him down. To subject him to our will. And in this maniacal conscious hunt of ourselves we get dark races and pale to help us, red, yellow, and black, east and west, Quaker and fire-worshipper, we get them all to help us in this ghastly maniacal hunt which is our doom and our suicide.

The last phallic being of the white man. Hunted into the death of upper consciousness and the ideal will. Our blood-self subjected to our will. Our blood-consciousness sapped by a parasitic mental or ideal consciousness.

Hot-blooded sea-born Moby Dick. Hunted by monomaniacs of the idea.

Oh God, oh God, what next, when the *Pequod* has sunk?

She sank in the war, and we are all flotsam.

Now what next?

Who knows? *Quien sabe? Quien sabe, señor?*

Neither Spanish nor Saxon America has any answer.

The *Pequod* went down. And the *Pequod* was the ship of the white American soul. She sank, taking with her negro and Indian and Polynesian, Asiatic and Quaker and good, businesslike Yankees and Ishmael: she sank all the lot of them.

Boom! as Vachel Lindsay would say.

To use the words of Jesus, IT IS FINISHED.

Consummatum est!

But *Moby Dick* was first published in 1851. If the Great White Whale sank the ship of the Great White Soul in 1851, what's been happening ever since?

Post-mortem effects, presumably.

Because, in the first centuries, Jesus was Cetus, the Whale. And the Christians were the little fishes. Jesus, the Redeemer, was Cetus, Leviathan. And all the Christians all his little fishes.

D. H. Lawrence on

THOMAS HARDY

This is supposed to be a book[1] about the people in Thomas Hardy's novels. But if one wrote everything they give rise to, it would fill the Judgment Book.

One thing about them is that none of the heroes and heroines care very much for money, or immediate self-preservation, and all of them are struggling hard to come into being. What exactly the struggle into being consists in, is the question. But most obviously, from the Wessex novels, the first and chiefest factor is the struggle into love and the struggle with love: by love, meaning the love of a man for a woman and a woman for a man. The *via media* to being, for man or woman, is love, and love alone. Having achieved and accomplished love, then the man passes into the unknown. He has become himself, his tale is told. Of anything that is complete there is no more tale to tell. The tale is about becoming complete, or about the failure to become complete.

It is urged against Thomas Hardy's characters that they do unreasonable things—quite, quite unreasonable things. They are always going off unexpectedly and doing something that nobody would do. That is quite true, and the charge is amusing. These people of Wessex are always bursting suddenly out of bud and taking a wild flight into flower, always shooting suddenly out of a tight convention, a tight, hide-bound cabbage state into something quite madly personal. It would be amusing to count the number of special marriage licenses taken out in Hardy's books. Nowhere, except perhaps in Jude, is there the slightest development of personal action in the characters: it is all explosive. Jude, however, does see more or less what he is doing, and acts from choice. He is more

[1] *Study of Thomas Hardy.*

consecutive. The rest explode out of the convention. They are people each with a real, vital, potential self, even the apparently wishy-washy heroines of the earlier books, and this self suddenly bursts the shell of manner and convention and commonplace opinion, and acts independently, absurdly, without mental knowledge or acquiescence.

And from such an outburst the tragedy usually develops. For there does exist, after all, the great self-preservation scheme, and in it we must all live. Now to live in it after bursting out of it was the problem these Wessex people found themselves faced with. And they never solved the problem, none of them except the comically, insufficiently treated Ethelberta.

This because they must subscribe to the system in themselves. From the more immediate claims of self-preservation they could free themselves: from money, from ambition for social success. None of the heroes or heroines of Hardy cared much for these things. But there is the greater idea of self-preservation, which is formulated in the State, in the whole modelling of the community. And from this idea, the heroes and heroines of Wessex, like the heroes and heroines of almost anywhere else, could not free themselves. In the long run, the State, the Community, the established form of life remained, remained intact and impregnable, the individual, trying to break forth from it, died of fear, of exhaustion, or of exposure to attacks from all sides, like men who have left the walled city to live outside in the precarious open.

This is the tragedy of Hardy, always the same: the tragedy of those who, more or less pioneers, have died in the wilderness, whither they had escaped for free action, after having left the walled security, and the comparative imprisonment, of the established convention. This is the theme of novel after novel: remain quite within the convention, and you are good, safe, and happy in the long run, though you never have the vivid pang of sympathy on your side: or, on the other hand, be passionate, individual, wilful, you will find the security of the convention a walled prison, you will escape, and you will die, either of your own lack of strength to bear the isolation and the exposure, or by direct revenge from the community, or from both. This is the tragedy, and only this:

it is nothing more metaphysical than the division of a man against himself in such a way: first, that he is a member of the community, and must, upon his honour, in no way move to disintegrate the community, either in its moral or its practical form; second, that the convention of the community is a prison to his natural, individual desire, a desire that compels him, whether he feel justified or not, to break the bounds of the community, lands him outside the pale, there to stand alone, and say: "I was right, my desire was real and inevitable; if I was to be myself I must fulfil it, convention or no convention," or else, there to stand alone, doubting, and saying: "Was I right, was I wrong? If I was wrong, oh, let me die!"—in which case he courts death.

The growth and the development of this tragedy, the deeper and deeper realisation of this division and this problem, the coming towards some conclusion, is the one theme of the Wessex novels. . . .

The Return of the Native . . . is the first tragic and important novel. Eustacia, dark, wild, passionate, quite conscious of her desires and inheriting no tradition which would make her ashamed of them, since she is of a novelistic Italian birth, loves, first, the unstable Wildeve, who does not satisfy her, then casts him aside for the newly returned Clym, whom she marries. What does she want? She does not know, but it is evidently some form of self-realisation; she wants to be herself, to attain herself. But she does not know how, by what means, so romantic imagination says: Paris and the *beau monde*. As if that would have stayed her unsatisfaction.

Clym has found out the vanity of Paris and the *beau monde*. What, then, does he want? He does not know; his imagination tells him he wants to serve the moral system of the community, since the material system is despicable. He wants to teach little Egdon boys in school. There is as much vanity in this, easily, as in Eustacia's Paris. For what is the moral system but the ratified form of the material system? What is Clym's altruism but a deep, very subtle cowardice, that makes him shirk his own being whilst apparently acting nobly; which makes him choose to improve mankind rather than to struggle at the quick of himself into being. He is not able to undertake his own soul, so he will take a commission for society to enlighten the souls of others. It is subtle equivocation. Thus both Eustacia and he sidetrack from themselves, and each leaves the other unconvinced, unsatisfied, unrealised. Eustacia, because she moves outside the convention, must die; Clym, because he identified himself with the community, is transferred from Paris to preaching. He had never become an integral man, because when faced with the demand to produce himself, he remained under cover of the community and excused by his altruism.

His remorse over his mother is adulterated with sentiment; it is exaggerated by the push of tradition behind it. Even in this he does not ring true. He is always according to pattern, producing his feelings more or less on demand, according to the accepted standard. Practically never is he able to act or even feel in his original self; he is always according to the convention. His punishment is his final loss of all his original self: he is left preaching, out of sheer emptiness.

Thomasin and Venn have nothing in them turbulent enough to push them to the bounds of the convention. There is always room for them inside. They are genuine people, and they get the prize within the walls.

Wildeve, shifty and unhappy, attracted always from outside and never driven from within, can neither stand with nor without the established system. He cares nothing for it, because he is unstable, has no positive being. He is an eternal assumption.

The other victim, Clym's mother, is the crashing-down of one of the old, rigid pillars of the system. The pressure on her is too great. She is weakened from the inside also, for her nature is non-conventional; it cannot own the bounds.

So, in this book, all the exceptional people, those with strong feelings and unusual characters, are reduced; only those remain who are steady and genuine, if commonplace. Let a man will for himself, and he is destroyed. He must will according to the established system.

The real sense of tragedy is got from the setting. What is the great, tragic power in the book? It is Egdon Heath. And who are the real spirits of the Heath? First, Eustacia, then

Clym's mother, then Wildeve. The natives have little or nothing in common with the place.

What is the real stuff of tragedy in the book? It is the Heath. It is the primitive, primal earth, where the instinctive life heaves up. There, in the deep, rude stirring of the instincts, there was the reality that worked the tragedy. Close to the body of things, there can be heard the stir that makes us and destroys us. The Heath heaved with raw instinct. Egdon, whose dark soil was strong and crude and organic as the body of a beast. Out of the body of this crude earth are born Eustacia, Wildeve, Mistress Yeobright, Clym, and all the others. They are one year's accidental crop. What matters if some are drowned or dead, and others preaching or married: what matter, any more than the withering heath, the reddening berries, the seedy furze, and the dead fern of one autumn of Egdon? The Heath persists. Its body is strong and fecund, it will bear many more crops beside this. Here is the sombre, latent power that will go on producing, no matter what happens to the product. Here is the deep, black source from whence all these little contents of lives are drawn. And the contents of the small lives are spilled and wasted. There is savage satisfaction in it: for so much more remains to come, such a black, powerful fecundity is working there that what does it matter?

Three people die and are taken back into the Heath; they mingle their strong earth again with its powerful soil, having been broken off at their stem. It is very good. Not Egdon is futile, sending forth life on the powerful heave of passion. It cannot be futile, for it is eternal. What is futile is the purpose of man.

Man has a purpose which he has divorced from the passionate purpose that issued him out of the earth into being. The Heath threw forth its shaggy heather and furze and fern, clean into being. It threw forth Eustacia and Wildeve and Mistress Yeobright and Clym, but to what purpose? Eustacia thought she wanted the hats and bonnets of Paris. Perhaps she was right. The heavy, strong soil of Egdon, breeding original native beings, is under Paris as well as under Wessex, and Eustacia sought herself in the gay city. She thought life there, in Paris, would be tropical, and all her energy and pas-

sion out of Egdon would there come into handsome flower.
And if Paris real had been Paris as she imagined it, no doubt
she was right, and her instinct was soundly expressed. But
Paris real was not Eustacia's imagined Paris. Where was her
imagined Paris, the place where her powerful nature could
come to blossom? Beside some strong-passioned, unconfined
man, her mate.

Which mate Clym might have been. He was born out of
passionate Egdon to live as a passionate being whose strong
feelings moved him ever further into being. But quite early
his life became narrowed down to a small purpose: he must
of necessity go into business, and submit his whole being,
body and soul as well as mind, to the business and to the
greater system it represented. His feelings, that should have
produced the man, were suppressed and contained, he worked
according to a system imposed from without. The dark struggle of Egdon, a struggle into being as the furze struggles into
flower, went on in him, but could not burst the enclosure of
the idea, the system which contained him. Impotent to *be*,
he must transform himself, and live in an abstraction, in a
generalisation, he must identify himself with the system. He
must live as Man or Humanity, or as the Community, or as
Society, or as Civilisation. "An inner strenuousness was prey-
ing on his outer symmetry, and they rated his look as singular. . . . His countenance was overlaid with legible meanings. Without being thought-worn, he yet had certain marks
derived from a perception of his surroundings, such as are
not infrequently found on man at the end of the four or five
years of endeavour which follow the close of placid pupilage.
He already showed that thought is a disease of the flesh, and
indirectly bore evidence that ideal physical beauty is incompatible with emotional development and a full recognition of
the coil of things. Mental luminousness must be fed with the
oil of life, even if there is already a physical seed for it; and
the pitiful sight of two demands on one supply was just showing itself here."

But did the face of Clym show that thought is a disease
of flesh, or merely that in his case a dis-ease, an un-ease, of
flesh produced thought? One does not catch thought like a
fever: one produces it. If it be in any way a disease of flesh,

it is rather the rash that indicates the disease than the disease itself. The "inner strenuousness" of Clym's nature was not fighting against his physical symmetry, but against the limits imposed on his physical movement. By nature, as a passionate, violent product of Egdon, he should have loved and suffered in flesh and in soul from love, long before this age. He should have lived and moved and had his being, whereas he had only his business, and afterwards his inactivity. His years of pupilage were past, "he was one of whom something original was expected," yet he continued in pupilage. For he produced nothing original in being or in act, and certainly no original thought. None of his ideas were original. Even he himself was not original. He was over-taught, had become an echo. His life had been arrested, and his activity turned into repetition. Far from being emotionally developed, he was emotionally undeveloped, almost entirely. Only his mental faculties were developed. And, hid, his emotions were obliged to work according to the label he put upon them: a ready-made label.

Yet he remained for all that an original, the force of life was in him, however much he frustrated and suppressed its natural movement. "As is usual with bright natures, the deity that lies ignominiously chained within an ephemeral human carcass shone out of him like a ray." But was the deity chained within his ephemeral human carcass, or within his limited human consciousness? Was it his blood, which rose dark and potent out of Egdon, which hampered and confined the deity, or was it his mind, that house built of extraneous knowledge and guarded by his will, which formed the prison?

He came back to Egdon—what for? To reunite himself with the strong, free flow of life that rose out of Egdon as from a source? No—"to preach to the Egdon eremites that they might rise to a serene comprehensiveness without going through the process of enriching themselves." As if the Egdon eremites had not already far more serene comprehensiveness than ever he had himself, rooted as they were in the soil of all things, and living from the root! What did it matter how they enriched themselves, so long as they kept this strong, deep root in the primal soil, so long as their instincts moved out to action and to expression? The system was big enough for them, and had no power over their instincts. They should have taught him rather than he them.

And Egdon made him marry Eustacia. Here was action and life, here was a move into being on his part. But as soon as he got her, she became an idea to him, she had to fit in his system of ideas. According to his way of living, he knew her already, she was labelled and classed and fixed down. He had got into this way of living, and he could not get out of it. He had identified himself with the system, and he could not extricate himself. He did not know that Eustacia had her being beyond his. He did not know that she existed un-touched by his system and his mind, where no system had sway and where no consciousness had risen to the surface. He did not know that she was Egdon, the powerful, eternal origin seething with production. He thought he knew. Egdon to him was the tract of common land, producing familiar rough herb-age, and having some few unenlightened inhabitants. So he skated over heaven and hell, and having made a map of the surface, thought he knew all. But underneath and among his mapped world, the eternal powerful fecundity worked on heedless of him and his arrogance. His preaching, his super-ficiality made no difference. . . . He did not know that the greater part of every life is underground, like roots in the dark in contact with the beyond. He preached, thinking lives could be moved like hen-houses from here to there. His blind-ness indeed brought on the calamity. But what matter if Eustacia or Wildeve or Mrs. Yeobright died: what matter if he himself became a mere rattle of repetitive words—what did it matter? It was regrettable; no more. Egdon, the primal impulsive body, would go on producing all that was to be produced, eternally, though the will of man should destroy the blossom yet in bud, over and over again. At last he must learn what it is to be at one, in his mind and will, with the primal impulses that rise in him. Till then, let him perish or preach. The great reality on which the little tragedies en-act themselves cannot be detracted from. The will and words which militate against it are the only vanity.

This is a constant revelation in Hardy's novels: that there exists a great background, vital and vivid, which matters more than the people who move upon it. Against the background of dark, passionate Egdon, of the leafy, sappy passion and sentiment of the woodlands, of the unfathomed stars, is drawn the lesser scheme of lives: *The Return of the Native, The Woodlanders,* or *Two on a Tower.* Upon the vast, incomprehensible pattern of some primal morality greater than ever the human mind can grasp, is drawn the little, pathetic pattern of man's moral life and struggle, pathetic, almost ridiculous. The little fold of law and order, the little walled city within which man has to defend himself from the waste enormity of nature, becomes always too small, and the pioneers venturing out with the code of the walled city upon them, die in the bonds of that code, free and yet unfree, preaching the walled city and looking to the waste.

This is the wonder of Hardy's novels, and gives them their beauty. The vast, unexplored morality of life itself, what we call the immorality of nature, surrounds us in its eternal incomprehensibility, and in its midst goes on the little human morality play, with its queer frame of morality and its mechanised movement; seriously, portentously, till some one of the protagonists chances to look out of the charmed circle, weary of the stage, to look into the wilderness raging round. Then he is lost, his little drama falls to pieces, or becomes mere repetition, but the stupendous theatre outside goes on enacting its own incomprehensible drama, untouched. There is this quality in almost all Hardy's work, and this is the magnificent irony it all contains, the challenge, the contempt. Not the deliberate ironies, little tales of widows or widowers, contain the irony of human life as we live it in our self-aggrandised gravity, but the big novels, *The Return of the Native,* and the others.

And this is the quality Hardy shares with the great writers, Shakespeare or Sophocles or Tolstoi, this setting behind the small action of his protagonists the terrific action of unfathomed nature; setting a smaller system of morality, the one grasped and formulated by the human consciousness within the vast, uncomprehended and incomprehensible morality of nature or of life itself, surpassing human consciousness. The difference is, that whereas in Shakespeare or Sophocles the greater, uncomprehended morality, or fate, is actively transgressed and gives active punishment, in Hardy and Tolstoi the lesser, human morality, the mechanical system is actively transgressed, and holds, and punishes the protagonist, whilst the greater morality is only passively, negatively transgressed, it is represented merely as being present in background, in scenery, not taking any active part, having no direct connexion with the protagonist. Oedipus, Hamlet, Macbeth set themselves up against, or find themselves set up against, the unfathomed moral forces of nature, and out of this unfathomed force comes their death. Whereas Anna Karenina, Eustacia, Tess, Sue, and Jude find themselves up against the established system of human government and morality, they cannot detach themselves, and are brought down. Their real tragedy is that they are unfaithful to the greater unwritten morality, which would have bidden Anna Karenina be patient and wait until she, by virtue of greater right, could take what she needed from society; would have bidden Vronsky detach himself from the system, become an individual, creating a new colony of morality with Anna; would have bidden Eustacia fight Clym for his own soul, and Tess take and claim her Angel, since she had the greater light; would have bidden Jude and Sue endure for very honour's sake, since one must bide by the best that one has known, and not succumb to the lesser good.

Had Oedipus, Hamlet, Macbeth been weaker, less full of real, potent life, they would have made no tragedy; they would have comprehended and contrived some arrangement of their affairs, sheltering in the human morality from the great stress and attack of the unknown morality. But being, as they are, men to the fullest capacity, when they find themselves, daggers drawn, with the very forces of life itself, they can only fight till they themselves are killed, since the morality of life, the greater morality, is eternally unalterable and invincible. It can be dodged for some time, but not opposed. On the other hand, Anna, Eustacia, Tess or Sue—what was there in their position that was necessarily tragic? Necessarily painful it was, but they were not at war with God, only with Society. Yet they were all cowed by the mere judgment of man upon them, and all the while by their own souls they were right. And the judgment of man killed them, not the judgment of their own souls or the judgment of Eternal God.

Which is the weakness of modern tragedy, where transgression against the social code is made to bring destruction, as though the social code worked our irrevocable fate. Like Clym, the map appears to us more real than the land. Shortsighted almost to blindness, we pore over the chart, map out journeys, and confirm them: and we cannot see life itself giving us the lie the whole time. . . .

Looking over the Hardy novels, it is interesting to see which of the heroes one would call a distinct individuality, more or less achieved, which an unaccomplished potential individuality, and which an impure, unindividualised life embedded in the matrix, either achieving its own lower degree of distinction, or not achieving it.

In *Desperate Remedies* there are scarcely any people at all, particularly when the plot is working. The tiresome part about Hardy is that, so often, he will neither write a morality play nor a novel. The people of the first book, as far as the plot is concerned, are not people: they are the heroine, faultless and white; the hero, with a small spot on his whiteness; the villainess, red and black, but more red than black; the villain, black and red; the Murderer, aided by the Adulteress, obtains power over the Virgin, who, rescued at the last moment by the Virgin Knight, evades the evil clutch. Then the Murderer, overtaken by vengeance, is put to death, whilst Divine Justice descends upon the Adulteress. Then the Virgin unites with the Virgin Knight, and receives Divine Blessing.

That is a morality play, and if the morality were vigorous and original, all well and good. But, between-whiles, we see that the Virgin is being played by a nice, rather ordinary girl.

In *The Laodicean*, there is all the way through a *prédilection d'artiste* for the aristocrat, and all the way through a moral condemnation of him, a substituting the middle- or lower-class personage with bourgeois virtues into his place. This was the root of Hardy's pessimism. Not until he comes to Tess and Jude does he ever sympathise with the aristocrat —unless it be in *The Mayor of Casterbridge*, and then he sympathises only to slay. He always, always represents them

the same, as having some vital weakness, some radical inef-
fectuality. From first to last it is the same.

Miss Aldclyffe and Manston, Elfride and the sickly lord
she married, Troy and Farmer Boldwood, Eustacia Vye and
Wildeve, de Stancy in *The Laodicean*, Lady Constantine in
Two on a Tower, the Mayor of Casterbridge and Lucetta,
Mrs. Charmond and Dr. Fitzpiers in *The Woodlanders*, Tess
and Alec d'Urberville, and, though different, Jude. There is
also the blond, passionate, yielding man: Sergeant Troy,
Wildeve, and, in spirit, Jude.

These are all, in their way, the aristocrat-characters of
Hardy. They must every one die, every single one.

Why has Hardy this *prédilection d'artiste* for the aristocrat, and why, at the same time, this moral antagonism to
him?

It is fairly obvious in *The Laodicean*, a book where, the
spirit being small, the complaint is narrow. The heroine, the
daughter of a famous railway engineer, lives in the castle of
the old de Stancys. She sighs, wishing she were of the de
Stancy line: the tombs and portraits have a spell over her.
"But," says the hero to her, "have you forgotten your father's
line of ancestry: Archimedes, Newcomen, Watt, Tylford,
Stephenson?"—"But I have a *prédilection d'artiste* for ancestors of the other sort," sighs Paula. And the hero despairs of
impressing her with the list of his architect ancestors: Phid-
ias, Ictinus and Callicrates, Chersiphron, Vitruvius, Wilars of
Cambray, William of Wykeham. He deplores her marked
preference for an "animal pedigree".

But what is this "animal pedigree"? If a family pedigree of
her ancestors, working-men and burghers, had been kept,
Paula would not have gloried in it, animal though it were.
Hers was a *prédilection d'artiste*.

And this because the aristocrat alone has occupied a position where he could afford to *be*, to be himself, to create
himself, to live as himself. That is his eternal fascination. This
is why the preference for him is a *prédilection d'artiste*. The
preference for the architect line would be a *prédilection de
savant*, the preference for the engineer pedigree would be a
prédilection d'économiste.

The *prédilection d'artiste*—Hardy has it strongly, and it is rooted deeply in every imaginative human being. The glory of mankind has been to produce lives, to produce vivid, independent, individual men, not buildings or engineering works or even art, not even the public good. The glory of mankind is not in a host of secure, comfortable, law-abiding citizens, but in the few more fine, clear lives, beings, individuals, distinct, detached, single as may be from the public.

And these the artist of all time has chosen. Why, then, must the aristocrat always be condemned to death, in Hardy? Has the community come to consciousness in him, as in the French Revolutionaries, determined to destroy all that is not the average? Certainly in the Wessex novels, all but the average people die. But why? Is there the germ of death in these more single, distinguished people, or has the artist himself a bourgeois taint, a jealous vindictiveness that will now take revenge, now that the community, the average, has gained power over the aristocrat, the exception?

It is evident that both is true. Starting with the bourgeois morality, Hardy makes every exceptional person a villain, all exceptional or strong individual traits he holds up as weaknesses or wicked faults. So in *Desperate Remedies, Under the Greenwood Tree, Far from the Madding Crowd, The Hand of Ethelberta, The Return of the Native* (but in *The Trumpet-Major* there is an ironical dig in the ribs to this civic communal morality), *The Laodicean, Two on a Tower, The Mayor of Casterbridge,* and *Tess,* in steadily weakening degree. The blackest villain is Manston, the next, perhaps, Troy, the next Eustacia, and Wildeve, always becoming less villainous and more human. The first show of real sympathy, nearly conquering the bourgeois or commune morality, is for Eustacia, whilst the dark villain is becoming merely a weak, pitiable person in Dr. Fitzpiers. In *The Mayor of Casterbridge* the dark villain is already almost the hero. There is a lapse in the maudlin, weak but not wicked Dr. Fitzpiers, duly condemned, Alec d'Urberville is not unlikeable, and Jude is a complete tragic hero, at once the old Virgin Knight and Dark Villain. The condemnation gradually shifts over from the dark villain to the blond bourgeois virgin hero, from Alec d'Urberville to Angel Clare, till in Jude they are united and loved, though the preponderance is of a dark villain, now dark, beloved, passionate hero. The condemnation shifts over at last from the dark villain to the white virgin, the bourgeois in soul: from Arabella to Sue. Infinitely more subtle and sad is the condemnation at the end, but there it is: the virgin knight is hated with intensity, yet still loved; the white virgin, the beloved, is the arch-sinner against life at last, and the last note of hatred is against her.

It is a complete and devastating shift-over, it is a complete *volte-face* of moralities. Black does not become white, but it takes white's place as good; white remains white, but it is found bad. The old, communal morality is like a leprosy, a white sickness: the old, anti-social, individualist morality is alone on the side of life and health.

But yet, the aristocrat must die, all the way through: even Jude. Was the germ of death in him at the start? Or was he merely at outs with his times, the times of the Average in triumph? Would Manston, Troy, Farmer Boldwood, Eustacia, de Stancy, Henchard, Alec d'Urberville, Jude have been real heroes in heroic times, without tragedy? It seems as if Manston, Boldwood, Eustacia, Henchard, Alec d'Urberville, and almost Jude, might have been. In an heroic age they might have lived and more or less triumphed. But Troy, Wildeve, de Stancy, Fitzpiers, and Jude have something fatal in them. There is a rottenness at the core of them. The failure, the misfortune, or the tragedy, whichever it may be, was inherent in them: as it was in Elfride, Lady Constantine, Marty South in *The Woodlanders*, and Tess. They have all passionate natures, and in them all failure is inherent. . . .

This, then, is the moral conclusion drawn from the novels:

1. The physical individual is in the end an inferior thing which must fall before the community: Manston, Henchard, etc.

2. The physical and spiritual individualist is a fine thing which must fall because of its own isolation, because it is a sport, not in the true line of life: Jude, Tess, Lady Constantine.

3. The physical individualist and spiritual bourgeois or communist is a thing, finally, of ugly, undeveloped, non-distinguished or perverted physical instinct, and must fall

physically. Sue, Angel Clare, Clym, Knight. It remains, however, fitted into the community.

4. The undistinguished, bourgeois or average being with average or civic virtues usually succeeds in the end. If he fails, he is left practically uninjured. If he expire during probation, he has flowers on his grave.

By individualist is meant, not a selfish or greedy person, anxious to satisfy appetites, but a man of distinct being, who must act in his own particular way to fulfil his own individual nature. He is a man who, being beyond the average, chooses to rule his own life to his own completion, and as such is an aristocrat.

The artist always has a predilection for him. But Hardy, like Tolstoi, is forced in the issue always to stand with the community in condemnation of the aristocrat. He cannot help himself, but must stand with the average against the exception, he must, in his ultimate judgment, represent the interests of humanity, or the community as a whole, and rule out the individual interest.

To do this, however, he must go against himself. His private sympathy is always with the individual against the community: as is the case with the artist. Therefore he will create a more or less blameless individual and, making him seek his own fulfilment, his highest aim, will show him destroyed by the community, or by that in himself which represents the community, or by some close embodiment of the civic idea. Hence the pessimism. To do this, however, he must select his individual with a definite weakness, a certain coldness of temper, inelastic, a certain inevitable and inconquerable adhesion to the community.

This is obvious in Troy, Clym, Tess, and Jude. They have naturally distinct individuality but, as it were, a weak life-flow, so that they cannot break away from the old adhesion, they cannot separate themselves from the mass which bore them, they cannot detach themselves from the common. Therefore they are pathetic rather than tragic figures. They have not the necessary strength: the question of their unfortunate end is begged in the beginning.

Whereas Oedipus or Agamemnon or Clytemnestra or Orestes, or Macbeth or Hamlet or Lear, these are destroyed by their own conflicting passions. Out of greed for adventure, a desire to be off, Agamemnon sacrifices Iphigenia: moreover he has his love-affairs outside Troy: and this brings on him death from the mother of his daughter, and from his pledged wife. Which is the working of the natural law. Hamlet, a later Orestes, is commanded by the Erinyes of his father to kill his mother and his uncle: but his maternal filial feeling tears him. It is almost the same tragedy as Orestes, without any goddess or god to grant peace.

In these plays, conventional morality is transcended. The action is between the great, single, individual forces in the nature of Man, not between the dictates of the community and the original passion. The Commandment says: "Thou shalt not kill." But doubtless Macbeth had killed many a man who was in his way. Certainly Hamlet suffered no qualms about killing the old man behind the curtain. Why should he? But when Macbeth killed Duncan, he divided himself in twain, into two hostile parts. It was all in his own soul and blood: it was nothing outside himself: as it was, really, with Clym, Troy, Tess, Jude. Troy would probably have been faithful to his little unfortunate person, had she been a lady, and had he not felt himself cut off from society in his very being, whilst all the time he cleaved to it. Tess allowed herself to be condemned, and asked for punishment from Angel Clare. Why? She had done nothing particularly, or at least irrevocably, unnatural, were her life young and strong. But she sided with the community's condemnation of her. And almost the bitterest, most pathetic, deepest part of Jude's misfortune was his failure to obtain admission to Oxford, his failure to gain his place and standing in the world's knowledge, in the world's work.

There is a lack of sternness, there is a hesitating betwixt life and public opinion, which diminishes the Wessex novels from the rank of pure tragedy. It is not so much the eternal, immutable laws of being which are transgressed, it is not that vital life-forces are set in conflict with each other, bringing almost inevitable tragedy—yet not necessarily death, as we see in the most splendid Aeschylus. It is, in Wessex, that the individual succumbs to what is in its shallowest, public opinion, in its deepest, the human compact by which we live together, to form a community. . . .

Thomas Hardy's metaphysic is something like Tolstoi's. "There is no reconciliation between Love and the Law," says Hardy. "The spirit of Love must always succumb before the blind, stupid, but overwhelming power of the Law."

Already as early as *The Return of the Native* he has come to this theory, in order to explain his own sense of failure. But before that time, from the very start, he has had an overweening theoretic antagonism to the Law. "That which is physical, of the body, is weak, despicable, bad," he said at the very start. He represented his fleshy heroes as villains, but very weak and maundering villains. At its worst, the Law is a weak, craven sensuality: at its best, it is a passive inertia. It is the gap in the armour, it is the hole in the foundation.

Such a metaphysic is almost silly. If it were not that man is much stronger in feeling than in thought, the Wessex novels would be sheer rubbish, as they are already in parts. *The Well-Beloved* is sheer rubbish, fatuity, as is a good deal of *The Dynasts* conception.

But it is not as a metaphysician that one must consider Hardy. He makes a poor show there. For nothing in his work is so pitiable as his clumsy efforts to push events into line with his theory of being, and to make calamity fall on those who represent the principle of Love. He does it exceedingly badly, and owing to this effort his form is execrable in the extreme.

His feeling, his instinct, his sensuous understanding is, however, apart from his metaphysic, very great and deep, deeper than that, perhaps, of any other English novelist. Putting aside his metaphysic, which must always obtrude when he thinks of people, and turning to the earth, to landscape, then he is true to himself.

Always he must start from the earth, from the great source of the Law, and his people move in his landscape almost insignificantly, somewhat like tame animals wandering in the wild. The earth is the manifestation of the Father, of the Creator, Who made us in the Law. God still speaks aloud in His Works, as to Job, so to Hardy, surpassing human conception and the human law. "Dost thou know the balancings of the clouds, the wondrous works of him which is perfect in knowledge? How thy garments are warm, when he quieteth the earth by the south wind? Hast thou with him spread out the sky, which is strong?"

This is the true attitude of Hardy—"With God is terrible majesty." The theory of knowledge, the metaphysic of the man, is much smaller than the man himself. So with Tolstoi.

"Knowest thou the time when the wild goats of the rock bring forth? Or canst thou mark when the hinds do calve? Canst thou number the months that they fulfil? Or knowest thou the time when they bring forth? They bow themselves, they bring forth their young ones, they cast out their sorrows. Their young ones are good in liking, they grow up with corn; they go forth, and return not unto them."

There is a good deal of this in Hardy. But in Hardy there is more than the concept of Job, protesting his integrity. Job says in the end: "Therefore have I uttered that I understood not; things too wonderful for me, which I knew not.

"I have heard of thee by hearing of the ear; but now mine eye seeth thee.

"Wherefore I abhor myself, and repent in dust and ashes."

But Jude ends where Job began, cursing the day and the services of his birth, and in so much cursing the act of the Lord, "Who made him in the womb."

It is the same cry all through Hardy, this curse upon the birth in the flesh, and this unconscious adherence to the flesh. The instincts, the bodily passions are strong and sudden in all Hardy's men. They are too strong and sudden. They fling Jude into the arms of Arabella, years after he has known Sue, and against his own will.

For every man comprises male and female in his being, the male always struggling for predominance. A woman likewise consists in male and female, with female predominant.

And a man who is strongly male tends to deny, to refute the female in him. A real "man" takes no heed for his body, which is the more female part of him. He considers himself only as an instrument, to be used in the service of some idea.

The true female, on the other hand, will eternally hold herself superior to any idea, will hold full life in the body to be the real happiness. The male exists in doing, the female in being. The male lives in the satisfaction of some purpose achieved, the female in the satisfaction of some purpose contained. . . .

So Aeschylus adheres still to the Law, to Right, to the Creator who created man in His Own Image, and in His Law. What he has learned of Love, he does not yet quite believe.

Hardy has the same belief in the Law, but in conceit of his own understanding, which cannot understand the Law, he says that the Law is nothing, a blind confusion.

And in conceit of understanding, he deprecates and destroys both women and men who would represent the old primeval Law, the great Law of the Womb, the primeval Female principle. The Female shall not exist. Where it appears, it is a criminal tendency, to be stamped out.

This in Manston, Troy, Boldwood, Eustacia, Wildeve, Henchard, Tess, Jude, everybody. The women approved of are not Female in any real sense. They are passive subjects to the male, the re-echo from the male. As in the Christian religion, the Virgin worship is no real Female worship, but worship of the Female as she is passive and subjected to the male. Hence the sadness of Botticelli's Virgins.

Thus Tess sets out, not as any positive thing, containing all purpose, but as the acquiescent complement to the male. The female in her has become inert. Then Alec d'Urberville comes along, and possesses her. From the man who takes her Tess expects her own consummation, the singling out of herself, the addition of the male complement. She is of an old line, and has the aristocratic quality of respect for the other being. She does not see the other person as an extension of herself, existing in a universe of which she is the centre and pivot. She knows that other people are outside her. Therein she is an aristocrat. And out of this attitude to the other person came her passivity. It is not the same as the passive quality in the other little heroines, such as the girl in *The Woodlanders*, who is passive because she is small.

Tess is passive out of self-acceptance, a true aristocratic quality, amounting almost to self-indifference. She knows she is herself incontrovertibly, and she knows that other people are not herself. This is a very rare quality, even in a woman. And in a civilisation so unequal, it is almost a weakness.

Tess never tries to alter or to change anybody, neither to alter nor to change nor to divert. What another person decides, that is his decision. She respects utterly the other's right to be. She is herself always.

But the others do not respect her right to be. Alec d'Urberville sees her as the embodied fulfilment of his own desire: something, that is, belonging to him. She cannot, in his conception, exist apart from him nor have any being apart from his being. For she is the embodiment of his desire.

This is very natural and common in men, this attitude to the world. But in Alec d'Urberville it applies only to the woman of his desire. He cares only for her. Such a man adheres to the female like a parasite.

It is a male quality to resolve a purpose to its fulfilment. It is the male quality, to seek the motive power in the female, and to convey this to a fulfilment; to receive some impulse into his senses, and to transmit it into expression.

Alec d'Urberville does not do this. He is male enough, in his way; but only physically male. He is constitutionally an enemy of the principle of self-subordination, which principle is inherent in every man. It is this principle which makes a man, a true male, see his job through, at no matter what cost. A man is strictly only himself when he is fulfilling some purpose he has conceived: so that the principle is not of self-subordination, but of continuity, of development. Only when insisted on, as in Christianity, does it become self-sacrifice. And this resistance to self-sacrifice on Alec d'Urberville's part does not make him an individualist, an egoist, but rather a non-individual, an incomplete, almost a fragmentary thing.

There seems to be in d'Urberville an inherent antagonism to any progression in himself. Yet he seeks with all his power for the source of stimulus in woman. He takes the deep impulse from the female. In this he is exceptional. No ordinary man could really have betrayed Tess. Even if she had had an illegitimate child to another man, to Angel Clare, for example, it would not have shattered her as did her connexion with Alec d'Urberville. For Alec d'Urberville could reach some of the real sources of the female in a woman, and draw from them. Troy could also do this. And, as a woman instinctively knows, such men are rare. Therefore they have a power over a woman. They draw from the depth of her being.

And what they draw, they betray. With a natural male, what he draws from the source of the female, the impulse he receives from the source he transmits through his own being into utterance, motion, action, expression. But Troy and Alec d'Urberville, what they received they knew only as gratification in the senses; some perverse will prevented them from submitting to it, from becoming instrumental to it.

Which was why Tess was shattered by Alec d'Urberville, and why she murdered him in the end. The murder is badly done, altogether the book is botched, owing to the way of thinking in the author, owing to the weak yet obstinate theory of being. Nevertheless, the murder is true, the whole book is true, in its conception.

Angel Clare has the very opposite qualities to those of Alec d'Urberville. To the latter, the female in himself is the only part of himself he will acknowledge: the body, the senses, that which he shares with the female, which the female shares with him. To Angel Clare, the female in himself is detestable, the body, the senses, that which he will share with a woman, is held degraded. What he wants really is to receive the female impulse other than through the body. But his thinking has made him criticise Christianity, his deeper instinct has forbidden him to deny his body any further, a deadlock in his own being, which denies him any purpose, so that he must take to hand, labour out of sheer impotence to resolve himself, drives him unwillingly to woman. But he must see her only as the Female Principle, he cannot bear to see her as the Woman in the Body. Her he thinks degraded. To marry her, to have a physical marriage with her, he must overcome all his ascetic revulsion, he must, in his own mind, put off his own divinity, his pure maleness, his singleness, his pure completeness, and descend to the heated welter of the flesh. It is objectionable to him. Yet his body, his life, is too strong for him.

Who is he, that he shall be pure male, and deny the existence of the female? This is the question the Creator asks of him. Is then the male the exclusive whole of life?—is he even the higher or supreme part of life? Angel Clare thinks so: as Christ thought.

Yet it is not so, as even Angel Clare must find out. Life, that is Two-in-One, Male and Female. Nor is either part greater than the other.

It is not Angel Clare's fault that he cannot come to Tess when he finds that she has, in his words, been defiled. It is the result of generations of ultra-Christian training, which had left in him an inherent aversion to the female, and to all in himself which pertained to the female. What he, in his Christian sense, conceived of as Woman, was only the servant and attendant and administering spirit to the male. He had no idea that there was such a thing as positive Woman, as the Female, another great living Principle counterbalancing his own male principle. He conceived of the world as consisting of the One, the Male Principle.

Which conception was already gendered in Botticelli, whence the melancholy of the Virgin. Which conception reached its fullest in Turner's pictures, which were utterly bodiless; and also in the great scientists or thinkers of the last generation, even Darwin and Spencer and Huxley. For these last conceived of evolution, of one spirit or principle starting at the far end of time, and lonelily traversing Time. But there is not one principle, there are two, travelling always to meet, each step of each one lessening the distance between the two of them. And Space, which so frightened Herbert Spencer, is as a Bride to us. And the cry of Man does not ring out into the Void. It rings out to Woman, whom we know not.

This Tess knew, unconsciously. An aristocrat she was, developed through generations to the belief in her own self-establishment. She could help, but she could not be helped. She could give, but she could not receive. She could attend to the wants of the other person, but no other person, save another aristocrat—and there is scarcely such a thing as another aristocrat—could attend to her wants, her deepest wants.

So it is the aristocrat alone who has any real and vital sense of "the neighbour", of the other person; who has the habit of submerging himself, putting himself entirely away before the other person: because he expects to receive nothing from the other person. So that now he has lost much of his initiative force, and exists almost isolated, detached, and without the surging ego of the ordinary man, because he has controlled his nature according to the other man, to exclude him.

And Tess, despising herself in the flesh, despising the deep Female she was, because Alec d'Urberville had betrayed her very source, loved Angel Clare, who also despised and hated the flesh. She did not hate d'Urberville. What a man did, he did, and if he did it to her, it was her look-out. She did not conceive of him as having any human duty towards her.

The same with Angel Clare as with Alec d'Urberville. She was very grateful to him for saving her from her despair of contamination, and from her bewildered isolation. But when he accused her, she could not plead or answer. For she had no right to his goodness. She stood alone.

The female was strong in her. She was herself. But she was out of place, utterly out of her element and her times. Hence her utter bewilderment. This is the reason why she was so overcome. She was outwearied from the start, in her spirit. For it is only by receiving from all our fellows that we are kept fresh and vital. Tess was herself, female, intrinsically a woman.

The female in her was indomitable, unchangeable, she was utterly constant to herself. But she was, by long breeding, intact from mankind. Though Alec d'Urberville was of no kin to her, yet, in the book, he has always a quality of kinship. It was as if only a kinsman, an aristocrat, could approach her. And this to her undoing. Angel Clare would never have reached her. She would have abandoned herself to him, but he would never have reached her. It needed a physical aristocrat. She would have lived with her husband, Clare, in a state of abandon to him, like a coma. Alec d'Urberville forced her to realise him, and to realise herself. He came close to her, as Clare could never have done. So she murdered him. For she was herself.

And just as the aristocratic principle had isolated Tess, it had isolated Alec d'Urberville. For though Hardy consciously made the younger betrayer a plebeian and an imposter, unconsciously, with the supreme justice of the artist, he made him the same as de Stancy, a true aristocrat, or as Fitzpiers, or Troy. He did not give him the tiredness, the touch of exhaustion necessary, in Hardy's mind, to an aristocrat. But he gave him the intrinsic qualities.

With the men as with the women of old descent: they have nothing to do with mankind in general, they are exceedingly personal. For many generations they have been accustomed to regard their own desires as their own supreme laws. They have not been bound by the conventional morality: this they have transcended, being a code unto themselves. The other person has been always present to their imagination, in the spectacular sense. He has always existed to them. But he has always existed as something other than themselves.

Hence the inevitable isolation, detachment of the aristocrat. His one aim, during centuries, has been to keep himself detached. At last he finds himself, by his very nature, cut off.

Then either he must go his own way, or he must struggle towards reunion with the mass of mankind. Either he must be an incomplete individualist, like de Stancy, or like the famous Russian nobles, he must become a wild humanitarian and reformer.

For as all the governing power has gradually been taken from the nobleman, and as, by tradition, by inherent inclination, he does not occupy himself with profession other than government, how shall he use that power which is in him and which comes into him?

He is, by virtue of breed and long training, a perfect instrument. He knows, as every pure-bred thing knows, that his root and source is in his female. He seeks the motive power in the woman. And, having taken it, has nothing to do with it, can find, in this democratic, plebeian age, no means by which to transfer it into action, expression, utterance. So there is a continual gnawing of unsatisfaction, a constant seeking of another woman, still another woman. For each time the impulse comes fresh, everything seems all right.

It may be, also, that in the aristocrat a certain weariness makes him purposeless, vicious, like a form of death. But that is not necessary. One feels that in Manston, and Troy, and Fitzpiers, and Alec d'Urberville, there is good stuff gone wrong. Just as in Angel Clare, there is good stuff gone wrong in the other direction.

There can never be one extreme of wrong, without the other extreme. If there had never been the extravagant Puritan idea, that the Female Principle was to be denied, cast out by man from his soul, that only the Male Principle, of Abstraction, of Good, of Public Good, of the Community, embodied in "Thou shalt love thy neighbour as thyself," really existed, there would never have been produced the extreme Cavalier type, which says that only the Female Principle endures in man, that all the Abstraction, the Good, the Public Elevation, the Community, was a grovelling cowardice, and that man lived by enjoyment, through his senses, enjoyment which ended in his senses. Or perhaps better, if the extreme Cavalier type had never been produced, we should not have had the Puritan, the extreme correction.

The one extreme produces the other. It is inevitable for Angel Clare and for Alec d'Urberville mutually to destroy the woman they both loved. Each does her the extreme of wrong, so she is destroyed.

The book is handled with very uncertain skill, botched and bungled. But it contains the elements of the greatest tragedy: Alec d'Urberville, who has killed the male in himself, as Clytemnestra symbolically for Orestes killed Agamemnon; Angel Clare, who has killed the female in himself, as Orestes killed Clytemnestra: and Tess, the Woman, the Life, destroyed by a mechanical fate, in the communal law.

There is no reconciliation. Tess, Angel Clare, Alec d'Urberville, they are all as good as dead. For Angel Clare, though still apparently alive, is in reality no more than a mouth, a piece of paper, like Clym left preaching.

There is no reconciliation, only death. And so Hardy really states his case, which is not his consciously stated metaphysic, by any means, but a statement how man has gone wrong and brought death on himself: how man has violated the Law, how he has supererogated himself, gone so far in his male conceit as to supersede the Creator, and win death as a reward. Indeed, the works of supererogation of our male assiduity help us to a better salvation.

D. H. LAWRENCE

"I always say, my motto is 'Art for my sake.'" The words are from a letter written by Lawrence before the war. "If I *want* to write, I write—and if I don't want to, I won't. The difficulty is to find exactly the form one's passion—work is produced by passion with me, like kisses—is it with you?—wants to take."

"Art for my sake." But even though for my sake, still art. Lawrence was always and unescapably an artist. Yes, unescapably is the word; for there were moments when he wanted to escape from his destiny. "I wish from the bottom of my heart that the fates had not stigmatized me 'writer.' It is a sickening business." But against the decree of fate there is no appeal. Nor was it by any means all the time that Lawrence wanted to appeal. His complaints were only occasional, and he was provoked to make them, not by any hatred of art as such, but by hatred of the pains and humiliations incidental to practising as an artist. Writing to Edward Garnett, "Why, why," he asks, "should we be plagued with literature and suchlike tomfoolery? Why can't we live decent, honourable lives, without the critics in the Little Theatre fretting us?" The publication of a work of art is always the exposure of a nakedness, the throwing of something delicate and sensitive to the "asses, apes and dogs." Mostly, however, Lawrence loved his destiny, loved the art of which he was a master—as who, that is a master, can fail to do? Besides, art, as he practised it, and as, at the bottom, every artist, even the most pharisaically "pure" practises it, was "art for my sake." It was useful to him, pragmatically helpful. "One sheds one's sicknesses in books —repeats and presents again one's emotions to be master of them." And, anyhow, liking or disliking were finally irrelevant in the face of the fact that Lawrence was in a real sense possessed by his creative genius. He could not help himself. "I am doing a novel," he writes in an early letter, "a novel which I have never grasped. Damn its eyes, there I am at p. 145 and I've no notion what it's about. I hate it. F. says it is good. But it's like a novel in a foreign language I don't know very well—I can only just make out what it's about." To this strange force within him, to this power that created his works of art, there was nothing to do but submit. Lawrence submitted, completely and with reverence. "I often think one ought to be able to pray before one works—and then leave it to the Lord. Isn't it hard work to come to real grips with one's imagination—throw everything overboard. I always feel as though I stood naked for the fire of Almighty God to go through me—and it's rather an awful feeling. One has to be so terribly religious to be an artist." Conversely, he might have added, one has to be terribly an artist, terribly conscious of "inspiration" and the compelling force of genius, to be religious as Lawrence was religious.

It is impossible to write about Lawrence except as an artist. He was an artist first of all, and the fact of his being an artist explains a life which seems, if you forget it, inexplicably strange. In *Son of Woman*, Mr. Middleton Murry has written at great length about Lawrence—but about a Lawrence whom you would never suspect, from reading that curious essay in destructive hagiography, of being an artist. For Mr. Murry almost completely ignores the fact that his subject—his victim, I had almost said—was one whom "the fates had stigmatized 'writer.'" His book is *Hamlet* without the Prince of Denmark—for all its metaphysical subtleties and its Freudian ingenuities, very largely irrelevant. The absurdity of his critical method becomes the more manifest when we reflect that nobody would ever have heard of a Lawrence who was not an artist.

An artist is the sort of artist he is, because he happens to possess certain gifts. And he leads the sort of life he does in fact lead, because he is an artist, and an artist with a particular kind of mental endowment. Now there are general abilities and there are special talents. A man who is born with a great share of some special talent is probably less deeply affected by nurture than one whose ability is generalized. His gift is his fate, and he follows a predestined course, from which no ordinary power can deflect him. In spite of Helvétius and Dr. Watson, it seems pretty obvious that no amount of education—including under that term everything from the Oedipus complex to the English Public School system—could have prevented Mozart from being a musician, or musicianship from being the central fact in Mozart's life. And how would a different education have modified the expression of, say, Blake's gift? It is, of course, impossible to answer. One can only express the unverifiable conviction that an art so profoundly individual and original, so manifestly "inspired," would have remained fundamentally the same whatever (within reasonable limits) had been the circumstances of Blake's upbringing. Lawrence, as Mr. F. R. Leavis insists, has many affinities with Blake. "He had the same gift of knowing what he was interested in, the same power of distinguishing his own feelings and emotions from conventional sentiment, the same 'terrifying honesty.'" Like Blake, like any man possessed of great special talents, he was predestined by his gifts. Explanations of him in terms of a Freudian hypothesis of nurture may be interesting, but they do not explain. That Lawrence was profoundly affected by his love for his mother and by her excessive love for him, is obvious to anyone who has read *Sons and Lovers*. None the less it is, to me at any rate, almost equally obvious that even if his mother had died when he was a child, Lawrence would still have been, essentially and fundamentally, Lawrence. Lawrence's biography does not account for Lawrence's achievement. On the contrary, his achievement, or rather the gift that made the achievement possible, accounts for a great deal of his biography. He lived as he lived, because he was, intrinsically and from birth, what he was. If we would write intelligibly of Lawrence, we must answer, with all their implications, two questions: first, what sort of gifts did he have? and secondly, how did the possession of these gifts affect the way he responded to experience?

Lawrence's special and characteristic gift was an extraordinary sensitiveness to what Wordsworth called "unknown modes of being." He was always intensely aware of the mystery of the world, and the mystery was always for him a *numen*, divine. Lawrence could never forget, as most of us almost continuously forget, the dark presence of the otherness that lies beyond the boundaries of man's conscious mind. This special sensibility was accompanied by a prodigious power of rendering the immediately experienced otherness in terms of literary art.

Such was Lawrence's peculiar gift. His possession of it accounts for many things. It accounts, to begin with, for his attitude towards sex. His particular experiences as a son and as a lover may have intensified his preoccupation with the subject; but they certainly did not make it. Whatever his experiences, Lawrence *must* have been preoccupied with sex; his gift made it inevitable. For Lawrence, the significance of the sexual experience was this: that, in it, the immediate, non-mental knowledge of divine otherness is brought, so to speak, to a focus—a focus of darkness. Parodying Matthew Arnold's famous formula, we may say that sex is something not ourselves that makes for—not righteousness, for the essence of religion is not righteousness; there is a spiritual world, as Kierkegaard insists, beyond the ethical—rather, that makes for life, for divineness, for union with the mystery. Paradoxically, this something not ourselves is yet a something lodged within us; this quintessence of otherness is yet the quintessence of our proper being. "And God the Father, the Inscrutable, the Unknowable, we know in the flesh, in Woman. She is the door for our in-going and our out-coming. In her we go back to the Father; but like the witnesses of the transfiguration, blind and unconscious." Yes, blind and unconscious; otherwise it is a revelation, not of divine otherness, but of very human evil. "The embrace of love, which should bring darkness and oblivion, would with these lovers (the hero and heroine of one of Poe's tales) be a daytime thing, bringing more heightened consciousness, visions, spectrum-visions, prismatic. The evil thing that daytime love-making is, and all sex-palaver!" How Lawrence hated Eleonora and Ligeia and Roderick Usher and all such soulful Mrs. Shandies, male as well as female! What a horror, too, he had of all Don Juans, all knowing sensualists and conscious libertines! (About the time he was writing *Lady Chatterley's Lover* he read the memoirs of Casanova, and was profoundly shocked.)

And how bitterly he loathed the Wilhelm-Meisterish view of love as an education, as a means to culture, a Sandow-exerciser for the soul! To *use* love in this way, consciously and deliberately, seemed to Lawrence wrong, almost a blasphemy. "It seems to me queer," he says to a fellow writer, "that you prefer to present men chiefly—as if you cared for women not so much for what they were in themselves as for what the men saw in them. So that after all in your work women seem not to have an existence, save they are the projections of the men. . . . It's the *positivity* of women you seem to deny—make them sort of instrumental." The instrumentality of Wilhelm Meister's women shocked Lawrence profoundly.

(Here, in a parenthesis, let me remark on the fact that Lawrence's doctrine is constantly invoked by people, of whom Lawrence himself would passionately have disapproved, in defence of a behaviour, which he would have found deplorable or even revolting. That this should have happened is by no means, of course, a condemnation of the doctrine. The same philosophy of life may be good or bad according as the person who accepts it and lives by it is intrinsically fine or base. Tartufe's doctrine was the same, after all, as Pascal's. There have been refined fetish-worshippers, and unspeakably swinish Christians. To the preacher of a new way of life the most depressing thing that can happen is, surely, success. For success permits him to see how those he has converted distort and debase and make ignoble parodies of his teaching. If Francis of Assisi had lived to be a hundred, what bitterness he would have tasted! Happily for the saint, he died at forty-five, still relatively undisillusioned, because still on the threshold of the great success of his order. Writers influence their readers, preachers their auditors—but always, at bottom, to be more themselves. If the reader's self happens to be intrinsically similar to the writer's, then the influence is what the writer would wish it to be. If he is intrinsically unlike the writer, then he will probably twist the writer's doctrine into a rationalization of beliefs, an excuse for behaviour, wholly alien to the beliefs and behaviour approved by the writer. Lawrence has suffered the fate of every man whose

works have exercised an influence upon his fellows. It was inevitable and in the nature of things.)

For someone with a gift for sensing the mystery of otherness, true love must necessarily be, in Lawrence's vocabulary,
nocturnal. So must true knowledge. Nocturnal and tactual—
a touching in the night. Man inhabits, for his own conven-
ience, a home-made universe within the greater alien world
of external matter and his own irrationality. Out of the il-
limitable blackness of that world the light of his customary
thinking scoops, as it were, a little illuminated cave—a tunnel
of brightness, in which, from the birth of consciousness to its
death, he lives, moves and has his being. For most of us this
bright tunnel is the whole world. We ignore the outer darkness; or if we cannot ignore it, if it presses too insistently
upon us, we disapprove, being afraid. Not so Lawrence. He
had eyes that could see, beyond the walls of light, far into
the darkness, sensitive fingers that kept him continually
aware of the environing mystery. He could not be content
with the home-made, human tunnel, could not conceive that
anyone else should be content with it. Moreover—and in this
he was unlike those others, to whom the world's mystery is
continuously present, the great philosophers and men of science—he did not want to increase the illuminated area; he
approved of the outer darkness, he felt at home in it. Most
men live in a little puddle of light thrown by the gig-lamps
of habit and their immediate interest; but there is also the
pure and powerful illumination of the disinterested scientific
intellect. To Lawrence, both lights were suspect, both seemed
to falsify what was, for him, the immediately apprehended
reality—the darkness of mystery. "My great religion," he was
already saying in 1912, "is a belief in the blood, the flesh,
as being wiser than the intellect. We can go wrong in our
minds. But what the blood feels, and believes, and says, is
always true." Like Blake, who had prayed to be delivered
from "single vision and Newton's sleep": like Keats, who had
drunk destruction to Newton for having explained the rainbow, Lawrence disapproved of too much knowledge, on the
score that it diminished men's sense of wonder and blunted
their sensitiveness to the great mystery. His dislike of science
was passionate and expressed itself in the most fantastically

unreasonable terms. "All scientists are liars," he would say, when I brought up some experimentally established fact, which he happened to dislike. "Liars, liars!" It was a most convenient theory. I remember in particular one long and violent argument on evolution, in the reality of which Lawrence always passionately disbelieved. "But look at the evidence, Lawrence," I insisted, "look at all the evidence." His answer was characteristic. "But I don't care about evidence. Evidence doesn't mean anything to me. I don't feel it *here*." And he pressed his two hands on his solar plexus. I abandoned the argument and thereafter never, if I could avoid it, mentioned the hated name of science in his presence. Lawrence could give so much, and what he gave was so valuable, that it was absurd and profitless to spend one's time with him disputing about a matter in which he absolutely refused to take a rational interest. Whatever the intellectual consequences, he remained through thick and thin unshakably loyal to his own genius. The *daimon* which possessed him was, he felt, a divine thing, which he would never deny or explain away, never even ask to accept a compromise. This loyalty to his own self, or rather to his gift, to the strange and powerful *numen* which, he felt, used him as its tabernacle, is fundamental in Lawrence and accounts, as nothing else can do, for all that the world found strange in his beliefs and his behaviour. It was not an incapacity to understand that made him reject those generalisations and abstractions by means of which the philosophers and the men of science try to open a path for the human spirit through the chaos of phenomena. Not incapacity, I repeat; for Lawrence had, over and above his peculiar gift, an extremely acute intelligence. He was a clever man as well as a man of genius. (In his boyhood and adolescence he had been a great passer of examinations.) He could have understood the aim and methods of science perfectly well if he had wanted to. Indeed, he did understand them perfectly well; and it was for that very reason that he rejected them. For the methods of science and critical philosophy were incompatible with the exercise of his gift—the immediate perception and artistic rendering of divine otherness. And their aim, which is to push back the frontier of the unknown, was not to be reconciled with his aim, which was to remain as intimately as possible in contact with the surrounding darkness. And so, in spite of their enormous prestige, he rejected science and critical philosophy; he remained loyal to his gift. Exclusively loyal. He would not attempt to qualify or explain his immediate knowledge of the mystery, would not even attempt to supplement it by other, abstract knowledge. "These terrible, conscious birds, like Poe and his Ligeia, deny the very life that is in them; they want to turn it all into talk, into *knowing*. And so life, which will not be known, leaves them." Lawrence refused to *know* abstractly. He preferred to live; and he wanted other people to live.

No man is by nature complete and universal; he cannot have first-hand knowledge of every kind of possible human experience. Universality, therefore, can only be achieved by those who mentally simulate living experience—by the knowers, in a word, by people like Goethe (an artist for whom Lawrence always felt the most intense repugnance).

Again, no man is by nature perfect, and none can spontaneously achieve perfection. The greatest gift is a limited gift. Perfection, whether ethical or æsthetic, must be the result of knowing and of the laborious application of knowledge. Formal æsthetics are an affair of rules and the best classical models; formal morality, of the ten commandments and the imitation of Christ.

Lawrence would have nothing to do with proceedings so "unnatural," so disloyal to the gift, to the resident or visiting *numen*. Hence his æsthetic principle, that art must be wholly spontaneous, and, like the artist, imperfect, limited and transient. Hence, too, his ethical principle that a man's first moral duty is not to attempt to live above his human station, or beyond his inherited psychological income.

The great work of art and the monument more perennial than brass are, in their very perfection and everlastingness, inhuman—too much of a good thing. Lawrence did not approve of them. Art, he thought, should flower from an immediate impulse towards self-expression or communication, and should wither with the passing of the impulse. Of all building materials Lawrence liked adobe the best; its extreme plasticity and extreme impermanence endeared it to him.

There could be no everlasting pyramids in adobe, no mathematically accurate Parthenons. Nor, thank heaven, in wood. Lawrence loved the Etruscans, among other reasons, because they built wooden temples, which have not survived. Stone oppressed him with its indestructible solidity, its capacity to take and indefinitely keep the hard uncompromising forms of pure geometry. Great buildings made him feel uncomfortable, even when they were beautiful. He felt something of the same discomfort in the presence of any highly finished work of art. In music, for example, he liked the folk-song, because it was a slight thing, born of immediate impulse. The symphony oppressed him; it was too big, too elaborate, too carefully and consciously worked out, too "would-be"—to use a characteristic Lawrencian expression. He was quite determined that none of his writings should be "would-be." He allowed them to flower as they liked from the depths of his being and would never use his conscious intellect to force them into a semblance of more than human perfection, or more than human universality. It was characteristic of him that he hardly ever corrected or patched what he had written. I have often heard him say, indeed, that he was incapable of correcting. If he was dissatisfied with what he had written, he did not, as most authors do, file, clip, insert, transpose; he re-wrote. In other words, he gave the *daimon* another chance to say what it wanted to say. There are, I believe, three complete and totally distinct manuscripts of *Lady Chatterley's Lover*. Nor was this by any means the only novel that he wrote more than once. He was determined that all he produced should spring direct from the mysterious, irrational source of power within him. The conscious intellect should never be allowed to come and impose, after the event, its abstract pattern of perfection.

It was the same in the sphere of ethics as in that of art. "They want me to have form: that means, they want me to have *their* pernicious, ossiferous, skin-and-grief form, and I won't." This was written about his novels; but it is just as applicable to his life. Every man, Lawrence insisted, must be an artist in life, must create his own moral form. The art of living is harder than the art of writing. "It is a much more delicate thing to make love, and win love, than to declare love." All the more reason, therefore, for practising this art with the most refined and subtle sensibility; all the more reason for not accepting that "pernicious skin-and-grief form" of morality, which *they* are always trying to impose on one. It is the business of the sensitive artist in life to accept his own nature as it is, not to try to force it into another shape. He must take the material given him—the weaknesses and irrationalities, as well as the sense and the virtues; the mysterious darkness and otherness no less than the light of reason and the conscious ego—must take them all and weave them together into a satisfactory pattern; *his* pattern, not somebody else's pattern. "Once I said to myself: 'How can I blame—why be angry?' . . . Now I say: 'When anger comes with bright eyes, he may do his will. In me he will hardly shake off the hand of God. He is one of the archangels, with a fiery sword. God sent him—it is beyond my knowing.'" This was written in 1910. Even at the very beginning of his career Lawrence was envisaging man as simply the locus of a polytheism. Given his particular gifts of sensitiveness and of expression it was inevitable. Just as it was inevitable that a man of Blake's peculiar genius should formulate the very similar doctrine of the independence of states of being. All the generally accepted systems of philosophy and of ethics aim at policing man's polytheism in the name of some Jehovah of intellectual and moral consistency. For Lawrence this was an indefensible proceeding. One god had as much right to exist as another, and the dark ones were as genuinely divine as the bright. Perhaps (since Lawrence was so specially sensitive to the quality of dark godhead and so specially gifted to express it in art), perhaps even more divine. Anyhow, the polytheism was a democracy. This conception of human nature resulted in the formulation of two rather surprising doctrines, one ontological and the other ethical. The first is what I may call the Doctrine of Cosmic Pointlessness. "There is no point. Life and Love are life and love, a bunch of violets is a bunch of violets, and to drag in the idea of a point is to ruin everything. Live and let live, love and let love, flower and fade, and follow the natural curve, which flows on, pointless."

Ontological pointlessness has its ethical counterpart in the doctrine of insouciance. "They simply are eaten up with caring. They are so busy caring about Fascism or Leagues of Nations or whether France is right or whether Marriage is threatened, that they never know where they are. They certainly never live on the spot where they are. They inhabit abstract space, the desert void of politics, principles, right and wrong, and so forth. They are doomed to be abstract. Talking to them is like trying to have a human relationship with the letter *x* in algebra." As early as 1911 his advice to his sister was: "Don't meddle with religion. I would leave all that alone, if I were you, and try to occupy myself fully in the present."

Reading such passages—and they abound in every book that Lawrence wrote—I am always reminded of that section of the *Pensées*, in which Pascal speaks of the absurd distractions, with which men fill their leisure, so that there shall be no hole or cranny left for a serious thought to lodge itself in their consciousness. Lawrence also inveighs against *divertissements*, but not against the same *divertissements* as Pascal. For him, there were two great and criminal distractions. First, work, which he regarded as a mere stupefacient, like opium. ("Don't exhaust yourself too much," he writes to an industrious friend; "it is immoral." Immoral, because, among other reasons, it is too easy, a shirking of man's first duty, which is to live. "Think of the rest and peace, the positive sloth and luxury of idleness that work is." Lawrence had a real puritan's disapproval of the vice of working. He attacked the gospel of work for the same reasons as Chrysippus attacked Aristotle's gospel of pure intellectualism—on the ground that it was, in the old Stoic's words, "only a kind of amusement" and that real living was a more serious affair than labour or abstract speculations.) The other inexcusable distraction, in Lawrence's eyes, was "spirituality," that lofty musing on the ultimate nature of things which constitutes, for Pascal, "the whole dignity and business of man." Pascal was horrified that human beings could so far forget the infinite and the eternal as to "dance and play the lute and sing and make verses." Lawrence was no less appalled that they could so far forget all the delights and difficulties of immediate living as to remember eternity and infinity, to say nothing of the League of Nations and the Sanctity of Marriage. Both were great artists; and so each is able to convince us that he is at any rate partly right. Just how far each is right, this is not the place to discuss. Nor, indeed, is the question susceptible of a definite answer. "Mental consciousness," wrote Lawrence, "is a purely individual affair. Some men are born to be highly and delicately conscious." Some are not. Moreover, each of the ages of man has its suitable philosophy of life. (Lawrence's, I should say, was not a very good philosophy for old age or failing powers.) Besides, there are certain conjunctions of circumstances in which spontaneous living is the great distraction and certain others in which it is almost criminal to divert oneself with eternity or the League of Nations. Lawrence's peculiar genius was such that he insisted on spontaneous living to the exclusion of ideals and fixed principles; on intuition to the exclusion of abstract reasoning. Pascal, with a very different gift, evolved, inevitably, a very different philosophy.

Lawrence's dislike of abstract knowledge and pure spirituality made him a kind of mystical materialist. Thus, the moon affects him strongly; therefore it cannot be a "stony cold world, like a world of our own gone cold. Nonsense. It is a globe of dynamic substance, like radium or phosphorus, coagulated upon a vivid pole of energy." Matter must be intrinsically as lively as the mind which perceives it and is moved by the perception. Vivid and violent spiritual effects must have correspondingly vivid and violent material causes. And, conversely, any violent feeling or desire in the mind must be capable of producing violent effects upon external matter. Lawrence could not bring himself to believe that the spirit can be moved, moved if need be, to madness, without imparting the smallest corresponding movement to the external world. He was a subjectivist as well as a materialist; in other words, he believed in the possibility, in some form or another, of magic. Lawrence's mystical materialism found characteristic expression in the curious cosmology and physiology of his speculative essays, and in his restatement of the strange Christian doctrine of the resurrection of the body. To his mind, the survival of the spirit was not enough; for the spirit is a man's conscious identity, and Lawrence did not want to be always identical to himself; he wanted to know otherness—to know it by being it, know it in the living flesh, which is always essentially *other*. Therefore there must be a resurrection of the body.

Loyalty to his genius left him no choice; Lawrence had to insist on those mysterious forces of otherness which are scattered without, and darkly concentrated within, the body and mind of man. He had to, even though, by doing so, he imposed upon himself, as a writer of novels, a very serious handicap. For according to his view of things most of men's activities were more or less criminal distractions from the proper business of human living. He refused to write of such distractions; that is to say, he refused to write of the main activities of the contemporary world. But as though this drastic limitation of his subject were not sufficient, he went still further and, in some of his novels, refused even to write of human personalities in the accepted sense of the term. *The Rainbow* and *Women in Love* (and indeed to a lesser extent all his novels) are the practical applications of a theory, which is set forth in a very interesting and important letter to Edward Garnett, dated June 5th, 1914. "Somehow, that which is physic—non-human in humanity, is more interesting to me than the old-fashioned human element, which causes one to conceive a character in a certain moral scheme and make him consistent. The certain moral scheme is what I object to. In Turgenev, and in Tolstoi, and in Dostoievsky, the moral scheme into which all the characters fit—and it is nearly the same scheme—is, whatever the extraordinariness of the characters themselves, dull, old, dead. When Marinetti writes: 'It is the solidity of a blade of steel that is interesting by itself, that is, the incomprehending and inhuman alliance of its molecules in resistance to, let us say, a bullet. The heat of a piece of wood or iron is in fact more passionate, for us, than the laughter or tears of a woman'—then I know what he means. He is stupid, as an artist, for contrasting the heat of the iron and the laugh of the woman. Because what is interesting in the laugh of the woman is the same as the binding of the molecules of steel or their action in heat: it is the inhuman will, call it physiology, or like Marinetti, physiology of matter, that fascinates me. I don't so much care about what the woman *feels*—in the ordinary usage of the word. That presumes an *ego* to feel with. I only care about what the woman *is*—what she is—inhumanly, physiologically, materially—according to the use of the word. . . . You mustn't look in my novel for the old stable *ego* of the character. There is another *ego*, according to whose action the individual is unrecognisable, and passes through, as it were, allotropic states which it needs a deeper sense than any we've been used to exercise, to discover are states of the same single radically unchanged element. (Like as diamond and coal are the same pure single element of carbon. The ordinary novel would trace the history of the diamond—but I say, 'Diamond, what! This is carbon.' And my diamond might be coal or soot, and my theme is carbon.)"

The dangers and difficulties of this method are obvious. Criticising Stendhal, Professor Saintsbury long since remarked on "that psychological realism which is perhaps a more different thing from psychological reality than our clever ones for two generations have been willing to admit, or, perhaps, able to perceive."

Psychological reality, like physical reality, is determined by our mental and bodily make-up. Common sense, working on the evidence supplied by our unaided senses, postulates a world in which physical reality consists of such things as solid tables and chairs, bits of coal, water, air. Carrying its investigations further, science discovers that these samples of physical reality are "really" composed of atoms of different elements, and these atoms, in their turn, are "really" composed of more or less numerous electrons and protons arranged in a variety of patterns. Similarly, there is a commonsense, pragmatic conception of psychological reality; and also an un-commonsense conception. For ordinary practical purposes we conceive human beings as creatures with characters. But analysis of their behaviour can be carried so far, that they cease to have characters and reveal themselves as collections of psychological atoms. Lawrence (as might have been expected of a man who could always perceive the otherness behind the most reassuringly familiar phenomenon) took the un-commonsense view of psychology. Hence the strangeness of his novels; and hence also, it must be admitted, certain qualities of violent monotony and intense indistinctness, qualities which make some of them, for all their richness and their unexpected beauty, so curiously difficult to get through. Most of us are more interested in diamonds and coal than in undifferentiated carbon, however vividly described. I have known readers whose reaction to Lawrence's books was very much the same as Lawrence's own reaction to the theory of evolution. What he wrote meant nothing to them because they "did not feel it *here*"—in the solar plexus. (That Lawrence, the hater of scientific knowing, should have applied to psychology methods which he himself compared to those of chemical analysis, may seem strange. But we must remember that his analysis was done, not intellectually, but by an immediate process of intuition; that he was able, as it were, to *feel* the carbon in diamonds and coal, to *taste* the hydrogen and oxygen in his glass of water.)

Lawrence, then, possessed, or, if you care to put it the other way round, was possessed by, a gift—a gift to which he was unshakably loyal. I have tried to show how the possession and the loyalty influenced his thinking and writing. How did they affect his life? The answer shall be, as far as possible, in Lawrence's own words. To Catherine Carswell Lawrence once wrote: "I think you are the only woman I have met who is so intrinsically detached, so essentially separate and isolated, as to be a real writer or artist or recorder. Your relations with other people are only excursions from yourself. And to want children, and common human fulfilments, is rather a falsity for you, I think. You were never made to 'meet and mingle,' but to remain intact, *essentially*, whatever your experiences may be."

Lawrence's knowledge of "the artist" was manifestly personal knowledge. He knew by actual experience that "the real writer" is an essentially separate being, who must not desire to meet and mingle and who betrays himself when he hankers too yearningly after common human fulfilments. All artists know these facts about their species, and many of them have recorded their knowledge. Recorded it, very often, with distress; being intrinsically detached is no joke. Lawrence certainly suffered his whole life from the essential solitude to which his gift condemned him. "What ails me," he wrote to the psychologist, Dr. Trigant Burrow, "is the absolute frustration of my primeval societal instinct. . . . I think societal instinct much deeper than sex instinct—and societal repression much more devastating. There is no repression of the sexual individual comparable to the repression of the societal man in me, by the individual ego, my own and everybody else's. . . . Myself, I suffer badly from being so cut off. . . . At times one is *forced* to be essentially a hermit. I don't want to be. But anything else is either a personal tussle, or a money tussle; sickening: except, of course, just for ordinary acquaintance, which remains acquaintance. One has no real human relations—that is so devastating." One has no real human relations: it is the complaint of every artist. The artist's first duty is to his genius, his *daimon*; he cannot serve two masters. Lawrence, as it happened, had an extraordinary gift for establishing an intimate relationship with almost anyone he met. "Here" (in the Bournemouth boarding-house where he was staying after his illness, in 1912), "I get mixed up in people's lives so—it's very interesting, sometimes a bit painful, often jolly. But I run to such close intimacy with folk, it is complicating. But I love to have myself in a bit of a tangle." His love for his art was greater, however, than his love for a tangle; and whenever the tangle threatened to compromise his activities as an artist, it was the tangle that was sacrificed: he retired. Lawrence's only deep and abiding human relationship was with his wife. ("It is hopeless for me," he wrote to a fellow artist, "to try to do anything without I have a woman at the back of me. . . . Böcklin—or somebody like him—daren't sit in a café except with his back to the wall. I daren't sit in the world without a woman behind me. . . . A woman that I love sort of keeps me in direct communication with the unknown, in which otherwise I am a bit lost.") For the rest, he was condemned by his gift to an essential separateness. Often, it is true, he blamed the world for his exile. "And it comes to this, that the *oneness* of mankind is destroyed in me (by the war). I am I, and you are you, and all heaven and hell lie in the chasm between. Believe me, I am infinitely hurt by being thus torn off from the body of mankind, but so it is and it is right." It was right because, in reality, it was not the war that had torn him from the body of mankind; it was his own talent, the strange divinity to which he owed his primary allegiance. "I will not live any more in this time," he wrote on another occasion. "I know what it is. I reject it. As far as I possibly can, I will stand outside this time. I will live my life and, if possible, be happy. Though the whole world slides in horror down into the bottomless pit . . . I believe that the highest virtue is to be happy, living in the greatest truth, not submitting to the falsehood of these personal times." The adjective is profoundly significant. Of all the possible words of disparagement which might be applied to our uneasy age "personal" is surely about the last that would occur to most of us. To Lawrence it was the first. His gift was a gift of feeling and rendering the unknown, the mysteriously other. To one possessed by such a gift, almost any age would have seemed unduly and dangerously personal. He had to reject and escape. But when he had escaped, he could not help deploring the absence of "real human relationships." Spasmodically, he tried to establish contact with the body of mankind. There were the recurrent projects for colonies in remote corners of the earth; they all fell through. There were his efforts to join existing political organisations; but somehow "I seem to have lost touch altogether with the 'Progressive' clique. In Croydon, the Socialists are so stupid and the Fabians so flat." (Not only in Croydon, alas.) Then, during the war, there was his plan to co-operate with a few friends to take independent political action; but "I would like to be remote, in Italy, writing my soul's words. To have to speak in the body is a violation to me." And in the end he wouldn't violate himself; he remained aloof, remote, "essentially separate." "It isn't scenery one lives by," he wrote from Cornwall in 1916, "but the freedom of moving about alone." How acutely he suffered from this freedom by which he lived! *Kangaroo* describes a later stage of the debate between the solitary artist and the man who wanted social responsibilities and contact with the body of mankind. Lawrence, like the hero of his novel, decided against contact. He was by nature not a leader of men, but a prophet, a voice crying in the wilderness—the wilderness of his own isolation. The desert was his place, and yet he felt himself an exile in it. To Rolf Gardiner he wrote, in 1926: "I should love to be connected with something, with some few people, in something. As far as anything *matters*, I have always been very much alone, and regretted it. But I can't belong to clubs, or societies, or Free-masons, or any other damn thing. So if there is, with you, an activity I *can* belong to, I shall thank my stars. But, of course, I shall be wary beyond words, of committing myself." He was in fact so wary that he never committed himself, but died remote and unconnected as he had lived. The *daimon* would not allow it to be otherwise.

(Whether Lawrence might not have been happier if he had disobeyed his *daimon* and forced himself at least into me-chanical and external connection with the body of mankind, I forbear to speculate. Spontaneity is not the only and in-fallible secret of happiness; nor is a "would-be" existence necessarily disastrous. But this is by the way.)

It was, I think, the sense of being cut off that sent Law-rence on his restless wanderings round the earth. His travels were at once a flight and a search: a search for some society with which he could establish contact, for a world where the times were not personal and conscious knowing had not yet perverted living; a search and at the same time a flight from the miseries and evils of the society into which he had been born, and for which, in spite of his artist's detachment, he could not help feeling profoundly responsible. He felt him-self "English in the teeth of all the world, even in the teeth of England": that was why he had to go to Ceylon and Aus-tralia and Mexico. He could not have felt so intensely English in England without involving himself in corporative political action, without belonging and being attached; but to attach himself was something he could not bring himself to do, something that the artist in him felt as a violation. He was at once too English and too intensely an artist to stay at home. "Perhaps it is necessary for me to try these places, perhaps it is my destiny to know the world. It only excites the outside of me. The inside it leaves more isolated and stoic than ever. That's how it is. It is all a form of running away from oneself and the great problems, all this wild west and the strange Australia. But I try to keep quite clear. One forms not the faintest inward attachment, especially here in America."

His search was as fruitless as his flight was ineffective. He could not escape either from his homesickness or his sense of responsibility; and he never found a society to which he could belong. In a kind of despair, he plunged yet deeper into the surrounding mystery, into the dark night of that otherness whose essence and symbol is the sexual experience. In *Lady Chatterley's Lover* Lawrence wrote the epilogue to his travels and, from his long and fruitless experience of flight and search, drew what was, for him, the inevitable moral. It is a strange and beautiful book; but inexpressibly sad. But then so, at bottom, was its author's life.

Lawrence's psychological isolation resulted, as we have seen, in his seeking physical isolation from the body of mankind. This physical isolation reacted upon his thoughts. "Don't mind if I am impertinent," he wrote to one of his correspondents at the end of a rather dogmatic letter. "Living here alone one gets so different—sort of ex-cathedra." To live in isolation, above the medley, has its advantages; but it also imposes certain penalties. Those who take a bird's-eye view of the world often see clearly and comprehensively; but they tend to ignore all tiresome details, all the difficulties of social life and, ignoring, to judge too sweepingly and to condemn too lightly. Nietzsche spent his most fruitful years perched on the tops of mountains, or plunged in the yet more abysmal solitude of boarding-houses by the Mediterranean. That was why, a delicate and sensitive man, he could be so bloodthirstily censorious—so wrong, for all his gifts, as well as so right. From the deserts of New Mexico, from rustic Tuscany or Sicily, from the Australian bush, Lawrence observed and judged and advised the distant world of men. The judgments, as might be expected, were often sweeping and violent; the advice, though admirable so far as it went, inadequate. Political advice from even the most greatly gifted of religious innovators is always inadequate; for it is never, at bottom, advice about politics, but always about something else. Differences in quantity, if sufficiently great, produce differences of quality. This sheet of paper, for example, is qualitatively different from the electrons of which it is composed. An analogous difference divides the politician's world from the world of the artist, or the moralist, or the religious teacher. "It is the business of the artist," writes Lawrence, "to follow it (the war) to the heart of the individual fighters —not to talk in armies and nations and numbers—but to track it home—home—their war—and it's at the bottom of almost every Englishman's heart—the war—the desire of war—the *will* to war—and at the bottom of every German heart." But an appeal to the individual heart can have very little effect on politics, which is a science of averages. An actuary can tell you how many people are likely to commit suicide next year; and no artist or moralist or Messiah can, by an appeal to the individual heart, prevent his forecast from being remarkably correct. If the things which are Caesar's differ from the things which are God's, it is because Caesar's things are numbered by the thousands and millions, whereas God's things are single individual souls. The things of Lawrence's Dark God were not even individual souls; they were the psychological atoms whose patterned coming together constitutes a soul. When Lawrence offers political advice, it refers to matters which are not really political at all. The political world of enormous numbers was to him a nightmare, and he fled from it. Primitive communities are so small that their politics are essentially unpolitical; that, for Lawrence, was one of their greatest charms. Looking back from some far-away and underpopulated vantage point at the enormous, innumerable modern world, he was appalled by what he saw. He condemned, he advised, but at bottom and finally he felt himself impotent to deal with Caesar's alien and inhuman problems. "I wish there were miracles," was his final despairing comment. "I am tired of the old laborious way of working things to their conclusions." But, alas, there are no miracles, and faith, even the faith of a man of genius, moves no mountains.

Enough of explanation and interpretation. To those who knew Lawrence, not *why*, but *that* he was what he happened to be, is the important fact. I remember very clearly my first meeting with him. The place was London, the time 1915. But Lawrence's passionate talk was of the geographically remote and of the personally very near. Of the horrors in the middle distance—war, winter, the town—he would not speak. For he was on the point, so he imagined, of setting off to Florida—to Florida, where he was going to plant that colony of escape, of which up to the last he never ceased to dream. Sometimes the name and site of this seed of a happier and different world were purely fanciful. It was called Rananim, for example, and was an island like Prospero's. Sometimes it had its place on the map and its name was Florida, Cornwall, Sicily, Mexico and again, for a time, the English countryside. That wintry afternoon in 1915 it was Florida. Before tea was over he asked me if I would join the colony, and though I was an intellectually cautious young man, not at all inclined to enthusiasms, though Lawrence had startled and embarrassed me with sincerities of a kind to which my upbringing had not accustomed me, I answered yes.

Fortunately, no doubt, the Florida scheme fell through. Cities of God have always crumbled; and Lawrence's city—his village, rather, for he hated cities—his Village of the Dark God would doubtless have disintegrated like all the rest. It was better that it should have remained, as it was always to remain, a project and a hope. And I knew this even as I said I would join the colony. But there was something about Lawrence which made such knowledge, when one was in his presence, curiously irrelevant. He might propose impracticable schemes, he might say or write things that were demonstrably incorrect or even, on occasion (as when he talked about science), absurd. But to a very considerable extent it didn't matter. What mattered was always Lawrence himself, was the fire that burned within him, that glowed with so strange and marvellous a radiance in almost all he wrote.

My second meeting with Lawrence took place some years later, during one of his brief revisitings of that after-war England, which he had come so much to dread and to dislike. Then in 1925, while in India, I received a letter from Spotorno. He had read some essays I had written on Italian travel; said he liked them; suggested a meeting. The next year we were in Florence and so was he. From that time, till his death, we were often together—at Florence, at Forte dei Marmi, for a whole winter at Diablerets, at Bandol, in Paris, at Chexbres, at Forte again, and finally at Vence where he died.

In a spasmodically kept diary I find this entry under the date of December 27th, 1927: "Lunched and spent the p.m. with the Lawrences. D. H. L. in admirable form, talking wonderfully. He is one of the few people I feel real respect and admiration for. Of most other eminent people I have met I feel that at any rate I belong to the same species as they do. But this man has something different and superior in kind, not degree."

"Different and superior in kind." I think almost everyone who knew him well must have felt that Lawrence was this. A being, somehow, of another order, more sensitive, more highly conscious, more capable of feeling than even the most gifted of common men. He had, of course, his weaknesses and defects; he had his intellectual limitations—limitations which he seemed to have deliberately imposed upon himself. But these weaknesses and defects and limitations did not affect the fact of his superior otherness. They diminished him quantitively, so to speak; whereas the otherness was qualitative. Spill half your glass of wine and what remains is still wine. Water, however full the glass may be, is always tasteless and without colour.

To be with Lawrence was a kind of adventure, a voyage of discovery into newness and otherness. For, being himself of a different order, he inhabited a different universe from that of common men—a brighter and intenser world, of which, while he spoke, he would make you free. He looked at things with the eyes, so it seemed, of a man who had been at the brink of death and to whom, as he emerges from the darkness, the world reveals itself as unfathomably beautiful and mysterious. For Lawrence, existence was one continuous convalescence; it was as though he were newly re-born from a mortal illness every day of his life. What these convalescent eyes saw his most casual speech would reveal. A walk with him in the country was a walk through that marvellously rich and significant landscape which is at once the background and the principal personage of all his novels. He seemed to know, by personal experience, what it was like to be a tree or a daisy or a breaking wave or even the mysterious moon itself. He could get inside the skin of an animal and tell you in the most convincing detail how it felt and how, dimly, inhumanly, it thought. Of Black-Eyed Susan, for example, the cow at his New Mexican ranch, he was never tired of speaking, nor was I ever tired of listening to his account of her character and her bovine philosophy.

"He sees," Vernon Lee once said to me, "more than a human being ought to see. Perhaps," she added, "that's why he hates humanity so much." Why also he loved it so much. And not only humanity: nature too, and even the supernatural. For wherever he looked, he saw more than a human being ought to see; saw more and therefore loved and hated more. To be with him was to find oneself transported to one of the frontiers of human consciousness. For an inhabitant of the safe metropolis of thought and feeling it was a most exciting experience.

One of the great charms of Lawrence as a companion was that he could never be bored and so could never be boring. He was able to absorb himself completely in what he was doing at the moment; and he regarded no task as too humble for him to undertake, nor so trivial that it was not worth his while to do it well. He could cook, he could sew, he could darn a stocking and milk a cow, he was an efficient wood-cutter and a good hand at embroidery, fires always burned when he had laid them and a floor, after Lawrence had scrubbed it, was thoroughly clean. Moreover, he possessed what is, for a highly strung and highly intelligent man, an even more remarkable accomplishment: he knew how to do nothing. He could just sit and be perfectly content. And his contentment, while one remained in his company, was infectious.

As infectious as Lawrence's contented placidity were his high spirits and his laughter. Even in the last years of his life, when his illness had got the upper hand and was killing him inchmeal, Lawrence could still laugh, on occasion, with something of the old and exuberant gaiety. Often, alas, towards the end, the laughter was bitter, and the high spirits almost terrifyingly savage. I have heard him sometimes speak of men and their ways with a kind of demoniac mockery, to which it was painful, for all the extraordinary brilliance and profundity of what he said, to listen. The secret consciousness of his dissolution filled the last years of his life with an over-powering sadness. (How tragically the splendid curve of the letters droops, at the end, towards the darkness!) It was, however, in terms of anger that he chose to express this sadness. Emotional indecency always shocked him profoundly, and, since anger seemed to him less indecent as an emotion than a resigned or complaining melancholy, he preferred to be angry. He took his revenge on the fate that had made him sad by fiercely deriding everything. And because the sadness of the slowly dying man was so unspeakably deep, his mockery was frighteningly savage. The laughter of the earlier Lawrence and, on occasion, as I have said, even the later Lawrence was without bitterness and wholly delightful.

Vitality has the attractiveness of beauty, and in Lawrence there was a continuously springing fountain of vitality. It went on welling up in him, leaping, now and then, into a great explosion of bright foam and iridescence, long after the time when, by all the rules of medicine, he should have been dead. For the last two years he was like a flame burning on in miraculous disregard of the fact that there was no more fuel to justify its existence. One grew, in spite of constantly renewed alarms, so well accustomed to seeing the flame blazing away, self-fed, in its broken and empty lamp that one almost came to believe that the miracle would be prolonged, indefinitely. But it could not be. When, after several months of separation, I saw him again at Vence in the early spring of 1930, the miracle was at an end, the flame guttering to extinction. A few days later it was quenched.

Graham Greene on

The technical qualities of Henry James's novels have been so often and so satisfactorily explored, notably by Mr. Percy Lubbock, that perhaps I may be forgiven for ignoring James as the fully conscious craftsman in order to try to track the instinctive, the poetic writer back to the source of his fantasies. In all writers there occurs a moment of crystallization when the dominant theme is plainly expressed, when the private universe becomes visible even to the least sensitive reader. Such a crystallization is Hardy's often-quoted phrase: 'The President of the Immortals . . . had ended his sport with Tess', or that passage in his preface to *Jude the Obscure*, when he writes of 'the fret and fever, derision and disaster, that may press in the wake of the strongest passion known to humanity'. It is less easy to find such a crystallization in the works of James, whose chief aim was always to dramatize, who was more than usually careful to exclude the personal statement, but I think we may take the sentence in the scenario of *The Ivory Tower*, in which James speaks of 'the black and merciless things that are behind great possessions' as an expression of the ruling fantasy which drove him to write: a sense of evil religious in its intensity.

'Art itself', Conrad wrote, 'may be defined as a single-minded attempt to render the highest kind of justice to the visible universe', and no definition in his own prefaces better describes the object Henry James so passionately pursued, if the word visible does not exclude the private vision. If there are times when we feel, in *The Sacred Fount*, even in the exquisite *Golden Bowl*, that the judge is taking too much into consideration, that he could have passed his sentence on less evidence, we have always to admit as the long record of human corruption unrolls that he has never allowed us to lose sight of the main case; and because his mind is bent on rendering even evil 'the highest kind of justice', the symmetry of his thought lends the whole body of his work the importance of a system.

No writer has left a series of novels more of one moral piece. The differences between James's first works and his last are only differences of art as Conrad defined it. In his early work perhaps he rendered a little less than the highest kind of justice; the progress from *The American* to *The Golden Bowl* is a progress from a rather crude and inexperienced symbolization of truth to truth itself: a progress from evil represented rather obviously in terms of murder to evil *in propria persona*, walking down Bond Street, charming, cultured, sensitive—evil to be distinguished from good chiefly in the complete egotism of its outlook. They are complete anarchists, these later Jamesian characters, they form the immoral background to that extraordinary period of haphazard violence which anticipated the first world war: the attempt on Greenwich Observatory, the siege of Sidney Street. They lent the tone which made possible the cruder manifestations presented by Conrad in *The Secret Agent*. Merton Densher, who planned to marry the dying Milly Theale for her money, plotting with his mistress who was her best friend; Prince Amerigo, who betrayed his wife with her friend, her father's wife; Horton, who swindled his friend Gray of his money: the last twist (it is always the friend, the intimate who betrays) is given to these studies of moral corruption. They represent an attitude which had been James's from very far back; they are not the slow painful fruit of experience. The attitude never varied from the time of *The American* onwards. Mme de Bellegarde, who murdered her husband and sold her daughter, is only the first crude presentation of a woman gradually subtilized, by way of Mme Merle in *The Portrait of a Lady*, into the incomparable figures of evil, Kate Croy and Charlotte Stant.

This point is of importance. James has been too often regarded as a novelist of superficial experience, as a painter of social types, who was cut off by exile from the deepest roots of experience (as if there were something superior in the Sussex or Shropshire of the localized talent to James's international scene). But James was not in that sense an exile; he could have dispensed with the international scene as easily as he dispensed with all the world of Wall Street finance. For the roots were not in Venice, Paris, London; they were in himself. Densher, the Prince, just as much as the redhaired valet Quint and the adulterous governess, were rooted in his own character. They were there when he wrote *The American* in 1876; all he needed afterwards to perfect his work to his own impeccable standard was technical subtlety and that other subtlety which comes from superficial observation, the ability to construct convincing masks for his own personality.

I do not use superficial in any disparaging sense. If his practice pieces, from *The Europeans* to *The Tragic Muse*, didn't engage his full powers, and were certainly not the vehicle for his most urgent fantasies, they were examples of sharp observation, the fruits of a direct objective experience, unsurpassed in their kind. He never again proved himself capable of drawing a portrait so directly, with such command of relevant detail. We know Charlotte Stant, of course, more thoroughly than we know Miss Birdseye in *The Bostonians*, but she emerges gradually through that long book, we don't 'see' her with the immediacy that we see Miss Birdseye:

> She was a little old lady with an enormous head; that was the first thing Ransom noticed—the vast, fair, pro-tuberant, candid, ungarnished brow, surmounting a pair of weak, kind, tired-looking eyes. . . . The long practice of philanthropy had not given accent to her features; it had rubbed out their transitions, their meanings. . . . In her large countenance her dim little smile scarcely showed. It was a mere sketch of a smile, a kind of in-stalment, or payment on account; it seemed to say that she would smile more if she had time, but that you could see, without this, that she was gentle and easy to beguile. . . . She looked as if she had spent her life on platforms, in audiences, in conventions, in phalansteries, in seances; in her faded face there was a kind of re-flexion of ugly lecture-lamps.

No writer's apprentice work contains so wide and brilliant

a range of portraits from this very early Miss Birdseye to Mrs. Brookenham in *The Awkward Age*:

> Mrs. Brookenham was, in her forty-first year, still charmingly pretty, and the nearest approach she made at this moment to meeting her son's description of her was by looking beautifully desperate. She had about her the pure light of youth—would always have it; her head, her figure, her flexibility, her flickering colour, her lovely, silly eyes, her natural, quavering tone, all played together towards this effect by some trick that had never yet been exposed. It was at the same time remarkable that—at least in the bosom of her family—she rarely wore an appearance of gaiety less qualified than at the present juncture; she suggested for the most part the luxury, the novelty of woe, the excitement of strange sorrows and the cultivation of fine indifferencies. This was her special sign—an innocence dimly tragic. It gave immense effect to her other resources. . . .

The Awkward Age stands formidably between the two halves of James's achievement. It marks his decision to develop finally from *The American* rather than from *The Europeans*. It is the surrender of experience to fantasy. He hadn't found his method, but he had definitely found his theme. One may regret, in some moods, that his more superficial books had so few successors (English literature has too little that is light, lucid and witty), but one cannot be surprised that he discarded many of them from the collected edition while retaining so crude a fiction as *The American*, discarded even the delicate, feline *Washington Square*, perhaps the only novel in which a man has successfully invaded the feminine field and produced work comparable to Jane Austen's.

How could he have done otherwise if he was to be faithful to his deeper personal fantasy? He wrote of 'poor Flaubert' that

> he stopped too short. He hovered for ever at the public door, in the outer court, the splendour of which very properly beguiled him, and in which he seems still to stand as upright as a sentinel and as shapely as a statue.

But that immobility and even that erectness were paid
too dear. The shining arms were meant to carry further,
the outer doors were meant to open. He should at least
have listened at the chamber of the soul. This would
have floated him on a deeper tide; above all it would
have calmed his nerves.

His early novels, except *The American*, certainly belonged
to the outer court. They had served their purpose, he had
improved his masks, he was never to be more witty; but when
he emerged from them again to take up his main study of
corruption in *The Wings of the Dove* he had amazingly advanced: instead of murder, the more agonizing mental violence; instead of Mme de Bellegarde, Kate Croy; instead of
the melodramatic heroine Mme de Cintré, the deeply felt,
subjective study of Milly Theale.

For to render the highest justice to corruption you must
retain your innocence: you have to be conscious all the time
within yourself of treachery to something valuable. If Peter
Quint is to be rooted in you, so must the child his ghost
corrupts; if Osmond, Isabel Archer too. These centres of innocence, these objects of treachery, are nearly always women:
the lovely daring Isabel Archer, who goes out in her high-
handed wealthy way to meet life and falls to Osmond; Nanda,
the young girl 'coming out', who is hemmed in by a vicious
social set; Milly Theale, sick to death just at the time when
life has most to offer, surrendering to Merton Densher and
Kate Croy (apart from Quint and the Governess the most
driven and 'damned' of all James's characters); Maggie
Verver, the unsophisticated 'good' young American who encounters her particular corruption in the Prince and Charlotte Stant; the child Maisie tossed about among grown-up
adulteries. These are the points of purity in the dark picture.

The attitude of mind which dictated these situations was
a permanent one. Henry James had a marvellous facility for
covering up his tracks (can we be blamed if we assume he
had a reason?). In his magnificent prefaces he describes the
geneses of his stories, where they were written, the method
he adopted, the problems he faced: he seems, like the con-
jurer with rolled sleeves, to show everything. But you have to

go further back than the anecdote at the dinner-table to trace
the origin of such urgent fantasies. In this exploration his
prefaces, even his autobiographies, offer very little help. Certainly they give his model for goodness; he is less careful to
obliterate *that* trail back into youth (if one can speak of care
in connexion with a design which was probably only half-
conscious if it was conscious at all). His cousin, Mary Temple,
was the model, a model in her deadly sickness and her high
courage, above all in her hungry grip on life, for Milly Theale
in particular.

> She had [James wrote of her] beyond any equally
> young creature I have known a sense for verity of char-
> acter and play of life in others, for their acting out of
> their force or their weakness, whatever either might be,
> at no matter what cost to herself. . . . Life claimed her
> and used her and beset her—made her range in her
> groping: her naturally immature and unlighted way
> from end to end of the scale. . . . She was absolutely
> afraid of nothing she might come to by living with
> enough sincerity and enough wonder; and I think it is be-
> cause one was to see her launched on that adventure in
> such bedimmed, such almost tragically compromised
> conditions that one is caught by her title to the heroic
> and pathetic mask.

Mary Temple then, whatever mask she wore, was always
the point of purity, but again one must seek further if one
is to trace the source of James's passionate distrust in human
nature, his sense of evil. Mary Temple was experience, but
that other sense, one feels, was born in him, was his in-
heritance.

It cannot but seem odd how little in his volumes of reminiscence, *A Small Boy and Others* and *Notes of a Son and
Brother*, Henry James really touches the subject of his family. His style is at its most complex: the beauty of the books
is very like the beauty of Turner's later pictures: they are all
air and light: you have to look a long while into their glow
before you discern the most tenuous outline of their subjects.
Certainly of the two main figures, Henry James, Senior, and
William James, you learn nothing of what must have been

to them of painful importance: their sense of daemonic possession.

James was to draw the figure of Peter Quint with his little red whiskers and his white damned face, he was to show Densher and Kate writhing in their hopeless infernal sundering success; evil was overwhelmingly part of his visible universe; but the sense (we get no indication of it in his reminiscences) was a family sense. He shared it with his father and brother and sister. One may find the dark source of his deepest fantasy concealed in a family life which for sensitive boys must have been almost ideally free from compulsions, a tolerant cultured life led between Concord and Geneva. For nearly two years his father was intermittently attacked by a sense of 'perfectly insane and abject terror' (his own words); a damned shape seemed to squat beside him raying out 'a fetid influence'. Henry James's sister, Alice, was a prey to suicidal tendencies, and William James suffered in much the same way as his father.

I went one evening into a dressing-room in the twilight to procure some article that was there; when suddenly there fell upon me without any warning, just as if it came out of the darkness, a horrible fear of my own existence. Simultaneously there arose in my mind the image of an epileptic patient whom I had seen in the asylum, a black-haired youth with greenish skin, entirely idiotic, who used to sit all day on one of the benches, or rather shelves against the wall, with his knees drawn up against his chin, and the coarse grey undershirt, which was his only garment, drawn over them enclosing his entire figure. . . . This image and my fear entered into a species of combination with each other. *That shape am I*, I felt potentially. Nothing that I possess can defend me against that fate, if the hour for it should strike for me as it struck for him. There was such a horror of him, and such a perception of my own merely momentary discrepancy from him, that it was as if something hitherto solid within my breast gave way entirely, and I became a mass of quivering fear. After this the universe was changed for me altogether. I awoke morn-

ing after morning with a horrible dread at the pit of my
stomach, and with a sense of the insecurity of life, that
I never knew before. . . . It gradually faded, but for
months I was unable to go out into the dark alone.

This epileptic idiot, this urge towards death, the damned
shape, are a more important background to Henry James's
novels than Grosvenor House and late Victorian society. It is
true that the moral anarchy of the age gave him his material,
but he would not have treated it with such intensity if it
had not corresponded with his private fantasy. They were
materialists, his characters, but you cannot read far in Henry
James's novels without realizing that their creator was not a
materialist. If ever a man's imagination was clouded by the
Pit, it was James's. When he touches this nerve, the fear of
spiritual evil, he treats the reader with less than his usual
frankness: 'a fairy-tale pure and simple', something season-
able for Christmas, is a disingenuous description of *The Turn
of the Screw*. One cannot avoid a conviction that here he
touched and recoiled from an important inhibition.

It was just because the visible universe which he was so
careful to treat with the highest kind of justice was determined for him at an early age that his family background is
of such interest. There are two other odd gaps in his autobiographies; his two brothers, Wilky and Bob, play in them
an infinitesimal part. To Miss Burr, the editor of Alice
James's Journal, we owe most of our knowledge of these almost commonplace, almost low-brow members of a family
intellectual even to excess. To Wilky 'the act of reading was
inhuman and repugnant'; he wrote from his brigade, 'Tell
Harry that I am waiting anxiously for his "next". I can find
a large sale for any blood-and-thunder tale among the darks.'
From his brigade: that was the point. It was the two failures,
Wilky and Bob, who at eighteen and seventeen represented
the family on the battlefields of the Civil War. William's eyesight was always bad, and Henry escaped because of an accident, the exact nature of which has always remained a
mystery. One is glad, of course, that he escaped the obvious
effects of war: Wilky was ruined physically, Bob nervously;
both drifted in the manner of war-time heroes from farming

in Florida to petty business careers in Milwaukee; and it is not improbable that the presence of these ruined heroes helped to keep Henry James out of America.

It is possible that through Wilky and Bob we can trace the source of James's main fantasy, the idea of treachery which was always attached to his sense of evil? James had not, so far as we know, been betrayed, like Monteith, like Gray, like Milly Theale and Maggie Verver and Isabel Archer, by his best friend, and it would have taken surely a very deep betrayal to explain an impulse which dictated *The American* in 1876 and *The Golden Bowl* in 1905, which attached itself to the family sense of supernatural evil and produced his great gallery of the damned. It takes some form of self-betrayal to dip so deep, and one need not go, like some of his modern critics, to a 'castration complex' to find the reason. There are psychological clues which point to James having evaded military service with insufficient excuse. A civil war is not a continental squabble; its motives are usually deeper, represent less superficial beliefs on the part of the ordinary combatant, and the James family at Concord were at the very spot where the motives of the North sounded at their noblest. His accident has an air of mystery about it (that is why some of his critics have imagined a literal castration), and one needs some explanation of his almost hysterical participation in the Great War on the side of a civilization about which he had no illusions, over whose corruption he had swapped amusing anecdotes with Alice. It will be remembered that in his magnificent study of treachery, *A Round of Visits*, Monteith's betrayer, like all the others, was a very near friend. 'To live thus with his unremoved, undestroyed, engaging, treacherous face, had been, as our traveller desired, to live with all of the felt pang.' His unremoved face, the felt pang: it is not hard to believe that James suffered from a long subconscious uneasiness about a personal failure.

This, then, was his visible universe: visible indeed if it faced him daily in his glass: the treachery of friends, the meanest kind of lies, 'the black and merciless things', as he wrote in the scenario of *The Ivory Tower*, 'that are behind great possessions'. But it is perhaps the measure of his greatness, of the wideness and justice of his view, that critics of an older generation, Mr. Desmond MacCarthy among them, have seen him primarily as a friendly, rather covetous follower of the 'best' society. The sense of evil never obsessed him, as it obsessed Dostoievsky; he never ceased to be primarily an artist, unlike those driven geniuses, Lawrence and Tolstoy, and he could always throw off from the superfluity of his talent such exquisite amiable fragments as *Daisy Miller* and *The Pension Beaurepas*: satire so gentle, even while so witty, that it has the quality of nostalgia, a looking back towards a way of life simple and unreflecting, with a kind of innocence even in its greed. 'Common she might be,' he wrote of Daisy Miller, 'yet what provision was made by that epithet for her queer little native grace.' It is in these diversions, these lovely little marginalia, that the Marxist critic, just as much as Mr. MacCarthy, finds his material. He was a social critic only when he was not a religious one. No writer was more conscious that he was at the end of a period, at the end of the society he knew. It was a revolution he quite explicitly foresaw; he spoke of

> the class, as I seemed to see it, that had had the longest and happiest innings in history . . . and for whom the future wasn't going to be, by most signs, anything like so bland and benedictory as the past. . . . I cannot say how vivid I felt the drama so preparing might become—that of the lapse of immemorial protection, that of the finally complete exposure of the immemorially protected.

But the Marxists, just as much as the older critics, are dwelling on the marginalia. Wealth may have been almost invariably connected with the treacheries he described, but so was passion. When he was floating on his fullest tide, 'listening' as he put it, 'at the chamber of the soul', the evil of capitalist society is an altogether inadequate explanation of his theme. It was not the desire for money alone which united Densher and Kate, and the author of *The Spoils of Poynton* would no more have condemned passion than the author of *The Ambassadors* would have condemned private wealth. His lot and his experience happened to lie among the great possessions, but 'the black and merciless things' were no more intrinsically part of a capitalist than of a socialist system: they belonged to human nature. They amounted really to this: an egotism so complete that you could believe that something inhuman, supernatural, was working there through the poor devils it had chosen.

In *The Jolly Corner* Bridon, the cultured American expatriate, returned to his New York home and found it haunted. He hunted the ghost down. It was afraid of him (the origin of that twist is known to us. In *A Small Boy* James has described the childish dream he built his story on). He drove it to bay in its evening dress under the skylight in the hall, discovered in the 'evil, odious, blatant, vulgar' features the reflection of himself. This was what he would have been if he had stayed and joined the Wall Street racket and prospered. It is easy to take the mere social criticism implied, but I have yet to find socialist or conservative who can feel any pity for the evil *he* denounces, and the final beauty of James's stories lies in their pity: 'The poetry is in the pity.' His egotists, poor souls, are as pitiable as Lucifer. The woman Bridon loved had also seen the ghost; he had not appeared less blatant, less vulgar to her with his ruined sight and maimed hand and million a year, but the emotion she chiefly felt was pity.

'He has been unhappy, he has been ravaged,' she said.

'And haven't I been unhappy? Am not I—you've only to look at me!—ravaged?'

'Ah, I don't say I like him *better*,' she granted after a thought. 'But he's grim, he's worn—and things have happened to him. He doesn't make shift, for sight, with your charming monocle.'

James wasn't a prophet, he hadn't a didactic purpose; he wished only to render the highest kind of justice, and you cannot render the highest kind of justice if you hate. He was a realist: he had to show the triumphs of egotism; he was a realist: he had to show that a damned soul has its chains. Milly Theale, Maggie Verver, these 'good' people had their escapes, they were lucky in that they loved, could sacrifice themselves like Wilky and Bob, they were never quite alone

n the bench of desolation. But the egotists had no escape,
here was no tenderness in their passion and their pursuit
f money was often no more than an interest, a hobby: they
vere, inescapably, themselves. Kate and Merton Densher get
he money for which they'd schemed; they don't get each
ther. Charlotte Stant and the Prince satisfy their passion at
he expense of a lifetime of separation.

This is not 'poetic justice'; it was not as a moralist that
ames designed his stories, but as a realist. His family background, his personal failure, determined his view of the visible universe when he first began to write, and there was noth-
ng in the society of his time to make him reconsider his
view. He had always been strictly just to the truth as he saw
it, and all that his deepening experience had done for him
was to alter a murder to an adultery, but while in *The American* he had not pitied the murderer, in *The Golden Bowl*
he had certainly learned to pity the adulterers. There was no
victory for human beings, that was his conclusion; you were
punished in your own way, whether you were of God's or the
Devil's party. James believed in the supernatural, but he saw
evil as an equal force with good. Humanity was cannon fodder
in a war too balanced ever to be concluded. If he had been
guilty himself of the supreme egotism of preserving his own
existence, he left the material, in his profound unsparing
analysis, for rendering even egotism the highest kind of justice, of giving the devil his due.

It brought Spencer Brydon to his feet. 'You "like"
that horror—?'
'I *could* have liked him. And to me,' she said, 'he was
no horror, I had accepted him.'

'I had accepted him.' James, who had never taken a great
interest in his father's Swedenborgianism, had gathered
enough to strengthen his own older more traditional heresy.
For his father believed, in his own words, that 'the evil or
hellish element in our nature, even when out of divine order
. . . is yet not only no less vigorous than the latter, but on
the contrary much more vigorous, sagacious and productive
of eminent earthly uses' (so one might describe the acquisi-
tion of Milly Theale's money). The difference, of course, was

greater than the resemblance. The son was not an optimist, he didn't share his father's hopes of the hellish element, he only pitied those who were immersed in it; and it is in the final justice of his pity, the completeness of an analysis which enabled him to pity the most shabby, the most corrupt, of his human actors, that he ranks with the greatest of creative writers. He is as solitary in the history of the novel as Shakespeare in the history of poetry.

George Moore
ON
Henry James and
W. D. Howells:

Henry James went to France and read Turgenev. W. D. Howells stayed at home and read Henry James.

H. G. Wells on

JAMES JOYCE

An eminent novelist was asked recently by some troublesome newspaper what he thought of the literature of 1916. He answered publicly and loudly that he had heard of no literature in 1916; for his own part he had been reading "science." This was kind neither to our literary nor our scientific activities. It was not intelligent to make an opposition between literature and science. It is no more legitimate than an opposition between literature and "classics" or between literature and history. Good writing about the actualities of the war too has been abundant, that was only to be expected; it is an ungracious thing in the home critic to sit at a confused feast and bewail its poverty when he ought to be sorting out his discoveries. Criticism may analyze, it may appraise and attack, but when it comes to the mere grumbling of veterans no longer capable of novel perceptions, away with it! There is indeed small justification for grumbling at the writing of the present time. Quite apart from the books and stories about the war, a brilliant literature in itself, from that artless assured immortal Arthur Green (the *Story of a Prisoner of War*) up to the already active historians, there is a great amount of fresh and experimental writing that cannot be ignored by anyone still alive to literary interests. There are, for instance, Miss Richardson's *Pointed Roofs*, and *Backwater*, amusing experiments to write as the Futurists paint, and Mr. Caradoc Evans' invention in *My People*, and *Capel Sion*, of a new method of grimness, a pseudo-Welsh idiom that is as pleasing in its grotesque force to the intelligent story-reader as it must be maddening to every sensitive Welsh patriot. Nowhere have I seen anything like adequate praise for the romantic force and beauty of Mr. Thomas Burke's *Limehouse Nights*. In the earlier 'nineties when Henley was alive and discovering was in fashion that book would have made a very big reputation indeed. Even more considerable is *A Portrait of the Artist as a Young Man*, by James Joyce. It is a book to buy and read and lock up, but it is not a book to miss. Its claim to be literature is as good as the claim of the last book of *Gulliver's Travels*.

It is no good trying to minimize a characteristic that seems to be deliberately obtruded. Like Swift and another living Irish writer, Mr. Joyce has a cloacal obsession. He would bring back into the general picture of life aspects which modern drainage and modern decorum have taken out of ordinary intercourse and conversation. Coarse, unfamiliar words are scattered about the book unpleasantly, and it may seem to many, needlessly. If the reader is squeamish upon these matters, then there is nothing for it but to shun this book, but if he will pick his way, as one has to do at times on the outskirts of some picturesque Italian village with a view and a church and all sorts of things of that sort to tempt one, then it is quite worth while. And even upon this unsavory aspect of Swift and himself, Mr. Joyce is suddenly illuminating. He tells at several points how his hero Stephen is swayed and shocked and disgusted by harsh and loud *sounds*, and how he is stirred to intense emotion by music and the rhythms of beautiful words. But no sort of smell offends him like that. He finds olfactory sensations interesting or aesthetically displeasing, but they do not make him sick or excited as sounds do. This is a quite understandable turn over from the more normal state of affairs. Long ago I remember pointing out in a review the difference in the sensory basis of the stories of Robert Louis Stevenson and Sir J. M. Barrie; the former visualized and saw his story primarily as picture, the latter mainly heard it. We shall do Mr. Joyce an injustice if we attribute a normal sensory basis to him and then accuse him of deliberate offense.

But that is by the way. The value of Mr. Joyce's book has little to do with its incidental insanitary condition. Like some of the best novels in the world it is the story of an education; it is by far the most living and convincing picture that exists of an Irish Catholic upbringing. It is a mosaic of jagged fragments that does altogether render with extreme completeness the growth of a rather secretive, imaginative boy in Dublin. The technique is startling, but on the whole it succeeds. Like so many Irish writers from Sterne to Shaw Mr. Joyce is a bold experimentalist with paragraph and punctuation. He breaks away from scene to scene without a hint of the change of time and place; at the end he passes suddenly from the third person to the first; he uses no inverted commas to mark off his speeches. The first trick I found sometimes tiresome here and there, but then my own disposition, perhaps acquired at the blackboard, is to mark off and underline rather fussily, and I do not know whether I was so much put off the thing myself as anxious, which after all is not my business, about its effect on those others; the second trick, I will admit, seems entirely justified in this particular instance by its success; the third reduces Mr. Joyce to a free use of dashes. One conversation in this book is a superb success, the one in which Mr. Dedalus carves the Christmas turkey; I write with all due deliberation that Sterne himself could not have done it better; but most of the talk flickers blindingly with these dashes, one has the same wincing feeling of being flicked at that one used to have in the early cinema shows. I think Mr. Joyce has failed to discredit the inverted comma.

The interest of the book depends entirely upon its quintessential and unfailing reality. One believes in Stephen Dedalus as one believes in few characters in fiction. And the peculiar lie of the interest for the intelligent reader is the convincing revelation it makes of the limitations of a great mass of Irishmen. Mr. Joyce tells us unsparingly of the adolescence of this youngster under conditions that have passed almost altogether out of English life. There is an immense shyness, a profound secrecy, about matters of sex, with its inevitable accompaniment of nightmare revelations and furtive scribblings in unpleasant places, and there is a living belief in a real hell. The description of Stephen listening without a doubt to two fiery sermons on that tremendous theme, his agonies of fear, not disgust at dirtiness such as unorthodox children feel but just fear, his terror-inspired confession of his sins of impurity to a strange priest in a distant part of the city, is like nothing in any boy's experience who has been trained under modern conditions. Compare its stuffy horror with Conrad's account of how under analogous circumstances Lord Jim wept. And a second thing of immense significance is the fact that everyone in this Dublin story, every human being, accepts as a matter of course, as a thing in nature like the sky and the sea, that the English are to be hated. There is no discrimination in that hatred, there is no gleam of recognition that a considerable number of Englishmen have displayed a very earnest disposition to put matters right with Ireland, there is an absolute absence of any idea of a discussed settlement, any notion of helping the slow-witted Englishman in his three-cornered puzzle between North and South. It is just hate, a cant cultivated to the pitch of monomania, an ungenerous violent direction of the mind. That is the political atmosphere in which Stephen Dedalus grows up, and in which his essentially responsive mind orients itself. I am afraid it is only too true an account of the atmosphere in which a number of brilliant young Irishmen have grown up. What is the good of pretending that the extreme Irish "patriot" is an equivalent and parallel of the English or American liberal? He is narrower and intenser than any English Tory. He will be the natural ally of the Tory in delaying British social and economic reconstruction after the war. He will play into the hands of the Tories by threatening an outbreak and providing the excuse for a militarist reaction in England. It is time the American observer faced the truth of that. No reason is that why England should not do justice to Ireland, but excellent reason for bearing in mind that these bright-green young people across the Channel are something quite different from the liberal English in training and tradition, and absolutely set against helping them. No single book has ever shown how different they are, as completely as this most memorable novel.

ARNOLD BENNETT

I first knew Arnold Bennett in 1904 when we were both living in Paris. I had taken a very small flat near the Lion de
Belfort, on the fifth floor, from which I had a spacious view
of the cemetery of Montparnasse; I used to dine at the *Chat
Blanc* in the rue d'Odessa. A number of painters, sculptors
and writers were in the habit of dining there and we had a
little room to ourselves. We got a very good dinner, *vin
compris*, for two francs fifty, and it was usual to give four
sous to Marie, the good-humoured and sharp-tongued maid
who waited on us. We were of all nationalities and the conversation was carried on indifferently in English and French.
Sometimes a painter would bring his mistress and her mother,
whom he introduced politely to the company as *ma belle
mère*, but for the most part we were men only. We discussed every subject under the sun, generally with heat, and
by the time we came to coffee (with which I seem to remember a *fine* was thrown in) and lit our cigars, *demi
londrès* at three sou apiece, the air was heady. We differed
with extreme acrimony. Arnold used to come there once a
week. He reminded me years later that the first time we met,
which was at this restaurant, I was white with passion. The
conversation was upon the merits of Heredia. I asserted that
there was no sense in him and a painter who was there scornfully replied that you didn't want sense in poetry. From this
an argument arose upon the objects and limitations of poetry
which soon embroiled the whole company. I exercised such
powers as I had of sarcasm, invective and vituperation; and
my antagonist, a taciturn Irishman, than whom there is no
man more difficult to cope with, was coldly and bitingly
virulent. The entire table took up the dispute and I have
still a dim recollection of Arnold, smiling a little, calm and

a trifle Olympian, putting in now and then a brief, dogmatic, but, I am certain, judicious remark. He was older than most of us. He was then a thin man, with dark hair very smoothly done in a fashion that suggested the private soldier of the day. He was much more neatly dressed than the rest of us and more conventionally. He looked like a managing clerk in a city office. At that time the only book he had written that we knew of was *The Grand Babylon Hotel* and our attitude towards him was somewhat patronising. We were very highbrow. Some of us had read the book and enjoyed it, which was enough for us to decide that there was nothing in it, but the rest shrugged their shoulders, though with good nature, and declined to waste their time over such trash. Had you read *Bubu de Montparnasse?* That was the stuff to give the troops.

Arnold lived in Montmartre, I think in the rue des Dames, and he had a small dark apartment filled with Empire furniture. He was exceedingly proud of it. It was very tidy. Everything was in its place. It was not very comfortable and you could not imagine anyone making himself at home in it. It gave you the impression of a man who saw himself in a certain role, which he was playing carefully, but into the skin of which he had not quite got. As everyone knows Arnold had then given up the editing of a magazine called *Woman* and had settled in Paris to train himself for the profession of literature. He was reading Stendhal and Flaubert, but chiefly Balzac, and I think he told me that in a year he had read through the whole of the *Comédie Humaine*. He was just beginning on the Russians and talked with enthusiasm of *Anna Karenina.* He thought it at that time the greatest novel ever written. I am under the impression that he did not discover Chekov till much later. When he did he began to admire Tolstoi less. Like everyone who lives in Paris he had come across a particular little restaurant where you could get a better meal for less money than anywhere else. This one was on the first floor, somewhere in Montmartre, and now and then I used to go over to dine, Dutch Treat, with him. After dinner we went back to his apartment and he would play Beethoven on a cottage piano. Through Marcel Schwob he had got to know a good many of the French writers of the day and I seem to remember his telling me that Schwob had taken him to Anatole France who was then the high priest of French letters. Arnold's plan of campaign was cut and dried. He proposed to make his annual income by writing novels and by writing plays to make provision for his old age. Because I had lately had my first play produced he gave me one of his to read. I thought it dull. He had made up his mind to write two or three books to get his hand in and then to write a masterpiece. I listened to him, but attached no importance to what he said. I did not think him capable of writing anything of consequence. When I asked him what sort of book his masterpiece was going to be he said, something on the lines of *A Great Man*; but this, he added, had brought him in nothing at all and he couldn't afford to go on in that style till he was properly established.

Arnold was good company and I always enjoyed spending an evening with him, but I did not much like him. He was very cocksure and bumptious, and he was rather common. I do not say this of him depreciatingly, but as I might say of someone else that he was short or fat. I left Paris and it was many years before I saw much of him again.

The Stage Society produced a play of his which I liked. I wrote and told him so, and he wrote a letter to me, thanking me, in which he laid out the critics who had not thought so well of the play as I did. He wrote one or two books which I did not read. At last I came across *The Old Wives' Tale*. I was astounded to discover that it was a great book. I was thrilled. I was enchanted. I was deeply impressed. It would be impertinent of me to say anything in praise of it. I have read many appreciations of it, and I think everything has been said but one thing, and that is that it is eminently readable. I should not mention a merit that is so obvious except that many great books do not possess it. It is the greatest gift of the story-teller and one that Arnold Bennett had even in his slightest and most trivial pieces. I thought at first that he owed it to his journalistic training, but since the other writer of our day in whom I find this characteristic most marked is Marcel Proust, it is clear that this is not the reason; and now I am under the impression that it is due to the intense interest the author has in what he is writing at the moment. Even when Proust is at his dullest he is so absorbed in his subject that you cannot help but read on, eager to know what is coming next; and with Arnold (to my mind) in the same way, though you felt sometimes that what you were reading was rather childish, you were constrained to turn over one page after the other till you reached the end. The success of *The Old Wives' Tale* came slowly. I think I am right in saying that it was reviewed favourably, but not with frantic eulogies, and that its circulation was moderate. For a time it looked as though it would have no more than a *succès d'éstime* and be forgotten as all but one novel out of a thousand are forgotten. By a happy chance which would take too long to narrate *The Old Wives' Tale* was brought to the attention of Mr. George Doran who had bought sheets of it; he forthwith acquired the American rights, set it up and launched it on its triumphal course. It was not till after its great success in America that it was taken over by another publisher in England and attracted the attention of the British public. For many years, what with one thing and another, I do not think I met Arnold, or if I did it was only at a party, literary or otherwise, at which I had the opportunity to say no more than a few words to him; but after the war and until his death I saw much of him. Much has been written of him during these later years and I have little to add. He was become a great figure. He was very different from the thin, rather insignificant man, looking like a city clerk, with his black hair plastered down on his head, that I had known in Paris. He had grown stout. His hair, very gray, was worn much longer and he had cultivated the amusing cock's comb that the caricaturists made famous. He had always been neat in his dress, disconcertingly even, but now he was grand. He wore frilled shirts in the evening and took an immense pride in his white waistcoats. He has related the story of a picnic I took him on while he was staying with me in the South of France when, a storm preventing us from leaving the island on which we were, he took stock with his humorous detachment of the reactions of the various persons present to the slight danger we found ourselves faced with. He did not say that the women were all in pyjamas and the men in tennis shirts, duck trousers and *espadrilles*; but that he, refusing to permit himself such *sans gêne*, was arrayed in a check suit of a sort of mustard colour, wore fancy socks and fancy shoes, a starched collar, a striped shirt and a foulard tie; and that when at six next morning we all got home, bedraggled, unshaven and looking like nothing on earth, he, in his smart shirt and neat suit, looked, as he had looked eighteen hours before, as though he had just come out of a band-box. To the end of the experience he remained dignified, self-possessed, good-tempered and interested.

But it was not only in appearance that he was a very different man from the one that I had known in Paris. I dare say it was all there then and perhaps it was only my stupidity and youth that prevented me from seeing it. Perhaps also it was that life had changed him. I think it possible that at first he was hampered by his extreme diffidence, and his bumptiousness was a protection he assumed to his own timidity, and that success had given him confidence. It had certainly mellowed him. He had acquired a very sensible assurance of his own merit. He told me once that there were only two novels written during the last thirty years that he was confident would survive and one of these was *The Old Wives' Tale*. It was impossible to know him without liking him. He was a character. His very oddities were endearing. Indeed it was to them that the great affection in which he was universally held was partly due, for people laughed at foibles in him which they were conscious of not possessing themselves and thus mitigated the oppression which admiration for his talent must otherwise have made them feel. He was never what in England is technically known as a gentleman, but he was not vulgar any more than the traffic surging up Ludgate Hill is vulgar. His common sense was matchless. He was entirely devoid of envy. He was generous. He was courageous. He always said with perfect frankness what he thought and because it never struck him that he could offend he never did; but if, with his quick sensitiveness, he imagined that he had hurt somebody's feelings he did everything in reason to salve the wound. His kindness glowed like a halo about a saint.

I was surprised to see how patronising on the whole were the obituary notices written at his death. A certain amount

of fun was made of his obsession with grandeur and luxury,
and the pleasure he took in *trains de luxe* and first-class
hotels. He never quite grew accustomed to the appurtenances
of wealth. Once he said to me, "If you've ever really been
poor you remain poor at heart all your life. I've often walked,"
he added, "when I could very well afford to take a taxi because I simply couldn't bring myself to waste the shilling it
would cost." He admired and disapproved of extravagance.

The criticism to which he devoted much time during his
later years came in for a good deal of adverse comment. He
loved his position on *The Evening Standard*. He liked the
power it gave him and enjoyed the interest his articles
aroused. The immediate response, like the applause an actor
receives after an effective scene, gratified his appetite for ac-
tuality. It gave him the illusion, peculiarly pleasant to the
author whose avocation necessarily entails a sense of apart-
ness, that he was in the midst of things. He read as a man
of letters and whatever he thought he said without fear or
favour. He had no patience with the precious, the affected
or the pompous. If he thought little of certain writers who
are now more praised than read it is not certain that he
thought wrong. He was more interested in life than in art.
In criticism he was an amateur. The professional critic is
probably somewhat shy of life, for otherwise it is unlikely
that he would devote himself to the reading and judging of
books rather than to the stress and turmoil of living. He is
more at ease with it when the sweat has dried and the acrid
odour of humanity has ceased to offend the nostrils. He can
be sympathetic enough to the realism of Defoe and the tumultuous vitality of Balzac, but when it comes to the productions of his own day he feels more comfortable with works
in which a deliberately literary attitude has softened the
asperities of reality. That is why, I suppose, the praise that
was accorded to Arnold Bennett for *The Old Wives' Tale*
after his death was cooler than one would have expected.
Some of the critics said that notwithstanding everything he
had a sense of beauty and they quoted passages to show his
poetic power and his feeling for the mystery of existence. I
do not see the point of making out that he had something
of what you would like him to have had a great deal more of

and ignoring that in which his power and value was. He was neither mystic nor poet. He was interested in material things and in the passions common to all men. He described life, as every writer does, in the terms of his own temperament. He was more concerned with the man in the street than with the exceptional person. Everyone knows that Arnold was afflicted with a very bad stammer; it was painful to watch the struggle he had sometimes to get the words out. It was torture to him. Few realised the exhaustion it caused him to speak. What to most men was as easy as breathing to him was a constant strain. It tore his nerves to pieces. Few knew the humiliations it exposed him to, the ridicule it excited in many, the impatience it aroused, the awkwardness of feeling that it made people find him tiresome; and the minor exasperation of thinking of a good, amusing or apt remark and not venturing to say it in case the stammer ruined it. Few knew the distressing sense it gave rise to of a bar to complete contact with other men. It may be that except for the stammer which forced him to introspection Arnold would never have become a writer. But I think it is not the least proof of his strong and sane character that notwithstanding this impediment he was able to retain his splendid balance and regard the normal life of man from a normal point of view.

The Old Wives' Tale is certainly the best book he wrote. He never lost the desire to write another as good and because it was written by an effort of will he thought he could repeat it. He tried in *Clayhanger*, and for a time it looked as though he might succeed. I think he failed only because his material fizzled out. After *The Old Wives' Tale* he had not enough left to complete the vast structure he had designed. No writer can get more than a certain amount of ore out of one seam; when he has got that, though it remains, miraculously, as rich as before, it is only others who can profitably work it. He tried again in *Lord Raingo* and he tried for the last time in *Imperial Palace*. Here I think the subject was at fault. Because it profoundly interested him he thought it was of universal interest. He gathered his data systematically, but they were jotted down in note-books and not garnered (as were those of *The Old Wives' Tale*) unconsciously and preserved, not in black and white, but as old memories in his bones, in his nerves, in his heart. But that Arnold should have spent the last of his energy and determination in the description of a hotel seems to me to have a symbolical significance. For I feel that he was never quite at home in the world. It was to him perhaps a sumptuous hotel, with marble bathrooms and a marvellous cuisine, in which he was a transient guest. For all his assurance and his knowing air I felt that he was, here among men, impressed, delighted, but a little afraid of doing the wrong thing and never entirely at his ease. Just as his little apartment in the rue des Dames years before had suggested to me a rôle played carefully, but from the outside, I feel that to him life was a rôle that he played conscientiously, and with ability, but into the skin of which he never quite got.

Katherine Anne Porter on

WILLA CATHER

I never knew her at all, nor anyone who did know her; do not to this day. When I was a young writer in New York I knew she was there, and sometimes wished that by some charming chance I might meet up with her; but I never did, and it did not occur to me to seek her out. I had never felt that my condition of beginning authorship gave me a natural claim on the attention of writers I admired, such as Henry James and W. B. Yeats. Some proper instinct told me that all of any importance they had to say to me was in their printed pages, mine to use as I could. Still it would have been nice to have seen them, just to remember how they looked. There are three or four great ones, gone now, that I feel, too late, I should not have missed. Willa Cather was one of them.

There exist large numbers of critical estimates of her work, appreciations; perhaps even a memoir or two, giving glimpses of her personal history—I have never read one. She was not, in the popular crutch-word to describe almost any kind of sensation, "exciting"; so far as I know, nobody, not even one of the Freudian school of critics, ever sat up nights with a textbook in one hand and her works in the other, reading between the lines to discover how much sexual autobiography could be mined out of her stories. I remember only one photograph—Steichen's—made in middle life, showing a big plain smiling woman, her arms crossed easily over a girl-scout sort of white blouse, with a ragged part in her hair. She seemed, as the French say, "well seated" and not very outgoing. Even the earnestly amiable, finely shaped eyes, the left one faintly askew, were in some mysterious way not expressive, lacking as they did altogether that look of strangeness which a strange vision is supposed to give to the eye of any real artist, and very often does. One doesn't have to be a genius absolutely to get this look, it is often quite enough merely to believe one is a genius; and to have had the wild vision only once is enough—the afterlight stays, even if, in such case, it is phosphorescence instead of living fire.

Well, Miss Cather looks awfully like somebody's big sister, or maiden aunt, both of which she was. No genius ever looked less like one, according to the romantic popular view, unless it was her idol, Flaubert, whose photographs could pass easily for those of any paunchy country squire indifferent to his appearance. Like him, none of her genius was in her looks, only in her works. Flaubert was a good son, adoring uncle of a niece, devoted to his friends, contemptuous of the mediocre, obstinate in his preferences, fiercely jealous of his privacy, unyielding to the death in his literary principles and not in the slightest concerned with what was fashionable. No wonder she loved him. She had been rebuffed a little at first, not by his astronomical standards in art—none could be too high for her—but by a certain coldness of heart in him. She soon got over that; it became for her only another facet of his nobility of mind.

Very early she had learned to reverence that indispensable faculty of aspiration of the human mind toward perfection called, in morals and the arts, nobility. She was born to the idea and brought up in it: first in a little crowded farmhouse in Virginia, and later, the eldest of seven children, in a little crowded ranch house in Nebraska. She had, as many American country people did have in those times and places, literate parents and grandparents, soundly educated and deeply read, educated, if not always at schools, always at their own firesides. Two such, her grandmothers, taught her from her infancy. Her sister, Mrs. Auld, in Palo Alto, California, told it like this:

"She mothered us all, took care of us, and there was a lot to do in such a big family. She learned Greek and Latin from our grandmothers before she ever got to go to school. She used to go, after we lived in Red Cloud, to read Latin and Greek with a little old man who kept a general store down the road. In the evenings for entertainment—there was nowhere to go, you know, almost nothing to see or hear—

she entertained us, it was good as a theater for us! She told us long stories, some she made up herself, and some were her versions of legends and fairy tales she had read; she taught us Greek mythology this way, Homer; and tales from the Old Testament. We were all story tellers," said her sister, "all of us wanted to be the one to tell the stories, but she was the one who told them. And we loved to listen all of us to her, when maybe we would not have listened to each other."

She was not the first nor the last American writer to be formed in this system of home education; at one time it was the customary education for daughters, many of them never got to school at all or expected to; but they were capable of educating their grandchildren, as this little history shows. To her last day Willa Cather was the true child of her plain-living, provincial farming people, with their aristocratic ways of feeling and thinking; poor, but not poverty-stricken for a moment; rock-based in character, a character shaped in an old school of good manners, good morals, and the unchallenged assumption that classic culture was their birthright; the belief that knowledge of great art and great thought was a good in itself not to be missed for anything; she subscribed to it all with her whole heart, and in herself there was the vein of iron she had inherited from a long line of people who had helped to break wildernesses and to found a new nation in such faiths. When you think of the whole unbelievable history, how did anything like this survive? Yet it did, and this life is one of the proofs.

I have not much interest in anyone's personal history after the tenth year, not even my own. Whatever one was going to be was all prepared for before that. The rest is merely confirmation, extension, development. Childhood is the fiery furnace in which we are melted down to essentials and that essential shaped for good. While I have been reading again Willa Cather's essays and occasional papers, and thinking about her, I remembered a sentence from the diaries of Anne Frank, who died in the concentration camp in Bergen-Belsen just before she was sixteen years old. At less than fifteen, she wrote: "I have had a lot of sorrow, but who hasn't, at my age?"

In Miss Cather's superb little essay on Katherine Mansfield, she speaks of childhood and family life: "I doubt whether any contemporary writer has made one feel more keenly the many kinds of personal relations which exist in an everyday 'happy family' who are merely going on with their daily lives, with no crises or shocks or bewildering complications. . . . Yet every individual in that household (even the children) is clinging passionately to his individual soul, is in terror of losing it in the general family flavor . . . the mere struggle to have anything of one's own, to be oneself at all, creates an element of strain which keeps everybody almost at breaking point.

". . . Even in harmonious families there is this double life . . . the one we can observe in our neighbor's household, and, underneath, another—secret and passionate and intense— which is the real life that stamps the faces and gives character to the voices of our friends. Always in his mind each member is escaping, running away, trying to break the net which circumstances and his own affections have woven about him. One realizes that human relationships are the tragic necessity of human life; that they can never be wholly satisfactory, that every ego is half the time greedily seeking them, and half the time pulling away from them."

This is masterly and water-clear and autobiography enough for me: my mind goes with tenderness to the big lonely slow-moving girl who happened to be an artist coming back from reading Latin and Greek with the old storekeeper, helping with the housework, then sitting by the fireplace to talk down an assertive brood of brothers and sisters, practicing her art on them, refusing to be lost among them—the longest-winged one who would fly free at last.

I am not much given to reading about authors, or not until I have read what they have to say for themselves. I found Willa Cather's books for myself, early, and felt no need for intermediaries between me and them. My reading went on for a good many years, one by one as they appeared: *O Pioneers!*; *The Song of the Lark*; *My Antonia*; *Youth and the Bright Medusa*; *Death Comes for the Archbishop*; *Obscure Destinies*; just these, and no others, I do not know why, and never anything since, until I read her notebooks about two years ago. Those early readings began in Texas, just before

World War I, before ever I left home; they ended in Paris, twenty years later, after the longest kind of journey.

With her first book I was reading also Henry James, W. B. Yeats, Joseph Conrad, my introduction to "modern" literature, for I was brought up on solid reading, too, well aged. About the same time I read Gertrude Stein's *Tender Buttons*, for sale at a little bookshop with a shoeshine stand outside; inside you could find magazines, books, newspapers in half-a-dozen languages, *avant-garde* and radical and experimental; this in a Texas coast town of less than ten thousand population but very polyglot and full of world travelers. I could make little headway with Miss Stein beyond the title. It was plain that she meant "tender buds" and I wondered why she did not say so. It was the beginning of my quarrel with a certain school of "modern" writing in which poverty of feeling and idea were disguised, but not well enough, in tricky techniques and disordered syntax. A year or two after *Tender Buttons* I was reading Joyce's *Dubliners*, and maybe only a young beginning writer of that time, with some preparation of mind by the great literature of the past, could know what a revelation that small collection of matchless stories could be. It was not a shock, but a revelation, a further unfolding of the deep world of the imagination. I had never heard of Joyce. By the pure chance of my roving curiosity, I picked up a copy of the book at that little shoeshine bookstore. It was a great day.

By the time I reached Paris, I had done my long apprenticeship, published a small book of my own, and had gone like a house afire through everything "new"—that word meant something peculiar to the times—absolutely everything "new" that was being published; also in music; also painting. I considered almost any painting with the varnish still wet, the artist standing by, so to speak, as more interesting than anything done even the year before. But some of the painters were Klee, Juan Gris, Modigliani. . . . I couldn't listen to music happily if it wasn't hot from the composer's brain, preferably conducted or played by himself. Still, some of the music was Stravinsky's. I was converted to the harpsichord by the first New York recital of Wanda Landowska. In the theater I preferred dress rehearsals, or even just rehearsals, to the finished performance; I was mad about the ballet and took lessons off and on with a Russian for two years; I even wrote a ballet libretto way back in 1920 for a young Mexican painter and scene designer who gave the whole thing to Pavlova, who danced it in many countries but not in New York, because the scenery was done on paper, was inflammable and she was not allowed to use it in New York. I saw photographs, however, and I must say they did not look in the least like anything I had provided for in the libretto. It was most unsatisfactory.

What has this to do with Willa Cather? A great deal. I had had time to grow up, to consider, to look again, to begin finding my way a little through the inordinate clutter and noise of my immediate day, in which very literally everything in the world was being pulled apart, torn up, turned wrong side out and upside down; almost no frontiers left unattacked, governments and currencies falling; even the very sexes seemed to be changing back and forth and multiplying weird, unclassifiable genders. And every day, in the arts, as in schemes of government and organized crime, there was, there had to be, something New.

Alas, or thank God, depending on the way you feel about it, there comes that day when today's New begins to look a little like yesterday's New, and then more and more so; you begin to suffer slightly from a sense of sameness or repetition: that painting, that statue, that music, that kind of writing, that way of thinking and feeling, that revolution, that political doctrine—is it really New? The answer is simply no, and if you are really in a perverse belligerent mood, you may add a half-truth—no, and it never was. Looking around at the debris, you ask has newness merely for its own sake any virtue? And you find that all along you had held and wound in your hand through the maze an unbreakable cord on which one by one, hardly knowing it, you had strung your life's treasures; it was as if they had come of themselves, while you were seeking and choosing and picking up and tossing away again, down all sorts of bypaths and up strange stairs and into queer corners; and there they were, things old and new, the things you loved first and those you loved last, all together and yours, and no longer old or new, but outside of time and beyond the reach of change, even your own; for that part of your life they belong to was in some sense made by them; if they went, all that part of your life would be mutilated, unrecognizable. While you hold and wind that cord with its slowly accumulating, weightless, unaccountable riches, the maze seems a straight road; you look back through all the fury you have come through, when it seemed so much, and so dismayingly, destruction, and so much just the pervasively trivial, stupid, or malignant-dwarfish tricks: fur-lined cups as sculpture, symphonies written for kitchen batteries, experiments on language very similar to the later Nazi surgical experiments of cutting and uniting human nerve ends never meant to touch each other: so many perversities crowding in so close you could hardly see beyond them. Yet look, you shared it, you were part of it, you even added to the confusion, so busy being new yourself. The fury and waste and clamor was, after all, just what you had thought it was in the first place, even if you had lost sight of it later—life, in a word, and great glory came of it, and splendid things that will go on living cleared of all the rubbish thrown up around their creation. Things you would have once thought incompatible to eternity take their right places in peace, in proper scale and order, in your mind—in your blood. They become that marrow in your bones where the blood is renewed.

I had liked best of all Willa Cather's two collections of short stories. They live still with morning freshness in my memory, their clearness, warmth of feeling, calmness of intelligence, an ample human view of things; in short the sense of an artist at work in whom one could have complete confidence: not even the prose attracted my attention from what the writer was saying—really saying, and not just in the words. Also I remember well my deeper impression of reserve—a reserve that was personal because it was a matter of temperament, the grain of the mind; yet conscious too, and practiced deliberately: almost a method, a technique, but not assumed. It was instead a manifesting, proceeding from the moral nature of the artist, morality extended to aesthetics—not aes-

thetics as morality but simply a development of both faculties along with all the others until the whole being was
indivisibly one, the imagination and its expression fused and
fixed.

A magnificent state, no doubt, at which to arrive; but it
should be the final one, and Miss Cather seemed to be there
almost from the first. What was it? For I began to have an
image of her as a kind of lighthouse, or even a promontory,
some changeless phenomenon of art or nature or both. I have
a peculiar antipathy to thinking of anyone I know in symbols
or mythical characters and this finally quietly alienated me
from her, from her very fine books, from any feeling that
she was a living, working artist in our time. It is hard to
explain, for it was a question of tone, of implication, and
what else? Finally, after a great while, I decided that Miss
Cather's reserve amounted to a deliberate withholding of
some vital part of herself as artist; not as if she had hidden
herself at the center of her mystery but was still there to be
disclosed at last; no, she had absented herself willfully.

I was quite wrong of course. She is exactly at the center
of her own mystery, where she belongs. My immoderate reading of our two or three invaluably afflicted giants of contemporary literature, and their abject army of camp followers and
imitators, had blurred temporarily my perception of that thin
line separating self-revealment from self-exhibition. Miss
Cather had never any intention of using fiction or any other
form of writing as a device for showing herself off. She was
not Paul in travesty, nor the opera singer in "The Diamond
Mine," nor that girl with the clear eyes who became an
actress: above all, not the Lost Lady. Of course she was all
of them. How not? She made all of them out of herself,
where else could they have taken on life?

Her natural lack of picturesqueness was also a good protective coloring: it saved her from the invasive prying of
hangers-on: and no "school" formed in her name. The young
writers did not swarm over her with flattery, manuscripts in
hand, meaning to use her for all she was worth; publishers
did not waylay her with seductions the instant her first little
book appeared; all S. S. McClure could think of to do for
her, after he published The Troll Garden, was to offer her

a job as one of his editors on *McClure's Magazine*, where she worked hard for six mortal years before it seems to have occurred to her that she was not being a writer, after all, which was what she had started out for. So she quit her job, and the next year, more or less, published *Alexander's Bridge*, of which she afterward repented, for reasons that were to last her a lifetime. The scene, London, was strange and delightful to her; she was trying to make a novel out of some interesting people in what seemed to her exotic situations, instead of out of something she really knew about with more than the top of her mind. "London is supposed to be more engaging than, let us say, Gopher Prairie," she remarks, "even if the writer knows Gopher Prairie very well and London very casually."

She realized at once that *Alexander's Bridge* was a mistake, her wrong turning, which could not be retraced too instantly and entirely. It was a very pretty success, and could have been her finish, except that she happened to be Willa Cather. For years she still found people who liked that book, but they couldn't fool her. She knew what she had done. So she left New York and went to Arizona for six months, not for repentance but for refreshment, and found there a source that was to refresh her for years to come. Let her tell of her private apocalypse in her own words: "I did no writing down there, but I recovered from the conventional editorial point of view."

She then began to write a book for herself—*O Pioneers!*—and it was "a different process altogether. Here there was no arranging or 'inventing'; everything was spontaneous and took its own place, right or wrong. This was like taking a ride through a familiar country on a horse that knew the way, on a fine morning when you felt like riding. The other was like riding in a park, with someone not altogether congenial, to whom you had to be talking all the time."

What are we to think? For certainly here is a genius who simply will not cater to our tastes for drama, who refuses to play the role in any way we have been accustomed to seeing it played. She wrote with immense sympathy about Stephen Crane: "There is every evidence that he was a reticent and unhelpful man, with no warmhearted love of giving out opinions." If she had said "personal confidences" she could as well have been writing about herself. But she was really writing about Stephen Crane and stuck to her subject. Herself, she gave out quite a lot of opinions, not all of them warmhearted, in the course of two short little books, the second a partial reprint of the first. You hardly realize how many and how firm and how cogent while reading her fine pure direct prose, hearing through it a level, well-tempered voice saying very good, sensible right things with complete authority—things not in fashion but close to here and now and always, not like a teacher or a mother—like an artist—until, after you have closed the book, her point of view begins to accumulate and take shape in your mind.

Freud had happened: but Miss Cather continued to cite the old Hebrew prophets, the Greek dramatists, Goethe, Shakespeare, Dante, Tolstoy, Flaubert, and such for the deeper truths of human nature, both good and evil. She loved Shelley, Wordsworth, Walter Pater, without any reference to their public standing at the time. In her essay, "The Novel Demeublé," she had the inspired notion to bring together for purposes of comparison Balzac and Prosper Merimée; she preferred Merimée on the ground quite simply that he was the better artist: you have to sort out Balzac's meanings from a great dusty warehouse of irrelevant vain matter—furniture, in a word. Once got at, they are as vital as ever. But Merimée is as vital, and you cannot cut one sentence without loss from his stories. The perfect answer to the gross power of the one, the too-finished delicacy of the other was, of course, Flaubert.

Stravinsky had happened; but she went on being dead in love with Wagner, Beethoven, Schubert, Gluck, especially *Orpheus*, and almost any opera. She was music-mad, and even Ravel's *La Valse* enchanted her; perhaps also even certain later music, but she has not mentioned it in these papers.

The Nude had Descended the Staircase with an epoch-shaking tread but she remained faithful to Puvis de Chavannes, whose wall paintings in the Panthéon of the legend of St. Genevieve inspired the form and tone of *Death Comes for the Archbishop*. She longed to tell old stories as simply as that, as deeply centered in the core of experience without extraneous detail as in the lives of the saints in *The Golden*

Legend. She loved Courbet, Rembrandt, Millet and the sixteenth-century Dutch and Flemish painters, with their "warmly furnished interiors" but always with a square window open to the wide gray sea, where the masts of the great Dutch fleets were setting out to "ply quietly on all the waters of the globe. . . ."

Joyce had happened: or perhaps we should say, *Ulysses,* for the work has now fairly absorbed the man we knew. I believe that this is true of all artists of the first order. They are not magnified in their work, they disappear in it, consumed by it. That subterranean upheaval of language caused not even the barest tremor in Miss Cather's firm, lucid sentences. There is good internal evidence that she read a great deal of contemporary literature, contemporary over a stretch of fifty years, and think what contemporaries they were—from Tolstoy and Hardy and James and Chekhov to Gide and Proust and Joyce and Lawrence and Virginia Woolf, to Sherwood Anderson and Theodore Dreiser: the first names that come to mind. There was a regiment of them; it was as rich and fruitfully disturbing a period as literature has to show for several centuries. And it did make an enormous change. Miss Cather held firmly to what she had found for herself, did her own work in her own way as all the others were doing each in his unique way, and did help greatly to save and reassert and illustrate the validity of certain great and dangerously threatened principles of art. Without too much fuss, too—and is quietly disappearing into her work altogether, as we might expect.

Mr. Maxwell Geismar wrote a book about her and some others, called *The Last of the Provincials.* Not having read it I do not know his argument; but he has a case: she is a provincial; and I hope not the last. She was a good artist, and all true art is provincial in the most realistic sense: of the very time and place of its making, out of human beings who are so particularly limited by their situation, whose faces and names are real and whose lives begin each one at an individual unique center. Indeed, Willa Cather was as provincial as Hawthorne or Flaubert or Turgenev, as little concerned with aesthetics and as much with morals as Tolstoy, as obstinately reserved as Melville. In fact she always reminds me of very good literary company, of the particularly admirable masters who formed her youthful tastes, her thinking and feeling.

She is a curiously immovable shape, monumental, virtue itself in her art and a symbol of virtue—like certain churches, in fact, or exemplary women, revered and neglected. Yet like these again, she has her faithful friends and true believers, even so to speak her lovers, and they last a lifetime, and after: the only kind of bond she would recognize or require or respect.

Willa Cather
ON
D. H. Lawrence:

Can one imagine anything more terrible than the story of Romeo and Juliet rewritten in prose by D. H. Lawrence?

Ford Madox Hueffer
ON
Henry James:

Mr. James presents you with the proposition, not so much that there are no such things as oppressors and oppressed, but that, even in the act of oppressing, the oppressor isn't having a very much better time than his victims. He does not, that is to say, picture for you starvations, gaols, workhouse wards, and slave-drivers brandishing whips. That is not his business. His subjects in the end are selected instances of long chains of embarrassments, and his tragic note is rather that of the nightmare than of the murder.

During the whole seventy years of his life . . . Mr. James has had just one immense mission—the civilizing of America.

André Gide
ON
Stendhal:

The great secret of Stendhal, his great shrewdness, consisted in writing at once. . . . Whence that element of alertness and spontaneity, of incongruity, of suddenness and nakedness, that always delights us anew in his style. It would seem that his thought does not take time to put on its shoes before beginning to run.

Hemingway
ON
Mark Twain:

All modern American literature comes from one book by Mark Twain called Huckleberry Finn.

For a year and a half, the writer of this appreciation was Ring Lardner's most familiar companion; after that geography made separations and our contacts were rare. When my wife and I last saw him in 1931 he looked already like a man on his deathbed—it was terribly sad to see that six feet three inches of kindness stretched out ineffectual in the hospital room. His fingers trembled with a match, the tight skin on his handsome skull was marked as a mask of misery and nervous pain.

He gave a very different impression when we first saw him in 1921—he seemed to have an abundance of quiet vitality that would enable him to outlast anyone, to take himself for long spurts of work or play that would ruin an ordinary constitution. He had recently convulsed the country with the famous kitten-and-coat saga (it had to do with a world's series bet and with the impending conversion of some kittens into fur), and the evidence of the betting, a beautiful sable, was worn by his wife at the time. In those days he was interested in people, sports, bridge, music, the stage, the newspapers, the magazines, the books. But though I did not know it, the change in him had already begun—the impenetrable despair that dogged him for a dozen years to his death.

He had practically given up sleeping, save on short vacations deliberately consecrated to simple pleasures, most frequently golf with his friends, Grantland Rice or John Wheeler. Many a night we talked over a case of Canadian ale until bright dawn when Ring would rise and yawn:

"Well, I guess the children have left for school by this time—I might as well go home."

The woes of many people haunted him—for example the doctor's death sentence pronounced upon Tad, the cartoonist (who, in fact, nearly outlived Ring)—it was as if he believed he could and ought to do something about such things. And as he struggled to fulfill his contracts, one of which, a comic strip based on the character of "the busher," was a terror indeed, it was obvious that he felt his work to be direction-less, merely "copy." So he was inclined to turn his cosmic sense of responsibility into the channel of solving other peo-ple's problems—finding someone an introduction to a theatri-cal manager, placing a friend in a job, maneuvering a man into a golf club. The effort made was often out of proportion to the situation; the truth back of it was that Ring was getting off—he was a faithful and conscientious workman to the end, but he had stopped finding any fun in his work ten years before he died.

About that time (1922) a publisher undertook to reissue his old books and collect his recent stories and this gave him a sense of existing in the literary world as well as with the public, and he got some satisfaction from the reiterated state-ments of Mencken and F.P.A. as to his true stature as a writer. But I don't think he cared then—it is hard to under-stand but I don't think he really gave a damn about anything except his personal relations with a few people. A case in point was his attitude to those imitators who lifted every-thing except the shirt off his back—only Hemingway has been so thoroughly frisked—it worried the imitators more than it worried Ring. His attitude was that if they got stuck in the process he'd help them over any tough place.

Throughout this period of huge earnings and in increas-ingly solid reputation on top and beneath, there were two ambitions more important to Ring than the work by which he will be remembered: he wanted to be a musician—sometimes he dramatized himself ironically as a thwarted composer—and he wanted to write shows. His dealings with managers would make a whole story: they were always commis-sioning him to do work which they promptly forgot they had ordered, and accepting librettos that they never produced. (Ring left a short ironic record of Ziegfeld.) Only with the aid of the practical George Kaufman did he achieve his am-bition, and by then he was too far gone in illness to get a proper satisfaction from it.

The point of these paragraphs is that whatever Ring's achievement was it fell short of the achievement he was capable of, and this because of a cynical attitude toward his work. How far back did that attitude go—back to his youth in a Michigan village? Certainly back to his days with the Cubs. During those years, when most men of promise achieve an adult education, if only in the school of war, Ring moved in the company of a few dozen illiterates playing a boy's game. A boy's game, with no more possibilities in it than a boy could master, a game bounded by walls which kept out novelty or danger, change or adventure. This material, the observation of it under such circumstances, was the text of Ring's schooling during the most formative period of the mind. A writer can spin on about his adventures after thirty, after forty, after fifty, but the criteria by which these adventures are weighed and valued are irrevocably settled at the age of twenty-five. However deeply Ring might cut into it, his cake had exactly the diameter of Frank Chance's diamond.

Here was his artistic problem, and it promised future trouble. So long as he wrote within that inclosure the result was magnificent: within it he heard and recorded the voice of a continent. But when, inevitably, he outgrew his interest in it, what was Ring left with?

He was left with his fine etymological technique—and he was left rather helpless in those few acres. He had been formed by the very world on which his hilarious irony had released itself. He had fought his way through to knowing what people's motives are and what means they are likely to resort to in order to attain their goals. But now he had a new problem—what to do about it. He went on seeing, and the sights traveled back the optic nerve, but no longer to be thrown off in fiction, because they were no longer sights that could be weighed and valued by the old criteria. It was never that he was completely sold on athletic virtuosity as the be-all and end-all of problems; the trouble was that he could find nothing finer. Imagine life conceived as a business of beautiful muscular organization—an arising, an effort, a good break, a sweat, a bath, a meal, a love, a sleep—imagine it achieved; then imagine trying to apply that standard to the horribly complicated mess of living where nothing, even the greatest conceptions and workings and achievements, is else but messy, spotty, tortuous—and then one can imagine the confusion that Ring faced coming out of the ball park.

He kept on recording but he no longer projected, and this accumulation, which he has taken with him to the grave, crippled his spirit in the latter years. It was not the fear of Niles, Michigan, that hampered him—it was the habit of silence formed in the presence of the "ivory" with which he lived and worked. Remember it was not humble ivory—Ring has demonstrated that—it was arrogant, imperative, often megalomaniacal ivory. He got a habit of silence, then the habit of repression that finally took the form of his odd little crusade in *The New Yorker* against pornographic songs. He had agreed with himself to speak only a small portion of his mind.

The present writer once suggested to him that he organize some *cadre* within which he could adequately display his talents, suggesting that it should be something deeply personal, and something on which Ring could take his time, but he dismissed the idea lightly; he was a disillusioned idealist but he had served his Fates well, and no other ones could be casually created for him—"This is something that can be printed," he reasoned, "this, however, belongs with that bunch of stuff that can never be written."

He covered himself in such cases with protests of his inability to bring off anything big, but this was specious, for he was a proud man and had no reason to rate his abilities cheaply. He refused to "tell all" because in a crucial period of his life he had formed the habit of not doing it—and this he had elevated gradually into a standard of taste. It never satisfied him by a damn sight.

So one is haunted not only by a sense of personal loss but by a conviction that Ring got less percentage of himself on paper than any other American author of the first flight. There is "You Know Me, Al," and there are about a dozen wonderful short stories, (My God, he hadn't even saved them —the material of "How to Write Short Stories" was obtained by photographing old issues of magazines in the public library!) and there is some of the most uproarious and inspired nonsense since Lewis Carroll. Most of the rest is mediocre stuff, with flashes, and I would do Ring a disservice to suggest it should be set upon an altar and worshiped, as have been the most casual relics of Mark Twain. Those three volumes should seem enough—to everyone who didn't know Ring. But I venture that no one who knew him but will agree that the personality of the man overlapped it. Proud, shy, solemn, shrewd, polite, brave, kind, merciful, honorable—with the affection these qualities aroused he created in addition a certain awe in people. His intentions, his will, once in motion were formidable factors in dealing with him—he always did every single thing he said he would do. Frequently he was the melancholy Jacques, and sad company indeed, but under any conditions a noble dignity flowed from him, so that time in his presence always seemed well spent.

On my desk, at the moment, I have the letters that Ring wrote to us; here is a letter one thousand words long, here is one of two thousand words—theatrical gossip, literary shop talk, flashes of wit but not much wit, for he was feeling thin and saving the best of that for his work, anecdotes of his activities. I reprint the most typical one I can find:

The Dutch Treat show was a week ago Friday night. Grant Rice and I had reserved a table, and a table holds ten people and no more. Well, I had invited, as one guest, Jerry Kern, but he telephoned at the last moment that he couldn't come. I then consulted with Grant Rice, who said he had no substitute in mind, but that it was a shame to waste our extra ticket when tickets were at a premium. So I called up Jones, and Jones said yes, and would it be all right for him to bring along a former Senator who was a pal of his and had been good to him in Washington. I said I was sorry, but our table was filled and besides, we didn't have an extra ticket. "Maybe I could dig up another ticket somewhere," said Jones. "I don't believe so," I said, "but anyway the point is that we haven't room at our table." "Well," said Jones, "I could have the Senator eat somewhere else and join us in time for the show." "Yes," I said, "but we have no ticket for him." "Well, I'll think up something," he said. Well, what he thought up was to bring himself and the Senator and I had a hell of a time getting an extra ticket and shoving the Senator in at another table where he wasn't wanted, and later in the evening, the Senator thanked Jones and said he was the greatest fella in the world and all I got was goodnight.

Well, I must close and nibble on a carrot. R.W.L.

Even in a telegram Ring could compress a lot of himself. Here is one:

When are you coming back and why please answer
Ring Lardner.

This is not the moment to recollect Ring's convivial aspects, especially as he had, long before his death, ceased to find amusement in dissipation, or indeed in the whole range of what is called entertainment—save for his perennial interest in songs. By grace of the radio and of the many musicians who, drawn by his enormous magnetism, made pilgrimages to his bedside, he had a consolation in the last days, and he made the most of it, hilariously rewriting Cole Porter's lyrics in *The New Yorker*. But it would be an evasion for the present writer not to say that when he was Ring's neighbor a decade ago, they tucked a lot under their belts in many weathers, and spent many words on many men and things. At no time did I feel that I had known him enough, or that anyone knew him—it was not the feeling that there was more stuff in him and that it should come out, it was rather a qualitative difference, it was rather as though, due to some inadequacy in one's self, one had not penetrated to something unsolved, new and unsaid. That is why one wishes that Ring had written down a larger proportion of what was in his mind and heart. It would have saved him longer for us, and that in itself would be something. But I would like to know what it was, and now I will go on wishing—what did Ring want, how did he want things to be, how did he think things were?

A great and good American is dead. Let us not obscure him by the flowers, but walk up and look at that fine medallion, all abraded by sorrows that perhaps we are not equipped to understand. Ring made no enemies, because he was kind, and to many millions he gave release and delight.

Glenway Wescott on

F. Scott Fitzgerald is dead, aged forty-four. *Requiescat in pace; ora pro nobis.* In the twenties, his heyday, he was a kind of king of our American youth; and as the news of his end appeared in the papers there were strange coincidences along with it. A number of others—a younger writer who was somewhat of his school and, like him, had committed his talent unfortunately to Hollywood, and that writer's pretty, whimsical wife, and another young woman who was a famous horse-trainer, and the young leader of a popular jazz-band— also met sudden deaths that week. I was reminded of the holocausts by which primitive rulers were provided with an escort, servants and pretty women and boon companions, for eternity. The twenties were heaven, so to speak, often enough; might not heaven be like the twenties? If it were, in one or two particulars, Scott Fitzgerald would be sorry; sorry once more.

His health failed, and with a peculiar darkness and dead-weight in mind and heart, some five years ago. Then in a wonderful essay entitled *The Crack-up* he took stock of himself, looking twenty years back for what flaws were in him or in the day and age, what early damage had been done, and how. Thanks to that, one can speak of his weaknesses without benefit of gossip, without impertinence. And so I do, asking for charity toward him and clarity about him; and a little on my own mortal account; and for certain innocent immature American writers' benefit.

My theme is as usual personality rather than esthetics; but my sentiment on this occasion is not personal. Aside from our Midwestern birth and years of foreign residence, you could scarcely find two men of the same generation less alike than we two. Neither our virtues nor our vices appeared to overlap at all. I did not have the honor of his particular friendship. I have only one vivid memory of conversation with him, which was on a Mediterranean beach. Across the Bay of Angels and over the big good-for-nothing city of Nice, some of the Alps hung in the air as pearly as onions; and that air and that sea, which has only delicate tides, quivered with warm weather. It was before the publication of *The Sun Also Rises*, the summer of 1925 or 1926, and Hemingway was what he wanted to talk to me about. He came abruptly and drew me a little apart from our friends and relations, into the shade of a rock.

Hemingway had published some short stories in the dinky de luxe way in Paris; and I along with all the literary set had discovered him, which was fun; and when we returned to New York we preached the new style and peculiar feeling of his fiction as if it were evangel. Still, that was too slow a start of a great career to suit Fitzgerald. Obviously Ernest was the one true genius of our decade, he said; and yet he was neglected and misunderstood and, above all, insufficiently remunerated. He thought I would agree that *The Apple of the Eye* and *The Great Gatsby* were rather inflated market values just then. What could I do to help launch Hemingway? Why didn't I write a laudatory essay on him? With this questioning, Fitzgerald now and then impatiently grasped and shook my elbow.

There was something more than ordinary art-admiration about it, but on the other hand it was no mere matter of affection for Hemingway; it was so bold, unabashed, lacking in sense of humor. I have a sharp tongue and my acquaintances often underestimate my good nature; so I was touched and flattered by Fitzgerald's taking so much for granted. It simply had not occurred to him that unfriendliness or pettiness on my part might inhibit my enthusiasm about the art of a new colleague and rival. As a matter of fact, my enthusiasm was not on a par with his; and looking back now, I am glad for my sake that it was not. He not only said but, I believe, honestly felt that Hemingway was inimitably, essentially superior. From the moment Hemingway began to appear in print, perhaps it did not matter what he himself produced or failed to produce. He felt free to write just for profit, and to live for fun, if possible. Hemingway could be entrusted with the graver responsibilities and higher rewards such as glory, immortality. This extreme of admiration—this excuse for a morbid belittlement and abandonment of himself—was bad for Fitzgerald, I imagine. At all events he soon began to waste his energy in various hack-writing.

I was told last year that another talented contemporary of ours had grown so modest in the wage-earning way, fallen so far from his youthful triumph, that he would sign a friend's stories and split the payment. Under the friend's name it would have been hundreds of dollars, and under his, a thousand or thousands. Perhaps this was not true gossip, but it is a good little exemplary tale, and of general application. It gives me goose-flesh. A signature which has been so humiliated is apt never to be the same again, in the signer's own estimation. As a rule the delicate literary brain, the aching creative heart, cannot stand that sort of thing. It is better for a writer even to fancy himself a Messiah, against the day when writing or life goes badly. And there is more to this than the matter of esthetic integrity. For if his opinion of himself is divided by disrespect—sheepish, shameful, cynical —he usually finds his earning capacity as well as his satisfaction falling off. The vast public, which appears to have no taste, somehow senses when it is being scornfully talked down to. The great hacks are innocent, and serenely class themselves with Tolstoy and Dickens. Their getting good enough to compare with P. G. Wodehouse or Zane Grey may depend upon that benign misapprehension.

Probably Fitzgerald never fell into any abuse of his reputation as unwise and unwholesome as the above-mentioned confrères. His standard of living did seem to the rest of us high. Publishers in the twenties made immense advances to novelists who had and could lend prestige; and when in the thirties Fitzgerald's popularity lapsed, movies had begun to be talkies, which opened up a new lucrative field of literary operation. Certainly he did write too much in recent years with his tongue in his cheek; his heart in his boots if not in his pocket. And it was his opinion in 1936 that the competition and popular appeal of the films—"a more glittering, a grosser power," as he put it—had made the God-given form of the novel archaic; a wrong thought indeed for a novelist.

This is not the ideal moment to reread and appraise his collectable works. With the mind at a loss, muffled like a drum—the ego a little inflamed as it always is by presentness of death—we may exaggerate their merit or their shortcomings. I remember thinking, when the early best sellers were published, that his style was a little too free and easy; but I was a fussy stylist in those days. His phrasing was almost always animated and charming; his diction excellent. He wrote very little in slang or what I call babytalk: the pitfall of many who specialized in American contemporaneity after him. But for other reasons—obscurity of sentiment, facetiousness—a large part of his work may not endure, as readable reading matter for art's sake. It will be precious as documentary evidence, instructive example. That is not, in the way of immortality, what the writer hopes; but it is much more than most writers of fiction achieve.

This Side of Paradise haunted the decade like a song, popular but perfect. It hung over an entire youth-movement like a banner, somewhat discolored and wind-worn now; the wind has lapsed out of it. But a book which college boys really read is a rare thing, not to be dismissed idly or in a moment of severe sophistication. Then there were dozens of stories, some delicate and some slap-dash; one very odd, entitled *Head and Shoulders*. I love *The Great Gatsby*. Its very timeliness, as of 1925, gave it a touch of the old-fashioned a few years later; but I have reread it this week and found it all right; pleasure and compassion on every page. A masterpiece often seems a period-piece for a while; then comes down out of the attic, to function anew and to last. There is a great deal to be said for and against his final novel, *Tender Is the Night*. On the whole I am warmly for it. To be sane or insane is a noble issue, and very few novels take what might be called an intelligent interest in it; this does, and gives a fair picture of the entertaining expatriate habit of life besides.

In 1936, in three issues of *Esquire*, he published the autobiographical essay, *The Crack-up*, as it were swan-song. I first read it at my barber's, which, I suppose, is according to the editorial devices of that magazine, a medium of advertising for men's ready-made clothing. There is very little in world literature like this piece: Max Jacob's *Defense de Tartuffe;* the confidential chapter of *The Seven Pillars of Wisdom,* perhaps; Sir Walter Raleigh's verse-epistle before his beheading, in a way. Fitzgerald's theme seems more dreadful, plain petty stroke by stroke; and of course his treatment lacks the good grace and firmness of the old and old-style authors. Indeed it is cheap here and there, but in embarrassment rather than in crudity or lack of courage. Or perhaps Fitzgerald as he wrote was too sensitive to what was to appear along with it in the magazine: the jokes, the Petty girls, the haberdashery. He always suffered from an extreme environmental sense. Still it is fine prose and naturally his timeliest piece today: self-autopsy and funeral sermon. It also, with an innocent air, gravely indicts our native idealism in some respects, our common code, our college education. And in general—for ailing civilization as well as one dead Fitzgerald—this is a day of wrath.

He had made a great recovery from a seemingly mortal physical illness; then found everything dead or deadish in his psyche, his thought all broken, and no appetite for anything on earth. It was not from alcohol, he said, evidently proud of the fact that he had not had any for six months, not even beer. We may be a little doubtful of this protestation; for protestation indeed is a kind of sub-habit of the alcoholic. Six months is no time at all, in terms of the things that kill us. Alcohol in fact never exclusively causes anything. Only, just as it will heighten a happy experience, it will deepen a rut or a pit, in the way of fatigue chiefly. Who cares, when a dear one is dying of a chest-cold or an embolism, whether he is a drunkard or a reformed ex-drunkard?—Yes, I know, the dying one himself cares! But when Fitzgerald wrote his essay he still had five years to live, quite a long time. It was not about ill health, and of course he was as sane as an angel. His trouble just then and his subject was only his lassitude of imagination; his nauseated spirit; that self-hypnotic state of not having any will-power; and nothing left of the intellect but inward observation and dislike. Why, he cried, why was I "identified with the objects of my horror and compassion"?

He said it was the result of "too much anger and too many tears." That was his snap-judgment; blunt sentimentality of a boy or ex-boy. But since he was a storyteller above all, he did not stop at that; he proceeded to tell things about the past in which the mystery showed extraordinarily.

The Crack-up has never been issued in book form; and perhaps because the pretty pictures in *Esquire* are so exciting to thumb-tack up on the wall, back numbers of it are not easy to come by. So I am tempted to try to summarize it all; but no, it must be published. Especially the first half is written without a fault: brief easy fiery phrases—the thinking that he compared to a "moving about of great secret trunks," and "the heady villainous feeling"—one quick and thorough paragraph after another, with so little shame and so little emphasis that I have wondered if he himself knew how much he was confessing.

He still regretted his bad luck in not getting abroad into the trenches as an army officer in 1918, and even his failure at football in 1913 or 1914. On certain of those unlucky days of his youth he felt as badly as in 1936, and badly in the same way; he makes a point of the similarity. Perhaps the worst of the early crises came in his junior year, when he lost the presidency of one of the Princeton clubs. Immediately afterward, as an act of desperation and consolation, he made love for the first time; and also that year, not until then, he turned to literary art, as the best of a bad bargain. Ominous! Fantastic, too, that a man who is dying or at least done with living—one who has had practically all that the world affords, fame and prosperity, work and play, love and friendship, and lost practically all—should still think seriously of so much fiddledeedee of boyhood! Very noble convictions underlay Fitzgerald's entire life, and he explains them nobly. But when he comes to the disillusionment, that too is couched in alumnal imagery; it is along with "the shoulder-pads worn for one day on the Princeton freshman football field and the overseas cap never worn overseas" that his ideals are relegated to the junk-heap, he says. It is strange and baroque; like those large bunches of battle-trappings which appear decoratively in seventeenth-century architecture, empty helmets and empty cuirasses and firearms laid crossways, sculptured up on the lintels of barracks and on the lids of tombs. Those condemned old European societies which have been too much militarized, too concerned with glory and glorious death, scarcely seem more bizarre than this: a kind of national consciousness revolving to the bitter end around college; and the latter also seems a precarious basis for a nation.

Aside from his literary talent—literary genius, self-taught —I think Fitzgerald must have been the worst educated man in the world. He never knew his own strength; therefore nothing inspired him very definitely to conserve or budget it. When he was a freshman, did the seniors teach him a manly technique of drinking, with the price and penalty of the several degrees of excess of it? If they had, it might never have excited him as a vague, fatal moral issue. The rest of us, his writing friends and rivals, thought that he had the best narrative gift of the century. Did the English department at Princeton try to develop his admiration of that fact about himself, and make him feel the burden and the pleasure of it? Apparently they taught him rather to appreciate this or that other writer, to his own disfavor. Did any worldly-wise critic ever remind him that beyond a certain point, writing for profit becomes unprofitable; bad business as well as bad art? Another thing: my impression is that only as he wrote, or just before writing, *Tender Is the Night*, did he discover certain causes and gradations of mental illness which, nowadays, every boy ought to be taught as soon as he has mastered the other facts of life.

Even the army failed to inculcate upon Lieutenant Fitzgerald one principle that a good army man must accept: heroism is a secondary virtue in an army. Lieutenant Fitzgerald had no business pining for the front-line trenches in advance of his superior officers' decision that it was the place for him. The point of soldiering is to kill; not a mere willingness to be killed. This seems important today, and again too much is made of the spirit of self-sacrifice and embattlement of ideals; and not enough of the mere means of victory. And with reference to literature, too, as Fitzgerald drops out of our insufficient little regiment, we writers particularly blame him for that all-out idealism of his. No matter what he died for

—if he died *for* anything—it was in too great a hurry; it was not worth it at his age.

In several of the obituary notices of Fitzgerald I detect one little line of mistaken moralizing, which I think is not uncommon; and his example and his fiction may have done something to propagate it. They seem to associate all rebellious morality somehow with a state of poor health. This is an unfair attack, and on the other hand a too easy alibi. Bad behavior is not always a feeble, pitiful, fateful thing. Malice of mind, strange style, offensive subject matter, do not always derive from morbid psyche or delicate physique. Wickedness is not necessarily weakness; and *vice versa*. For there is will-power in humanity. Its genuine manifestation is only in the long run; but, with knowledge, it can have the last word. Modern psychology does not deny it. Whether one is a moralist or an immoralist—a vengeful daily preacher like Mr. Westbrook Pegler, or an occasional devil's advocate like myself, or the quietest citizen—these little distinctions ought to be kept clear.

Fitzgerald was weak; we have the proof of it now in his demise. Fitzgerald, the outstanding aggressor in the little warfare which divided our middle classes in the twenties—warfare of moral emancipation against moral conceit, flaming youth against old guard—definitely has let his side down. The champion is as dead as a doornail. Self-congratulatory moral persons may crow over him if they wish.

There is bound to be a slight anger at his graveside; cursewords amid our written or spoken obsequies. The whole school of writers who went to France has been a bit maligned while the proletarian novelist and the politico-critics have enjoyed the general applause. Some of us are reckless talkers, and no doubt we have maligned each other and each himself as well. It was the beautiful, talented Miss Stein in her Paris salon who first called us "the lost generation." It was Hemingway who took up the theme and made it a popular refrain. The twenties were in fact a time of great prosperity and liberty, a spendthrift and footloose time; and especially in France you got your American money's worth of everything if you were clever. Still I doubt whether, in dissipation and unruly emotion, we strayed much farther out of the way than young Americans ordinarily do, at home as abroad. I think we were somewhat extraordinarily inclined to make youthful rebelliousness, imprudent pursuit of pleasure or ambition, a little easier for our young brothers. Heaven knows how it will be for our sons.

In any case, time is the real moralist; and a great many of the so-called lost are still at hand, active and indeed conspicuous: Bishop and Hemingway and Bromfield and Cummings and V. Thomson and Tate, Gordon and Porter and Flanner and others, the U. S. A.'s odd foreign legion. We were a band of toughs in fact, indestructible, which perhaps is the best thing to be said for us at this point. For the next step is to age well. Relatively speaking, I think we are aging well; giving evidence of toughness in the favorable sense as well: tenacity and hardiness, and a kind of worldly wisdom that does not have to change its platform very often, and skepticism mixed in with our courage to temper it and make it last. Sometimes we are still spoken of as the young or youngish or "younger" writers, but there can be no sense in that, except by lack of competition; every last one of us is forty. That is the right age to give advice to the immature and potential literary generation. For their sake, lest they feel unable to take our word for things, it seems worth while to protest against the strange bad name we have had.

In any case we are the ones who know about Fitzgerald. He was our darling, our genius, our fool. Let the young people consider his untypical case with admiration but great caution; with qualms and a respect for fate, without fatalism. He was young to the bitter end. He lived and he wrote at last like a scapegoat, and now has departed like one. As you might say, he was Gatsby, a greater Gatsby. Why not? Flaubert said, "*Madame Bovary, c'est moi!*" On the day before Christmas, in a sensible bitter obituary, *The New York Times* quoted a paragraph from *The Crack-up* in which the deceased likened himself to a plate. "Sometimes, though, the cracked plate has to be kept in service as a household necessity. It can never be warmed up on the stove nor shuffled with the other plates in the dishpan; it will not be brought out for company but it will do to hold crackers late at night or to go into the ice-box with the left-overs." A deadly little prose-poem! No doubt the ideals Fitzgerald acquired in college and in the army—and put to the test on Long Island and in the Alpes-Maritimes and in Hollywood—always were a bit second-hand, fissured, cracked, if you like. But how faithfully he reported both idealization and ordeal; and how his light smooth earthenware style dignifies it!

The style in which others have written of him is different. On the day after Christmas, in his popular column in *The New York World-Telegram*, Mr. Westbrook Pegler remarked that his death "recalls memories of a queer bunch of undisciplined and self-indulgent brats who were determined not to pull their weight in the boat and wanted the world to drop everything and sit down and bawl with them. A kick in the pants and a clout over the scalp were more like their needing. . . ." With a kind of expert politeness throughout this *in memoriam*, Mr. Pegler avoids commenting upon the dead man himself exactly. His complaint is of anonymous persons: the company Fitzgerald kept, readers who let themselves be influenced by him, and his heroes and heroines: "Sensitive young things about whom he wrote and with whom he ran to fires not only because he could exploit them for profit in print but because he found them congenial. . . ." I suppose Mr. Pegler's column is profitable too; and if I were doing it I should feel easier in my mind, surer of my aim, if I knew and liked my exploitees. Joking aside, certainly this opinion of his does not correspond in the least to my memory of the gay twenties. Certainly if sensitive young men and women of the thirties believe Pegler, they will not admire Fitzgerald or like the rest of us much.

Too bad; there should be peace between the generations now, at least among the literary. Popularity or no popularity, we have none too many helpful friends; and in a time of world war there may be panic and conservatism and absent-mindedness and neglect of literature in general, and those slight acts of obscure vengeance so easy to commit when fellow citizens have begun to fear and imagine and act as a mass. There should not be any quarrel between literature and journalism either. Modernly conceived and well done—literary men sticking to the truth and newspapermen using imagination—they relate to each other very closely, and may sustain and inspire each other back and forth. In a time of solemn subject matter it is more and more needful that they should.

In any case Mr. Pegler's decade is out as well as ours; the rude hard-working thirties as well as the wild twenties. The forties have come. Those of us who have been youthful too long—which, I suppose, is the real point of his criticism—now certainly realize our middle age; no more time to make ready or dawdle, nor energy to waste. That is one universal effect of war on the imagination: time, as a moral factor, instantly changes expression and changes pace. Everyman suddenly has a vision of sudden death.

What is the difference, from the universal angle? Everyone has to die once; no one has to die twice. But now that mortality has become the world's worst worry once more, there is less sophistication of it. Plain as day we see that the bull in the arena is no more fated than the steer in the slaughterhouse. The glamorous gangster's cadaver with bellyful of bullets is no deader than the commonplace little chap overcome by pernicious anemia. Napoleon III at the battle of Sedan, the other battle of Sedan, rouged his cheeks in order not to communicate his illness and fright to his desperate army. An unemployed young actor, a friend of a friend of mine, lately earned a living for a while by rouging cheeks of well-off corpses at a smart mortician's. All this equally—and infinitude of other things under the sun—is jurisdiction of death. The difference between a beautiful death and an ugly death is in the eye of the beholder, the heart of the mourner, the brain of the survivor.

The fact of Scott Fitzgerald's end is as bad and deplorable as could be; but the moral of it is good enough, and warlike. It is to enliven the rest of the regiment. Mere tightening the belt, stiffening the upper lip, is not all I mean; nor the simple delight of being alive still, the dance on the grave, the dance between holocausts. As we have it—documented and prophesied by his best work, commented upon in the newspaper with other news of the day—it is a deep breath of knowledge, fresh air, and an incitement to particular literary virtues.

For the private life and the public life, literary life and real life, if you view them in this light of death—and now we have it also boding on all the horizon, like fire—are one and the same. Which brings up another point of literary criticism; then I have done. The great thing about Fitzgerald was his candor; verbal courage; simplicity. One little man with eyes really witnessing; objective in all he uttered, even about himself in a subjective slump; arrogant in just one connection, for one purpose only, to make his meaning clear. The thing, I think, that a number of recent critics have most disliked about him is his confessional way, the personal tone, the *tête-à-tête* or man-to-man style, first person singular. He remarked it himself in *The Crack-up*: "There are always those to whom all self-revelation is contemptible."

I on the other hand feel a real approval and emulation of just that; and I recommend that all our writers give it serious consideration. It might be the next esthetic issue and new mode of American letters. It is American enough; our greatest fellows, such as Franklin and Audubon and Thoreau and Whitman, were self-expressers in so far as they knew themselves. This is a time of greater knowledge, otherwise worse; an era which has as many evil earmarks as, for example, the Renaissance: awful political genius running amok and clashing, migrations, races whipped together as it were by a titanic egg-beater, impatient sexuality and love of stimulants and cruelty, sacks, burnings and plagues. Fine things eventually may be achieved amid all this, as in that other century. I suggest revelation of man as he appears to himself in his mirror—not as he poses or wishes or idealizes—as one thing to try a revival of, this time. Naked truth about man's nature in unmistakable English.

In the Renaissance they had anatomy: Vesalius in Paris at midnight under the gallows-tree, bitten by the dogs as he disputed with them the hanged cadavers which they wanted to eat and he wanted to cut up. They had anatomy and we have psychology. The throws of dice in our world—at least the several dead-weights with which the dice appear to be loaded against us—are moral matters; and no one ever learns much about all that except in his own person, at any rate in private. In public, in the nation and the inter-nation and the anti-nation, one just suffers the weight of the morality of others like a dumb brute. This has been a dishonest century above all: literature lagging as far behind modern habits as behind modern history; democratic statesmanship all vitiated by good form, understatement, optimism; and the nations which could not afford democracy, finally developing their supremacy all on a basis of the deliberate lie. And now is the end, or another beginning.

Writers in this country still can give their little examples of truth-telling; little exercises for their fellow citizens, to develop their ability to distinguish truth from untruth in other connections when it really is important. The importance arises as desperately in the public interest as in private life. Even light fiction can help a society get together and agree upon its vocabulary; little strokes of the tuning-fork, for harmony's sake. And for clarity's sake, let us often use, and sanction the use of, words of one syllable. The shortest and most potent is the personal pronoun: I. The sanctified priest knows that, he says *credo*; and the trustworthy physician only gives his opinion, not a panacea. The witness in the courtroom does not indulge in the editorial we; the judge and the lawyers will not allow it; and indeed, if the case is important, if there is life or liberty or even a large amount of money at stake, not even supposition or hearsay is admitted as evidence. Our worldwide case is important.

Not only is Anglo-Saxondom all at war with the rest of the world in defense of its accustomed power and prosperity, and of the luxuries of the spirit such as free speech, free publication, free faith—for the time being, the United States is the likeliest place for the preservation of the Mediterranean and French ideal of fine art and writing: which puts a new, peculiar obligation upon us ex-expatriates. The land of the free should become and is becoming a city of refuge; but there is cultural peril even in that. France has merely committed her tradition to our keeping, by default; whereas Germany has exiled to us her most important professors and brilliant writers. Perhaps the latter are bound to introduce into our current literature a little of that mystically philosophic, obscurely scientific mode which somewhat misled or betrayed them as a nation. Therefore we must keep up more strictly and energetically than ever, our native specific skeptical habit of mind; our plainer and therefore safer style.

In any consideration of the gravity of the work of art and letters—and upon any solemn occasion such as the death of a good writer like Scott Fitzgerald—I think of Faust, and that labor he dreamed of when he was blind and dying, keeping the devil waiting. It was the drainage of a stinking sea-marsh and the construction of a strong dyke. Fresh fields amid the eternally besieging sea: room for a million men to live, not in security—Goethe expressly ruled out that hope of which we moderns have been too fond—but free to do the best they could for themselves. Does it seem absurd to compare a deceased best seller with that mythic man: former wholesome Germany's demigod? There must always be some pretentiousness about literature, or else no one would take its pains or endure its disappointments. Throughout this article I have mixed bathos with pathos, joking with tenderness, in order to venture here and there a higher claim for literary art than is customary now. I am in dead earnest. Bad writing is in fact a rank feverish unnecessary slough. Good writing is a dyke, in which there is a leak for every one of our weary hands. And honestly I do see the very devil standing world-wide in the decade to come, bound to get some of us. I realize that I have given an exaggerated impression of Fitzgerald's tragedy in recent years: all the above is based on his confession of 1936, and he was not so nearly finished as he thought. But fear of death is one prophecy that never fails; and now his strength is only in print, and his weakness of no account, except for our instruction.